United States Edition RNAB 2011 Year A

Workbook for Lectors, Gospel Readers, and Proclaimers of the Word

Mary A. Ehle, PHD

and Margaret Nutting Ralph, PHD

LTP
LITURGY
TRAINING
PUBLICATIONS

Liturgy Training Publications, 3949 South Racine Avenue, Chicago IL 60609, 1-800-933-1800, fax 1-800-933-7094, orders@ltp.org, www.LTP.org.

Editor: Lorie Simmons
Production Editor: Kris Fankhouser
Typesetter: Jim Mellody-Pizzato
Original book design: Jill Smith
Revised design: Anna Manhart and Jim Mellody-Pizzato
Cover art: Barbara Simcoe
Interior art: Anna Manhart

LTP now prints the text of *Workbook for Lectors, Gospel Readers, and Proclaimers of the Word* with ink that contains renewable linseed oil on paper that is 100% recycled and contains a minimum of 40% postconsumer waste. The paper for this product was de-inked by a process that uses PCF (Processed Chlorine Free) technologies, unlike many de-inking proesses that use toxic bleach.

The printing process used to manufacture this book uses a non-heatset process that significantly reduces emission of volatile organic compounds (VOCs) into the atmosphere.

LTP continues to work toward responsible stewardship of the environment. For more information on our efforts, please go to www.LTP.org/environment.

Printed in the United States of America.
ISBN 978-1-56854-883-8
WL11

CONTENTS

EASTER SEASON

ORDINARY TIME

The Authors

Mary A. Ehle holds a doctorate in Religious Studies from Marquette University in Milwaukee, Wisconsin, as well as degrees from St. John's University in Collegeville, Minnesota, and St. Norbert College in De Pere, Wisconsin. She is an experienced liturgist, pastoral musician, and director of faith formation. Mary is the author of *Workbook for Lectors 2009*. She resides in Albuquerque, New Mexico. Mary has written the commentaries for Ordinary Time and the Christmas season.

Margaret Nutting Ralph, PHD, has taught grade school, college, graduate school, and adult education throughout the country. She currently directs the Master of Arts in Pastoral Studies program for Catholics at Lexington Theological Seminary. Margaret is the author of ten books on scripture, including *And God Said What?* and the *Breaking Open the Lectionary* series published by Paulist Press. She has written the commentaries for Advent, Lent, and Easter seasons.

In accordance with c. 827, permission to publish was granted on March 29, 2010, by the Very Reverend John F. Canary, Vicar General of the Archdiocese of Chicago. Permission to publish is an official declaration of ecclesiastical authority that the material is free from doctrinal and moral error. No legal responsibility is assumed by the grant of this permission.

INTRODUCTION

The liturgy is the public prayer of the Church. Prayer itself involves a relationship—a relationship between God and you, the person praying. In public prayer such as the liturgy, the relationship also includes members of the assembly, those present and those not present. The *Catechism of the Catholic Church* states, the liturgy is "a participation in Christ's own prayer addressed to the Father in the Holy Spirit. In the liturgy, all Christian prayer finds its source and goal" (1073).

As a proclaimer of the word, your ministry helps facilitate the public prayer of the Church in the Liturgy of the Word. This is a tremendous responsibility, but one which need take on by yourself. Other proclaimers of the word, along with the ordained ministers and lay ecclesial ministers in your parish community, are present to help form you so that you will be able to carry out your ministry of proclamation and prayer. You also belong to a church community that has called you forth and recognized that you have gifts that suit you for this ministry. Through your continued participation in the Church's liturgy, your involvement in workshops for proclaimers of the word, your own preparation, and above all, your willingness to grow in your relationship with God, you will hone your proclamation skills and gifts. And in this day and age, when people are often more comfortable interacting through e-mail or cell phones, you will make possible genuine human interaction through the sharing of God's word as you proclaim it to the best of your ability.

The Liturgy of the Word as Prayer

The Second Vatican Council's Dogmatic Constitution on Divine Revelation, or *Dei Verbum* (DV), teaches us that the Liturgy of the Word and the Liturgy of the Eucharist are to be regarded with the same reverence: "The Church has always venerated the divine Scriptures as she venerated the Body of the Lord, in so far as she never ceases, particularly in the sacred liturgy, to partake of the bread of life and to offer it to the faithful from the one table of the Word of God and the Body of Christ" (DV, 21). In imparting the word of the Lord to the assembly, you feed them with the Bread of Life, and provide nourishment for them to continue their life of prayer and to develop further their relationship with the Lord.

The way in which the Liturgy of the Word is celebrated can foster a deepening of peoples' relationship with God. You have an important role to play in this. But first, as a proclaimer of the word, you yourself always need to be mindful that the Liturgy of the Word is prayer, a dialogue between God and his people. Aware of this, your presence and your proclamation of the word will nurture the assembly's prayer. In the Introduction to the Lectionary (#28) we read of the Liturgy of the Word as meditation, a form of prayer:

> The liturgy of the word must be celebrated in a way that fosters meditation; clearly, any sort of haste that hinders recollection must be avoided. The dialogue between God and his people taking place through the Holy Spirit demands short intervals of silence, suited to the assembled congregation, as an opportunity to take the word of God to heart and to prepare a response to it in prayer.

The General Instruction of the Roman Missal (#29) also reflects on the dialogue of prayer that occurs in the Liturgy of the Word:

In the beginning was the Word, and the Word was with God, and the Word was God.

When the Sacred Scriptures are read in the Church, God himself speaks to his people, and Christ, present in his own word, proclaims the Gospel.

The Holy Spirit works through the words you proclaim and in the hearts of believers who are recalling the saving works of God in history (CCC, 1103). Your presence, the variations in tone and volume you use, and the different paces and rhythms you employ, all serve to provide room for the Spirit to work in people's hearts, leading them to prayer. Depending on the time in the liturgical year, the events of a person's life, and world events, this prayer might be one of praise, thanksgiving, desire, forgiveness, pleading, or joyful expectation. Your aim is to support that prayer of the assembly and not to distract from it by drawing attention to yourself. You do not want to place any barriers between the assembly and the Holy Spirit, who is making present God's marvelous deeds through your proclamation.

You have been called forth to serve as a proclaimer of God's word. The Council Fathers said that those who serve in the ministry of the word should immerse themselves in the scriptures through study and reflection, and during the proclamation at liturgy, and they also remind us that "prayer should accompany the reading of sacred Scripture, so that a dialogue takes place between God and man" (DV, 25). Your communication of God's word during the public prayer of the Church is proclamation. Yet it is also proclamation in the context of prayer. This sometimes is forgotten. One way to be attentive to your proclamation as prayer is to center your preparation on prayer—on your conversation with God.

Preparation as Prayer

Saint Augustine in one of his sermons spoke of the necessity of coming to the ministry of the word from one's personal prayer. Although he was referring to clergy, his thought applies today to all who proclaim the word of God. He asserted that one is "an empty preacher of the Word of God to others, not being a hearer of the Word in his own heart" (*Sermon*, 179). In other words, you have to listen to God through the prayer of your heart if you want to be a sincere and truthful proclaimer of the word. You might want to ask yourself is, "How can I be more attentive to the

God so loved the world that he gave his only Son, so that everyone who believes in him might not perish but might have eternal life.

Word of God in my own heart so I can communicate the Word to the assembly gathered before me to pray?"

Spiritual preparation as a proclaimer of the word is essential. Because of the weightiness of the ministry you perform, the preparation required is twofold, spiritual, and technical. The Introduction to the Lectionary describes the lector's preparation as "above all" spiritual. This spiritual preparation "presupposes at least a biblical and liturgical formation." According to paragraph 55 of the Introduction,

> The biblical formation is to give readers the ability to understand the readings in context and to perceive by the light of faith the central point of the revealed message. The liturgical formation ought to equip the readers to have some grasp of the meaning and structure of the liturgy of the word and of the significance of its connection with the liturgy of the Eucharist.

If you are an experienced proclaimer of the word, you might have already developed a method of spiritual preparation that works well for you. Newcomers to the ministry might want to experiment with different methods of preparation. Whatever the method you choose, it is important to have a regular method of spiritual preparation. Center this preparation on prayer. Converse with God about how best you can be the conduit in proclaiming his presence to the assembly. Some parishes provide opportunities for their ministers of the word, or all their liturgical ministers for a given Sunday, to come together during the week prior to the Sunday to pray and reflect on the scripture readings for the Sunday on which they will be serving. If group preparation is not feasible, you might prepare by praying with reflection questions based on the readings. Very often, parishes print reflection questions for the next week in the current week's bulletin or publish them on the parish Web site. If you don't know where to find reflection questions on the readings, you might ask a member of the parish staff.

The preparation you as a proclaimer of the word need to do before a liturgical celebration is more involved than the preparation of your other liturgical minister colleagues. While it would be good for all liturgical ministers to prepare spiritually for the liturgy at which they will serve, your spiritual preparation goes beyond simple reflection on the readings. As the last quote from the Introduction to the Lectionary mentioned, spiritual preparation also involves biblical and liturgical formation. The biblical preparation entails developing an understanding of the readings in their context. For this, some tools of the lector's ministry are essential. Try preparing with the Bible and *Workbook* by your side. With the Bible you will be able to read the readings in the context of the entire chapter or book in which they are contained. Sometimes the introductions at the beginning of each book of the Bible provide beneficial information. Frequently, the footnotes are useful in developing a better understanding of the meaning of a passage.

The commentaries located beneath the scripture readings in *Workbook* aid in both your biblical and liturgical formation. They provide historical and critical background to assist you in understanding the reading in its original context. They also draw connections between the readings and the time in the liturgical year, so that as a proclaimer of the word, you are better able to appreciate why particular readings are proclaimed on the days they are. Furthermore, the commentaries offer pastoral suggestions for helping you make connections between the reading and

This is my commandment: love one another as I love you.

our world and Church today. By understanding the original intention of the author in writing the inspired words of scripture and by relating them to the contemporary context, you will communicate God's presence in the word to the assembly. Your ministry will then effectively deepen your own prayer and that of those present in your community.

One way of looking at the goal of the spiritual preparation of the proclaimer of the word is in relation to the early Church fathers and mothers of the desert. These men and women of prayer were so devoted to cultivating their relationship with God through the scriptures that they simply wanted to "become prayer."[1] They wanted their entire life—their presence and their actions to show forth the presence of God. But, what does this mean for a minister of the Word to "become prayer" in the twenty-first century? First, it entails openness to the Spirit of the Lord working in your own life. In your preparation time, as well as in the ordinary events of your life, cultivate an awareness of the presence of God in yourself and in others you meet. The direction with which you live your life is both inward and outward toward God—open to the Spirit of God within you and in others. Second, immerse yourself in the practice of your faith. Participate consistently in the Sunday eucharistic liturgy of the Church. Pray as a conversation with God, but also with the traditional prayers of the Church. Third, let the scriptures be your guide in talking with God. God never stops inviting us to closer union with him through his word.

As you prepare the readings, perhaps you will want to start out the Monday of the Sunday before you are scheduled to proclaim the word simply by reading over the passages, and getting a sense of their themes or main points. As you go through your life during the week, perhaps there is a phrase that you will want to remember and draw on during the week. Let this phrase be your prayer every time it comes to mind. Use it as the direction for living your life during the week—at home, at work, in the community, and in the parish. The word of God is living and active—it's not meant to remain on the written page.

If proclaimers truly work at "becoming prayer," they will always be welcoming and generous—to their fellow ministers, to those seeking to enter the ministry, and to the entire parish. In a way, every liturgical minister is a minister of hospitality. Ministers of the word must be willing to greet those they meet before and after the liturgy, welcoming those they know and reaching out to those who are newcomers or who clearly need their assistance. Consonance between the word of God the proclaimed and the word of God lived out is, in the end, what it means to "become prayer."

When we are able to witness to the word of God in our words and actions, then we are closer to "becoming prayer" in our day and age. Then, your proclamation of the word of God in the context of the Church's public prayer, the liturgy, will be a proclamation filled with integrity. The assembly gathered to worship with you will sense the genuineness of your proclamation. They will know you have prepared both spiritually as well as technically.

Prayerfulness and Practical Matters

The spirit of prayerfulness in the Liturgy of the Word is reflected both in the way ministers of the word present themselves and in the manner in which they proclaim the word of God. There are many practical matters in relation to the minister of the word that affect the celebration of the Liturgy of the Word. Even for the seasoned proclaimer, a reminder every so often about some of these matters is helpful. As you read through these comments, be aware that some details are specific to the parish in which you serve, particularly matters concerning the sound system and microphones. In order to address issues such as these, many parishes already have implemented yearly or semiannual formational gatherings with all the ministers of the word.

When you are scheduled to be a minister of the word, make sure to arrive at least twenty minutes before the liturgy is scheduled to begin. You do not want to be rushing out the door and arriving at the church at the last minute. This creates unnecessary anxiety both for you, and for those who are expecting you to be present. You do not want to leave anyone wondering whether or not you are coming. Arriving early also provides you with time to check the Lectionary, making sure your reading is marked correctly so that you do not need to turn unnecessary pages trying to locate the reading after you approach the ambo. Before the liturgy begins, you will also want to find out if there are any additional rites taking place during the Mass that would affect the time when you need to approach the ambo, for example, dismissal for Children's Liturgy of the Word, Rite of Acceptance, Baptism, and so forth. Being aware of any changes in this regard will help you do your part to keep the flow of the liturgy going and will leave no one waiting for the you to move into place.

Some ministers of the word will want to sit in silence and prayer either in the sacristy or in the church before the celebration of the liturgy begins. Others will want to greet members of the assembly or welcome other liturgical ministers. For some, this interaction with the community enables them to sense the presence of God and to remember that the faith we profess and the God we worship in the liturgy is present among us, in each other. Find a method of immediate preparation that works best for you and which lets you center yourself in God before the liturgy. No matter the method of immediate preparation you choose, you will want to be focused as the liturgy begins.

Your posture, both when you are proclaiming the word of God and during the rest of the liturgy when you are not carrying out your specific ministry, is

Magnify the LORD with me; let us exalt his name together.

Blessed are the poor in spirit, for theirs is the kingdom of heaven.

very important. As you approach the ambo, make sure you are standing tall and erect. You want to exude confidence, but not overconfidence or arrogance. The manner in which you comport yourself lets the assembly know you have something important to tell them. When you are seated in the assembly or the sanctuary area, sit upright, actively listening and responding, involving yourself in the prayer of the liturgy.

As a minister of the word, you also have the role of being an example for the rest of the community. People will recognize you before, during, and after the liturgy. How you present yourself at times other than when you are proclaiming the word is as important as how you appear in front of the assembly when it is your turn to execute your ministry. So sing, pray, and listen attentively throughout the liturgy as part of the assembly. Through your Baptism you are first a part of the assembly; then, you are called forth from the assembly because you have a specific gift the Church recognizes and you are willing to share. But you always remain part of the assembly. Anything that would set you apart as "better than" others or not in unity with those in the assembly will detract from your ministry. Conversely, your full, conscious, and active participation will help lead others to the same. So, even though your gift might be in public speaking and not public singing, still participate in the sung prayer of the community!

After you arrive at the ambo, take a brief moment to focus yourself. Many ministers of the word are nervous when they read. This energy, when channeled correctly, can help convey the message of the reading. One way that works for some proclaimers of the word is to take an unnoticeable, deep breath after arriving at the ambo. While taking that breath, you might want to say a short prayer offering your proclamation of the reading to God. Doing so reminds you that the reading is not about you, but about God. When you are focused, begin with the announcement of the reading in a confident, strong tone of voice. Both the announcement at the beginning of the reading and the acclamation at the end of the reading are important liturgically, so deliver them with care. Making eye contact with the assembly and speaking in a strong, deliberate way will engage your listeners.

If you make a mistake when you are proclaiming the word, keep your composure. You do not want to look frustrated, laugh, or draw attention to yourself and the mistake. Depending on the mistake, you might want to return to the beginning of the sentence. The assembly's comprehension of the reading will be aided with this method. If you clearly mispronounce or stumble over a word, simply restate that word and proceed. Do not attempt to work out the correct pronunciation by saying it over and over again. This makes it obvious to everyone that you have not prepared. More than that, however, it results in a lack of reverence for the word and disrupts people's train of thought as they attempt to understand the meaning of the reading. Because we are human beings, we all make mistakes. Your ability to maintain your composure in itself reverences the word of God.

Our natural human anxiety causes us to read faster when we are in front of people. Indeed, most ministers of the word tend to speak too fast; some even race, wanting to finish the reading quickly. Many whose pace is rapid are not even aware that this is the case. A good reminder for most proclaimers, then, is slow down, slow down, slow down. A slower pace will help the assembly to understand the meaning of the reading. In a culture that has so much visual stimulation, we are becoming less proficient at processing auditory information. This challenges you to always be aware of your pace, to take your time communicating the word to the assembly.

Your appearance also reflects the reverence you have for the word of God and for God's presence in the Eucharist and the assembly. Although different parishes have different guidelines for dress, your appearance needs to speak of the importance of the liturgy itself and your particular ministry. Choose attire that is neither flashy nor shabby so as not to make yourself the center of attention. In addition, choose attire that is practical—especially shoes. It is not wise to carry out your ministry in big winter boots or shoes with high or noisy heels. People in the assembly will be looking at what you are wearing, rather than listening to what you are proclaiming. Take a quick look in the mirror before the liturgy to correct anything that is amiss. This is particularly important for those ministers of the word who serve at the very early morning Masses and sometimes have to trudge through inclement weather to do so, as well as for those who are called on to proclaim at the last minute!

The LORD's word is true; all his works are trustworthy.

In addition to its role in spiritual formation—liturgical and biblical formation, *Workbook* is also meant to assist you in the correct and expressive delivery of the reading. The bolded text of the readings suggests words to emphasize, although all need not be given the same degree of emphasis. The margin notes on the left side of the readings provide pronunciations for difficult or uncommon words and names, explanations of certain words or phrases from the reading, and suggestions for how to proclaim the reading (such as when to take pauses and what tone of voice to use). Use *Workbook* as a guide, not as a manual with definitive pronouncements as to how to proclaim the readings. Your own technical preparation and the feedback you receive from the assembly and parish staff can also assist you in becoming a better minister of the word.

When you have addressed the practical matters, you will be able to concentrate on praying with the community. You will be able to remember that your proclamation of the Word is part of the Church's liturgy. It deepens your relationship with God and moves those in the assembly to grow in theirs as well. Through your ministry, then, you will offer praise to God and draw others to that same praise in the liturgy and in the ordinary events of their lives. You will have helped to lead the assembly to the full, active, and conscious participation the Church desires. You and the assembly will have "become prayer" and God will have been glorified because of the ministry you do.

Prepared to Proclaim

As the liturgy approaches, ask yourself, "Am I prepared to proclaim the word well?" Think about the following questions: Do I understand the main points in the reading? How would I express the meaning of the passage in my own words? How do I understand the relationship between this reading and the season of the liturgical year, the feast or solemnity on which it will be proclaimed? Am I able to pronounce all the words in the reading without hesitating? Can I articulate the difficult words smoothly and with confidence? If I were to proclaim the reading to others, would they be able to tell me the message of the reading? Would they have difficulty understanding any section of the reading? What are one or two ways I could live the message of the scriptures in my own life this week? What will be my prayer to God as I approach the ambo to carry out the ministry of the word?

Perhaps time got away from you this week, and you didn't prepare as thoroughly as you would have liked. If this is the case, resolve to plan more time to prepare the next time you are scheduled. In fact, consider setting aside some regular time each week, whether or not you are scheduled, to prepare "as if" you were the scheduled proclaimer. This is one of the best ways to grow in your skills, confidence, and spirituality—and to be sure that you will be well prepared to listen or to proclaim at Sunday's liturgy.

For now, as the liturgy approaches, offer a prayer to God expressing that you will do the best you can in your ministry. Draw on your experience from the other occasions on which you have proclaimed the word to give yourself confidence. Communicate calm to the assembly as you undertake your ministry.

Proclaiming the reading well is very important, but sometimes, in spite of the best intentions, mistakes will be made and preparation will be lacking. Yet all is not lost. The presence of God is still ours to communicate, in word and in the dignity with which we carry out our ministry.

After the liturgy, evaluate your own proclamation and solicit feedback from a few people whose opinion you trust. Ask questions such as: What is your initial reaction to the proclamation of the word I gave? How was the pacing of my proclamation, the volume, and so on? Did I emphasize words appropriately and in a way that helped communicate the meaning of the passage? Did my oral punctuation help express the meaning of the reading? Was my body language reverent? Did anything I did distract from the reading? Express your gratitude for any feedback, positive or negative, that you receive. Assure yourself and others that you are always working to improve your proclamation skills, to better understand the word you proclaim, and to help others in the assembly do the same. Go forth from the liturgy knowing that you are a child of God, created in his image and likeness. You have offered yourself as prayer to your parish community and you go into the world to do the same.

Pronunciation Key

bait = bayt	thin = thin
cat = kat	vision = VIZH*n
sang = sang	ship = ship
father = FAH-ther	sir = ser
care = kair	gloat = gloht
paw = paw	cot = kot
jar = jahr	noise = noyz
easy = EE-zee	poison = POY-z*n
her =her	plow = plow
let = let	although = ahl-THOH
queen = kween	church = cherch
delude = deh-LOOD	fun = fun
when = hwen	fur = fer
ice = īs	flute = floot
if = if	foot = foot
finesse = fih-NES	

Recommended Works

Church Documents

"Introduction to the Lectionary." In *Lectionary for Mass: Study Edition.* Chicago: Liturgy Training Publications (LTP), 1998.

Resources for Proclaiming God's Word

Meagher, Virginia, and Paul Turner. *Guide for Lectors.* Chicago: LTP, 2007.

Pronunciation Guide for the Lectionary. Chicago: LTP, 2010.

Rosser, Aelred R. *A Well-Trained Tongue: Formation in the Ministry of the Reader.* Chicago: LTP, 1996.

Prayers for a Lector (pamphlet, Catholic Pocket Prayers). Chicago: LTP, 2008.

General Reference Works on the Bible

Boadt, Lawrence. *Reading the Old Testament: An Introduction.* New York, New York/Mahwah, New Jersey: Paulist Press, 1984.

Brown, Raymond E. *Christ in the Gospels of the Liturgical Year.* Collegeville, Minnesota: Liturgical Press, 2008.

_______. *An Introduction to the New Testament.* The Anchor Bible Reference Library. New York, New York: Doubleday, 1997.

The New Jerome Biblical Commentary. Raymond E. Brown, Joseph Fitzmyer and Roland E. Murphy, eds. Englewood Cliffs, New Jersey: Prentice Hall, 1990.

Perkins, Pheme. *Reading the New Testament: An Introduction.* New York, New York/Mahwah, New Jersey: Paulist Press, 1988.

Commentaries on the Gospel according to Matthew

Byrne, SJ, Brendan. *Lifting the Burden: Reading Matthew's Gospel in the Church Today.* Collegeville, Minnesota: The Liturgical Press, 2004.

Harrington, SJ, Daniel J. *The Gospel of Matthew.* Sacra Pagina Series. Collegeville, Minnesota: The Liturgical Press, 2007.

Reid, Barbara E. *The Gospel according to Matthew.* New Collegeville Bible Commentary. New Testament, vol. 1. Collegeville, Minnesota: The Liturgical Press, 2005.

Notes

1. *The Roots of Christian Mysticism: Texts from the Patristic Era with Commentary.* Translated by Theodore Berkeley, OCSO, and Jeremy Hummerston. Hyde Park, New York: New City Press, 1993.

1ST SUNDAY OF ADVENT

Lectionary #1

READING I Isaiah 2:1–5

The first sentence simply gives information.
Isaiah = Ī-ZAY-uh; Amoz = AY-muhz
Judah = JOO-duh
Jerusalem = juh-ROO-suh-lem
Pause before reading this proclamation.

A reading from the Book of the Prophet Isaiah

This is what **Isaiah**, son of **Amoz**,
saw concerning **Judah** and **Jerusalem**.
In days to come,
the mountain of the LORD's **house**
shall be established as the **highest mountain**
and raised **above** the **hills**.
All nations shall **stream** toward it;
many peoples shall come and say:

This invitation should be offered with enthusiasm.
Jacob = JAY-kuhb

"**Come**, let us **climb** the **LORD's mountain**,
to the **house** of the **God** of **Jacob**,
that he may instruct us in **his** ways,
and we may walk in his paths."

Now a note of solemnity.
Zion = ZĪ-ahn

For from **Zion** shall go forth **instruction**,
and the **word** of the LORD from **Jerusalem**.
He shall judge between the **nations**,
and impose terms on **many peoples**.

This promise of peace calls for a lowered but confident voice.

They shall beat their **swords** into **plowshares**
and their **spears** into **pruning hooks**;
one nation shall **not** raise the **sword** against another,
nor shall they **train** for **war** again.

Again, this invitation should be offered with enthusiasm, and now urgency.

O house of Jacob, **come**,
let us **walk** in the **light** of the LORD!

READING I By the time Isaiah, son of Amoz, was prophesying, the Israelite nation had divided into two: Israel in the north; Judah in the south, with Jerusalem as its capital. Isaiah (742 BC–700 BC) prophesied in Judah at a time when both nations were being threatened by the Assyrians. In the face of this threat to their very existence as nations, Isaiah offered hope to God's people.

What hope did Isaiah offer? In today's reading we hear Isaiah assure the people that God has a purpose for the nation, Judah. If the people are faithful to their covenant with God, if they walk in God's paths, then not only will Judah survive, but all nations will stream to Judah. Why? Not to conquer Judah. They will come in peace: "They shall beat their swords into plowshares / and their spears into pruning hooks." Other nations will stream to Judah to learn from Judah how to walk in the light of the Lord.

Isaiah pleads with the people: "come, / let us walk in the light of the Lord!" The people of Judah must live in fidelity to their covenant with God not only to survive but to be an example that other nations can and will follow.

The Church proclaims Isaiah's words to the universal Church on the first Sunday of Advent so that we, too, will be filled with hope. However, in order for God's will, both for ourselves and for the world, to be fulfilled in and through us, we too must walk in the light of the Lord.

Isaiah's words should be read first with quiet authority, then with joyful confidence, and finally with urgent pleading. An invitation is being offered, but it is an urgent invitation.

READING II Romans 13:11–14

A reading from the Letter of Saint Paul to the Romans

Speak with affection and intimacy.

Brothers and sisters:
You **know** the time;
it is the hour **now** for you to **awake** from **sleep**.
For our salvation is **nearer now** than when we **first believed**;
the **night** is **advanced**, the **day** is at **hand**.

Speak a little faster here to convey urgency.

Let us then **throw off** the works of **darkness**
and **put on** the **armor** of **light**;

Speak with a slower pace here, with pauses.
orgies = OHR-jeez
promiscuity = proh-mis-KEW-ih-tee

let us conduct ourselves **properly** as in the **day**,
not in **orgies** and **drunkenness**,
not in **promiscuity** and **lust**,
not in **rivalry** and **jealousy**.

Speak firmly as you proclaim this direction.

But put on the **Lord Jesus Christ**,
and make **no provision** for the **desires** of the **flesh**.

READING II When Paul wrote his letter to the Romans, he expected the Son of Man to return in glory on the clouds of heaven during his lifetime. That is why he, too, addresses his audience with some urgency: "it is the hour now for you to awake from sleep." Because the day of the Lord draws near the people must not put off acting on their good intentions. Now is the time to act, to "put on the armor of light."

A person who converts to Christ no longer engages in drunkenness, promiscuity, rivalry, or jealousy. Instead, he or she "put[s] on the Lord Jesus Christ." A life lived in Christ calls for entirely different behavior, both for the Romans and for us.

As you read Romans be careful not to sound like you are scolding the congregation. The reading begins, "Brothers and sisters . . . ." The tone should be both affectionate and firm.

GOSPEL Matthew's Gospel was compiled about AD 80. In contrast, Paul's letter to the Romans was written about AD 58, over 20 years earlier. Obviously, the return of the Son of Man on the clouds of heaven had not occurred as early as was expected. As we read today's Gospel we see that the message about being prepared for the coming of the Son of Man is just as urgent, but accommodation has been made for the fact that the expectation of an imminent return has not been confirmed by events.

As Matthew describes the coming of the Son of Man he says: "Two men will be out in the field; one will be taken, and one will be left. Two women will be grinding at the mill; one will be taken, and one will be left." This description does not seem to be

GOSPEL Matthew 24:37–44

A reading from the holy Gospel according to Matthew

This is simply introductory information.

Jesus said to his **disciples**:

Jesus is warning the disciples. His tone is firm.

Noah = NOH-ah

"**As it was** in the days of **Noah**,
so it will be at the **coming** of the **Son of Man**.
In those days before the **flood**,
they were **eating** and **drinking**,
marrying and **giving in marriage**,
up to the day that **Noah** entered the **ark**.
They **did not know** until the **flood** came and carried them
all away.

This line is spoken with solemnity.

So will it be also at the **coming** of the **Son of Man**.

Read slowly here.

Two men will be out in the **field**;
one will be **taken**, and **one** will be **left**.
Two women will be **grinding** at the **mill**;
one will be **taken**, and **one** will be **left**.

Now read a little louder and more quickly.

Therefore, **stay awake**!
For **you do not know** on **which day** your **Lord** will come.

Lower your voice; speak with intimacy.

Be sure of this: if the **master** of the house
had known the **hour** of **night** when the **thief** was coming,
he would have **stayed awake**
and **not let** his house be broken into.

Speak slowly and firmly.

So too, you also must be prepared,
for at an hour you do **not expect**, the **Son of Man will come**."

about the end time, but about personal death: one will be left on earth.

Matthew is warning the people that they must not be like those who lived during Noah's time, giving no thought to anything but the present. "They were eating and drinking, / marrying and giving in marriage, / up to the day that Noah entered the ark." Because they gave no thought to the future they did not survive the flood: "the flood came and carried them all away."

Matthew's audience must stay awake. Because no one knows when the Son of Man will come, nor when one's life on earth will end, one must be ready always. As Jesus tells his disciples: "So, too, you must be prepared, for at an hour you do not expect, the Son of Man will come."

In Matthew's Gospel, today's Lectionary reading is part of a long eschatological (about the end times) talk that Jesus has with his disciples near the end of his ministry. The tone of the conversation is both urgent and intimate.

Why does the Church begin a new liturgical year and the season of Advent with readings about the end times? Because Advent is a time to prepare for the coming of the Lord, not just as a babe who was born in Bethlehem many years ago, but also as a risen Savior who comes into the lives of each person and each generation.

In Advent we not only recall the birth of our Savior, but we prepare for the coming of that Savior into our lives today. We once again dedicate ourselves to walk in the light of the Lord so that God's purposes throughout history may be fulfilled in us, in our children, and in our children's children. Then we will always be ready for the coming of the Lord, every day and at the end of time.

2ND SUNDAY OF ADVENT

Lectionary #4

READING I Isaiah 11:1–10

Isaiah is offering hope with great confidence.

Jesse = JES-ee

A reading from the Book of the Prophet Isaiah

On **that day**, a shoot shall **sprout** from the **stump** of **Jesse**,
and from **his** roots a **bud** shall **blossom**.
The **spirit of the LORD** shall rest upon **him**:

Read slowly, with pauses.

a spirit of **wisdom** and of **understanding**,
a spirit of **counsel** and of **strength**,
a spirit of **knowledge** and of **fear of the LORD**,
and his **delight** shall be the **fear of the LORD**.

Read a little faster here.

Not by **appearance** shall he **judge**,
nor by **hearsay** shall he **decide**,

Slowly, again.

but he shall judge the **poor** with **justice**,
and decide **aright** for the land's **afflicted**.

Increase your volume here.

He shall strike the **ruthless** with the **rod** of his **mouth**,
and with the **breath** of his **lips** he shall **slay** the **wicked**.
Justice shall be the **band** around his **waist**,
and **faithfulness** a **belt** upon his **hips**.

Use a softer voice: this is a vision of peace and tranquility.

Then the **wolf** shall be a guest of the **lamb**,
and the **leopard** shall lie down with the **kid**;
the **calf** and the **young lion** shall browse **together**,
with a **little child** to **guide** them.
The **cow** and the **bear** shall be **neighbors**,
together their young shall **rest**;
the **lion** shall eat hay like the **ox**.
The **baby** shall play by the **cobra's den**,
and the **child** lay his **hand** on the **adder's lair**.

READING I Today we again proclaim words of Isaiah, the eighth-century prophet who offered hope to Judah. Isaiah prophesied during the reign of King Ahaz, a bad king because he did not trust God's promise of protection to the house of David. He chose instead to make Judah a vassal state of Assyria. In today's reading, Isaiah is looking forward to a future time, "that day," when a future king, unlike Ahaz, will be faithful to God's covenant promises.

Isaiah refers to the future good king as a "blossom" from the "stump of Jesse." Jesse was the father of King David, who was the greatest king that the Israelites had ever had. Through the prophet Nathan, God had promised David that his kingdom and his line would be secure forever (2 Samuel 7:16). Ahaz is a mere stump of Jesse, because he is such a bad king. However, even if Ahaz is unfaithful to covenant love, God is not. A blossom from the stump of Jesse, a good king descended from Ahaz, will surely come.

Isaiah describes this future king as one full of "the spirit of the LORD." He will be gifted with what Catholics often call the gifts of the Holy Spirit: wisdom, understanding, counsel, strength, knowledge, and fear of the Lord. These gifts will enable the future king to act with justice: he will secure the rights of the poor and punish the wicked.

This future, faithful king will bring peace to the country: "Then the wolf shall be a guest of the lamb." On that day, God's purposes throughout history will be accomplished: the Gentiles will seek out the root of Jesse, the people descended from King David.

There shall be **no harm** or **ruin** on **all** my holy mountain;
for the **earth** shall be **filled** with **knowledge** of the LORD,
as **water covers** the sea.

Increase your volume again for the final lines. Speak with confidence.

Gentiles = JEN-tīls

On that day, the **root** of **Jesse**,
set up as a **signal** for the **nations**,
the **Gentiles** shall **seek out**,
for his **dwelling** shall be **glorious**.

READING II Romans 15:4–9

A reading from the Letter of Saint Paul to the Romans

As always, Paul's sentence structure is complex. Read slowly, with pauses.

Brothers and sisters:
Whatever was written **previously** was written for our **instruction**,
that by **endurance** and by the **encouragement** of the **Scriptures**
we might have **hope**.

Here Paul is offering a kind of blessing.

May the God of **endurance** and **encouragement**
grant you to think in **harmony** with one another,
in keeping with **Christ Jesus**,
that with **one accord** you may with **one voice**
glorify the **God** and **Father** of our **Lord Jesus Christ**.

Now Paul is giving instructions.

Welcome one another, then, as **Christ** welcomed **you**,
for the **glory** of **God**.
For I say that Christ became a **minister** of the **circumcised**
to show God's **truthfulness**,

Jesus, as Joseph's adopted son, is of the house of David. By proclaiming Isaiah's words during Advent, the Church is professing our belief that Isaiah's words have been fulfilled in Jesus Christ. A tone of hopeful confidence is appropriate for this reading.

READING II Today's second reading, from Paul's letter to the Romans, is also offering hope. Paul is assuring the Romans that "what was written previously," that is, scripture passages like the one we just read from Isaiah, offer not only instruction, but hope. Behind this statement is the presumption, accepted by both Paul and by the Church of every generation, that scripture is not simply an historic word describing the lives of our ancestors in faith, but is a living word that is also addressed to us.

The hope that Paul is offering is hope that both Jews and Gentiles will be united in "glorify[ing] the God and Father of our Lord Jesus Christ." Like Isaiah, Paul believes that the Jews, the circumcised, are fulfilling God's loving purposes when they welcome Gentiles into their midst. Through Christ, God has both fulfilled his promises to the patriarchs and has invited the Gentiles into a relationship of covenant love. Therefore, as God, through Christ, has welcomed Gentiles, so should the Jews living in Rome welcome them also.

Today's reading ends with a quotation from 2 Samuel (also Psalm 18:49). In 2 Samuel, David prays: "Therefore will I proclaim you, O Lord among the nations, / and I will sing praise to your name" (2 Samuel 22:50). By quoting David, Paul is teaching that the Gentiles were always intended to be included in God's plan. It is God's plan and God's will that Jewish Christians and

to confirm the **promises** of the **patriarchs**,
but so that the **Gentiles** might **glorify God** for his **mercy**.
As it is written:

Read this quotation as a proclamation.

Therefore, I will **praise** *you among the* **Gentiles**
and sing **praises** *to your* **name**.

GOSPEL Matthew 3:1–12

A reading from the holy Gospel according to Matthew

Judea = joo-DEE-uh; joo-DAY-uh
Say John's words with authority and urgency.

John the **Baptist** appeared, **preaching** in the desert of **Judea**
and saying, "**Repent**, for the **kingdom** of **heaven** is at **hand**!"

Drop your voice for this line.
Isaiah = ī-ZAY-uh

It was of him that the prophet **Isaiah** had spoken when he said:

Increase your volume here.

A voice of one **crying out** *in the desert,*
Prepare *the* **way** *of the* **Lord**,
make **straight** *his* **paths**.

Now the narrator's voice is simply giving us information.

John wore clothing made of **camel's hair**
and had a **leather belt** around his **waist**.
His **food** was **locusts** and **wild honey**.

Jerusalem = juh-ROO-suh-lem; juh-ROO-zuh-lem
Jordan = JOHR-d*n

At that time **Jerusalem**, **all Judea**,
and the **whole region** around the **Jordan**
were going **out** to him
and were being **baptized** by him in the **Jordan River**
as they **acknowledged** their **sins**.

Gentile Christians welcome each other and live in harmony with each other.

Paul's words should be read slowly with appropriate pauses.

GOSPEL On the Second Sunday of Advent we always hear the story of John the Baptist preparing the way for Jesus. In Matthew's account, John's message is identical to Jesus' message. Both say, "Repent, for the kingdom of heaven is at hand" (see also Matthew 4:17).

The Gospel according to Matthew was addressed primarily to Jewish Christians who wanted to be faithful to their covenant relationship with God. They were asking whether or not becoming a disciple of Jesus Christ was an act of fidelity. After all, Jesus had been rejected by some of their religious leaders and had died by crucifixion. In addition, Gentiles who didn't even obey the law were becoming disciples of Christ. In answer to their question, Matthew is always and everywhere stressing that fidelity to Jesus Christ is fidelity to the Israelite's 2,000-year tradition of covenant relationship with God.

For instance, Matthew claims that the words of the prophet Isaiah were fulfilled in John the Baptist. In Isaiah we read: "A voice cries out: / In the desert prepare the way of the Lord! / Make straight in the wasteland a highway for our God" (Isaiah 40:3)! These words date to the time of the Babylonian exile (587 BC–537 BC). The prophet, known as Second Isaiah, was offering hope to the exiles that God would save them and lead them home.

In Second Isaiah, the word "Lord" refers to Yahweh. In this Gospel, Matthew attributes Second Isaiah's words to John

Pharisees = FAYR-uh-seez
Saddducees = SAD-yoo-seez
John is accusing the Pharisees and Sadducees.

When he saw many of the **Pharisees** and **Sadducees**
coming to his **baptism**, he said to them, "You **brood of vipers**!
Who warned you to **flee** from the coming **wrath**?
Produce **good fruit** as evidence of your **repentance**.
And do **not presume** to say to yourselves,
'We have **Abraham** as **our** father.'

Here John is mimicking the Pharisees and Sadducees' defending themselves.

For I tell you,

Again, John speaks forcefully. He is threatening the Pharisees and Sadducees with punishment.

God can **raise up children** to **Abraham** from these **stones**.
Even now the **ax** lies at the **root** of the **trees**.
Therefore **every tree** that does not bear **good fruit**
will be **cut down** and **thrown** into the **fire**.

The tone changes here. Use less volume.

I am baptizing you with **water**, for **repentance**,
but the **one who is coming after** me is **mightier** than I.

Say this softly.

I am **not worthy** to carry his **sandals**.

Now, increase your volume to the end of the reading.

He will baptize you with the **Holy Spirit** and **fire**.
His **winnowing** fan is in his **hand**.
He will **clear** his **threshing floor**
and **gather** his **wheat** into his **barn**,

The reading ends with a return to a threatening tone.

but the **chaff** he will **burn** with **unquenchable fire**."

the Baptist, and by having the person for whom John is preparing be Jesus, Matthew is making a claim about Jesus' identity: that Jesus is Lord.

The description of John's clothing is important. He wore "clothing made of camel's hair and had a leather belt around his waist." This is an allusion to the prophet Elijah who is described as, "Wearing a hairy garment . . . with a leather girdle about his loins" (2 Kings 1:8). Elijah was taken up to heaven in a fiery chariot (2 Kings 2:11). He was expected to return before the day of the Lord: "Lo, I will send you/ Elijah, the prophet, / Before the day of the Lord comes . . ." (Malachi 3:23a). John the Baptist is presented as the new Elijah, preparing the way of the Lord.

John the Baptist speaks very harshly to "many of the Pharisees and Sadducees" who were coming to be baptized. He calls them a "brood of vipers," and warns them about "the coming wrath." In Matthew's account the Pharisees and Sadducees will be presented as Jesus' adversaries. Jesus will be in the right, and they in the wrong.

If those in Matthew's audience are in doubt about what the great John the Baptist thinks about Jesus Christ, Matthew answers their question forcefully. John says, "the one who is coming after me is mightier than I. I am not worthy to carry his sandals." John then urges his followers to become Jesus' followers: "He will baptize you with the Holy Spirit and fire."

However, in order to receive Baptism, one must truly repent. As we prepare for the coming of the Lord we, too, must repent. It is your role to deliver John's message to your assembly. The kingdom of God is at hand.

IMMACULATE CONCEPTION

Lectionary #689

READING I Genesis 3:9–15, 20

A reading from the Book of Genesis

The narrator's voice is simply setting the stage.

After the **man**, **Adam**, had **eaten** of the **tree**,
the LORD God **called** to the man and **asked** him,

God doesn't yet know that anything is wrong.

"Where are you?"

The man, as he says, is afraid and hiding.

He answered, "I **heard** you in the garden;
but I was **afraid**, because I was **naked**,
so I **hid** myself."

God is, at first, puzzled.

Then he asked, "**Who told you** that you were **naked**?

Now God begins to understand the awful truth.

You have **eaten**, then,
from the **tree** of which I had **forbidden** you to eat!"

The man is blaming.

The man replied, "The **woman** whom you put here with me—
she gave me fruit from the tree, and so **I ate it**."

God is gentle and inquiring.

The LORD God then asked the woman,
"**Why** did you **do** such a thing?"

The woman, too, is blaming.

The woman answered, "The **serpent tricked** me into it, so **I ate it**."

Here God is firm and compassionate. God is explaining the ramifications of what the serpent has done.

Then the **LORD God** said to the **serpent**:
"**Because you have done this**, you shall be **banned**
from **all** the **animals**
and from **all** the **wild creatures**;
on your **belly** shall you **crawl**,
and **dirt** shall you **eat**
all the days of your **life**.

READING I On the Solemnity of the Immaculate Conception, the Old Testament reading is one part of a great story of sin, and we are tuning in on this story after the sin has been committed. The man and woman have both eaten from the "tree of knowledge of good and bad" (see Genesis 2:17). The plot of this story makes it obvious that the kind of writing we are reading is neither historical nor scientific. The author uses symbols to explore a great mystery: why do human beings suffer? At the beginning of the story, in Genesis 2:25, we see the man and woman in a place of no suffering. However, there is a moral order that is part of the very fabric of their lives, a moral order that God explains to the man and woman when he warns them not to eat of the tree of knowledge of good and bad.

The author has presented temptation in the form of a personified serpent that convinces the woman who convinces the man to eat. Their eyes are opened, and they are ashamed. They cover their nakedness and hide from the Lord. Our Lectionary reading introduces us to the middle of the story by adding the phrase, "After the man, Adam, had eaten of the tree. . . ."

Notice that God is not presented as all-knowing in the story. God comes for a walk and talk, and realizes something is wrong when the man cannot relate to God in his usual loving fashion. The reading shows the terrible results of sin: The man and woman are suddenly ashamed of who they are and then blame others for what they freely chose to do. God explains to the man, the woman, and the serpent that they have brought suffering upon themselves.

I will put **enmity** between **you** and the **woman**,
and between **your offspring** and **hers**;
he will strike at **your** head,
while **you** strike at **his** heel."

The narrator concludes the story.

The man called his wife **Eve**,
because she became the **mother** of **all** the **living**.

READING II Ephesians 1:3–6, 11–12

A reading from the Letter of Saint Paul to the Ephesians

Brothers and sisters:

This is said with great gratitude.

Blessed be the **God** and **Father** of our **Lord Jesus Christ**,
who has **blessed** us in **Christ**
with **every spiritual blessing** in the heavens,

Read slowly, with pauses.

as he **chose us** in **him**, **before** the **foundation** of the world,
to be **holy** and **without blemish** before him.
In love he **destined** us for **adoption** to himself
through Jesus Christ,
in accord with the **favor** of his **will**,

Increase your volume as you proclaim this line.

for the **praise** of the **glory** of his **grace**
that he **granted us** in the beloved.

Now back to an explanatory tone.

In him we were **also chosen**,
destined in accord with the purpose of the One
who accomplishes **all things** according to the intention
of his will,

Again, emphasize "praise of his gory" by increasing your volume.

so that we might exist for the **praise** of **his glory**,
we who **first hoped** in **Christ**.

The story of the man and woman in the garden is a story about the human condition: when we choose sin we bring suffering upon ourselves and others because we lessen our ability to be in right relationship with ourselves, others, and God.

Still there is a note of hope: Humanity will struggle against evil. By the time this story took shape (1000 BC), Israel had a strong sense of itself as a chosen nation. Eve's offspring, the nation Israel, will strike at the serpent's head. Christians saw in this passage a reference to Mary, the new Eve, whose offspring, Jesus Christ, struck at the serpent's head. That is why statues of Mary often depict her standing on a serpent.

As you read this story, try to reflect the emotions of each character: God, loving but disappointed; the man, afraid; the woman, blaming.

READING II Paul, in his letter to the Ephesians, is praising God for the great gifts God has given to the people (see above: "Blessed be . . . who has blessed us . . . foundation of the world"). By the time Paul is living, the followers of Jesus Christ have come to realize that it has been God's will since "before the foundation of the world" to include Gentiles in God's redemptive plan.

Not only Mary, but the Ephesians, and we ourselves have been chosen "to be holy and without blemish" before God. This holiness is accomplished only through God's saving power and grace. The tone in this reading moves from exuberance, to awe, to conviction. Imagine! Not only Mary, but we also, have been chosen to fulfill God's purposes for the human race.

GOSPEL Luke 1:26–38

A reading from the holy Gospel according to Luke

The narrator's voice sets the stage.
Gabriel = GAY-bree-uhl
Galilee = GAL-ih-lee
Nazareth = NAZ-uh-reth

The angel **Gabriel** was sent from **God**
to a town of **Galilee** called **Nazareth**,
to a **virgin** betrothed to a man named **Joseph**,
of the house of **David**,
and the virgin's name was **Mary**.
And coming to her, he said,

The angel speaks with authority, but gently.

"**Hail, full of grace**! The **Lord** is **with** you."
But she was greatly **troubled** at what was said
and **pondered** what sort of **greeting** this might be.
Then the angel said to her,

The angel is both calming and encouraging Mary.

"Do not be **afraid**, Mary,
for you have found **favor** with **God**.
Behold, you will **conceive** in your womb and **bear** a **son**,
and you shall **name** him **Jesus**.

Here increase your volume for a proclamation.
Jacob = JAY-kuhb

He will be **great** and will be called **Son of the Most High**,
and the **Lord God** will give him the throne of **David** his father,
and he will **rule** over the house **of Jacob forever**,
and of his **Kingdom** there will be **no end**."

GOSPEL Today we read Luke's beautiful story of the annunciation to Mary. Only in Luke's Gospel do we hear what Catholics call Mary's *fiat*, Mary's response of total trust, total self-giving.

Although Catholics treasure this story for the picture it gives us of Mary, the primary purpose of the story is to teach something about Jesus. Scripture scholars believe that the stories surrounding Jesus' birth are Christological stories that developed later in the oral tradition than did stories about Jesus' Passion, death, and Resurrection, or about his mighty acts of power. The birth and infancy stories are responding to the question, "Who is Jesus?" They teach the post-Resurrection understanding that Jesus is God's own son, and the fulfillment of all of God's promises to the Chosen People.

In the story of the annunciation, when Mary responds to the angel's announcement of her pregnancy with "How can this be . . . ?" the angel replies with an explanation for Mary and for Luke's audience. The Holy Spirit and the Most High will make this happen so that the child will be "the Son of God." Through the words of the angel, Luke is teaching the post-Resurrection understanding that Jesus is divine.

In addition to being divine, Jesus is the fulfillment of God's promises to the chosen people. Luke tells us that Joseph is "of the house of David" and the angel says that Mary's son will have "the throne of David his father . . . and of his kingdom there will be no end."

To understand this passage we need to remember what the Jews understood God to have promised David and his posterity. In 2 Samuel we read that the Lord spoke to Nathan, the prophet during David's

Mary is truly puzzled.

Again, the angel is calming but speaks with authority.

Elizabeth = ee-LIZ-uh-beth

Read Mary's response slowly and emphasize each word.

The narrator makes a concluding remark.

But Mary said to the angel,
"**How can this be**,
since I have no **relations** with a **man**?"
And the **angel** said to her in reply,
"The **Holy Spirit** will come **upon you**,
and the **power** of the **Most High** will **overshadow you**.
Therefore the **child** to be **born**
will be called **holy**, the **Son of God**.
And behold, **Elizabeth**, your relative,
has **also conceived** a **son** in her old age,
and this is the **sixth month** for her who was called **barren**;
for **nothing** will be **impossible** for God."
Mary said, "**Behold, I am the handmaid of the Lord**.
May it be done **to me** according to **your** word."
Then the angel departed from her.

reign, instructing him to tell David: " 'And when your time comes and you rest with your ancestors, I will raise up your heir after you . . . and I will make his kingdom firm. It is he who shall build a house for my name. And I will make his royal throne firm forever' " (2 Samuel 7:12–13).

Because the Israelites were in a relationship of covenant love with God, and God had promised to protect them, whenever they were facing difficulty they expected God to send someone, a messiah, to save them. David was such a person—he saved them from the Philistines. Based on God's promise through Nathan, the Jews of Mary's time were expecting one from the house of David to come and save them from the Romans. By emphasizing that Jesus is from the house of David, Luke is teaching that Jesus is the fulfillment of all the hopes of the generations. Jesus will establish an endless kingdom.

On the solemnity of the Immaculate Conception, we celebrate our belief that Mary, as God's chosen instrument, was holy from the moment of her conception in her mother's womb. This reading is perfectly suited for today's celebration because in it the angel greets Mary with the words, "Hail, full of grace! The Lord is with you." This grace-filled state was true of Mary not only when she conceived Jesus, but from the moment when she herself was conceived.

As you proclaim Luke's story of the annunciation to Mary, remember that there are three speakers: the narrator, the angel, and Mary. The tone for the narrator's lines should be somewhat matter of fact; they are informational. The angel speaks with gentle authority. Mary speaks first with puzzlement, then with total conviction and trust.

DECEMBER 12, 2010

3RD SUNDAY OF ADVENT

Lectionary #7

READING I Isaiah 35:1–6a, 10

Isaiah = Ī-ZAY-uh

These lines are full of joy and hope.
steppe = step

Lebanon = LEB-uh-nuhn
Carmel = KAHR-m*l
Sharon = SHAYR-uhn

Here a direction is being given.

Emphasize every word.
Speak with firmness and conviction.
vindication = vin-dih-KAY-shuhn
recompense = REK-uhm-pens

Again, the tone is joy and confidence.

A reading from the Book of the Prophet Isaiah

The **desert** and the **parched land** will **exult**;
the **steppe** will **rejoice** and **bloom**.
They will bloom with **abundant flowers**,
and **rejoice** with **joyful song**.
The **glory** of **Lebanon** will be **given** to them,
the **splendor** of **Carmel** and **Sharon**;
they will **see** the **glory** of the **LORD**,
the **splendor** of our **God**.
Strengthen the hands that are **feeble**,
make **firm** the knees that are **weak**,
say to those whose hearts are frightened:
Be strong, fear not!
Here is your God,
he comes with **vindication**;
with **divine recompense**
he comes to **save** you.
Then will the **eyes** of the **blind** be **opened**,
the **ears** of the **deaf** be **cleared**;
then will the **lame leap** like a **stag**,
then the **tongue** of the **mute** will **sing**.

READING I Once more we read a prophecy of hope from the book of Isaiah, which contains the prophecies of three great prophets who lived at different times. During this Advent we have already heard from two of them: First Isaiah, the eighth-century prophet who offered hope of a future, good king, and Second Isaiah, the sixth-century prophet who offered the exiles hope that God would lead them back to the Holy Land.

At the time of today's prophecy, the Assyrians have conquered the northern kingdom, and the Babylonians have conquered the southern kingdom. The temple has been destroyed, the upper-class citizens have been forced into exile in Babylon, and the land has been ravaged. The people are asking, "Where is God? Are we God's people, or not?"

This prophecy offers hope that there will be a great reversal in the people's future. The ravaged land that they have left will exult, bloom, and rejoice. Why? Because "they will see the glory of the LORD." The feeble must now be strong, the weak, firm, the frightened, without fear. They are about to experience the presence of this God whom they feared had abandoned them: "Here is your God, / he comes with vindication; / . . . he comes to save you." This is good news, indeed.

READING II James, too, is preparing people for the coming of the Lord. The Lord about whom James is speaking, however, is Jesus Christ. The coming to which he is referring is the return of the Son of Man at the end time.

Zion = ZĪ-ahn

Those whom the LORD has **ransomed** will **return**
and enter **Zion** singing,
crowned with **everlasting joy**;
they will meet with **joy** and **gladness**,
sorrow and **mourning** will **flee**.

READING II James 5:7–10

A reading from the Letter of Saint James

The tone is persuasive. Speak slowly, since patience is being recommended.

Be **patient**, brothers and sisters,
until the **coming of the Lord**.
See how the farmer **waits** for the precious **fruit** of the **earth**,
being **patient** with it
until it receives the early and the late rains.

Emphasize each word of this line.

You too must be patient.
Make your hearts **firm**,

Slightly increase your pace.

because the **coming of the Lord** is at **hand**.

Again, the tone is persuasive, conciliatory.

Do not **complain**, brothers and sisters, about one **another**,
that you may not be **judged**.

Now, speak with firmness.

Behold, the **Judge** is **standing** before the **gates**.
Take as an example of **hardship** and patience, brothers and sisters,
the **prophets** who **spoke** in the **name** of the **Lord**.

This second coming was expected to occur during the lifetime of Jesus' contemporaries. By the time the letter of James was written, that coming was overdue. James recommends patience.

He looks to nature, God's creation, as a model from which to interpret events. The farmer has to be patient for the crop to grow. So does James' audience have to be patient. In the mean time, the people should make their "hearts firm, because the coming of the Lord is at hand."

While they are waiting, the people should not complain. They should look to the prophets as examples of hardship and patience, and they should always remember that they are accountable for their actions: "Behold, the Judge is standing before the gates."

James is one of the Church's "Catholic Epistles"; that is, the letter is addressed to the whole Church (the word *catholic* means *universal*), rather than to a specific community. The letter is named after its sender, not its receiver. The tone of this reading moves from patience, to encouragement, to authority, and back to patience.

GOSPEL In last Sunday's Gospel, John the Baptist was preparing the way of the Lord. This Sunday, John the Baptist is in prison and seems unsure about who the Lord is. He sends his disciples to ask Jesus, "Are you the one who is to come?" In the Gospel according to Matthew, John is imprisoned before Jesus' public ministry (Matthew 4:12), and John is evidently dependent on his disciples for information.

GOSPEL Matthew 11:2–11

A reading from the holy Gospel according to Matthew

The narrator's voice sets the stage.

When **John the Baptist** heard in **prison** of the **works** of the **Christ**,
he sent his disciples to **Jesus** with this **question**,

John's disciples' are perplexed.

"Are **you** the **one** who is to **come**,
or should we look for another?"

Jesus said to them in **reply**,

Jesus speaks with friendly authority. Pause after each line.

"Go and tell John what you **hear** and **see**:
the **blind** regain their **sight**,
the **lame walk**,

lepers = LEP-erz
cleansed = klenzd

lepers are **cleansed**,
the **deaf hear**,
the **dead** are **raised**,

proclaimed = proh-KLAYMD

and the **poor** have the **good news proclaimed** to them.
And **blessed** is the one who takes **no offense at me**."

Again, the narrator gives background information.

As they were going off,
Jesus began to speak to the **crowds** about **John**,

Jesus is not puzzled. These are Socratic questions used to teach.

"What did you go out to the **desert** to see?
A **reed** swayed by the **wind**?
Then what did you go out to **see**?
Someone dressed in **fine clothing**?
Those who wear **fine clothing** are in **royal palaces**.

prophet = PROF-uht

Then **why** did you go **out**? To see a **prophet**?

Jesus speaks with conviction.

Yes, I tell you, and more than a prophet.
This is the one about whom it is **written**:

Read the quotation as a proclamation.

Behold*, I am sending my* ***messenger ahead*** *of you;*
he *will prepare* ***your*** *way* ***before*** *you.*

Speak Jesus' concluding words with gentle conviction.

Amen, I say to you,
among those born of **women**
there has been **none greater** than **John the Baptist**;
yet the least in the kingdom of heaven is greater than he."

Notice that Jesus answers John's disciples' question by pointing to his works. Among them are the signs of the coming of the Lord that we just read in Isaiah: "the blind regain their sight, the lame walk," and so forth. If these are the signs of the coming of the Lord, and Jesus is performing them, who does John the Baptist think Jesus is? Only one conclusion can be drawn: Jesus is the one who is to come.

After John's disciples leave, Jesus addresses the crowd about John. He is not only a prophet, but he is the one about whom the prophet Malachi spoke when he said, "Lo, I am sending my messenger / to prepare the way before me" (see Malachi 3:1). In Malachi, the one for whom the way is being prepared is God. In Matthew, it is Jesus. Once more, Matthew is claiming Jesus' divinity. Jesus is the one who is to come. This Advent we are the ones who are to prepare the way, both in our hearts and in the world.

There are three speakers in this reading: the narrator, John's disciples, and Jesus. The narrator simply gives information. John's disciples are puzzled. Jesus answers them as a teacher would, encouraging John and his disciples to reach their own conclusions based on the evidence. When addressing the crowd, Jesus' tone changes from questioning to forceful.

4TH SUNDAY OF ADVENT

Lectionary #10

FIRST READING Isaiah 7:10–14

Isaiah = ī-ZAY-uh

A reading from the Book of the Prophet Isaiah

The narrator sets the stage.
Ahaz = AY-haz

The LORD spoke to **Ahaz**, saying:

The Lord is pleading with Ahaz.
netherworld = NETH-er-werld

Ask for a **sign** from the **LORD**, your **God**;
let it be **deep** as the **netherworld**, or **high** as the **sky**!

Ahaz is adamant. Emphasize every word of his response.

But **Ahaz** answered,
"I will not ask! I will not tempt the LORD!"

Isaiah's words are commanding. He demands attention.

Then Isaiah said:
Listen, O house of **David**!
Is it not **enough** for you to weary **people**,
must you **also** weary my **God**?

Lower your voice here; speak slowly and with solemnity.
Emmanuel = ee-MAN-yoo-el

Therefore the **Lord himself** will give you **this sign**:
the **virgin** shall **conceive**, and **bear** a **son**,
and shall name him **Emmanuel**.

READING I Our reading begins: "The LORD spoke to Ahaz." After Ahaz's response, the reading continues: "Then Isaiah said. . . ." The conversation we are reading today is actually between Isaiah, the 8th century prophet, and Ahaz, the king of Judah. A prophet's words were often attributed to God. In fact, a prophet's message often begins, "The LORD says this. . . ." The word *prophet* means "one who speaks for another." In the context of scripture, the other for whom the prophet speaks is God.

Prophets did not foretell inevitable future events. Rather, they called the king and the nation to fidelity to covenant love. That is what Isaiah is doing in today's reading. He is reminding King Ahaz that he is David's descendent. Through the prophet Nathan, God promised David that his kingdom and his line would be secure forever (2 Samuel 7:16). Ahaz is being threatened by the Assyrians. What will he do? Will he trust God to protect the nation, or will he enter into a political alliance with two smaller nations (the Syro-Ephramite Alliance) in hopes of stopping the Assyrians?

Isaiah tries to persuade Ahaz to trust God. Ask for a sign! Ahaz refuses. Isaiah is worn out trying to persuade Ahaz to be faithful. But even if Ahaz is not faithful, God will be. Isaiah assures Ahaz that a virgin will bear a son and name him Emmanuel, which means God is with us.

Isaiah is telling Ahaz that his son will be a better king than Ahaz is. God will be with that future king as he has with past kings. We know that Isaiah is referring to Ahaz's son because, in a verse not included in the Lectionary, Isaiah says that before this child is very old "the land of

READING II Romans 1:1–7

A reading from the Letter of Saint Paul to the Romans

Paul is introducing himself. Read slowly and with pauses after each unit of thought.
apostle = uh-POS-*l

Paul, a **slave** of **Christ Jesus**,
called to be an **apostle** and **set apart** for the **gospel** of **God**,
which he **promised** previously through his **prophets** in the
holy Scriptures,
the **gospel** about his **Son**, descended from **David**
according to the **flesh**,

Increase your volume with "Son of God in power."

but established as **Son of God** in **power**
according to the **Spirit of holiness**
through **resurrection** from the **dead**, **Jesus Christ** our **Lord**.

Paul shares a teaching and an invitation; the tone is inviting.

Gentiles = JEN-tīls

Through **him** we have received the grace of **apostleship**,
to bring about the **obedience** of **faith**,
for the sake of **his name**, among **all** the **Gentiles**,
among whom are **you also**, who are called to **belong**
to **Jesus Christ**;
to all the **beloved of God** in Rome, **called** to be **holy**.

Here Paul offers a blessing.

Grace to you and **peace** from **God** our **Father**
and the **Lord Jesus Christ**.

those two kings whom you dread shall be deserted" (Isaiah 7:16b).

Isaiah's words did not lead anyone to expect a virginal conception or an incarnation. However, as we will see when we read today's Gospel, after these marvelous events occurred, Isaiah's words were used to teach that the virginal conception and the incarnation had been God's mysterious plan all along.

God's words in this reading should be read with persuasiveness. Ahaz's tone is defensive. Isaiah's proclamation should be read slowly and with authority.

READING II As Paul begins his letter to the Romans, he reminds them of the fact that we just noticed: the Gospel, the Good News of Jesus Christ, had been "promised previously through his prophets in the holy Scriptures." The hidden meaning of those promises, however, was understood only in hindsight, after Christ's Resurrection. True, Jesus is of David's family, but, in the light of the Resurrection, we now know that Jesus is God's Son: he was "established as Son of God in power . . . through resurrection from the dead, Jesus Christ our Lord."

Paul tells the Romans that he has been "called to be an apostle and set apart for the gospel of God" to bring the Good News of Jesus Christ to the Gentiles. Through Paul, the Romans are being called "to belong to Jesus Christ." They are being "called to be holy." These words are addressed just as much to us as they were to the Romans. We, too, are called to belong to Jesus Christ and to be holy.

The tone of Paul's letter is gracious. Paul does not know most of his audience but is passionate about his message.

GOSPEL Matthew 1:18–24

A reading from the holy Gospel according to Matthew

The narrator's voice sets the stage.
betrothed = bee-TROTHD
Joseph = JOH-sif or JOH-zuhf

This is how the **birth** of **Jesus Christ** came about.
When his mother **Mary** was betrothed to **Joseph**,
but **before** they lived together,
she was found with **child** through the **Holy Spirit**.

righteous = RĪ-chuhs

Joseph her husband, since he was a righteous man,
yet **unwilling** to **expose** her to **shame**,
decided to **divorce** her **quietly**.
Such was his **intention** when, **behold**,
the **angel of the Lord appeared** to him in a **dream** and said,

The angel speaks reassuringly and with authority.

"**Joseph, son of David**,
do not be afraid to take **Mary** your **wife** into your **home**.
For it is through the **Holy Spirit**
that this child has been **conceived** in **her**.
She will bear a **son** and **you** are to **name** him **Jesus**,
because he will **save** his **people** from their **sins**."

Again, the narrator explains the situation.

All this took place to **fulfill** what the **Lord** had said
through the **prophet**:

Read the quotation as a proclamation.
Emmanuel = ee-MAN-yoo-el

***Behold**, the **virgin** shall **conceive** and bear a **son**,*
*and they shall name him **Emmanuel**,*
which means "**God is with us**."

The narrator concludes the story.

When Joseph **awoke**,
he did as the **angel** of the **Lord** had **commanded** him
and took his **wife** into his **home**.

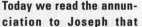

GOSPEL Today we read the annunciation to Joseph that appears only in Matthew's account. Matthew begins by telling us that Mary, who was betrothed to Joseph, but was not yet living with him, was "with child through the Holy Spirit." Joseph was "a righteous man." He did not want to expose Mary to shame. (According to the law, Joseph could have had Mary stoned to death; see Deuteronomy 22:21).

A second time we are told that Mary has conceived her child through the Holy Spirit, this time through the angel's words to Joseph. Joseph is to name the child Jesus, because he will save the people from their sins. It is extremely important that Joseph receives Mary into his home and names Jesus because these actions establish Jesus as being from the house of David. The name *Jesus* means "God saves." Jesus will save God's people, not from the Romans, as was expected, but from sin.

In the light of these marvellous things, Matthew then reinterprets the words of Isaiah that we just read. "A virgin shall conceive" is now understood to mean that a woman will conceive without having had a sexual relationship with a man. The name *Emmanuel* is now understood to mean that God will become incarnate. By finding this hidden meaning in Isaiah's words, Matthew is assuring his Jewish audience that Jesus is the fulfillment of God's promises to the Israelites.

The narrator's lines at the beginning and the end are informational. The angel speaks with compassion and authority.

NATIVITY OF THE LORD: VIGIL

Lectionary #13

READING I Isaiah 62:1–5

Isaiah = Ī-ZAY-uh

As the prophet will be neither silent nor quiet, let your voice, too, be neither silent nor quiet; let it come across with confidence. Speak loudly and clearly as you begin this passage.

diadem = DĪ-uh-dem

Make the contrast clear between the names "Forsaken" and "Desolate" and "My Delight" and "Espoused" by lightening the strength of your voice on the latter words to convey the happiness at being chosen by the Lord.

Make eye contact with the assembly as you proclaim the final line with joy.

A reading from the Book of the Prophet Isaiah

For **Zion's** sake I will **not** be silent,
for **Jerusalem's** sake I will **not** be quiet,
until her **vindication** shines forth like the **dawn**
and her **victory** like a burning **torch**.

Nations shall **behold your** vindication,
and **all** the kings your **glory**;
you shall be called by **a new** name
pronounced by the mouth of the LORD.
You shall be a **glorious crown** in the hand of the LORD,
a **royal diadem** held by your God.
No more shall people call you "**Forsaken**,"
or your land "**Desolate**,"
but you shall be called "**My Delight**,"
and your land "**Espoused**."
For the LORD delights in you
and makes your land his **spouse**.
As a **young man** marries a **virgin**,
your **Builder** shall marry **you**;
and as a **bridegroom** rejoices in his **bride**
so shall **your** God rejoice in you.

READING I Jerusalem's restoration and the return of the Hebrew people from exile is meant for all to see; her exoneration and return to glory is so beautiful and wondrous that everyone will witness it. Our own path to glory begins with Christmas and the birth of Jesus, the one we call "Messiah." It is the beginning of an intimate relationship with God in Jesus through the Church.

The contrast between the old names and the new names testifies to the significance and depth of what is transpiring in the relationship between God, Jerusalem, and its people. Names like "Forsaken" and "My Delight" are present elsewhere in Israelite history (1 Kings 22:42; 2 Kings 21:1). In the past, Israel and her people had been associated with fertility cults; the name "Espoused" means Israel has been forgiven for those associations.

These are not minor changes taking place in the relationship between God and Israel; they are life-altering. In human history, what transpired with the birth of the Messiah gave witness to how much God wants to bring the world close to him. The entire song from which the five verses of this reading come is found in Isaiah 62:1–12. The last two verses (11–12) are the reading for the Mass at Dawn on Christmas (see that commentary for more insights into the passage), and include the climax of the song: "your savior comes!" This conclusion is not included in your reading and therefore the assembly does not hear it at the Christmas Vigil Mass. However, the joy and confidence of your proclamation can help lead members of the assembly to this conclusion on their own.

READING II Acts 13:16–17, 22–25

Antioch = AN-tee-ahk
Pisidia = pih-SID-ee-uh
Pause noticeably after "said," so as to make it obvious that what follows is Paul's speech. Deliver Paul's speech making eye contact with the assembly as much as possible.

Speak Jesus' name clearly and with reverence on this evening when we celebrate the Vigil of Christmas.

Pause noticeably after "I am not he." Then, with humility in your voice, proclaim John's announcement of Jesus' coming.

A reading from the Acts of the Apostles

When **Paul** reached **Antioch** in **Pisidia** and entered the **synagogue**,
he **stood** up, **motioned** with his hand, and **said**,
"Fellow **Israelites** and you others who are God-fearing, **listen**.
The God of this people **Israel** chose our ancestors
and exalted the people during their **sojourn** in the land of **Egypt**.
With **uplifted** arm he **led** them out of it.
Then he **removed Saul** and **raised** up **David** as king;
of him he **testified**,
'I have found **David**, son of **Jesse**, a man after my own **heart**;
he will carry out my **every** wish.'
From this man's **descendants** God, according to his promise,
has brought to Israel a **savior**, **Jesus**.
John heralded his coming by proclaiming a **baptism** of **repentance**
to all the people of **Israel**;
and as John was completing his course, he would say,
'**What** do you suppose that I **am**? I am **not** he.
Behold, one is coming **after** me;
I am not **worthy** to unfasten the **sandals** of his **feet**.' "

This Christmas Eve, celebrate the continuation of Jerusalem's restored relationship with the Lord in your proclamation of the prophet's words. We who participate in the life of the Church are forever united with Christ in an everlasting covenant that was inaugurated by the Lord with the Israelites; God in Christ will never cease to care for the Church, his spouse. This relationship of love we celebrate with joy and delight on Christmas.

READING II It seems strange to be proclaiming a passage from the Acts of the Apostles at the Christmas Vigil liturgy. We usually hear from Acts, the book that describes the spread of the Gospel and the development of early Christian communities, during the Easter Season. Yet this reading in particular focuses on the Jewish heritage of our Christian belief in Jesus as the Savior. We have here a few verses from Paul's sermon in the Jewish synagogue at Antioch in Pisidia, the administrative center for the Roman province of Galatia. They are found in the section of the Acts that narrates the extension of Paul's mission beyond the Jerusalem community.

As you take time to understand these verses, look at the entire speech Paul gave (Acts 13:16–41). The verses you read today are from a section of the speech that details what God has done for the Chosen People of Israel. The missionary discourse is Paul's first in Acts and meant to persuade the Jewish audience that God has sent Israel a savior in the person of Jesus. Masterfully crafted, the discourse shows Paul reverencing the Jews as "fellow Israelites," a title that not only shows his

GOSPEL Matthew 1:1–25

Practice the names in the genealogy so that the assembly can sense the importance of history. Read the genealogy with care as if it were that of your own family or one of your parishioners. Pace yourself, not rushing, but not reading too slowly either.

Perez = PAYR-ez
Zerah = ZEE-rah
Tamar = TAY-mahr
Hezron = HEZ-ruhn
Ram = ram
Amminadab = uh-MIN-uh-dab
Nahshon = NAH-shuhn
Salmon = SAL-muhn
Boaz = BOH-az
Rahab = RAY-hab
Obed = OH-bed

Uriah = yoo-RĪ-uh
Rehoboam = ree-huh-BOH-uhm
Abijah = uh-BĪ-juh
Asaph = AY-saf
Jehoshaphat = jeh-HOH-shuh-fat
Joram = JOHR-uhm
Uzziah = uh-ZĪ-uh

A reading from the holy Gospel according to Matthew

The book of the **genealogy** of Jesus **Christ**,
the son of **David**, the son of **Abraham**.

Abraham became the father of **Isaac**,
Isaac the father of **Jacob**,
Jacob the father of **Judah** and his brothers.
Judah became the father of **Perez** and **Zerah**,
whose mother was **Tamar**.
Perez became the father of **Hezron**,
Hezron the father of **Ram**,
Ram the father of **Amminadab**.
Amminadab became the father of **Nahshon**,
Nahshon the father of **Salmon**,
Salmon the father of **Boaz**,
whose mother was **Rahab**.
Boaz became the father of **Obed**,
whose mother was **Ruth**.
Obed became the father of **Jesse**,
Jesse the father of **David** the king.

David became the father of **Solomon**,
whose mother had been the wife of **Uriah**.
Solomon became the father of **Rehoboam**,
Rehoboam the father of **Abijah**,
Abijah the father of **Asaph**.
Asaph became the father of **Jehoshaphat**,
Jehoshaphat the father of **Joram**,
Joram the father of **Uzziah**.

oneness with them (Paul is a Jew), but also honors the history of salvation already begun in the Chosen People. But for the evangelist Luke, the author of the Acts of the Apostles, a period of salvation history came to an end with John the Baptist ("as John was completing his course") and a new period began. The section of the speech after these verses shows how Jesus is the fulfillment of the promise to the Hebrew people, and the conclusion, which recounts all that God has done through the death and Resurrection of Jesus, calls people in the synagogue to faith.

For Christians, salvation history can neither be understood apart from the history of the Chosen People of Israel nor apart from the birth, life, death, and Resurrection of Jesus. Although Jews do not profess faith in Jesus as their Messiah, this passage gives us as Christians the opportunity to reflect on the intimate faith connection we have with Jews. God was active in history and in the lives of people before the birth of the Messiah and God is still active in the lives of those who do not profess Jesus as the Messiah.

Yet, we Christians have an obligation, like Paul, to evangelize, to spread the Good News of salvation to those who have not yet heard. We do this though, like Paul, in a way that recognizes God already present in their lives. Some in the assembly this evening will not have heard the Good News. Announce the Good News to them with humility and with respect for the presence of God already at work in them.

GOSPEL The genealogy of Jesus presents a core truth of our faith: Jesus Christ, Emmanuel—God with

Jotham = JOH-thuhm
Ahaz = AY-haz
Hezekiah = hez-eh-KĪ-uh
Manasseh = muh-NAS-uh
Amos = AY-m*s
Josiah = joh-SĪ-uh
Jechoniah = jek-oh-NĪ-uh

Shealtiel = shee-AL-tee-uhl
Zerubbabel = zuh-ROOB-uh-b*l
Abiud = uh-BĪ-uhd
Eliakim = ee-LĪ-uh-kim
Azor = AY-zohr
Zadok = ZAY-dok
Achim = AH-kim
Eliud = ee-LĪ-uhd
Eleazar = el-ee-AY-zer
Matthan = MATH-uhn

Take a deep, but inaudible, breath before the announcement of the birth of Jesus, "Of her was born Jesus who is called the Christ." Read the announcement slowly with solemnity.

Take another deep, but inaudible breath after the concluding phrase "fourteen generations" as you have finished the genealogy. The pause will also make apparent the beginning of a new section of the Gospel.

Uzziah became the father of **Jotham**,
Jotham the father of **Ahaz**,
Ahaz the father of **Hezekiah**.
Hezekiah became the father of **Manasseh**,
Manasseh the father of **Amos**,
Amos the father of **Josiah**.
Josiah became the father of **Jechoniah** and his brothers
at the time of the **Babylonian exile**.

After the **Babylonian exile**,
Jechoniah became the father of **Shealtiel**,
Shealtiel the father of **Zerubbabel**,
Zerubbabel the father of **Abiud**.
Abiud became the father of **Eliakim**,
Eliakim the father of **Azor**,
Azor the father of **Zadok**.
Zadok became the father of **Achim**,
Achim the father of **Eliud**,
Eliud the father of **Eleazar**.
Eleazar became the father of **Matthan**,
Matthan the father of **Jacob**,
Jacob the father of **Joseph**, the husband of **Mary**.
Of her was born **Jesus** who is called the **Christ**.

Thus the **total** number of generations
from **Abraham** to **David**
is **fourteen generations**;
from **David** to the **Babylonian exile**,
fourteen generations;
from the **Babylonian exile** to the **Christ**,
fourteen generations.

us—born of the Virgin Mary through the creative act of God, enters into human history—indeed, the history of the world. Jesus is fully human and fully divine. In this passage, Matthew offers us a theological truth similar to the one found in this evening's Second Reading: God works through human persons, men and women who sometimes have faith and sometimes do not yet believe.

Although Jesus comes from God, it is into and also through the ordinariness of human life that Jesus comes. The genealogy is intentionally composed of three sections of 14 names: from Abraham to David; David to the Babylonian captivity; and the Exile to Jesus, who is called the Christ, the Messiah. Both men and women (Tamar, Rahab, Ruth, Bathsheba, and Mary) are included, as are the names of those who were responsible for good and evil. Most of us are familiar with the stories of Abraham, Isaac, and Jacob, but perhaps not as much with the stories of Tamar, who deceived her father-in-law Judah into an incestuous relationship in order to obtain justice, and Bathsheba, who was the wife of Uriah and committed adultery with David. The upright and the sinful, the simplicity and the messiness of human nature are all evident in Matthew's genealogy. And the inclusion of Ruth shows that the ancestry of Jesus is not exclusively Jewish; Ruth was a Moabite who joined the Israelite community. All this is to affirm that Jesus came to save God's people, Jews and Gentiles alike, from their sins. Those saved through Jesus are from every

Now **this** is how the **birth** of **Jesus Christ** came about.
When his mother **Mary** was betrothed to **Joseph**,
but **before** they lived together,
she was found with **child** through the **Holy Spirit**.

Express the care and concern of Joseph for Mary as you read about his unwillingness to expose her to shame. Use a gentle tone of voice.

Joseph her **husband**, since he was a **righteous** man,
yet unwilling to expose her to **shame**,
decided to divorce her quietly.
Such was his intention when, **behold**,
the **angel** of the Lord **appeared** to him in a **dream** and said,
"**Joseph**, son of **David**,
do not be afraid to take **Mary** your **wife** into your home.
For it is through the **Holy Spirit**
that this child has been **conceived** in her.

Emphasize the name "Jesus" and its meaning by taking your time proclaiming the line "She will bear a son and you are to name him Jesus, because he will save his people from their sins." This is what Christmas is all about.

She will bear a **son** and you are to name him **Jesus**,
because he will save his **people** from their **sins**."
All this took place to **fulfill**
what the **Lord** had said through the **prophet**:
Behold, *the* ***virgin*** *shall* ***conceive*** *and bear a* ***son***,
and they shall name him ***Emmanuel***,
which means "**God** is **with** us."

Utter these words describing Joseph's act of will with the peace Joseph must have felt when he, like Mary, opened himself to doing the Lord's will.

When Joseph **awoke**,
he did as the **angel** of the Lord had **commanded** him
and took his wife into his home.
He had **no** relations with her until she bore a **son**,
and he **named** him **Jesus**.

[Shorter Form: Matthew 1:18–25]

race, nation, culture, gender, age, and background. For Matthew, Jesus is the Messiah-King of Israel, the son of David, the son of Abraham, and the son of Mary.

After the genealogy, Matthew's focus on Joseph in the Gospel story of Jesus' birth, provides us with a model of trust in uncertain and threatening circumstances. Joseph, like Mary in the Gospel according to Luke, listened to the voice of God in the angel and was obedient to God's will. Joseph trusted that God would be with him as he joined himself to Mary for the birth of Jesus. In the world of Joseph and Mary, a betrothed Jewish woman who was seemingly unfaithful would be stoned, as Jewish law dictated. But Joseph, despite thinking that Mary had not been loyal to him, chose to listen to God's will rather than bring shame upon her. In doing so, Joseph welcomed the presence of the Savior in Mary.

Offer your proclamation as a reminder that we are to live Christmas as Joseph did, by reverencing the presence of Emmanuel in all those with whom we come in contact, whether they are intimate spouses, close friends, or merely acquaintances. Both Mary and Joseph provide us with examples of what it means to trust that God is present at turning points in life's journey. Many in the assembly will be at crossroads in their own life journeys this Christmas. Allow your own faith and trust in God to be evident in your proclamation. This will lead others to trust with Mary and Joseph that God is with us as we live Christmas in the ordinariness, messiness, and beauty of human life.

NATIVITY OF THE LORD: MIDNIGHT

Lectionary #14

READING I Isaiah 9:1–6

Isaiah = Ī-ZAY-uh

Express the lines in the first section, "The people who walked in darkness have seen a great light" and "land of gloom a light has shone" with contentment. Relief from the darkness has come!

Pause before the section that begins "For the yoke that burdened them." Read this section with confidence that God has overcome the oppression his people faced.

Midian = MID-ee-uhn

Read each of the titles with different expression: 1) Wonder-Counselor with awe, 2) God-Hero, 3) Father-Forever with confidence and assurance, and 4) Prince of Peace with gentleness. Pause after the last title.

Convey the characteristics of the royal Messiah's dominion in the same way as you spoke the titles (although the structure is not exactly parallel): 1) "vast" with awe, 2) "peaceful" with gentleness, 3) "confirms and sustains" with confidence and assurance, and 4) "judgment and justice" with strength.

A reading from the Book of the Prophet Isaiah

The people who walked in **darkness**
    have seen a great **light**;
upon those who **dwelt** in the land of **gloom**
    a **light** has **shone**.
You have brought them **abundant** joy
    and great **rejoicing**,
as they **rejoice** before you as at the **harvest**,
    as people make **merry** when dividing spoils.
For the **yoke** that **burdened** them,
    the **pole** on their **shoulder**,
and the rod of their **taskmaster**
    you have **smashed**, as on the day of Midian.
For **every** boot that tramped in **battle**,
    every cloak rolled in **blood**,
    will be burned as **fuel** for **flames**.
For a **child** is **born** to **us**, a **son** is **given us**;
    upon his shoulder **dominion** rests.
They name him Wonder-**Counselor**, God-**Hero**,
    Father-**Forever**, Prince of **Peace**.
His dominion is **vast**
    and forever **peaceful**,

READING I The term "oracle" refers to prophetic statements that relate to a judgment or the future. An oracle is often preceded by the words "Thus says the Lord," a formula indicating that what follows is a divine message communicated word-for-word by a go-between such as a prophet. Today's First Reading is a messianic oracle that suggests the triumph of light over darkness and gloom. The Israelites faced much darkness and gloom in their history. In this selection from Isaiah, the yoke, pole, and rod are symbols of their oppression by the Assyrians. But for Isaiah, a prophet of hope, this oppression will be overcome. Even in their darkest moments, God will never abandon the Israelites. The prophet's message of hope is that a child will be born from the line of David and will continue the Davidic monarchy. This child and his dominion will be such that he can be named Wonder-Counselor, God-Hero, Father-Forever, and Prince of Peace.

Biblical scholars discuss whether this passage represents an account of the coronation of a king or an actual birth of a child. But no matter which interpretation is given, for the Israelites, the passage represents the hope for a better life through a new leader. Jews today still hold out the messianic hope of this passage. And, though the Christian belief that the messianic hope has been fulfilled in Jesus distinguishes us from our Jewish brothers and sisters, still together we rejoice when we see darkness and gloom overcome in the hearts of individuals and in the world. Let joy reign in your heart, be seen in your eyes, and heard in your voice as you proclaim this reading to the assembly.

from David's throne, and over his **kingdom**,
which he confirms and sustains
by **judgment** and **justice**,
both **now** and **forever**.

Zeal is strong and impassioned desire. Proclaim "The zeal of the Lord of hosts will do this!" with eagerness and certainty.

The **zeal** of the LORD of **hosts** will **do** this!

READING II Titus 2:11–14

Titus = TĪ-tus

A reading from the Letter of Saint Paul to Titus

Proclaiming a one-sentence reading is difficult. Thinking about the meaning of the sentence in terms of the past, present, and future will be more helpful than following the punctuation exactly.

Beloved:
The **grace** of **God** has **appeared**, saving **all**
and training us to reject **godless** ways and **worldly** desires
and to live **temperately**, **justly**, and **devoutly** in this age,
as we await the **blessed** hope,
the **appearance** of the **glory** of our great **God**
and savior **Jesus Christ**,
who gave himself for us to **deliver** us from all **lawlessness**
and to **cleanse** for himself a people as his own,
eager to do what is **good**.

GOSPEL Luke 2:1–14

Take your time with this familiar story.
Caesar Augustus = SEE-zer aw-GUHS-tuhs

A reading from the holy Gospel according to Luke

In those days a **decree** went out from Caesar **Augustus**
that the whole **world** should be **enrolled**.

Quirinius = kwih-RIN-ee-uhs
Syria = SEER-ee-u

This was the **first** enrollment,
when **Quirinius** was governor of **Syria**.

Let those who come to church only on Christmas sense how extraordinary is the Light coming into darkness which you proclaim during this late-night liturgy!

READING II **One sentence! At first glance this is all that this short reading from Titus seems to be! (Titus is one of the three pastoral letters—I Timothy and II Timothy are the others.) But it is so much more. In this one sentence, the author of this letter discloses the grace of God active in the past, present, and future. On Christmas we not only remember Jesus' first coming in history—his birth in Bethlehem, (the past) but we also affirm how he is God-with-us today (the present), and we look forward in blessed hope to his appearance again as the glory of God (the future).**

According to the author of Titus, when we celebrate Jesus' coming as the grace of God in history, then Jesus' saving works accomplished through his life, death, and Resurrection must be as near to our minds as his birth as an infant. The "grace of God" is the "savior Jesus Christ" who in his first coming showed us how to live, gave himself for us through his death to deliver us from sin, washed us clean in his death and Resurrection, and took us as his own people.

We, who accept as true the Savior's first coming in history, have ethical responsibilities, for Christ now lives in us. Often the Christmas season is the time of year when we take these ethical responsibilities seriously. However, for the author of Titus, the concern is the eagerness to which we are *always* ready to do what is good. This is what Jesus Christ has trained

Galilee = GAL-ih-lee

Judea = joo-DEE-uh

So **all** went to be enrolled, **each** to his **own** town.
And **Joseph** too went up from **Galilee** from the town
of **Nazareth**
to **Judea**, to the city of **David** that is called **Bethlehem**,
because he was of the house and family of **David**,
to be enrolled with **Mary**, his **betrothed**, who was with **child**.
While they were there,
the **time** came for her to **have** her child,
and she gave **birth** to her **firstborn son**.
She **wrapped** him in **swaddling** clothes and **laid** him in a **manger**,
because there was no **room** for them in the **inn**.

Now there were **shepherds** in that region living in the **fields**
and keeping the **night** watch over their **flock**.
The **angel** of the Lord **appeared** to them
and the **glory** of the Lord **shone** around them,
and they were struck with great **fear**.
The **angel** said to them,
"Do **not** be **afraid**;
for **behold**, I proclaim to you good **news** of great **joy**
that will be for **all** the **people**.
For **today** in the city of **David**
a **savior** has been born for you who is **Christ** and **Lord**.
And **this** will be a **sign** for **you**:
you will find an **infant** wrapped in **swaddling** clothes
and **lying** in a **manger**."
And **suddenly** there was a multitude of the heavenly **host** with
the angel,
praising **God** and saying:
"**Glory** to **God** in the **highest**
and on earth **peace** to those on whom his favor **rests**."

Emphasize the word "today" in "For today in the city of David." Look up and convey this line to your assembly as a solemn proclamation. While Jesus was born in Bethlehem some 2,000 years ago, he is present today in the assembly, in the word, in the celebrant, and in the Eucharist.

End on a joyful note as you proclaim the praises of the heavenly host with the angel. We have already sung the Gloria, so read the praises with the same exuberance with which the Gloria was sung. A look of joy reflected on your face is more than appropriate!

us to do through his own life. As a result of your well-prepared and skillfully delivered proclamation of this reading, others might be led to inquire about your belief in Jesus Christ as the Messiah and your blessed hope in his second coming.

GOSPEL Luke's account of the birth of Jesus shows us that we share in a graced humanity. For years people have been moved by the many details in this story. Many have passed on the Lucan story to their children and Christmas pageants often dramatize this narrative. Why? While our storytelling and Christmas pageants often emphasize details that may or may not be true historically, they do convey a profound truth of faith: God graced humanity with divinity.

While Luke emphasizes God's coming to all of humanity, he gives particular attention to the poor. In this story, his stress on the swaddling clothes in which the infant Jesus is wrapped and the shepherds being the first to hear the news of Jesus' birth and to visit him, shows that God graces those who are lowly and poor. The circumstances of Jesus' birth give testimony to a power that contrasts with that of the Roman ruler Caesar Augustus and affirms the intimate relationship between divinity and humanity.

Your task is to present this Christmas Gospel with awe at the momentous change the course of human history took some 2,000 years ago. Proclaim it with the belief of Christmas expressed in the Responsorial Psalm that, "Today is born our Savior, Christ the Lord" (Psalm 98).

DECEMBER 25, 2010

NATIVITY OF THE LORD: DAWN

Lectionary #15

READING I Isaiah 62:11–12

Isaiah = Ī-ZAY-uh

Look up as you proclaim the words "See, the Lord proclaims to the ends of the earth." "To the ends of the earth" includes all sides of the assembly, even the back rows and those standing!

Soften your voice on the name "holy people." Speak the title "redeemed of the Lord" with confidence. State the name "Frequented," which means "sought out" with reassurance, for Zion (Jerusalem)—and we—will not be forsaken.

A reading from the Book of the Prophet Isaiah

See, the **LORD** proclaims
to the **ends** of the **earth**:
say to daughter **Zion**,
your **savior** comes!
Here is his **reward** with him,
his **recompense** before him.
They shall be called the **holy** people,
the **redeemed** of the LORD,
and you shall be called "**Frequented**,"
a city that is **not forsaken**.

READING I **The historical context for this reading is the end of the Babylonian exile and the joyful return of the Israelites to Jerusalem. The city was restored and its people delivered back to their home. While the Israelites were not always faithful to God, God was always committed to them. Imagine the joy of the Israelites returning in procession to Jerusalem. In later times the joy of the reading is seen in the procession on the first day of major pilgrimage feasts such as the feast of Tabernacles.**

The prophet's announcement of salvation extends beyond Jerusalem and its people. All the ends of the earth will know newness of life. As dawn breaks on Christmas morning, we once again proclaim with conviction that the fullness of salvation has come through Jesus Christ, who himself was of Jewish descent. Just as the members of the community at Jerusalem could now be called "the holy people" and the "redeemed of the Lord" and Jerusalem called "Frequented," Christians also claim these titles, but in a new way. Jesus Christ makes us the redeemed of the Lord.

Make this announcement of salvation resound throughout the church and beyond, as if the doors were opened wide for the whole neighborhood to hear the joyful news! If you are able to memorize well, this would be a good text to commit to memory. It would not be wise, however, to try and proclaim a text from memory for the first time at a Christmas liturgy. You might try at least a line or two.

READING II Titus 3:4–7

Titus = Tī-tus

The phrase "When the kindness and generous love of God our savior appeared refers to Jesus Christ. Emphasize this as the first point of the reading by proclaiming it more slowly than what follows. The second point is "he saved us through the bath of rebirth . . . ." Read a little slower through "Holy Spirit."

Speak the words "so that we might be justified" with warmth as they refer to the gifts of justification and eternal life in Jesus, gifts your assembly receives.

A reading from the Letter of Saint Paul to Titus

Beloved:
When the **kindness** and **generous love**
of **God** our **savior** appeared,
not because of any **righteous deeds we** had done
but because of **his mercy**,
he **saved** us through the **bath** of **rebirth**
and **renewal** by the **Holy Spirit**,
whom he **richly** poured out on us
through **Jesus Christ** our **savior**,
so that we might be **justified** by his **grace**
and become **heirs** in **hope** of **eternal life**.

READING II **Christmas and Easter come together once again! In this brief passage, we hear that from his birth to his Resurrection, Jesus Christ saves. The four verses from the letter to Titus deal directly with what has been a central issue for Christians from the beginning: salvation.**

Some in the community on Crete, for which Titus was responsible, believed they could earn their salvation by the good deeds they performed. From the authentic Pauline letters through the later pastoral epistles (1 and 2 Timothy and Titus) and up to the present day, the Christian tradition has been clear that salvation is a gift from God. God freely chose to send his Son Jesus Christ as the Savior because God loved humanity unconditionally. No deeds or actions on our part can earn us salvation.

Yet we are called to respond to our gift of salvation by living our lives in a certain way. In the two verses that precede this selection from Titus, we hear Christians called to perform honest work, live in gentle obedience, respect authority, speak no evil, and be kind to all. During this time of year, which has its own built-in stress, we might find it difficult at times to respond in love to others, especially family members and close friends. As you prepare this reading, reflect on how God's gratuitous self-giving in Jesus Christ provides an example for us to live out our Easter faith. Prepare to proclaim, the reading well, but when you proclaim let go of the need for a perfect proclamation. Rather, allow the Holy Spirit to work through you so the assembly can know of their unmerited salvation in Jesus Christ.

GOSPEL Luke 2:15–20

A reading from the holy Gospel according to Luke

Let eagerness be heard in your voice as you speak the shepherds' words.

Pause after "Mary and Joseph." They are not lying in the manger with the infant!

Lower your voice and speak gently and slowly about Mary. Pause after describing Mary's response. Then, raise your voice and speak excitedly to deliver the narrative lines of the shepherds' response.

When the **angels** went away from them to **heaven**,
the **shepherds** said to one another,
"Let us go, then, to **Bethlehem**
to see this thing that has taken place,
which the **Lord** has made known to us."
So they went in haste and found **Mary** and **Joseph**,
and the **infant** lying in the **manger**.
When they saw this,
they made known the **message**
that had been told them about this **child**.
All who heard it were **amazed**
by what had been told them by the **shepherds**.
And **Mary** kept all these things,
reflecting on them in her **heart**.
Then the **shepherds** returned,
glorifying and **praising** God
for all they had **heard** and **seen**,
just as it had been told to them.

GOSPEL The Gospel reading this Christmas morning begins where the Gospel for the Mass at Midnight ended. At the end of the last night's Gospel, the heavenly hosts and angel praise God saying, "Glory to God. . . ." At the end of today's passage, the shepherds, after listening to the angel's message about the birth of a Savior, praise God for what they had seen in the manger, while Mary reflects in her heart on what has taken place. Both the shepherds and Mary are on their own distinct faith journeys, as we are today. In their own ways, the shepherds and Mary are both responding to the amazing news that a Savior has been born who is Christ and Lord. They simply express their amazement differently.

Some in the assembly before you will be natural evangelizers like the shepherds and want to go out into the world announcing the Good News of the Savior's birth. Others, like Mary, will take the Good News into their hearts, reflecting on what it means for them and for the world. While your tendency might be to proclaim this passage emphasizing the exuberance of the shepherds, this could overshadow Mary's response to the Good News. A balanced proclamation, which contrasts the two responses, can have the effect of affirming the genuineness of both responses in Christians today.

This brief Gospel is packed with meaning, so take your time communicating it. Fill your voice with the reverence, eagerness, and joy that permeate Luke's account of the Savior's birth. Doing so will assist many in hearing this familiar Gospel anew and lead them to express amazement at the Savior's birth through their unique personalities and gifts.

NATIVITY OF THE LORD: DAY

Lectionary #16

READING I Isaiah 52:7–10

Isaiah = Ī-ZAY-uh

A reading from the Book of the Prophet Isaiah

Speak the opening lines ("How beautiful upon the mountains . . .") slowly and serenely as if painting a picture for the assembly. Strengthen your voice incrementally as you come to the announcement of the King in the words "Your God is King!" Pause significantly after the announcement.

Sentinels = SEN-tih-nuls

How **beautiful** upon the **mountains**
are the **feet** of him who brings glad **tidings**,
announcing **peace**, bearing **good news**,
announcing **salvation**, and saying to **Zion**,
"Your God is **King**!"

Hark! Your **sentinels** raise a cry,
together they shout for **joy**,
for they see **directly**, before their eyes,
the LORD **restoring** Zion.

Even the ruins are singing about what God is doing! Speak so that enthusiasm, energy, and excitement are palpable. Moderate your voice as you describe why the ruins are singing.

Break out together in **song**,
O **ruins** of Jerusalem!
For the LORD **comforts** his people,
he **redeems** Jerusalem.
The LORD has **bared** his holy arm
in the sight of **all** the nations;

Memorize this last line if you can do so with ease.

all the **ends** of the **earth** will **behold**
the **salvation** of our **God**.

READING I In this reading, you are the messenger who is announcing peace and salvation. To the Hebrew people who sometimes forgot God and failed to live up to their part of the covenant, it must have seemed that God also had forgotten them, especially during the long days of the Babylonian exile. The traditional role of the messenger was to announce the advent (coming) of the king. The role of the messenger in this passage in no different. He had news: "God is king!" The Babylonians had been defeated by the Persians, a new day was dawning, God was back in power, and God was once again watching out for the people of Jerusalem.

Consistent in this reading is the affirmation that God is leading his people home. It is neither the exiles returning home nor the city of Jerusalem that attracts the attention of Second Isaiah (the author of chapters 40 through 55 of the book of Isaiah); instead the Lord is his focus. The author's lyrical and poetic style, along with his use of vivid images and active verbs, also focus on the Lord.

On Christmas Day, we are mindful of God's divine initiative in sending Jesus Christ to be King, the bringer of peace and salvation. Just as the author of this passage draws attention to the Lord, your challenge is to do the same. Let your proclamation exude praise for the salvation of our God—so much so that you leave the assembly eager to sing the refrain of the Responsorial Psalm, "All the ends of the earth have seen the saving power of God" (Psalm 98).

READING II Why do you proclaim this passage on Christmas Day? The short answer to this question is

READING II Hebrews 1:1–6

A reading from the Letter to the Hebrews

In the lines "In times past . . . in these last days" make sure and observe the commas to differentiate between how God spoke in the two different times.

Brothers and sisters:
In times **past**, God spoke in partial and various ways
to our **ancestors** through the **prophets**;
in these **last** days, he has spoken to **us** through the **Son**,
whom he made **heir** of all things
and **through** whom he created the **universe**,
who is the **refulgence** of his **glory**,
the very **imprint** of his **being**,
and who **sustains** all things by his mighty **word**.
When he had accomplished **purification** from **sins**,
he took his **seat** at the right hand of the **Majesty** on high,
as far **superior** to the **angels**
as the **name** he has inherited is more **excellent** than theirs.

By pausing significantly after the colons in the phrases "For to which of the angels did God ever say," you will make it clear that the author is offering three distinct quotations. The assembly will not be aware they are from the Old Testament, but they are from Psalm 2:7; 2 Samuel 7:14; and Deuteronomy 32:43. The first two the author writes in the form of a question; the third as a strong affirmation of the Son's identity. Let the difference be heard in the inflection of your voice.

For to ***which*** of the angels did God ever say:
You *are my* ***son****;* ***this*** *day I have* ***begotten*** *you?*
Or again:
I *will be a* ***father*** *to him, and* ***he*** *shall be a* ***son*** *to me?*
And again, when he leads the ***firstborn*** into the world, he says:
Let all the ***angels*** *of God* ***worship*** *him.*

because on Christmas day we assert with utmost conviction what we believe about Jesus Christ, the Son of the Father: that he is fully divine and fully human. The two together comprise our belief in the Incarnation of God in Jesus Christ and are equally important to celebrate in word and Eucharist on Christmas.

The entire letter to the Hebrews, including the introduction we read today, is a defense of who Christians believe the Son to be. While the letter itself does not provide specific information as to its author, the date of its composition, or its addressees, the content of the letter suggests it was written for Christians who were attracted to the values of the Jewish cult. These Christians struggled with remaining faithful when challenged by those who denied the fullness of Jesus' divinity.

To persuade readers of the Christian belief in the Son's divinity, the author of Hebrews develops the theme of Jesus' high priesthood. The Son is different from and superior to past prophets because God spoke completely through him (1:1–2), the Son is superior to the angels because he sacrificed himself for the purification of sins (1:4–5), and the Son is the "reflection of God's glory"—he is the only begotten Son of God (1:3). On the basis of these arguments, the author of Hebrews concludes that the new covenant established through Jesus offers a new and superior priesthood from the Levitical priesthood of the old covenant.

Early Christians needed to defend their belief in the preexistence and divinity of Jesus Christ because they were challenged by Jews and others in the Greco-Roman world who did not believe that God

GOSPEL John 1:1–18

A reading from the holy Gospel according to John

Read the section, "In the beginning was the Word, and the Word was with God, and the Word was God" as if you were telling a story and not teaching philosophy.

In the **beginning** was the **Word**,
and the Word was **with God**,
and the Word **was** God.
He was in the **beginning** with God.
All things came to be **through** him,
and **without** him **nothing** came to be.
What came to be through him was **life**,
and this life was the **light** of the human **race**;
the **light** shines in the **darkness**,
and the **darkness** has not overcome it.

Accentuate the contrasting images by putting lightness in your voice with "life" and "light," and heaviness with "darkness."
Pause before "A man named John was sent by God" to mark the Gospel's change in focus.

A man named **John** was sent from God.
He came for **testimony**, to testify to the **light**,
so that **all** might **believe** through him.
He was **not** the light,
but came to **testify** to the light.

Here is another transition, beginning with "The true light, which enlightens everyone." Pause before these words. Convey both the sadness and hope in this section by changing the tone in your voice appropriately.

The **true** light, which enlightens **everyone**,
was coming into the world.
He was **in** the world,
and the world came to be **through** him,
but the world did not **know** him.
He came to what was his own,
but his **own** people did **not** accept him.

But to those who **did** accept him
he gave **power** to become **children** of **God**,
to those who **believe** in his **name**,

could actually become human while retaining the fullness of divinity. But the truth for Christians is that God *did* do this in his Son. The later articulation of our theological beliefs about the Son's relationship to God will find many of its roots in the letter to the Hebrews.

We worship the Son as God. Let the last line of this reading be filled with your own conviction that Jesus Christ is the Son of God, the very reflection of God's glory—indeed, fully divine. Only because Jesus Christ is fully divine as well as fully human are we purified from our sins. Through the Eucharist, we share in Jesus' high priesthood of the new covenant. On Christmas we celebrate Jesus' priesthood and our participation in it.

GOSPEL There is much complicated theology and philosophy behind the prologue to the Gospel according to John. But we needn't understand it fully in order to communicate the prologue's fundamental meaning. In an age when some were denying the humanity of Jesus and others were rejecting his divinity, John begins his account of the Gospel with this hymn to incarnation which describes the divine becoming human in the Word made flesh.

John wrote in a time when most believed that the material world was evil and the spiritual world (the world of the divine) was good. The deep chasm that existed between the two worlds could never be bridged, lest the divine be contaminated with the vices of nature. While we are separated from John's time by thousands of years, many today still speak of the wickedness of the flesh and the evilness of human nature. Some even teach

who were born not by **natural** generation
nor by **human** choice nor by a **man's** decision
but of **God**.

This is Christmas: "And the Word became flesh!" Communicate the joy and wonder of this in your voice.

And the Word became **flesh**
and made his **dwelling** among us,
and we saw his **glory**,
the glory as of the Father's only **Son**,
full of **grace** and **truth**.

Pause again before "John testified to him and cried out." This is the second time the author deviates to narrate John's story and role. Use the same tone that you used in the first section that dealt with John.

John **testified** to him and cried out, saying,
"**This** was he of whom I said,
'The one who is coming **after** me ranks **ahead** of me
because he existed **before** me.'"
From his **fullness** we have **all received**,
grace in place of **grace**,
because while the **law** was given through **Moses**,
grace and **truth** came through Jesus **Christ**.

This, too, is Christmas: no one has seen God until the Son revealed God. State the concluding lines with faith and conviction, reading them slowly.

No one has ever **seen** God.
The only **Son**, God, who is at the Father's **side**,
has **revealed** him.
[Shorter Form: John 1:1–5, 9–14]

that to know God we must leave behind the flesh. How contrary to the truths of John's prologue and the truth of Christmas for Christians!

In the Word made flesh, the same Word who existed with God and was God from the very beginning, and through whom the world was created, God chose to bridge the chasm between the material and spiritual worlds. As John tells us, God chose to give out of his own grace, the fullness of himself—the Son, the Word. No longer would the physical world, of which we human persons are a part, be separated from the true face of God.

Humanity and divinity are united in a new way different from the grace given through the law of Moses. This new way allows for a relationship between all creation and its Creator that never before was possible. While it builds on the relationship God had with God's people as recounted in the Old Testament, it also changes that relationship, because all flesh has now seen the glory of God. As the early Church father, Saint Athanasius, puts it, "God became human so that we could become divine." (*On the Incarnation,* 54) The beauty of the Incarnation and the possibilities it holds out for us are what this passage from the Gospel according to John disclose. And these are the reasons we come together on Christmas to express our eternal gratitude. Your careful and solemn proclamation will lead the assembly to understand the gratitude due to God for the gift of the Word made flesh.

HOLY FAMILY OF JESUS, MARY, AND JOSEPH

Lectionary #17a

READING I Sirach 3:2–6, 12–14

Sirach = SEER-ak

Deliver the first section in a teacher-like tone of voice.

A reading from the Book of Sirach

God sets a **father** in **honor** over his **children**;
a **mother's authority** he **confirms** over her **sons**.
Whoever honors his **father** atones for **sins**,
and **preserves** himself from them.
When he **prays**, he is **heard**;
he stores up **riches** who **reveres** his **mother**.
Whoever **honors** his **father** is **gladdened** by **children**,
and, when he **prays**, is **heard**.
Whoever **reveres** his **father** will **live a** long **life**;
he who **obeys** his **father** brings **comfort** to his **mother**.

Pause noticeably before a new section begins with the words "My son." Use a gentle, personable tone of voice for the instructions that follow.

My **son**, take **care** of your father when he is **old**;
grieve him **not** as long as he **lives**.
Even if his mind **fail**, be **considerate** of him;
revile him **not** all the days of his life;
kindness to a **father** will not be **forgotten**,
firmly planted against the **debt** of your **sins**
—a **house** raised in **justice** to you.

Make eye contact with the assembly on the words "a house raised in justice to you."

READING I The Introduction to the Lectionary tells us that the first two readings on the feast of the Holy Family were chosen to disclose the virtues of family life (#95). The First Reading comes from the book of Sirach, which was written by Ben Sira in the late third and early second centuries BC. A scholar in the Jewish way of life, Ben Sira spent his life studying the teachings of the law and prophets and passing on his knowledge to his students at a school for young Jewish men. The topics covered in the book of Sirach are many and vary greatly, including humility, charity, anger, how to give alms, and how to provide loans.

In the book of Sirach, today's reading falls between the end of chapter 2 (which details a faithful person's duties toward God) and before the second half of chapter 3 (which gives instructions on how to live with humility). In context, then, the fundamental principle of family life that the First Reading reveals is that love of God and love of one's parents cannot be separated. Fidelity to God involves the children's responsibilities toward their parents.

Three times this reading refers to honoring one's father and once to revering one's mother. The final paragraph is solely about caring for one's father, although today, by extension, we would include caring for all those who are a part of our family or community of friends.

In your proclamation, try not to overemphasize the patriarchal dimension of the reading. Rather, draw out the consequences of caring for our parents and others in old age. The children who take care of those who have nurtured them will receive forgiveness of sins, riches, the

READING II Colossians 3:12–21

Colossians = kuh-LOSH-uhnz

Look up at the assembly for the greeting "Brothers and sisters" and pause noticeably after it, making sure you have their attention.

Read the list of virtues slowly, clearly enunciating each one.

A reading from the Letter of Saint Paul to the Colossians

Brothers and sisters:
Put on, as God's **chosen** ones, **holy** and **beloved**,
heartfelt **compassion**, **kindness**, **humility**, **gentleness**,
and **patience**,
bearing with one another and **forgiving** one another,
if one has a **grievance** against another;
as the **Lord** has forgiven **you**, so must **you** also **do**.
And over **all** these put on **love**,
that is, the **bond** of **perfection**.
And let the **peace** of Christ control your **hearts**,
the **peace** into which you were also **called** in one **body**.
And be **thankful**.
Let the **word** of Christ **dwell** in you **richly**,
as **in all wisdom** you **teach** and **admonish** one another,
singing **psalms**, **hymns**, and spiritual **songs**
with **gratitude** in your **hearts** to **God**.
And **whatever** you do, in **word** or in **deed**,
do **everything** in the **name** of the **Lord Jesus**,
giving **thanks** to God the **Father** through **him**.

Pause significantly after the concluding line "giving thanks to God the Father through him."

Proclaim the household code with love and humility, not authority and arrogance in your voice.

Wives, be **subordinate** to your **husbands**,
as is **proper** in the **Lord**.
Husbands, love your **wives**,
and avoid **any bitterness** toward them.

blessings of children, answered prayers, and a long life—and they will be a comfort to their mothers. All this is the foundation for the child's own house and will result in love returned to them.

As you proclaim the final section, be cognizant that many in the assembly have experience caring for elderly parents or relatives. Healthcare providers who have honored the dignity of Alzheimer's and other dementia patients will also be present. Let them know that the love they have shown has taken root and they can look forward to God's love returned in justice to them.

READING II On the feast of the Holy Family, the Second Reading provides a prescription for ideal family relations. The passage itself comes from the section of Colossians which urges the members of the body of Christ, the Church, to live according to the values of the community (3:5—4:6).

Lists of virtues and vices, as well as household codes, were common in Greek philosophical works of the first century. This author strongly urges the members of the Church to practice these virtues as the Lord intends them to (3:13). Christian families are to perform works of compassion, kindness, humility, gentleness, and patience, not for themselves, but rather in Christ's name (verse 17). When they do, the peace of Christ will lead them to gratitude and praise for all God has done.

The final four verses of the reading set out the manner in which a Christian household is to be ordered. The advice has its roots in the same social or household codes of the first century which held that slaves

Children, obey your **parents** in **everything**,
for this is **pleasing** to the **Lord**.
Fathers, do not **provoke** your **children**,
so they **may not** become **discouraged**.

[Shorter Form: Colossians 3:12–17]

GOSPEL Matthew 2:13–15, 19–23

A reading from the holy Gospel according to Matthew

Differentiate between the narrative lines and the quotations by pausing at the commas and looking up at the assembly as you read the quotation. For example, pause after "and said," and look up on the words "Rise, take the child. . . ."

When the **magi** had **departed**, **behold**,
the **angel** of the **Lord** appeared to **Joseph** in a **dream** and **said**,
"**Rise**, take the **child** and his **mother**, **flee** to **Egypt**,
and **stay** there until I **tell** you.
Herod is going to **search** for the child to **destroy** him."
Joseph **rose** and took the **child** and his **mother** by **night**
and departed for **Egypt**.
He **stayed** there until the **death** of **Herod**,
that what the Lord had said through the **prophet** might
be **fulfilled**,
*Out of **Egypt** I **called** my **son**.*

Make eye contact with the assembly on the quotation from Hosea ("Out of Egypt I called my son").

Use the same technique as in the opening section since a similar structure with "and said," followed by a quotation, occurs here.

When Herod had **died**, **behold**,
the **angel** of the **Lord** appeared in a **dream**
to **Joseph** in **Egypt** and **said**,
"**Rise**, take the **child** and his **mother** and **go** to the land
of **Israel**,
for those who **sought** the child's **life** are **dead**."

were subject to their masters. While this part of the reading might be difficult for you to proclaim, in your preparation try and focus on the dimension of love and care among family members that is present in these verses. Showing affection and paying attention to the feelings and desires of its members is the responsibility of each in the family who live their lives in Christ—wives, husbands, and children alike.

For Catholics, the household or family is the basic unit of the Church. Because of this, it is called the "domestic Church" (*Lumen Gentium,* Dogmatic Constitution on the Church, 11). In this Church, the love between parents and among parents and children identifies the family as a household of faith that gives thanks to God.

In your proclamation, use a consistent gentle and peaceful tone of voice throughout the reading, rather than switching to a didactic and authoritative tone for the household code. This will help keep the unity of the passage and will assist the assembly in understanding the code in relation to the Christian virtue of love.

GOSPEL Even though we have not yet celebrated the solemnity of Epiphany, in Matthew's account of the Gospel, this passage occurs immediately after the narrative of the magi following the star to Bethlehem and paying homage to the Christ-child. It is proclaimed on the feast of the Holy Family because in it we see Joseph, Mary, and Jesus as a family unit. In fidelity to God's direction, Joseph, together with Mary, takes the child Jesus from his place of birth to Egypt and eventually out of Egypt to the land of Israel.

Archelaus = ahr-keh-LAY-uhs

He **rose**, took the **child** and his **mother**,
and **went** to the land of **Israel**.
But when he **heard** that **Archelaus** was ruling over **Judea**
in **place** of his father **Herod**,
he was afraid to go back there.
And because he had been **warned** in a **dream**,
he **departed** for the region of **Galilee**.
He **went** and **dwelt** in a town called **Nazareth**,
so that what had been **spoken** through the **prophets**
might be **fulfilled**,
***He** shall be **called** a **Nazorean**.*

Pause again before the final line ("He shall be called a Nazorean"). Be confident in your delivery, for you are certain Jesus is the Savior.

Nazorean = naz-uh-REE-uhn

In the evangelist's view, it was necessary for the journey of the Holy Family to occur in this manner in order to show Jesus as the fulfillment of the law and the prophets. "My son" in the words quoted from Hosea 11:1, refers to Israel as God's Chosen People. In the Gospel, then, Joseph's faithfulness in guiding Mary and Jesus out of Egypt mirrors the exodus experience of the Israelites. Their freedom from slavery in Egypt offered the hope of a new day. In Jesus, this new day is fulfilled. He is the new Moses in whose life, death, and Resurrection there will be a new exodus.

Matthew's use of the expression "He shall be called a Nazorean" serves the dual purpose of affirming the tradition that the Holy Family resided in Nazareth and drawing a connection between Jesus and the Davidic king of the future referred to in Isaiah 11:1 as "a bud" in Hebrew. In other places in the Old Testament, the same term is used to identify Samson as a savior-like personage (Judges 13—16) and used for consecrated people who set themselves apart by taking vows to the Lord (Amos 2:11–12 and Numbers 6:1–21).

Your proclamation of this Gospel reading, backed by your confident belief in Jesus as the Savior of the world, will lead the families and individuals in the assembly to see that it is through the Holy Family that salvation has come, and that they too can be bearers of Jesus the Nazorean to others, wherever their family's life journey might take them.

MARY, MOTHER OF GOD

Lectionary #18

READING I Numbers 6:22–27

Clearly identify the Lord as the speaker by using a strong, declarative tone of voice.

Moses = MOH-ziz

Aaron = AIR-un

Israelites = IZ-ree-uh-līts

Pray the blessing, "The Lord bless you . . . and give you peace," slowly and with care, line by line, as if you were blessing the assembly. You are asking the Lord to take care of his people.

Pause at the end of the blessing before the Lord's words that are not a part of the actual blessing, "So shall they invoke my name upon the Israelites, and I will bless them."

A reading from the Book of Numbers

The **LORD** said to **Moses**:
"**Speak** to **Aaron** and his **sons** and **tell** them:
This is how you shall **bless** the **Israelites**.
Say to them:
The LORD **bless** you and **keep** you!
The LORD **let** his face **shine** upon
you, and be **gracious** to you!
The LORD **look** upon you **kindly** and
give you **peace**!
So shall they invoke my **name** upon the **Israelites**,
and I will **bless** them."

READING I **The liturgical celebration today focuses on the Incarnation from the perspective of Mary, the Mother of God. The brief passage from the book of Numbers you proclaim today comes at the end of a section on laws and regulations that the Hebrew people were to follow. One of the reasons this passage is proclaimed on the solemnity of Mary, the Mother of God is that it shows Mary to be deeply rooted in the ancient traditions of the Hebrew people. We see that Mary was a faithful Jew. The words of the blessing in these verses were probably not far from her heart, just as many Jews and Christians hold it dear.**

The three lines of the blessing ask that God take care of his people, that God reveal himself to them, and grant them peace. The expression "let his face shine" in Hebrew corresponds to our word "smile." To ask the Lord to let his face shine upon us means to see God happy. God has divine pleasure and contentment because he is in relationship with us. Even though God does not need our companionship, he is happy to freely choose a relationship with us. The Hebrew word for "peace" (*shalom*) includes not only a sense of serenity, but also happiness and prosperity. The peace that comes from God reaches into all areas of our life and leads us to experience the contentment that comes from living our life in God.

Offer this blessing as a prayer for the assembly before you. In your preparation, think about the ways in which the Lord has blessed you and given you peace. This will help you to achieve a tone of prayerfulness in your own voice as you impart the blessing to the assembly.

READING II Galatians 4:4–7

A reading from the Letter of Saint Paul to the Galatians

Brothers and sisters:
When the **fullness** of time had **come**, **God** sent his **Son**,
born of a **woman**, born under the law,
to **ransom** those under the law,
so that we might receive **adoption** as **sons**.
As **proof** that **you** are sons,
God sent the **Spirit** of his **Son** into our **hearts**,
crying out, "**Abba**, **Father**!"
So you are no longer a **slave** but a **son**,
and if a **son** then also an **heir**, through **God**.

Paul captures the entire Paschal Mystery in the single sentence: "When the fullness of time had come . . . adoption as sons." The commas are a good reading guide. "God sent his Son" is the main clause.

"Abba, Father!" are the same words that Jesus used while praying in Gethsemane (Mark 14:36). "Abba" is an Aramaic term that connotes intimacy between a father and his child. Express this intimacy by using a gentle, but audible, voice. Do not shout the words.

READING II This reading expresses the joy that comes from a life-giving transition. Paul wrote in a society in which slavery was reality, so he employed that image in making his point about the new position of Christians in relation to God. Prior to the Son's coming, the Galatians were a people who were slaves to sin. Paul often characterized this slavery as being bound by a shallow understanding of all the details of the Jewish law. When Jesus Christ came, everything changed. Faith—not superficial adherence to the law—was required in order to inherit the promises of Abraham.

Christ took on our humanity, being born of a woman and under the law. It was necessary that he take upon himself our human condition in order that we might now be able to call ourselves adopted sons and daughters of God. Because the Son redeemed humanity and its attachment to the law, we, like Galatians, have the possibility of a new, intimate relationship to God. We can use the Son's words "Abba, Father!" in our prayer to God. We no longer have to follow the letter of the law in order to be in right relationship with God.

Try to convey in your reading of this passage the dynamic movement from constraint to freedom that is behind Paul's words. In order to do this, it might be helpful to reflect on a time in your life when you experienced a change from an old way of life to a new way. What did it feel like for you to be set free from the old to embrace the new? Consider this change as living life more deeply in the Spirit of the Son whom God sent. Through your own growth, you are realizing more of your identity as

GOSPEL Luke 2:16–21

A reading from the holy Gospel according to Luke

Pause at the comma after "Mary and Joseph." They are not lying in the manger with the infant!

The **shepherds** went in **haste** to **Bethlehem** and found **Mary** and **Joseph**,
and the **infant** lying in the **manger**.
When they saw this,
they made **known** the message
that had been **told** them about this child.

Let amazement be in your voice for "all who heard" the news and felt the same.

All who **heard** it were **amazed**
by what had been **told** them by the **shepherds**.

Speak unhurriedly and with care as you describe Mary's actions in the words "And Mary kept all these things, reflecting on them in her heart." Mary is a focal point today and her response is well-known to many. Speaking these words slowly and in a considered fashion allows people to hear her response as if for the first time.

And **Mary** kept all these things,
reflecting on them in her **heart**.
Then the **shepherds** returned,
glorifying and **praising** God
for all they had **heard** and **seen**,
just as it had been told to them.

Pause before the final verse. Taking your time proclaiming it will highlight the important belief in it: Jesus is the fulfillment of Jewish law.

When **eight** days were completed for his **circumcision**,
he was named **Jesus**, the name given him by the **angel**
before he was **conceived** in the womb.

an adopted son or daughter of God; this is what you are calling the assembly to realize as well.

GOSPEL This is the same Gospel reading proclaimed during the Christmas Mass at Dawn, except it begins a verse later and ends with an additional verse. Today, we read the Gospel from the perspective of the solemnity of Mary, Mother of God.

Early Church leaders debated the identity of Mary and how Christians should refer to her. Should Mary be called the "Mother of Christ" (*Christotokos*) or the "Mother of God" (*Theotokos*)? Calling Mary the "Mother of Christ" emphasizes the human nature of Jesus, her child. On the other hand, the title "Mother of God" stresses his divine nature. The Council of Ephesus in 431 decided that Mary was to be referred to as the "Mother of God." At its core, this title of Mary affirms the truth about who Jesus Christ is for Christians: God incarnate.

The addition of the verse at the end of the Gospel reading shows us the significance of the Jewish law for Jesus' parents. Jesus was born at a particular time in history and in a particular religious tradition. Mary and Joseph raised him to be faithful to its laws and customs. For Luke, Jesus is the fulfillment of the hopes of the Chosen People for a messiah. He is the fulfillment of the law.

In your preparation reflect in your heart on who Jesus is for you and for the world. Knowing, then, that Mary gave birth to the Savior of the world, your proclamation will lead the assembly to a deeper faithfulness to him through the intercession of Mary, the Mother of God.

EPIPHANY OF THE LORD

Lectionary #20

READING I Isaiah 60:1–6

Let the ups and downs of this first section be heard in your voice. Raise your voice at first, lower it as you speak of darkness, and then raise it again as you state with joy that the Lord shines over Jerusalem.

Raise your eyes and look to different sides of the assembly as you proclaim, "Raise your eyes and look about; they all gather and come to you: your sons . . . and your daughters." When you turn to make eye contact with different sections of the assembly, be careful not to move away from the microphone.

Midian = MID-ee-uhn
Ephah = EE-fah
Sheba = SHEE-buh

The last phrase, "proclaiming the praises of the Lord," captures the main point of the passage. It is also the reason why both Jews and Christians continue to gather in prayer.

A reading from the Book of the Prophet Isaiah

Rise up in splendor, **Jerusalem**! Your **light** has come,
the **glory** of the **Lord** shines upon you.
See, **darkness** covers the earth,
and **thick** clouds cover the **peoples**;
but upon you the LORD **shines**,
and over **you** appears his **glory**.
Nations shall **walk** by your **light**,
and **kings** by your **shining** radiance.
Raise your **eyes** and **look** about;
they all **gather** and come to you:
your **sons** come from afar,
and your **daughters** in the arms of their **nurses**.

Then you shall be **radiant** at what you see,
your **heart** shall **throb** and **overflow**,
for the **riches** of the sea shall be **emptied out** before you,
the **wealth** of nations shall be **brought** to you.
Caravans of **camels** shall **fill** you,
dromedaries from **Midian** and **Ephah**;
all from **Sheba** shall come
bearing **gold** and **frankincense**,
and **proclaiming** the **praises** of the LORD.

READING I The solemnities of the Nativity and Epiphany, together with the feast of the Baptism of the Lord, are the three "manifestation" feasts. Epiphany was the original celebration of God's manifestation, and included both Jesus' birth and baptism. The celebration of Christmas as a manifestation came later, and in the West, eventually became the principal observance of Jesus' birth.

The words of the prophet Isaiah and the example of the magi in the Gospel reading teach us that those who see the glory of the Lord are accountable for what they see. Just as Jerusalem was called to "rise up" and be a light for other nations, we are to proclaim God's glory beyond our church buildings, in the streets and neighborhoods of our cities and towns.

This passage from Second Isaiah, the author of chapters 40 through 55 of the book of Isaiah, provides us with a description of the new Jerusalem. The Israelites return from the exile with the Lord's light shining on them and their city. The Lord's glory is so impressive that others want to join in singing God's praises.

Proclaim this reading with joy and excitement, praising God for the many ways in which he is present in your life, your parish community, the universal Church, and the world itself. Just as we hear of Israel's duty to be the light of the Lord to the world, your own joy will extol the assembly to reflect the Lord's shining glory in all they say and do. As a result of your ministry, many will want to stream to God.

READING II Saint Augustine, in an early fifth century sermon, said "Recently we celebrated the day on which

READING II Ephesians 3:2–3a, 5–6

Ephesians = ee-FEE-zhunz
Address the "You have heard" directly to the assembly by looking up and making eye contact with them.

A reading from the Letter of Saint Paul to the Ephesians

Brothers and sisters:
You have **heard** of the **stewardship** of God's **grace**
that was given to me for your **benefit**,
namely, that the **mystery** was made **known** to me by **revelation**.
It was not made known to people in **other** generations
as it has **now** been revealed
to his **holy apostles** and **prophets** by the **Spirit**:
that the **Gentiles** are **coheirs**, members of the **same body**,
and **copartners** in the **promise** in **Christ Jesus**
through the **gospel**.

Pause significantly after the colon in the line "to his holy apostles and prophets by the Spirit."
Gentiles = JEN-tīls
coheirs = co-ayrs

GOSPEL Matthew 2:1–12

Bethlehem = BETH-luh-hem
Judea = joo-DEE-uh
Herod = HAYR-ud

A reading from the holy Gospel according to Matthew

When **Jesus** was born in **Bethlehem** of Judea,
in the days of King **Herod**,
behold, **magi** from the **east** arrived in **Jerusalem**, saying,
"**Where** is the newborn **king** of the Jews?
We saw his **star** at its **rising**
and have **come** to do him **homage**."
When King **Herod** heard this,
he was greatly **troubled**,
and **all Jerusalem** with him.

As you proclaim the section that begins "When King Herod heard this . . ." express the cunning nature of King Herod in your tone of voice.

Christ was born among the Jews; today we celebrate the day on which He was adored by the Gentiles" (Sermon 199, 1). When Saint Paul speaks of the "stewardship of God's grace," he is referring to the realization of God's plan in Christ Jesus.

Through Christ, God manifested himself to *all*. Paul understood that the primary purpose of his ministry was to bring Jews and Gentiles together in adoration of Christ Jesus. Both are heirs to his promise. Both are members of the same body, the body of Christ.

In early Christian communities, Jews and Gentiles did not always want to accept each other fully into the body of Christ. In Christ, we are to work through our differences, accepting what is true, good, and beautiful in all religious traditions, cultures, and peoples. As Paul found out, working to bring people together as the body of Christ is a lifelong endeavor. This endeavor is possible for us to undertake because God is faithful—the Spirit of Christ remains with us in the work we do.

This same Spirit is present in your proclamation. Be conscious that your reading brings people together. Achieve this by not favoring one row or side of the assembly when you make eye contact. Look at women as well as men, people of different ethnic and racial heritages, and people of all ages to help each person know God is manifest in each.

GOSPEL **The Gospel story of the magi is rightly beloved by Christians; it is the story that is most associated with the solemnity of Epiphany. At times, however, placing the emphasis on the details of the number of wise men and**

Observing the commas (the comma and semicolon) before and after "In Bethlehem of Judea," will highlight the repetition of the place of Christ's birth.

King Herod really does not want to offer the child homage, despite his words "when you have found him, bring me word, that I too may go and do him homage." Try adding a little sarcasm to your tone of voice so that Herod's deceptive and fraudulent character comes through.

Impart the joy and relief of the magi in the lines "They were overjoyed at seeing the star, and on entering the house they saw the child with Mary his mother." They had succeeded in their journey! Take your time with the lines that tell us how the magi offered homage to the Christ child. Read them with homage in your own voice.

frankincense = FRAYNK-in-sens

myrrh = mer

Assembling all the chief priests and the scribes of the people,
he inquired of them where the **Christ** was to be **born**.
They said to him, "In **Bethlehem** of Judea,
for **thus** it has been **written** through the **prophet**:
*And **you**, **Bethlehem**, land of Judah,*
*are by no means **least** among the **rulers** of **Judah**;*
*since from you shall **come** a **ruler**,*
*who is to **shepherd** my people **Israel**."*
Then Herod **called** the **magi** secretly
and ascertained from them the **time** of the star's **appearance**.
He sent them to **Bethlehem** and said,
"**Go** and search **diligently** for the **child**.
When you have found him, **bring** me word,
that I **too** may go and **do** him **homage**."
After their **audience** with the **king** they set **out**.
And **behold**, the **star** that they had **seen** at its **rising**
preceded them,
until it **came** and **stopped** over the place where the **child** was.
They were **overjoyed** at seeing the **star**,
and on entering the house
they saw the **child** with **Mary** his **mother**.
They **prostrated** themselves and did him **homage**.
Then they **opened** their **treasures**
and **offered** him gifts of **gold**, **frankincense**, and **myrrh**.
And having been **warned** in a **dream not** to return to **Herod**,
they **departed** for their **country** by another **way**.

the names of their gifts diminishes the importance of the profound truth that the evangelist Matthew sought to convey.

In Matthew, the magi (who are Gentiles) are the first to adore Jesus. However, when some Jews, including King Herod, were notified about Jesus' birth, they remained unmoved, even caught up in the political import of the birth. Matthew's main point in framing his narrative in this way is that in Jesus, God is manifest to the whole world. God's promise of salvation is not reserved to a select few. It is available to all, to be accepted in faith just as the Gentile magi responded.

At the end of today's Gospel reading is the line often glossed over in proclamation that tells us the magi went back to their home country. They did not remain basking in the excitement from their adoration of Christ. Rather, their mission began in earnest as they journeyed back home to share their joy of seeing the Christ child.

In their explanation of the relationship between Christmas and Epiphany, liturgists sometimes refer to Guerric of Igny, a twelfth-century French abbot, who said, "That which we have celebrated up to today is the birth of Christ, that which we celebrate today is our own birth" (Sermon 14, 1). The magi's own birth, as followers of Jesus, occurred as they offered homage to Jesus. We too are born as Christians in our act of giving homage to Christ and in bringing his presence to the world. By your proclamation of the last line of this Gospel, the assembly will know that the praise of God includes manifesting Jesus in our cities, towns, and villages.

BAPTISM OF THE LORD

Lectionary #21a

READING I Isaiah 42:1–4, 6–7

Isaiah = Ī-ZAY-uh

Proclaim the first section of the reading as if you are making an announcement. You are telling the assembly of the servant's presence in their midst.

Proclaim the second section beginning with "I, the Lord, have called you . . ." in a personal tone of voice. Make eye contact with the assembly, for the Lord calls its members.

A reading from the Book of the Prophet Isaiah

Thus says the LORD:
Here is my **servant** whom I **uphold**,
my **chosen** one with whom I am **pleased**,
upon whom I have put my **spirit**;
he shall bring forth **justice** to the **nations**,
not **crying** out, not **shouting**,
not making his voice **heard** in the **street**.
A **bruised reed** he shall not **break**,
and a **smoldering wick** he shall not **quench**,
until he establishes **justice** on the **earth**;
the **coastlands** will wait for his **teaching**.

I, the LORD, have **called** you for the victory of **justice**,
I have **grasped you** by the **hand**;
I **formed you**, and set **you**
as a **covenant** of the **people**,
a light for the **nations**,
to open the **eyes** of the **blind**,
to bring out **prisoners** from **confinement**,
and from the **dungeon**, those who live in **darkness**.

READING I The First Reading on the feast of the Baptism of the Lord is one of four servant songs in Isaiah. Written by Second Isaiah in the sixth century, this song offers encouragement for the disheartened Israelites who thought their exile would never end.

The first section is written in the third person and provides a description of the servant's identity and mission. The servant, like Abraham, Moses, David, Israel, and all her leaders, is the Lord's chosen one. As kings were believed to be, he is filled with the Lord's own spirit. Yet, his mission contrasts starkly with that of political and military leaders. The servant would bring forth justice, that is, a reflection of God's love for his people and the earth.

The second section is written with the personal pronoun "you." The identity of the servant is unclear. The servant could be an individual, the prophet, or Israel herself. Regardless of the servant's identity, the Lord's words here are a direct address, the Lord's personal call of the servant and a declaration of the messianic task set before the servant. There are similarities between the descriptions of the servant's mission in the two sections of the reading. Note the repetition of the word justice and the references to images of light in both sections.

In your proclamation, accentuate the difference in the addressees of the two sections by delivering the first in a narrative style. In the second section, directly address the assembly, making much more eye contact with them. This will convey that through Baptism, each of us is personally called by God to participate in the Servant's mission of covenant, light, and freedom.

READING II Acts 10:34–38

Use a narrative tone of voice for the introductory line, pausing after the comma, to make sure you have the assembly's attention for Peter's words.
Cornelius = kohr-NEEL-yuhs

Lower your tone of voice on the parenthetical phrase "that he sent . . . Jesus Christ," so as to connect "the word" with "who is Lord of all."

Pause after "by the devil," as the comma indicates. Proclaim the words "for God was with him" slowly and making eye contact with the assembly. This will help the assembly understand the presence of God in Jesus that we celebrate on the feast of the Lord's Baptism.

A reading from the Acts of the Apostles

Peter proceeded to **speak** to those gathered
in the house of **Cornelius**, **saying**:
"In **truth**, I see that **God** shows **no partiality**.
Rather, in every nation whoever **fears** him and **acts uprightly**
is **acceptable** to him.
You **know** the word that he **sent** to the Israelites
as he proclaimed **peace** through Jesus **Christ**, who is Lord of **all**,
what has happened **all over Judea**,
beginning in **Galilee** after the **baptism**
that John preached,
how God **anointed** Jesus of Nazareth
with the **Holy Spirit** and **power**.
He went about doing **good**
and healing **all** those **oppressed** by the **devil**,
for **God** was **with** him."

READING II Christmas and Easter come together again on the feast of the Baptism of the Lord! Today's Second Reading from the Acts of the Apostles includes three verses that are a part of the First Reading proclaimed on Easter Sunday all three years of the Lectionary cycle.

The reading is from Peter's speech to Cornelius' household prior to their conversion and Baptism. After the opening statements about God's impartiality, the words "You know" suggest that Peter's teaching is intended primarily for the members of Luke's audience who are already Christian. What follows presents the continuity between the word God spoke to the Israelites and its fulfillment in the person and mission of Jesus Christ who, in his Baptism was anointed with the Holy Spirit and power.

In proclaiming the truth of how God's revelation in Jesus took place, you have the opportunity to assist the assembly in making the connection between Christmas and Easter. Accomplish this by speaking with great sincerity at the beginning of the reading about God's acceptance of all persons. Then, deliver the *kerygma* (the proclamation of Christ's teachings) with equal emphasis on each of its historical components. When you end the reading, leave the assembly wanting to hear the rest of the story—even though they know it.

Before we get to Easter in this liturgical year, we have to participate in spreading the Good News with Jesus as we journey to Jerusalem with him. All of this is involved in the mission we received at our Baptism.

GOSPEL One of the synoptic accounts of Jesus' Baptism is pro-

GOSPEL Matthew 3:13–17

A reading from the holy Gospel according to Matthew

Jesus came from **Galilee** to **John** at the **Jordan**
to be **baptized** by him.
John tried to **prevent** him, **saying,**
"**I** need to be baptized by **you,**
and yet **you** are coming to **me**?"
Jesus **said** to him in **reply,**
"**Allow** it **now,** for **thus** it is **fitting** for **us**
to **fulfill** all **righteousness.**"
Then he **allowed** him.
After Jesus was **baptized,**
he came **up** from the **water** and **behold,**
the **heavens** were **opened** for him,
and he saw the **Spirit** of **God** descending like a **dove**
and coming **upon** him.
And a **voice** came from the **heavens,** saying,
"**This** is my **beloved Son,** with **whom** I am well **pleased.**"

Deliver John's question with some strength and tension in your voice as the evangelist tells us John would have prevented Jesus' Baptism.

Offer Jesus' reply in a reassuring tone; his baptism is meant to occur.

Emphasizing the word "This," look up at the assembly and proclaim the Father's words with pride, as if you're introducing a newly baptized person to the assembly.

claimed each year on this feast. Each of them includes unique details which support the evangelist's particular portrait of Jesus. Matthew's account supports his understanding of Jesus as the new Moses, the fulfillment of the law. It does this in three small, but significant ways.

First, Matthew added the verses about John trying to stop Jesus from coming to him for baptism because he did not want Jesus to be identified as one of the sinners whom John baptized. Second, the coming of the Spirit upon Jesus is both personal and public. It is personal because only Jesus sees the Spirit descending and coming upon him, and public because the sight of the heavens opening was there for all to witness. As both personal and public, it testifies to Jesus' intimate relationship with the Father who sends him, and with the Holy Spirit, as the fulfillment of justice for all God's people.

Third, Matthew retains the introductory "This is" ("Here is") in his use of the Isaiah 42:1, the opening verse of today's First Reading, rather than changing it to "You are" as in Mark and Luke. In doing so, he introduces Jesus to his audience as the servant who fulfills Israel's hopes.

Through your proclamation of this Gospel, invite those in the assembly to renew their baptismal commitment and once again begin the journey of Ordinary Time together with God's beloved one sent forth in mission from his own baptism. Paying attention to the details noted above will help you extend this invitation with grace and the confidence which comes from knowing you, too, have been chosen by God.

2ND SUNDAY IN ORDINARY TIME

Lectionary #64a

READING I Isaiah 49:3, 5–6

Isaiah = Ī-ZAY-uh

Personalize the delivery of the Lord's words to the servant by making eye contact with the assembly as much as possible.

Convey the enthusiasm of a prophet renewed in his commission as you speak the words "and I am made glorious."

The Lord's mission for the servant is immense. Increase the boldness in your voice as you reach the end of the final line so that the back rows of the assembly know that the Lord's salvation reaches them.

A reading from the Book of the Prophet Isaiah

The **LORD** said to **me**: **You** are my **servant**,
Israel, through whom I **show** my **glory**.
Now the LORD has **spoken**
who **formed** me as his **servant** from the **womb**,
that **Jacob** may be brought **back** to him
and **Israel gathered** to him;
and **I** am made **glorious** in the sight of the **LORD**,
and my **God** is now my **strength**!
It is too **little**, the LORD **says**, for **you** to be my **servant**,
to raise **up** the tribes of **Jacob**,
and **restore** the survivors of Israel;
I will **make** you a **light** to the **nations**,
that my **salvation** may **reach** to the **ends** of the **earth**.

READING I On the eight Sundays of Ordinary Time before Lent begins, we hear from the prophet Isaiah four times. Today's reading is from the second of four servant songs in Isaiah (Isaiah 49:1–7). As in the second half of the servant song proclaimed last Sunday, the Lord addresses his servant personally.

In this song, Isaiah speaks in retrospect about his mission from the Lord. As it was for the prophet Jeremiah (Jeremiah 1:5), Isaiah's call is personal); the Lord has formed him from the womb and has made him glorious. The servant has held out hope for Israel and her people in the face of suffering. So afflicted were the Israelites that they felt the Lord who had chosen them had then abandoned them, leaving them exiled in Babylon.

The four small words that begin the second stanza, "It is too little," point to a new undertaking the Lord has in mind for his servant. The servant will not bring a new exodus himself, but he will announce it, first to Israel ("the tribes of Jacob") and her survivors (see Isaiah 49:8–13) and then to "the nations." The size and scope of the servant's mission grows exponentially! Yet in Isaiah's reflection, two thoughts keep the mission in perspective: God is the servant's strength and God will do the actual work of restoring Israel and bringing salvation.

As you proclaim this reading to the assembly, remember that both you and they are called to be the Lord's servants. When you speak the four small words of transition, think about how our mission extends beyond the doors of the church. Remember, your proclamation doesn't save, but through it God can lead others to salvation in Christ.

READING I 1 Corinthians 1:1–3

Corinthians = kohr-IN-thee-uhnz

Sosthenes = SOS-thuh-neez

Greet those in the assembly by looking up on the phrase "with all those everywhere."

Offer the words of "grace" and "peace" in Paul's greeting in a gentle, but clearly audible, tone of voice.

A reading from the first Letter of Saint Paul to the Corinthians

Paul, called to be an **apostle** of **Christ Jesus** by the will of **God**,
and **Sosthenes** our **brother**,
to the **church** of **God** that is in **Corinth**,
to **you** who have been **sanctified** in **Christ Jesus**,
called to be **holy**,
with **all** those **everywhere** who **call** upon the **name** of our
Lord Jesus **Christ**, **their** Lord and **ours**.
Grace to you and **peace** from God our **Father**
and the **Lord Jesus Christ**.

READING II For seven out of the next eight Sundays in Ordinary Time before Lent begins, the Second Reading is from First Corinthians. This letter was written to the Christian community in Corinth in the mid-50s. At the time, Corinth was a bustling commercial center filled with cultural and religious diversity and known for its sexual libertarianism, even promiscuity. The fledgling Christians at Corinth were divided about whether to believe the preaching of Paul or of others. Paul wrote to address this issue, among others, and help restore unity to the community.

Today's reading consists of the first three verses from Paul's letter. They function as the customary greeting used in letters of that time. Paul introduces himself and Sosthenes as coauthors. Sosthenes could be the synagogue official who was seized and beaten in Acts 18:17, but he could also be someone else who worked with Paul. From the start of the letter, Paul defends his own authority by definitively stating that God called him to be an apostle of Christ Jesus.

The final verse of the reading is familiar to us as a liturgical greeting. Its depth extends far beyond the welcome offered by two people meeting on the street. When you speak this greeting, think of the power of the peace of Christ, and offer it with warmth, sincerity, and reverence for the people before you. Paul's greeting reminds the Corinthians (and us), that despite divisions on some issues, they have been called to be holy and set apart by God, to live as Christ's disciples in unity with him.

GOSPEL John 1:29–34

A reading from the holy Gospel according to John

Proclaim John's words of witness ("Behold, the Lamb of God . . .") slowly and boldly.

Continue John's testimony with confidence, but with less boldness.

John the **Baptist** saw **Jesus** coming toward him and **said**,
"**Behold**, the **Lamb** of **God**, who takes **away** the sin
of the **world**.
He is the **one** of whom I **said**,
'A man is coming **after** me who ranks **ahead** of me
because he existed **before** me.'
I did not **know** him,
but the **reason** why I came **baptizing** with **water**
was that **he** might be made **known** to **Israel**."
John testified **further**, saying,
"I saw the **Spirit** come down like a **dove** from **heaven**
and **remain** upon him.

State John's point about the Spirit coming down on Jesus with the conviction similar to that which you used to proclaim John's opening statement. Then, continue John's words with less intensity in your voice.

I did not **know** him,
but the one who **sent** me to **baptize** with water **told** me,
'On **whomever** you see the **Spirit** come down and **remain**,
he is the **one** who will **baptize** with the **Holy Spirit**.'
Now I have **seen** and **testified** that he **is** the **Son** of **God**."

The strength with which you proclaim John's conclusion should parallel the tenor used for the opening testimony.

GOSPEL The Gospel reading for the Second Sunday of Ordinary Time helps us to transition from the end of the Christmas season to the beginning of Ordinary Time. On this Sunday and on all three years of the Lectionary cycle of readings, the Gospel comes from John's narrative and continues to focus on the manifestation of Jesus.

Today's passage begins shortly after the prologue in the Gospel according to John. The prologue itself ends by stating that no one has ever seen God, but the Son of God has revealed him (John 1:18). What follows is John the Baptist's testimony to having seen God revealed in Jesus Christ.

Through the testimony of John the Baptist, that Jesus is the Lamb of God, the Evangelist John could be making the connection between Jesus and one or all of the following: the apocalyptic lamb who will destroy the evil and darkness of the world (Revelation 5—7), the paschal lamb of the exodus sacrifice that freed Israel (Exodus 12), or the suffering servant who was led like a lamb to slaughter (Isaiah 53:7, 10). Whichever of the connections the evangelist intended, the Baptist's testimony reveals God in the person of Jesus Christ who, having overcome sin, is the Light of the world.

John also testifies that the Spirit has come upon Jesus. The coming of the Spirit is the heavenly sign that Jesus has been sent by God as the Messiah. It also links the Son of God to the suffering servant of Isaiah 52:1 who is filled with the spirit. Through the sacrament of Baptism, Christ's followers will be filled with the Holy Spirit and will brightly shine his light on the world.

3RD SUNDAY IN ORDINARY TIME

Lectionary #67a

READING I Isaiah 8:23—9:3

Isaiah = Ī-ZAY-uh
Zebulun = ZEB-yoo-luhn
Naphtali = NAF-tuh-lee
Make the contrasts between "degraded" and "glorified," "darkness" and "light," and "gloom" and "light" stand out in your proclamation. Try using a lighter tone of voice for the hopeful words.

A reading from the Book of the Prophet Isaiah

First the LORD **degraded** the land of **Zebulun**
and the land of **Naphtali**;
but in the **end** he has **glorified** the seaward **road**,
the **land** west of the **Jordan**,
the **District** of the **Gentiles**.

Anguish has taken **wing**, **dispelled** is **darkness**:
for there is **no gloom** where but **now** there was **distress**.
The **people** who **walked** in **darkness**
have **seen** a great **light**;
upon those who **dwelt** in the land of **gloom**
a **light** has **shone**.
You have **brought** them abundant **joy**
and great **rejoicing**,
as they rejoice before **you** as at the **harvest**,
as people make **merry** when dividing **spoils**.
For the **yoke** that **burdened** them,
the **pole** on their **shoulder**,
and the **rod** of their **taskmaster**
you have **smashed**, as on the **day** of **Midian**.

Continue a confident tone of voice through the lines that speak of the Lord's victory over oppression, for the Lord has overcome it! Speak the onomatopoeia ("smashed") with strength so that it truly imitates the action for which it stands.
Midian = MID-ee-uhn

READING I The book of Isaiah is the work of multiple authors, believed to have written three different sections of the book. They are referred to as First Isaiah (chapters 1 to 39), Second Isaiah (40 to 55), and Third Isaiah (56 to 66).

Today's First Reading comes from chapters 8 and 9; like all of chapters 1—11, these are considered to be the actual words of the prophet, First Isaiah. He wrote in the eighth century during the reign of King Ahaz, after the rise of Assyria. The first part of the reading speaks of the Lord's triumph over the lands that had been subject to Assyrian aggression and the light he brings to the territories in which Gentiles resided.

The three verses in the second half of today's reading are also proclaimed at the Christmas Mass at Midnight (see that commentary for more background). The light imagery of the first section continues here. Originally a hymn for the prince of peace who will come after Ahaz, these verses describe the freedom from oppression the prince will bring to the people. The hope for this prince stands in contrast to Ahaz who failed at listening to Isaiah's demand for trust in God. Instead, Ahaz made his kingdom a vassal of Assyria and the people suffered.

Ultimately, Christians believe that Jesus Christ is the Prince of Peace, the one who overcomes oppression once, for all. His light shines in the darkness the way no other can. In your proclamation, communicate the hope and joy that comes from believing in Christ. Leave the assembly ready to accept the invitation they will hear in today's Gospel, the invitation to come after him.

READING II 1 Corinthians 1:10–13, 17

Corinthians = kohr-IN-thee-uhnz

A reading from the first Letter of Saint Paul to the Corinthians

I **urge** you, brothers and sisters, in the **name** of our **Lord**
Jesus Christ,

Deliver Paul's instruction "that all of you agree . . ." directly to the assembly in a strong tone of voice.

that **all** of you **agree** in what you **say**,
and that there be **no divisions** among you,
but that you be united in the **same mind** and
in the **same purpose**.

Lower your tone of voice as you communicate the reports Paul has heard.

Chloe's = KLOH-eez

For it has been **reported** to me **about you**, my brothers and sisters,
by **Chloe's** people, that there are **rivalries** among you.
I mean that **each** of you is **saying**,
"**I** belong to **Paul**," or "**I** belong to **Apollos**,"
or "**I** belong to **Cephas**," or "**I** belong to **Christ**."

Ask Paul's questions as if you are trying to solicit a "no" response from the assembly.

Is **Christ divided**?
Was **Paul crucified** for you?
Or were you **baptized** in the name of **Paul**?
For **Christ** did not **send** me to **baptize** but to **preach** the **gospel**,
and **not** with the **wisdom** of human **eloquence**,
so that the **cross** of **Christ** might not be **emptied** of its **meaning**.

READING II Is Paul perhaps too idealistic as he tells the Corinthians not to be divided, to agree on everything they say, and to be united in the same mind and purpose? The opening lines of today's Second Reading disclose that the Christian community at Corinth was suffering real divisions over pastoral concerns. Here Paul is urging the Corinthians to work toward unity. For a community of believers in Christ, unity in the body is essential, because Christ himself is one.

We see in the letter that before Paul addresses the practical causes of discord among the Corinthians, he first takes up the question of to whom the ultimate allegiance of the Corinthians belongs. The passage mentions four competing loyalties in the community: to Paul himself, to Apollos, to Cephas, and to Christ. Paul learned of these rivalries from people who presumably worked for Chloe, a businesswoman from Ephesus (Acts 16:14). Apollos preached in Corinth when Paul was there and also accompanied him in Ephesus. "Cephas" is the Aramaic term for "rock"—Peter's name. Paul probably used "Cephas" to denote those Christians who strictly observed the Jewish law.

Including those who belong to Christ as one of the last of the rival factions is unusual, given that it seems to put the strength of this group on a par with the others. In doing so, however, Paul could be subtly demonstrating the exact problem he's exhorting the Corinthians to rectify: Christ is not one among many allegiances; he is the source of the body's unity.

Your forthright and direct proclamation of the reading will set the stage for the following five Sundays in which Paul will

GOSPEL Matthew 4:12–23

Galilee = GAL-ih-lee
Nazareth = NAZ-uh-reth
Capernaum = kuh-PER-nee-*m or kuh-PER-nay-*m or kuh-PER-n*m
Zebulun = ZEB-yoo-luhn
Naphtali = NAF-tuh-lee

Pause noticeably after the colon before Isaiah's words. This will help prepare the assembly to notice the parallel with the First Reading.

A reading from the holy Gospel according to Matthew

When Jesus **heard** that **John** had been **arrested**,
he **withdrew** to **Galilee**.
He left **Nazareth** and went to **live** in **Capernaum** by the **sea**,
in the region of **Zebulun** and **Naphtali**,
that what had been **said** through Isaiah the **prophet**
might be **fulfilled**:
*Land of **Zebulun** and land of **Naphtali**,*
*the way to the **sea**, beyond the **Jordan**,*
***Galilee** of the **Gentiles**,*
*the **people** who sit in **darkness** have **seen** a great **light**,*
*on those **dwelling** in a land **overshadowed** by **death***
***light** has **arisen**.*
From that time **on**, Jesus began to **preach** and say,
"**Repent**, for the kingdom of **heaven** is at **hand**."

As he was **walking** by the Sea of **Galilee**, he saw two **brothers**,
Simon who is called **Peter**, and his brother **Andrew**,
casting a **net** into the **sea**; they were **fishermen**.

further develop his argument about unity in Christ and his cross. Given our humanity, unity in the body of believers might be an ideal, but one worth proclaiming.

GOSPEL The longer form of today's Gospel reading has three sections. The first and third sections focus on Jesus' geographical movements in his ministry. The middle section details Jesus' call of the first disciples. All three sections are written in a narrative style with one modified quotation from the Old Testament in the opening section and two brief statements from Jesus, one each in the first two sections.

Matthew uses these quotations to effectively convey three main points: 1) Jesus is the fulfillment of the law and the prophets, 2) In Jesus, the kingdom of heaven is already present, and 3) Jesus' disciples follow him and participate in his mission and ministry.

First, Matthew's reworking of Isaiah 8:23, the opening verse of today's First Reading, informs us that the salvation promised by the prophet has come in Jesus. The darkness of oppression faced by the peoples of those lands and by nonbelievers is overcome by Jesus. Notice that Matthew has Jesus begin his public ministry in Galilee, a region that, at the time of Matthew's writing, was approximately half Gentile. By doing so, Matthew shows that Jesus' mission reaches out to Jews and Gentiles alike; he is the Servant of Isaiah whose mission, although it began with Israel and her people, was extended to the ends of the earth (see the First Reading from the Second Sunday in Ordinary Time, Isaiah 49:3, 5–6).

He **said** to them,
"Come after **me**, and I will **make** you fishers of **men**."

Allow the immediacy of Peter's and Andrew's response to Jesus' call to be heard in your voice.

At **once** they left their **nets** and **followed** him.
He walked along from **there** and saw two **other** brothers,
James, the son of **Zebedee**, and his brother **John**.
They were in a **boat**, with their father **Zebedee**,
mending their **nets**.

Let the same immediacy be heard in your voice as you proclaim the response of James and John.

He **called** them, and **immediately** they left their **boat**
and their **father**
and **followed** him.
He went around **all** of **Galilee**,

Although the final sentence of the Gospel is a summary statement, do not let your voice trail off; keep a confident, moderate tone, for the Gospel is being spread in word and deed.

teaching in their **synagogues**, **proclaiming** the gospel
of the **kingdom**,
and **curing** every **disease** and **illness** among the **people**.

Second, the first words that Jesus speaks in this Gospel ("Repent, for the kingdom of heaven is at hand") mirrors the preaching of John the Baptist, who announced Jesus' coming (Matthew 3:1). Yet Matthew, using an Old Testament citation from Isaiah 40:3, plainly identifies John as the one whose mission is to prepare the way of the Lord (Matthew 3:3; see the Gospel for the Third Sunday of Advent). Having Jesus say these words immediately after the citation from Isaiah formalizes the beginning of Jesus' ministry. The teaching and action which are to come will occur because Jesus, in his very person, is the presence of the kingdom, is God.

The second time Jesus speaks, he offers an invitation. His words are a personal call to Simon and his brother Andrew to follow him. As part of the call, the brothers are informed of what they will be taught to do. Because the disciples will "come after" him, presumably they will be performing the same acts Jesus does: teaching, proclaiming the good news of the kingdom, and healing. These are the activities listed at the end of the long form of today's Gospel.

Make it the goal of your proclamation to help the assembly recognize that they truly believe Jesus is the fulfillment of the Law, that in him the kingdom of heaven is present, and that they, through their own Baptism, have accepted Jesus' call to come after him. As the assembly hears the word of God proclaimed each week by those who are well-prepared, they are schooled and formed in how they, like the first disciples, can bring others to Jesus.

4TH SUNDAY IN ORDINARY TIME

Lectionary #70a

READING I Zephaniah 2:3; 3:12–13

Zef-uh-NĪ-uh

Offer the invitation to "Seek the Lord" with hospitality in your tone of voice. Even those in the assembly who are already observing the Lord's commands are called to draw closer to him. Let the strength of the word "justice" and the peacefulness of "humility" be heard in your voice.

Make eye contact with the assembly, inviting them to live so that they will be part of the remnant of Israel.

Paint the picture of the humble people tending their flocks by using a compassionate tone of voice.

A reading from the Book of the Prophet Zephaniah

Seek the **LORD**, all you **humble** of the **earth**,
who have **observed** his **law**;
seek **justice**, seek **humility**;
perhaps you may be **sheltered**
on the **day** of the LORD's **anger**.

But **I** will **leave** as a **remnant** in your **midst**
a people **humble** and **lowly**,
who shall take **refuge** in the **name** of the **LORD**:
the **remnant** of **Israel**.
They shall **do** no **wrong**
and **speak** no **lies**;
nor shall there be **found** in their **mouths**
a deceitful **tongue**;
they shall **pasture** and **couch** their **flocks**
with **none** to **disturb** them.

READING I After three Sundays of hearing the words of Isaiah, today we hear from the prophet Zephaniah. This is one of only two times in the Lectionary cycle of readings and the only time in Year A that the words of this prophet are proclaimed.

Zephaniah prophesied during the reign of King Josiah in the seventh century. The previous king, Manasseh, had not upheld the law, and so Zephaniah inherited and tried to overcome the faithlessness of the people. At the time, the oppression that the Kingdom of Judah faced from Assyria was waning, but another aggressive power, Babylon, was flexing its muscles.

The opening verse of today's reading is the final verse of an oracle about the salvation of Judah and Jerusalem. This verse appeals to the Israelites to remain faithful to the Lord before the day of his anger, the day of the Lord, comes. On this day, the Lord will win victory over the oppressors, but only those who have remained faithful to him—the remnant—will be spared. These followers of the Lord of justice and humility will be known by their actions. They will be people of righteousness, honesty, humility, and peace.

Endeavor to put across a sense of urgency and seriousness as you exhort the assembly to seek the Lord. They will want to be part of the remnant who believe in the Lord and live accordingly. In the way you comport yourself, not setting yourself above the assembly or seeing yourself as better than anyone in it, you too, will be seen as a humble and lowly person who pastures the flock, leading others to the Lord.

READING II 1 Corinthians 1:26–31

Corinthians = kohr-IN-thee-uhnz

A reading from the first Letter of Saint Paul to the Corinthians

Deliver the opening line directly to the assembly. Then lower your tone of voice as you help them to consider their calling according to Paul's words.

Consider your **own calling**, brothers and sisters.
Not **many** of you were **wise** by **human** standards,
not **many** were **powerful**,
not **many** were of **noble birth**.

Stress the contrast "foolish"/"wise" and "weak"/"strong." Do so in a way that is not demeaning because God calls all to himself.

Rather, God chose the **foolish** of the world to shame the **wise**,
and God chose the **weak** of the world to shame the **strong**,
and God chose the **lowly** and **despised** of the world,
those who count for **nothing**,
to reduce to **nothing** those who are **something**,
so that **no** human being might **boast** before **God**.

Pause before beginning the final section ("It is due to him . . ."). Direct the opening and closing of this section directly to the assembly by making eye contact with them. This will encourage invite them to consider whether their boasting is done in the Lord.

It is due to **him** that you **are** in Christ **Jesus**,
who **became** for us **wisdom** from God,
as well as **righteousness**, **sanctification**, and **redemption**,
so **that**, as it is **written**,
"Whoever **boasts**, should **boast** in the **Lord**."

READING II Between the conclusion of last week's reading and the beginning of this week's, Paul discusses the paradox of the cross (1:18—25). Reading these verses will help you understand the context of today's Second Reading. In them, Paul contrasts the truth of the Christian proclamation of Christ crucified with the signs demanded by Jews and the wisdom searched for by the Greeks.

Paul argues that although the wisdom of the cross is absurd to the world, to those who believe, it is true wisdom. In Christ, those who are strong and wise according to the world are now weak and foolish, and those who appear weak and foolish become strong and wise. This reversal of fortunes is the paradox of the cross. Around the paradox of the cross, Paul exhorts the Corinthians to foster their unity. The folly and weakness of those who profess Christ crucified triumphs because Christ has been raised (1 Corinthians 15:43).

When you proclaim this reading, strive to do so "in the Lord." You want to avoid becoming arrogant like the Corinthians. Their arrogance led them to boast in their human ways and to think they could rely solely on themselves. In humility, recognize that as a proclaimer of the word, set apart from the assembly because of your gift of proclamation, you are still one with them in the body of Christ. Together you live from the wisdom of the cross.

GOSPEL The entire Sermon on the Mount in the Gospel according to Matthew, from which today's Gospel reading is taken, begins immediately after Jesus calls the first disciples. In the sermon, the disciples are schooled in what it

GOSPEL Matthew 5:1–12a

Use a narrative tone of voice to set the scene for Jesus giving the Beatitudes.

Try proclaiming the first half of each beatitude in a stronger voice and then lightening the tenor of your voice slightly for the second half. Be careful that your proclamation does not become singsong. Pause significantly after each beatitude and allow time for the assembly to take in what they just heard.

Use the conclusion to the ninth beatitude as a climax to your proclamation by confidently instructing the assembly to rejoice in the reward they will receive for living the Beatitudes.

A reading from the holy Gospel according to Matthew

When **Jesus** saw the **crowds**, he went **up** the **mountain**,
and after he had sat **down**, his disciples **came** to him.
He began to **teach** them, saying:
"**Blessed** are the poor in **spirit**,
for **theirs** is the kingdom of **heaven**.
Blessed are they who **mourn**,
for they will be **comforted**.
Blessed are the **meek**,
for they will **inherit** the **land**.
Blessed are they who **hunger** and **thirst** for **righteousness**,
for they will be **satisfied**.
Blessed are the **merciful**,
for they will be **shown** mercy.
Blessed are the **clean** of **heart**,
for they will **see God**.
Blessed are the **peacemakers**,
for they will be **called children** of **God**.
Blessed are they who are **persecuted**
for the sake of **righteousness**,
for **theirs** is the kingdom of **heaven**.
Blessed are **you** when they **insult** you and **persecute** you
and utter every kind of **evil** against you **falsely**
because of **me**.
Rejoice and be **glad**,
for **your reward** will be **great** in **heaven**."

means to follow Jesus as students in the field of discipleship.

In the Gospel reading, the evangelist has Jesus position himself as a teacher by sitting down. Matthew then presents the disciples as eager to hear what their Master has to say by having them gather around him. What Jesus the Teacher says, however, might have come as a surprise to them. Known as the Beatitudes, Matthew's version includes nine blessing statements, whereas Luke's includes four blessings and four woes. These statements describe the life of a disciple, or more specifically, the qualities of the disciple as a person. They are paradoxical in relation to the world's expectations, just as Paul argues in today's Second Reading that the cross of Christ is paradoxical.

These nine blessings can be seen in the light of the First Reading, showing how the remnant left behind on the day of the Lord are to live and what their future will be. Like that remnant, the humble, honest, authentic, gentle, and kind people who live as Jesus' disciples will experience a great reward in the kingdom of heaven. In hope of this reward, they can rejoice and be glad!

More than half the liturgical year remains before the celebration of the solemnity of All Saints when this Gospel reading will again be proclaimed. By taking time and care with your proclamation of each blessing statement, the assembly will understand what it means to accept their call to holiness and sainthood and to live as Jesus' disciples throughout the liturgical year.

5TH SUNDAY IN ORDINARY TIME

Lectionary #73a

READING I Isaiah 58:7–10

Isaiah = ī-ZAY-uh

Use a peaceful, tender tone of voice on the instructions "share your bread . . . do not turn your back."

Switch to a stronger, declarative tone of voice to proclaim the breaking forth of your light. Speak these words directly to the assembly, making eye contact with its members.
vindication = vin-dih-KAY-shuhn

Convey a sense of responsibility to the assembly by emphasizing the words "If you" both times they occur.

Conclude the second half of the conditional statement "then light . . ." using the same peaceful and gentle tone with which you began the passage.

A reading from the Book of the Prophet Isaiah

Thus says the LORD:
Share your **bread** with the **hungry**,
shelter the **oppressed** and the **homeless**;
clothe the **naked** when you **see** them,
and do **not** turn your **back** on your **own**.
Then your **light** shall break **forth** like the **dawn**,
and your **wound** shall **quickly** be **healed**;
your **vindication** shall go **before** you,
and the **glory** of the LORD shall be **your** rear **guard**.
Then you shall **call**, and the LORD will **answer**;
you shall cry for **help**, and he will say: **Here I am**!
If you **remove** from your midst
oppression, false **accusation** and malicious **speech**;
if you **bestow** your **bread** on the **hungry**
and **satisfy** the **afflicted**;
then **light** shall **rise** for **you** in the **darkness**,
and the **gloom** shall **become** for you like **midday**.

READING I Today's First Reading is from a speech on true fasting found at Isaiah 58:1–14. The section from which the speech comes, chapters 56 to 66, was written by Third Isaiah after Israel had returned to her homeland from exile. It contains visions of a glorious future for God's Chosen People.

Today's reading has three distinct sections. In the first, the Lord commands his people to care for the physical needs of those who are hungry, oppressed, homeless, and unclothed. These imperatives strengthen the tone of instruction and they culminate in the broad but firm directive not to turn your back on your own people. As the Israelites began to worship in their new temple, conflicts arose: who would lead and how would worship be conducted? In the face of this, the Lord extols his people to build up their relationships with one another, for each Israelite ultimately belongs to the whole.

The second section of the reading is an announcement of salvation. When the Israelites act in the way the Lord has commanded, then their wounds will be healed and their goodness will be known to those around them like the light breaking forth at dawn. They will be protected from future harm: the justification and glory of the Lord will wrap around them, conveying God's presence whenever they cry out in need (see Isaiah 58:11).

The third section of the reading forms a bookend with the first section. It contains a conditional statement with two "if" clauses and one "then" clause. The "if" clauses are similar to the commands in the opening section of the reading. In case the Israelites wanted to dismiss their responsibility to act justly and compassionately,

READING II 1 Corinthians 2:1–5

Corinthians = kohr-IN-thee-uhnz

sublimity = suh-BLIM-ih-tee

Proclaim Paul's opening description of his own proclamation of the Gospel with humility in your voice.

Begin the second stanza with the same humble tone of voice as you ended the first, and build slightly in strength as you speak about the Spirit and power of God.

A reading from the first Letter of Saint Paul to the Corinthians

When I **came** to **you**, brothers and sisters,
proclaiming the mystery of **God**,
I did **not** come with sublimity of **words** or of **wisdom**.
For I **resolved** to know **nothing** while I was with **you**
except **Jesus Christ**, and him **crucified**.
I **came** to **you** in **weakness** and **fear** and much **trembling**,
and my **message** and my **proclamation**
were **not** with persuasive words of **wisdom**,
but with a **demonstration** of **Spirit** and **power**,
so that **your faith** might rest **not** on **human** wisdom
but on the **power** of **God**.

the prophet's reiteration of the connection between their actions and the light of salvation rising in the darkness makes the responsibility of the Lord's people clear. Your strong proclamation of this section will help the assembly hear what the Lord asks of them and decide for themselves if they will be open to the light that rises before them.

READING II Today's Second Reading from the beginning of chapter 2 of Paul's first letter to the Corinthians reads like an overly humble statement about how Paul comported himself in relation to the Corinthians. By characterizing himself as weak and fearful, he contrasts himself with the itinerant preachers and philosophers who were competing with him for the attention of the Corinthians.

In these brief verses, Paul continues to develop the theme of the wisdom and power of God. Last Sunday's Second Reading ended with the proclamation of Christ Jesus as the wisdom from God and Paul's call for those who follow the Lord to live from him, boasting only in him.

Today you proclaim that Paul himself embodied his own preaching. He lived from the Lord, proclaiming not his own power, as the pagan philosophers did, but the power of God. For him, human wisdom was no comparison to the wisdom of God evident in history and in the people of the Corinthian community.

Be humble, but not self-effacing, in your proclamation of Paul's words. Like Paul, you do not come to the assembly with sublimity of words and wisdom. You come

GOSPEL Matthew 5:13–16

A reading from the holy Gospel according to Matthew

Pause significantly after the colon to gain the assembly's attention.

With strength in your voice and making eye contact, clearly state the line "You are the salt . . ." directly to the assembly. Lower your tone of voice for the explanation ("But if salt loses . . .").

Repeat the same vocal pattern as in the previous note for the declaration "You are the light . . ." and the explanation "A city set . . . ."

Increase the strength in your voice again as you proclaim the climax of the reading and the ultimate purpose of shining our light: glorifying the heavenly Father.

Jesus **said** to his **disciples**:
"**You** are the **salt** of the **earth**.
But if salt **loses** its **taste**, with **what** can it be **seasoned**?
It is no longer **good** for **anything**
but to be **thrown** out and **trampled** underfoot.
You are the **light** of the **world**.
A **city** set on a **mountain** cannot be **hidden**.
Nor do they light a **lamp** and then **put** it under a bushel **basket**;
it is set on a **lampstand**,
where it gives **light** to **all** in the **house**.
Just so, **your** light must **shine** before **others**,
that they may **see** your good **deeds**
and **glorify** your heavenly **Father**."

instead to proclaim the power of Christ crucified—the power of the cross of life—which the assembly can take with them as they go into the world.

GOSPEL **Today's Gospel continues where last Sunday's left off. In this brief passage following the Beatitudes, Jesus uses two symbols from everyday life to illustrate the expectation he has for those who claim to be his followers. First, he directly teaches the disciples that just as salt is of no use in flavoring or preserving food if it has lost its own taste, so too the disciples are of no use if they fail to live as he teaches.**

Second, Jesus draws on the image of light from Isaiah 2:2–5 to instruct his disciples that they are personally called to bring the light of salvation to others. Notice that the lamp in the house gives light to all those in the house. A one-room house in Palestine at the time Matthew was writing housed an extended family. The lamp of a disciple was thus intended to provide light not only for the individual disciples, but for all those around.

Your proclamation of Jesus' teaching will be enhanced best by emphasizing its personal nature. As Jesus told his disciples directly that they were salt and light, communicate to the assembly that they are salt and light, not for a few, but for those in the house of the Church and those outside its walls—all for the greater glory of God.

6TH SUNDAY IN ORDINARY TIME

Lectionary #76a

READING I Sirach 15:15–20

Sirach = SEER-ak

A reading from the Book of Sirach

Closely follow the punctuation in the conditional clauses which begin with "If you . . ." by pausing at the commas.

Proclaim the line "he has set . . ." as a complete sentence, stopping after "water." Proclaim "to whichever . . ." as if it were the beginning of a new sentence. Make eye contact with the assembly as you do so, letting them know that they have a choice to make. Lessen the strength in your tone of voice as you offer the general explanatory statement "Before man . . . ."

The strength in your tone of voice and your eye contact with the assembly should convey the unambiguous nature of the final line "No one does . . . ."

If you **choose** you can **keep** the **commandments**,
they will **save** you;
if you **trust** in **God**, **you too** shall **live**;
he has set before you **fire** and **water**;
to whichever you **choose**, stretch **forth** your **hand**.
Before man are **life** and **death**, **good** and **evil**,
whichever he **chooses** shall be **given** him.
Immense is the **wisdom** of the **LORD**;
he is **mighty** in **power**, and all-seeing.
The eyes of **God** are on **those** who **fear** him;
he **understands** man's every **deed**.
No one does he **command** to act **unjustly**,
to **none** does he give **license** to **sin**.

READING II 1 Corinthians 2:6–10

Corinthians = kohr-IN-thee-uhnz

A reading from the first Letter of Saint Paul to the Corinthians

Acknowledge that both you and the assembly are included in the "we" who speak wisdom by making eye contact with people in different places in the assembly.

Brothers and sisters:
We speak a **wisdom** to those who are **mature**,
not a **wisdom** of this **age**,
nor of the **rulers** of this **age** who are passing **away**.

READING I Sirach, a book which belongs to the collection of writings known as Wisdom literature, was written in Hebrew in the late third to early second century BC by Ben Sira and thought to be his class notes from years of teaching philosophy in Jerusalem. The author is attempting to show how Jewish teachings and traditions offer the wisdom for living life in accord with God's wisdom.

Today's reading insists that following God's commandments and trusting in him will lead to life. The choice between fire and water, between life and death, lies solely on the shoulders of each individual.

By making it clear that the responsibility for our actions lies squarely on us, Ben Sira teaches that God cannot be blamed for the injustice and evil in the world. The immensity of his wisdom and power, referred to in theological terms as God's omnipotence and omniscience, does not make him responsible for sin in the world. God does not cause sin or even permit evil to exist.

This strong declaration about human free will demands that your proclamation be candid and forthright. Difficult life situations and losses may lead us to stray from using our free will to choose well, and may sometimes cause us to blame God for our suffering, even if momentarily. Your proclamation can remind us that the God of immense wisdom graciously gives us the free will to make the choice for life in all the situations we face.

READING II The First Reading tells us that God's wisdom is immense. Paul adds to the understanding of divine wisdom by contrasting it with

Clearly identify the wisdom we speak as "God's wisdom" by slowing down on your proclamation of those words. Observing a lengthier than average pause at the comma after those words will also help emphasize them.

Rather, we speak **God's** wisdom, **mysterious**, **hidden**,
which God **predetermined** before the **ages** for our **glory**,
and which **none** of the **rulers** of this age **knew**;
or, if they **had** known it,
they would **not** have crucified the Lord of **glory**.
But as it **is written**:

The quotation in italics is connected to the line "this God . . ." to make a complete sentence. Emphasize the word "this" by stating it strongly and making eye contact with the assembly for the entire line.

What ***eye*** *has not* ***seen****, and* ***ear*** *has not* ***heard****,*
and what has not ***entered*** *the human* ***heart****,*
what God has ***prepared*** *for those who* ***love*** *him,*
this *God has* ***revealed*** *to us through the* ***Spirit****.*

For the **Spirit** scrutinizes **everything**, even the **depths** of **God**.

GOSPEL Matthew 5:17–37

A reading from the holy Gospel according to Matthew

Direct the narrative line "Jesus said to his disciples" to today's disciples in the assembly by making eye contact with them.

Jesus **said** to his **disciples**:
"Do not **think** that I have **come** to **abolish** the **law**
or the **prophets**.
I have **come** not to **abolish** but to **fulfill**.
Amen, I **say** to you, until **heaven** and **earth** pass **away**,
not the smallest **letter** or the smallest **part** of a letter
will **pass** from the **law**,
until **all** things have taken **place**.

Proclaim the consequences of not following and of following the commandments with somberness and hopeful enthusiasm, respectively.

Therefore, whoever **breaks** one of the **least** of these
commandments
and teaches **others** to **do** so
will be called **least** in the kingdom of **heaven**.

earthly wisdom. He is thinking of the Greek philosophers of his time, but this earthly wisdom could include any worldly knowledge. The wisdom Paul preaches is not of this age; it does not belong to this or any historical time. The wisdom of earthly rulers is also not the wisdom of which Paul speaks. Like the earthly rulers who will pass away, so their wisdom will also.

Paul speaks instead of divine wisdom, which is mysterious and hidden. This wisdom God has known since before the beginning of time. "The rulers of this age" (perhaps a reference to Pilate or Herod or both) did not know this wisdom, for if they had, Jesus' Crucifixion would not have happened.

Familiar to many from the piece of liturgical music by Marty Haugen, "Eye Has Not Seen," what appears to be a quotation from the Old Testament in verse 9 is more likely simply inspired by Isaiah 6:1–3. Paul uses this citation to show the Corinthians and us that God's wisdom has been made known through the Spirit. To those who are receptive, the Holy Spirit will reveal the wisdom of God's plan of salvation in Christ.

In last Sunday's reading, Paul said that he did not come with wisdom, but he knew only Jesus Christ crucified. For Paul, this is the divine wisdom and power of God on which our faith rests. Lead the assembly to hear the distinction between the wisdom of this world and God's wisdom as you proclaim this reading. Let them know that God's wisdom is within their grasp if they open themselves to the Spirit.

GOSPEL This Sunday and next, the Gospel is Jesus' teaching to his disciples on what exactly it means

But whoever **obeys** and **teaches** these **commandments**
will be called **greatest** in the kingdom of **heaven**.
I **tell** you, unless **your** righteousness **surpasses**
that of the **scribes** and **Pharisees**,
you will not **enter** the **kingdom** of **heaven**.

Make eye contact with the assembly and state "You shall not kill" clearly. It marks the first of four commandments Jesus teaches about in the Gospel reading. Pause after the commandment and then emphasize "I" to make it evident that Jesus' own teaching follows.

Intensify the seriousness in your tone of voice as you proclaim the three statements about relating to one's brother and the increasing severity of consequences.

Raqa = ree-KAY or ree-kuh
Sanhedrin = san-HEE-druhn
Gehenna = geh-HEN-nah

Lower your tone of voice for the two sections on reconciliation.

"You have **heard** that it was **said** to your **ancestors**,
You shall not ***kill****; and whoever* ***kills*** *will be* ***liable***
to ***judgment****.*
But **I** say to **you**,
whoever is **angry** with his **brother**
will be **liable** to **judgment**;
and whoever **says** to his brother, '**Raqa**,'
will be **answerable** to the **Sanhedrin**;
and whoever says, 'You **fool**,'
will be **liable** to fiery **Gehenna**.
Therefore, if you **bring** your **gift** to the **altar**,
and there **recall** that your **brother**
has anything **against** you,
leave your gift **there** at the **altar**,
go **first** and be **reconciled** with your **brother**,
and then **come** and **offer** your **gift**.
Settle with your opponent **quickly** while on the way to **court**.
Otherwise your **opponent** will hand you over to the **judge**,
and the **judge** will hand you over to the **guard**,
and **you** will be **thrown** into **prison**.
Amen, I **say** to you,
you will **not** be **released** until you have **paid** the last **penny**.

Use the same technique as for the first commandment in this Gospel reading to proclaim "You shall not commit adultery."

"You have ***heard*** *that it was* ***said****,*
You shall **not** *commit* ***adultery****.*

for them to be the salt of the earth and the light of the world. They are to flavor the world and shine for others by conducting themselves in a manner that distinguishes them from the scribes and the Pharisees.

The Gospel begins with a general statement that expresses how Jesus has come, not to abolish the law but to fulfill it. Used in this context, "fulfill" means to complete. Jesus' teaching not only completes the law, but in him—in his very person, message, and mission—he completes and perfects the law.

After the general statement, four examples are given. Each begins with a statement of the Jewish law, which is followed by the words "But I say to you," which introduce Jesus' own teaching. The first example addresses the prohibition of murder (Exodus 21:12). Jesus' response broadens the law to address anger. Anger, including denigrating others by calling them names such as *raqa,* Aramaic for "imbecile" or "idiot," can cause harm to others. Jesus calls for reconciliation and the working out of differences before the anger leads one to the court of law or even to Gehenna.

The second example begins with the statement of the law prohibiting adultery from Exodus 20:14 and Deuteronomy 5:18. Jesus' teaching recognizes that adultery is a sin of the heart; a person uses his free will to decide in his heart to act in an adulterous way.

The example of adultery is followed by one on divorce (Deuteronomy 24:1–5). The exceptive clause Matthew includes in

But **I** say to **you**,
everyone who **looks** at a woman with **lust**
has **already** committed **adultery** with her in his **heart**.
If your right **eye** causes you to **sin**,
tear it **out** and throw it **away**.
It is **better** for you to **lose** one of your **members**
than to have your whole **body** thrown into **Gehenna**.
And if your right **hand** causes you to **sin**,
cut it **off** and throw it **away**.
It is **better** for you to **lose** one of your **members**
than to have your whole **body** go into **Gehenna**.

Again, follow the same technique for the third commandment ("Whoever divorces his wife . . .").

"It was **also** said,
Whoever ***divorces*** *his* ***wife*** *must give her a* ***bill*** *of* ***divorce***.
But **I** say to **you**,
whoever **divorces** his **wife**—unless the marriage is **unlawful**—
causes her to commit **adultery**,
and whoever **marries** a divorced **woman** commits **adultery**.

Follow the same technique for your proclamation of the fourth commandment ("Do not take a false oath . . .").

"**Again** you have **heard** that it was **said** to your **ancestors**,
Do ***not*** *take a* ***false*** *oath,*
but make ***good*** *to the* ***Lord*** *all that you* ***vow***.
But **I** say to **you**, do not **swear** at **all**;
not by **heaven**, for it is God's **throne**;
nor by the **earth**, for it is his **footstool**;
nor by **Jerusalem**, for it is the **city** of the great **King**.
Do not **swear** by your **head**,
for you cannot **make** a single **hair** white or black.
Let your **'Yes'** mean **'Yes**,' and your **'No'** mean **'No**.'
Anything **more** is from the **evil** one."

Personalize the responsibility entailed in the final line by making eye contact with the assembly. Let the strength in your voice convey the uncompromising nature of these words.

[Shorter Form: Matthew 5:20–22a, 27–28, 33–34a, 37]

Jesus' response has been the subject of much debate. Yet it seems to be the presupposition of the Old Testament law of divorce that Jesus denies. The Old Testament commandment which says that a man can give a woman a bill of divorce appears to legitimize divorce as an option. Thus, what Jesus denies is this option. The ideal of marriage, the permanence of the covenantal bond of personal love, he upholds.

The fourth example addresses the taking of oaths (see Exodus 20:7; Deuteronomy 5:11; Leviticus 19:12). While the Jewish law prohibits false oaths, Jesus is uncomplicated and straightforward, forbidding any swearing of oaths at all. Jesus concludes by exhorting his disciples to say "yes" and "no" and follow through on what they say.

In essence, Jesus calls his disciples, and your proclamation today calls the assembly, to speak the truth of Jesus—the unity of his person, message, and mission. Following the parallel structure of the four examples will help you achieve this goal and assist the assembly in knowing that they can be the greatest in the kingdom of heaven.

7TH SUNDAY IN ORDINARY TIME

Lectionary #79a

READING I Leviticus 19:1–2, 17–18

Leviticus = lih-VIT-ih-kuhs

Deliver the Lord's instruction to Moses in a conversational, not didactic, tone of voice as if the Lord were privately instructing Moses in what to do. Pause significantly after the colon.

Offer the instructions on how the whole Israelite community should be holy to the whole assembly before you, making eye contact after each instruction. Allow your voice to be firm and teacher-like, but try not to come across as moralizing or lecturing.

Proclaim the final command slowly and deliberately. Pause before delivering the Lord's self-declaration resolutely and with confidence.

A reading from the Book of Leviticus

The **LORD** said to **Moses**,
"Speak to the whole Israelite community and tell them:
Be **holy**, for **I**, the **LORD**, your **God**, am **holy**.
"**You** shall not bear **hatred** for your brother or sister in your **heart**.
Though you may have to **reprove** your fellow **citizen**,
do **not** incur **sin** because of **him**.
Take no **revenge** and cherish no **grudge** against **any** of your **people**.
You shall **love** your **neighbor** as **yourself**.
I am the **LORD**."

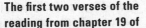

READING I The first two verses of the reading from chapter 19 of Leviticus (the third book of the Pentateuch) provide an introduction to the entire chapter. That chapter contains an assortment of laws on worship and how to relate to one's neighbor. These verses are particularly arresting because they present the commands as the Lord's own words. Read in context, the commands describe how the Israelites are to imitate the Lord's holiness.

In the two verses that comprise the second half of today's reading, holiness is linked to love of neighbor. At the time, a neighbor was a fellow citizen. Neighborly love could entail challenging law-breakers to follow the law; however, this must not result in grudges or revenge. The mark of true holiness is to be holy as God is holy through love for one another.

Notice that these words of the Lord's were first spoken to the people by Moses. Now through your compassionate, but instructive proclamation of these words, you call the assembly to assess how they are being holy.

READING II To develop the contrast between true wisdom and foolishness in today's Second Reading, Paul cites Job 5:13 and Psalm 94:11. The first quotation, "God catches the wise in their own ruses," comes from the first speech of Eliphaz the Temanite, in which he offers a response to Job's hopelessness (Job 4:1—5:27). In this speech, Eliphaz contends that the Lord never forgets those who are wise, act uprightly, and truly follow him, but he will punish those who are foolish and who engage in mischievous acts.

READING II 1 Corinthians 3:16–23

Corinthians = kohr-IN-thee-uhnz

Ask this rhetorical question with kindness in your voice, gently reminding each member of the assembly that he or she is the temple of God.

State Paul's first instruction ("Let no one deceive himself") in an assertive manner. Then lower your tone of voice as you offer Paul's explanation for how wisdom and foolishness can be deceptive. Be deliberate in your proclamation so as not to get tongue-tied with the repetition of forms of "wise" and "fool." Pause significantly before the quotations from Job 5:13 and Psalm 94:11 to set them off from Paul's words.

State Paul's second instruction ("So let no one boast . . .") using the same tone of voice as you used for the first. Pause significantly at the comma after "belongs to you" so as to connect this phrase to the repetition "all belong to you."

Apollos = uh-POL-ohs

Cephas = SEE-fuhs

Proclaim the concluding line of the reading slowly, pausing at the commas to give the assembly time to ponder the relationships Paul defines.

A reading from the first Letter of Saint Paul to the Corinthians

Brothers and sisters:
Do you not **know** that **you** are the **temple** of **God**,
and that the **Spirit** of **God dwells** in you?
If **anyone** destroys God's **temple**, **God** will **destroy** that **person**;
for the **temple** of **God**, which you **are**, is **holy**.

Let no **one** deceive **himself**.
If any **one** among you considers himself **wise** in this **age**,
let him become a **fool**, so as to become **wise**.
For the **wisdom** of this **world** is **foolishness** in the **eyes** of **God**,
for it is **written**:
__God__ catches the __wise__ in their own __ruses__,
and again:
The __Lord__ knows the __thoughts__ of the __wise__,
that __they__ are __vain__.
So let no **one** boast about human **beings**, for **everything** belongs
to **you**,
Paul or Apollos or Cephas,
or the world or life or death,
or the present or the future:
all belong to **you**, and **you** to **Christ**, and **Christ** to **God**.

Upon an initial read of Paul's use of this quote, it appears as if he has adopted Eliphaz's view, which at the end of the book of Job proves false. While wisdom and foolishness are analogous with good and bad in Eliphaz's argument, for Paul, wisdom and foolishness are more sophisticated concepts, not merely equated with human understanding. For Paul, one is truly wise if one can boast only in light of the cross of Jesus Christ. This wisdom the world does not understand.

Paul's use of the quote from Psalm 94 advances his argument beyond Eliphaz's speech. In it, the psalmist cries to the Lord, hoping the Lord will turn back the evil of the wicked and destroy them (verse 23). The wisdom of the psalmist is evident in his conviction that human plans, the plans of the wise, are simply vanity. Happiness is found only by those whom the Lord guides and teaches (94:12). For Paul, this is true wisdom, which comes to people when they recognize they are holy because they belong to the Lord.

When the Corinthians recognize their holiness, they recognize that they house God—they are God's temple. Your proclamation calls the assembly to recognize that your parish community is holy and as such, is God's temple.

GOSPEL **Following upon the four teachings from the law presented last Sunday, the master teacher presents two more this Sunday.**

The first, the legal rule about revenge rooted in Exodus 21:22–25, Leviticus 24:20, and Deuteronomy 19:21, Jesus completes by emphasizing kindness and compassion, true holiness in light of today's First

GOSPEL Matthew 5:38–48

A reading from the holy Gospel according to Matthew

Using the same technique as in last Sunday's Gospel reading, make eye contact with the assembly and state the first rule ("An eye for an eye . . .") clearly. Then lower your tone of voice and speak Jesus' teaching with compassion.

Jesus **said** to his **disciples**:
"You have **heard** that it was **said**,
An **eye** *for an* **eye** *and a* **tooth** *for a* **tooth**.
But **I** say to **you**, offer no **resistance** to one who is **evil**.
When someone **strikes** you on your right **cheek**,
turn the **other** one as well.
If anyone wants to go to **law** with you over your **tunic**,
hand **over** your **cloak** as **well**.
Should anyone **press** you into **service** for **one** mile,
go for **two** miles.
Give to the one who asks of **you**,
and do **not** turn your **back** on one who wants to **borrow**.

Again, deliver the second command ("You shall love . . .") with the same technique as the first. With more compassion—even empathy—offer Jesus' remarkable teaching.

"You have **heard** that it was **said**,
You shall ***love*** *your* ***neighbor*** *and* ***hate*** *your* ***enemy***.
But **I** say to **you**, **love** your **enemies**
and **pray** for those who **persecute** you,
that you may be **children** of your heavenly **Father**,
for he **makes** his sun **rise** on the **bad** and the **good**,
and **causes** rain to **fall** on the **just** and the **unjust**.

recompense = REK-uhm-pens

For if you **love** those who love **you**, what **recompense** will you **have**?
Do **not** the tax **collectors** do the **same**?

Pause after the second more specific rhetorical question so as to separate the first set of questions from the second.

And if you **greet** your brothers **only**,
what is **unusual** about **that**?
Do **not** the **pagans** do the **same**?

Make eye contact with the assembly as you call them to be perfect. Do so with a kindness and mercy in your voice that reminds them of God's own.

So be **perfect**, just as your heavenly **Father** is **perfect**."

Reading. Written in the singular (not two eyes and multiple teeth), this law was originally intended to curtail the extent of revenge by an evil person. However, at the time of Jesus, many already regarded this teaching as too severe. Yet Jesus' new teaching could have been similarly interpreted as too severe, erring on the side of pure charity, and thus disconnected entirely from the law of revenge.

The source of the second teaching Jesus addresses is Leviticus 19:18. Why the evangelist Matthew has Jesus leave out "as yourself" and expands the verse to include "hate your enemy" is uncertain. Growing tensions between Jewish leadership and Gentiles at the time Matthew was writing could be the reason. After the quotation, Jesus explains the morality his disciples are to live. Love extends beyond neighbors who think and act similarly, to those who disagree and dislike you, and even desire to do you harm.

The call of the Lord's disciples to be "perfect" or blameless, which serves as both the summary and climax of the last two Sunday's passages, is the call to be holy, imitating God's holiness fulfilled in Jesus. "Perfect" in this context is unrelated to the contemporary human need to strive for perfection. Inherent in this word, which occurs in the Lucan parallel to this passage (6:36) and again in Matthew 19:21, is the notion of the divine mercy that disciples are to extend to others who journey on the path to holiness, but occasionally falter. Extend this mercy through your proclamation of the Gospel and the manner in which you offer compassion to those in your assembly who journey on the path to true holiness.

8TH SUNDAY IN ORDINARY TIME

Lectionary #82a

READING I Isaiah 49:14–15

Isaiah = Ī-ZAY-uh

Zion = ZĪ-ahn

Ask the rhetorical question about the mother's relationship to the child in her womb with warmth and affection in your voice.

Take your time proclaiming the truth that the Lord will never forget his people. Make eye contact with the assembly as you do.

A reading from the Book of the Prophet Isaiah

Zion **said**, "The LORD has **forsaken me**;
my **Lord** has **forgotten** me."
Can a **mother** forget her **infant**,
be without **tenderness** for the **child** of her **womb**?
Even should she **forget**,
I will **never** forget **you**.

READING II 1 Corinthians 4:1–5

Corinthians = kohr-IN-thee-uhnz

Make eye contact with the assembly as you proclaim the opening statement directly to them.

Use a conversational tone of voice to convey Paul's lack of concern about human judgment. Deliver the conclusion of this section slowly, clearly, and boldly.

A reading from the first Letter of Saint Paul to the Corinthians

Brothers and sisters:
Thus should one regard **us**: as **servants** of **Christ**
and **stewards** of the **mysteries** of **God**.
Now it is of course **required** of **stewards**
that **they** be found **trustworthy**.
It does **not** concern me in the **least**
that **I** be judged by **you** or any **human** tribunal;
I do **not** even pass **judgment** on **myself**;
I am **not** conscious of **anything** against **me**,
but I do **not** thereby stand **acquitted**;
the **one** who judges **me** is the **Lord**.

READING I You will want to be sure to have the assembly's attention as you proclaim these brief two verses because they have not been proclaimed for 20 years. The Eighth Sunday of Ordinary Time, Year A, occurs this year for the first time since 1990 because Easter is the last Sunday in April and counting backward from that date until Ash Wednesday leaves eight Sundays between the end of the Christmas season and the beginning of Lent.

The two verses from Isaiah in today's First Reading are preceded by the announcement of a new exodus found in verses 8–13 and are the beginning of the announcement of Zion's salvation, verses 14–26. Reading the whole of chapter 49 as you prepare will help you understand more fully the context surrounding verses 14–15.

The newly commissioned prophet (49:1–7, the second servant song) offers these moving words of comfort to Zion/Jerusalem, who had long been grieving for her children in exile. Because Second Isaiah wrote after the Persian king, Cyrus, signed the verdict allowing the Israelites to return home, in context this passage conveys not only the mother's longing for her children en route back home, but also her distress over the reality that until the completion of the Jerusalem Temple and the development of the surrounding state in the sixth century, the mother cannot support all her children. The Lord, however, will never forget. The Lord will love with the constancy and tenderness of a mother.

READING II The subject of today's Second Reading from the beginning of chapter 4 in Paul's first letter to the Corinthians is the same as that in

Return to the conversational tone as you proclaim Paul's instructions to the Corinthians about when and how they are to judge.

Therefore do **not** make **any** judgment **before** the appointed **time**,
until the Lord **comes**,
for **he** will bring to **light** what is **hidden** in **darkness**
and will manifest the **motives** of our **hearts**,
and then **everyone** will receive **praise** from **God**.

Deliver the joyful news that "everyone will receive praise" from the Lord at the appointed time with eagerness and confidence, again making eye contact with the assembly.

GOSPEL Matthew 6:24–34

A reading from the holy Gospel according to Matthew

Be strong and direct as you convey Jesus' teaching "No one can serve two masters." Lower your tone of voice on the following explanatory sentence and then return to the strength and directness as you identify the two masters that cannot be served.

Jesus **said** to his **disciples**:
"No one can serve **two** masters.
He will either **hate** one and **love** the other,
or be **devoted** to one and **despise** the other.
You **cannot** serve **God** and **mammon**.

Fill your voice with calmness and serenity as you proclaim Jesus' teaching about the Father's care for his children

"**Therefore** I tell **you**, do not **worry** about your **life**,
what you will **eat** or **drink**,
or about your **body**, what you will **wear**.
Is not **life** more than **food** and the **body** more than **clothing**?
Look at the **birds** in the **sky**;
they do not **sow** or **reap**, they gather **nothing** into **barns**,
yet your heavenly **Father** feeds **them**.
Are not **you** more important than **they**?

Employ a slightly didactic tone of voice to proclaim Jesus' questions about why his disciples are anxious and why they seem to lack trust in God's providence.

Can **any** of you by **worrying** add a single **moment**
to your life-**span**?

3:5–9: how the Christians at Corinth should view their leaders. In the opening verse of this reading, Paul instructs the Corinthians that pastors such as he should be regarded as "servants of Christ and stewards of the mysteries of God." As a servant of Christ, he is a witness to the Gospel—the truth and merits of Christ's salvific death and Resurrection. As a steward of the divine mysteries, he takes care to preach about them authentically and so that those who profess belief in God's mysteries will live according to them.

In this section of his letter, Paul does not appear even slightly concerned about what the Corinthians think of him. Whether they judge him negatively carries no weight, for he does not serve on his own accord; his role as steward of God's mysteries does not come by appointment from the Corinthians or any other human community. Rather, he is "called to be an apostle of Christ Jesus by the will of God" (1 Corinthians 1:1).

The Corinthians should reserve judgment until the parousia, when the Lord will come again in glory. At the appointed time of the Lord's final judgment, he will show forth what is in the hearts and minds of all. Have we cooperated with those whom God has called to be servants and stewards? Have we lived our own lives according to Christ, the Wisdom of God, as servants and stewards of the Gospel? Leave people to ponder these questions as you conclude your proclamation of this reading with the joyful news of God praising those who have aligned their hearts' motives with him.

Why are you **anxious** about **clothes**?
Learn from the **way** the wild flowers **grow**.
They do not **work** or **spin**.
But **I** tell **you** that not even **Solomon** in all his **splendor**
was **clothed** like one of **them**.
If **God** so clothes the **grass** of the **field**,
which grows **today** and is thrown into the oven **tomorrow**,
will **he** not much more **provide** for **you**, O you of little **faith**?
So do not **worry** and **say**, 'What **are** we to **eat**?'
or 'What **are** we to **drink**?' or 'What **are** we to **wear**?'
All these things the pagans **seek**.
Your heavenly **Father** knows that you need them all.
But seek first the kingdom of **God** and his **righteousness**,
and **all** these **things** will be given you **besides**.
Do not **worry** about **tomorrow**; **tomorrow** will take care of **itself**.
Sufficient for a **day** is its own **evil**."

As you deliver the line "So do not worry . . ." return to the calmness and serenity that was in your voice when you proclaimed Jesus' initial teaching about not worrying.

Make eye contact and be confident proclaiming Jesus' instruction to seek first the kingdom of God.

Return again to calmness and serenity to communicate Jesus' conclusion and the third occurrence of "Do not worry . . ." Pause. Then be straightforward, but not fearful, about the day's evil.

GOSPEL

There is much to be anxious about in today's world. The 24/7 news cycle makes this patently obvious. While the specific anxieties in our world and the world of Jesus' time might not be identical, this Gospel passage shows us that people in the first century did experience the same human feeling of anxiety that we do.

Obviously, they were concerned about their basic human needs for food and drink, they were worried about their appearance, physical health, and having clothes to wear. Jesus consistently and compassionately tries to calm their fears.

Teaching both the inner circle of disciples always surrounding him in Matthew's account of the Gospel and the crowds gathered around on the mount, Jesus tries to get at the root of their anxiety, asking them why they are anxious (Matthew 6:28). His question is rhetorical, so neither the disciples nor crowds answer. Instead, Jesus uses an example from nature. Just as the Father feeds the birds in the sky, he clothes the grass of the field, and will clothe those who have faith.

The last verse of today's Gospel conveys the truth that each day already carries with it enough evil. Our personal anxieties and worries and those of people throughout the world will only multiply the force of this evil. Those who seek the kingdom of God will be fed by the Father's serenity and clothed in his peace. Serving only God and not mammon (the Semitic word for money or wealth) will show your fidelity to God and your trust in his constant care.

9TH SUNDAY IN ORDINARY TIME

Lectionary #85a

FIRST READING Deuteronomy 11:18, 26–28, 32

Deuteronomy = d<u>oo</u>-ter-AH-nuh-mee

Make eye contact with the assembly as you strongly proclaim the opening line, calling them to listen to the words that follow.

Distinguish between blessing and curse by using a lighter tone of voice for blessing and a darker, heavier tone for curse.

Pause noticeably before the final sentence. Offer Moses' general instructions with care. Make eye contact with the assembly as you do.

A reading from the Book of Deuteronomy

Moses told the **people**,
"Take these words of mine into your **heart** and **soul**.
Bind them at your **wrist** as a **sign**,
and let them be a **pendant** on your **forehead**.
"I set **before** you here, **this** day, a **blessing** and a **curse**:
a **blessing** for **obeying** the **commandments** of the **LORD**,
your God,
which I **enjoin** on you **today**;
a curse if you do **not** obey the **commandments** of the **LORD**,
your God,
but **turn aside** from the **way** I **ordain** for you **today**,
to follow **other** gods, whom you have **not** known.
Be carfeful to observe **all** the statutes and decrees
that I set before you **today**."

READING I The First Reading follows upon a section in Deuteronomy which recounts the way the Lord cared for his people by delivering them out of Egypt, leading them through the wilderness, and bringing them to the beautiful new land that they are about to enter (11:2–17). In today's passage, Moses makes clear the moral choice facing the Israelites: the reward of blessing comes from their fidelity to the Lord's commands. The book of the law, which begins where today's passage leaves off, details these commands—concerning purity and sanctuary laws, religious duties, responsibilities to the poor, consequences for idolatry, and various other legal and moral prescriptions.

We know from the first account of Creation in the book of Genesis that the Lord's word is active and creative. It contains the breath of life and is his bond with us. When we choose to follow the Lord's word, we create a bond with that word. The Israelites (and we also) are urged to commit to God's word, regardless of the cost.

As the Lord has cared for his Chosen People in the past, Moses explains, he will continue to do so if they choose to obey his commands. For Christians, the Lord's word became flesh and is living and active in Jesus Christ. He is God's bond of fidelity to us.

Moses tells the people that the choice between blessing and curse is set before them "this day." This day, the moment of now, is the time of choice for people today as well—and this Sunday it will be offered through you. This is the same choice to listen and heed that Jesus places before his disciples in today's Gospel. Before you proclaim this passage, ask yourself, have

READING II Romans 3:21–25, 28

Romans = ROH-muhnz

A reading from the Letter of Saint Paul to the Romans

Connect the opening phrase of the first sentence with the third phrase by lowering your tone of voice on the parenthetical phrase "though testified to . . . ."

Brothers and sisters,
Now the **righteousness** of **God** has been **manifested apart** from the law,
though **testified** to **by** the law and the prophets,
the **righteousness** of **God** through **faith** in **Jesus Christ**
for **all** who **believe**.
For there is **no** distinction;
all have **sinned** and are **deprived** of the **glory** of **God**.
They are **justified freely** by **his grace**
through the **redemption** in **Christ Jesus**,
whom God set forth as an **expiation**,
through **faith**, by **his blood**.
For we consider that a person is **justified** by **faith**
apart from **works** of the **law**.

Again, lower your tone of voice on the parenthetical phrase "whom God set forth . . . ."

Use a confident, strong voice to proclaim the final line to the assembly. Make eye contact as you do—you are proclaiming your and their belief in God's gratuitous justification through Christ by faith.

you yourself taken the words of the Lord into your heart and soul?

READING II **Paul says, "We consider that a person is justified by faith apart from works of the law." Is he contradicting the words of the Lord spoken through the prophet Moses in the First Reading? Although Paul may appear to negate the Mosaic law, he does not. Paul is saying that something new has happened in Christ that works in tandem with the essence of the law. For those who believe in Christ and the redemption offered through his death and Resurrection, justification is freely given. A few verses after our Lectionary reading ends, Paul will say, "Are we then annulling the law by this faith? Of course not! On the contrary, we are supporting the law" (31).**

Paul taught that "all have sinned," both Jews and Gentiles alike. All are in need of the justification offered in Jesus Christ. ("Justification," "righteousness," and "redemption" are words with similar meanings.) Receiving the free gift of justification, however, does not mitigate the responsibility one has for following the Lord's commands. Rather, the Lord's commands are now to be seen and interpreted in light of this grace newly received. Paul's teaching and Moses' words are congruent because both express the Lord's word.

God's care for the sinner—for those who miss the mark trying to follow the law—remains, and is present in a unique way once for all in the justification given through Jesus Christ for those who believe. This great gift compels believers to live the law, not because they fear the gift will be taken away, but because they wish to express heartfelt gratitude for it.

GOSPEL Matthew 7:21–27

Emphasize the contrast between "says" and "does" by placing stress on those words. Make eye contact with two different parts of the assembly to communicate the two sides of Jesus' teaching.

Follow a similar pattern of making eye contact with different parts of the assembly as you ask the three questions about prophesying, driving out demons, and doing mighty deeds. Stress the repetition of "in your name." Let a hint of sadness mark your proclamation of Jesus' solemn words "I never knew you."

Lower your tone of voice to share the parable and its explanation. Color your tone of voice with seriousness so as to make the grave consequences real to the assembly.

A reading from the holy Gospel according to Matthew

Jesus **said** to his **disciples**:
"Not **everyone** who says to me, '**Lord, Lord**,'
will **enter** the kingdom of **heaven**,
but **only** the one who does the **will** of my Father in **heaven**.
Many will say to me on that **day**,
'Lord, Lord, did we not **prophesy** in your **name**?
Did we not **drive** out **demons** in your **name**?
Did we not do **mighty deeds** in your **name**?'
Then **I** will **declare** to them solemnly,
'I **never** knew you. **Depart** from me, you **evildoers**.'

"**Everyone** who **listens** to these words of mine and **acts** on them
will be like a **wise** man who built his house on rock.
The **rain** fell, the **floods** came,
and the **winds** blew and buffeted the **house**.
But it did **not** collapse; it had been set **solidly** on **rock**.
And **everyone** who **listens** to these words of mine
but does **not** act on them
will be like a **fool** who built his house on **sand**.
The **rain** fell, the **floods** came,
and the **winds** blew and buffeted the house.
And it **collapsed** and was **completely** ruined."

GOSPEL Today's Gospel is from the conclusion to the Sermon on the Mount (7:13–27). Having instructed his disciples and the crowds who gathered around to hear him, Jesus now draws his teaching to an end.

The Gospel passage is eschatological in character, meaning that it addresses what will happen at the final judgment. Whether a person's house collapses in the end (the house is a symbol for one's life), coincides with the choice between blessing and curse that Moses offers to the Israelites in the First Reading. The sturdiness of one's house in the face of life's tribulations (the rains, floods, and winds) will be determined by one's choice to listen and act on Jesus' words.

For Jesus, consistency between what a disciple hears and how a disciple lives is essential. In this passage, Jesus confronts false prophets who choose to prophesy and perform acts of healing in his name, but who never "knew him." They never acknowledge him for who he is, the Son of God, the Messiah (see Matthew 10:33).

The blessing of being Jesus' disciple is the blessing of a relationship with him. This relationship buoys us for the suffering we might experience, teaches us how to align our own words and actions with his, and prepares us to receive the gift of eternal life.

With Lent about to begin, you have the opportunity to make clear to the assembly the consequences of following (or not) Jesus' teaching from the Sermon on the Mount. In doing so, your proclamation will help prepare them for the Lenten journey of repentance and forgiveness.

ASH WEDNESDAY

Lectionary #219

READING I Joel 2:12–18

A reading from the Book of the Prophet Joel

God speaks with urgency and longing.

mourning = MOR-ning

Here, the words are reassuring.

Even now, says the LORD,
return to me with your **whole heart**,
with **fasting**, and **weeping**, and **mourning**;
Rend your **hearts**, not your **garments**,
and **return** to the **LORD**, your **God**.
For **gracious** and **merciful** is he,
slow to **anger**, **rich** in **kindness**,
and **relenting** in **punishment**.
Perhaps he will again **relent**
and leave behind him a **blessing**,
Offerings and **libations**
for the **LORD**, your **God**.

relent = rih-LENT

libations = lī-BAY-shuhnz

This is a rallying cry.

Zion = ZĪ-ahn

assemble = uh-SEM-b*l

Blow the trumpet in **Zion**!
proclaim a **fast**,
call an **assembly**;
Gather the **people**,
notify the **congregation**;
Assemble the **elders**,
gather the **children**
and the **infants** at the breast;
Let the **bridegroom** quit his room,
and the **bride** her chamber.

READING I As today's reading from Joel begins, the prophet, speaking for God, says, "Even now . . . return to me with your whole heart." "Even now" implies after all that has happened. What has happened?

Joel was a prophet after the exile, about 400 BC. Life was terribly hard for those living in the Holy Land. In chapter one, Joel tells us that a plague of locusts had recently invaded the land and destroyed everything. There was not enough food for people or animals, much less food to offer in sacrifice to God. The people were truly suffering.

In today's reading, we read Joel's response to this natural disaster. He encourages the people to respond to God's constant call to live in fidelity to covenant love: "Return to the Lord, your God." Joel understands the locust plague to be a precursor of the great day of the Lord when other nations, who are God's enemies, will try to devastate the land, just as the locusts have. Now is the time to turn wholeheartedly to the Lord. The people's return to God must not be limited to participation in rituals. No, they must rend their hearts, not their garments.

Joel assures the people that there is every hope that God will intervene on the people's behalf because of who God is: God is "gracious," "merciful," "slow to anger, rich in kindness, and relenting in punishment." In describing God this way, Joel is alluding to Exodus, where God describes himself to Moses: "The LORD . . . a merciful and gracious God, slow to anger and rich in kindness and fidelity . . ." (Exodus 34:6b).

The priests' tone is beseeching.
reproach = rih-PROHCH

The reading ends with reassurance.

Between the porch and the altar
let the **priests**, the **ministers** of the LORD, **weep**,
And say, "**Spare**, O LORD, your **people**,
and make not **your heritage** a **reproach**,
with the **nations ruling** over them!
Why should they say among the peoples,
'**Where is their God**?'"
Then the LORD was **stirred to concern** for his land
and took **pity** on his **people**.

READING II 2 Corinthians 5:20 — 6:2

Here, Paul is appealing on God's behalf.
ambassadors = am-BAS-uh-derz or am-BAS-uh-dohrz
appealing = uh-PEEL-ing
Paul is imploring.
implore = im-PLOHR
reconciled = REK-uhn-sīld
Read slowly, pausing after each unit of thought.
righteousness = RĪ-chuhs-n*ss

A reading from the second Letter of Saint Paul to the Corinthians

Brothers and **sisters**:
We are ambassadors for Christ,
as if God were appealing through **us**.
We **implore you** on behalf of **Christ**,
be **reconciled** to God.
For **our sake** he made **him** to be **sin**
who did not know sin,
so that **we** might become the **righteousness**
of **God** in him.

Joel calls all of the people to participate in an assembly to ritualize their repentance. All must attend: the elders, the children, infants at the breast, even brides and bridegrooms. The newly married were usually exempt from public duties for one full year (see Deuteronomy 24:5). However, the present situation was too dire to allow any exceptions. All must be present.

As the priests pray for the people, they remind God that they are depending on him to be faithful to his promises. It certainly wouldn't look good if other nations could ask, "Where is their God?" In response to true penitence and prayer, God has pity on the people.

Joel's words are proclaimed on Ash Wednesday to call all of us to repentance. We, too, are to rend our hearts, not our garments. The tone of the reading changes: God's words are spoken with urgency and longing. The prophet's words, when describing God, are reassuring, but then become a rallying cry. The character of the priests' prayer is beseeching. The reading ends with a reassuring tone.

READING II Paul had a complicated and difficult relationship with the Corinthians. It is evident from Paul's letters that he and the Corinthians both hurt each other, and loved each other, deeply. One of Paul's reasons for writing the passage that we read today is to affirm that he and the Corinthians are reconciled. As is often true in Paul's pastoral letters, he uses an everyday experience as an opportunity to teach profound theological truths.

We do not know all that caused the hurt. One reason seems to be that Paul had not visited the Corinthians when expected

Paul is still appealing. However, you could speak more softly here.

Working together, then,
we **appeal** to you not to receive the **grace**
of **God** in **vain**.
For he says:

*In an acceptable time I **heard** you,*
*and on the day of salvation I **helped** you.*

Now increase your volume.

Behold, **now** is a **very acceptable time**;
behold, **now** is the **day of salvation**.

GOSPEL Matthew 6:1–6, 16–18

A reading from the holy Gospel according to Matthew

disciples = dih-SĪ-p*lz

Jesus is instructing, not correcting his disciples.

righteous = RĪ-chuhs

recompense = REK-uhm-pens

Jesus is drawing a contrast between his disciples and hypocrites.

Jesus said to his disciples:
"Take care **not** to perform **righteous deeds**
in order that **people** may **see** them;
otherwise, you will have **no recompense**
from your **heavenly Father**.
When you give **alms**,
do **not** blow a **trumpet** before you,
as the **hypocrites** do in the **synagogues**
and in the **streets**
to win the **praise** of **others**.

Emphasize each word in this line. This phrase signals that Jesus is speaking with authority.

Amen, I say to you,
they have **received** their **reward**.
But when you give **alms**,
do **not** let your **left hand know** what your **right** is **doing**,
so that your **almsgiving** may be **secret**.
And your **Father** who sees in **secret** will **repay you**.

(2 Corinthians 1:23). Rather than visit, Paul had written the Corinthians a tearful letter (2 Corinthians 2:4). Now, however, Paul has heard from Titus about the Corinthians "yearning . . . lament . . . and zeal" for Paul (2 Corinthians 7:7). This whole experience has caused Paul to reflect on the fact that both he and the Corinthians have been trusted with "the message of reconciliation" (2 Corinthians 5:19b). It is at this point that today's reading begins.

Paul reminds the Corinthians that both he and they are "ambassadors for Christ." An ambassador is a person who represents another and speaks on the other's behalf. Because they are ambassadors for Christ, God is appealing through them. They must both model and teach the necessity of reconciliation.

Paul implores the Corinthians to be reconciled to God. After all, Christ, who was sinless, suffered as sinful people do, for the purpose of reconciling them to God. They must not "receive the grace of God in vain; that is, they must not fail to accept this great gift. Now is the time to accept that gift; "now is the day of salvation."

As Paul writes to the Corinthians, he tells us his tone: Paul says, "We implore you . . . we appeal to you." Paul's words are a living word, calling each of us to be reconciled and to become ministers of reconciliation for others. An imploring, entreating tone is still appropriate. We, too, are being taught that now is the day of salvation.

GOSPEL **Today's reading from the Gospel according to Matthew is part of Jesus' long Sermon on the Mount, in which he says that he has not**

hypocrites = HIP-uh-kritz
synagogues = SIN-uh-gogz

"When **you** pray,
do not be like the **hypocrites**,
who love to **stand** and pray in the **synagogues**
and on **street corners**
so that others may **see** them.

Again, emphasize each word in this line.

Amen, **I say to you**,
they have **received** their **reward**.

From here to the end, speak with an intimate and affectionate tone.

But when **you** pray, go to your **inner room**,
close the **door**, and pray to your **Father** in **secret**.
And your **Father** who **sees** in secret will **repay** you.

"When **you** fast,
do not look **gloomy** like the **hypocrites**.
They neglect their **appearance**,
so that they may **appear to others** to be fasting.
Amen, **I say to you**, they have **received their** reward.
But when **you fast**,
anoint your head and **wash** your face,
so that you may **not appear** to be fasting,
except to your **Father** who is **hidden**.
And your **Father** who **sees** what is **hidden**
will **repay** you."

come to destroy the law and the prophets, but to fulfill them (Matthew 5:17). Jesus gives the disciples instructions on three traditional forms of repentance: almsgiving, prayer, and fasting. In each case, Jesus is encouraging his followers to make these practices a matter of the heart, not a matter of appearance. Jesus is teaching what Joel taught in our first reading: the disciples must rend their hearts, not their garments.

When the disciples give alms they are not to draw attention to themselves in order to earn human respect. Rather, Jesus instructs them to "not let your left hand know what your right is doing." The goal is to be in right relationship with God, not to impress other human beings. When they pray, they are not to act like hypocrites, making a huge public display. They are to pray in private where only God will see them.

At this point our Lectionary reading skips what Jesus says next: he teaches his disciples what we have come to call the Our Father, and impresses on them the absolute necessity of forgiving others.

Jesus then continues with the same message: when the disciples fast they must not, like the hypocrites, draw everyone's attention to their fasting. Fasting, too, should be done in secret. God, who sees what is hidden, will repay them.

The tone of today's Gospel is one of instruction and invitation. Jesus is not accusing the disciples of misbehavior; he is simply instructing them, and us, on the way to behave. Our Lenten practices should be undertaken to rectify bad habits and change our ways in order to draw close to God, not to impress other people.

1ST SUNDAY OF LENT

Lectionary #22a

READING I Genesis 2:7–9; 3:1–7

A reading from the Book of Genesis

The narrator is simply setting the stage.

The **LORD God** formed **man** out of the **clay** of the **ground**
and blew into his nostrils the **breath** of **life**,
and so **man** became a **living being**.

Eden = EE-d*n

Then the LORD God planted a **garden** in **Eden**, in the east,
and **placed** there the **man** whom he had **formed**.
Out of the **ground** the LORD God made **various trees grow**
that were **delightful** to **look** at and **good** for **food**,
with the **tree of life** in the middle of the garden
and the **tree of the knowledge of good and evil**.

Now the **serpent** was the **most cunning** of **all** the animals
that the LORD God had made.
The **serpent** asked the **woman**,

The serpent is cunning, ingratiating, and persuasive.

"Did **God really tell** you not to eat
from **any** of the trees in the garden?"
The woman answered the serpent:

Here the woman is defending God and showing that she is in the know.

"**We may eat** of the **fruit** of the **trees** in the **garden**;
it is **only** about the **fruit** of the **tree**
in the **middle** of the **garden** that God said,

Raise your volume and say this line with authority.

'You shall not **eat it** or **even touch it**, **lest you die**.'"
But the **serpent** said to the woman:

Now the serpent speaks with authority.

"You **certainly will not die**!

READING I In the Genesis reading, we hear the familiar story about how sin causes suffering. The Lectionary includes those parts of the story in which the woman and her husband succumb to temptation. This is to draw a contrast to the Gospel, in which Jesus does not succumb to temptation.

The Lectionary reading begins with the creation of man and the planting of the garden in Eden, including the tree of life and the tree of the knowledge of good and evil. We can tell from the details in the story that we are reading a symbol story composed to teach a lesson. The forbidden tree is not an apple tree; it is a tree of the knowledge of good and evil.

The Lectionary reading does not include the instructions that God gives the man concerning the forbidden fruit. When the woman repeats them later, she does not repeat them accurately. God tells the man: "From that tree you shall not eat; the moment you eat from it you are surely doomed to die" (Genesis 2:17b). The Lectionary reading also skips over the creation of the woman, whom God creates because, "It is not good for the man to be alone" (Genesis 2:18b). God wants the man to be happy, not only to be well fed and in right relationship with himself and God, but to have another person to be loved by and to love.

Our reading picks up the story again as the woman faces temptation, symbolized by a talking serpent. The conversation between the serpent and the woman dramatizes temptation, whether that temptation is experienced as a conversation with another person or as an internal debate: should I or shouldn't I?

No, God knows well that the **moment** you **eat** of it
your **eyes** will be **opened** and you will be like **gods**
who know what is **good** and what is **evil**."

The narrator's voice is reasonable. Read slowly when you describe the appearance of the fruit.

The woman **saw** that the tree was **good** for **food**,
pleasing to the **eyes**, and **desirable** for gaining **wisdom**.

Read more quickly now that the decision is made.

So she **took** some of its fruit and **ate it**;
and she also **gave** some to her **husband**, who was with her,
and **he ate** it.

The tone at the end is solemn. We know a tragedy has occurred.

Then the **eyes** of **both of them** were **opened**,
and they **realized** that they were **naked**;
so they sewed **fig leaves** together
and made **loincloths** for themselves.

READING II Romans 5:12–19

A reading from the Letter of Saint Paul to the Romans

Both Paul's sentence structure and his ideas are dense. Read slowly, pausing after each unit of thought.

Brothers and sisters:
Through **one man sin** entered the **world**,
and through **sin**, **death**,
and thus **death** came to **all men**, inasmuch as **all sinned**—

These two lines are a side comment; drop your voice.

for up to the time of the **law**, sin **was** in the **world**,
though sin is not **accounted** when there is no **law**.

Here Paul resumes his explanation.

reigned = raynd

But **death reigned** from **Adam** to **Moses**,
even over those who did **not sin**
after the **pattern** of the **trespass** of **Adam**,

Emphasize the word type.

who is the **type** of the **one** who was to **come**.

Paul is now naming the good news. Speak slightly more quickly.

transgression = trans-GRESH-uhn or tranz-GRESH-uhn

Slow down with "how much more . . ."

But the **gift** is **not like** the **transgression**.
For if by the **transgression** of the **one**, the **many died**,
how much more did the **grace** of **God**

The serpent asks the woman if God told them not to eat from any of the trees in the garden. The woman replies that they may eat of all of the trees except one. About that tree God said: "You shall not eat it or even touch it, lest you die." God did not say that the man was not to touch the tree, only that he was not to eat of its fruit. A very important lesson is present here, one that is also taught in the Gospels: it is not only those who are too lax who are prone to temptation and sin; those who are too strict are also vulnerable.

The serpent then questions whether or not God's warning about death is the real reason that God said not to eat of this tree. Behind this temptation is a profound question: "Is God loving or not?" Is the moral order that is imbedded in God's creation for our good, so that we may flourish, or for God's good, to keep us in our place? The woman begins to doubt that God's directions were for her good.

The forbidden fruit looks good, pleasing, and desirable. She eats it, gives some to her husband, and he eats it. Upon eating the fruit, they do die—spiritually. They are immediately ashamed of themselves. Their self-shame is symbolized by their suddenly becoming uncomfortable with their nakedness, with who they are. Sin is never a good choice. It always leads to suffering.

The story begins with the narrator's voice, simply setting the stage. The tone for the serpent's lines are at first cunning and persuasive. The woman is initially defending God's orders. The serpent next speaks with authority. As the narrator's voice finishes the story, the tone should reflect the fact that we know something tragic has occurred.

and the **gracious gift** of the **one man Jesus Christ**
overflow for the **many**.

Read as you did the similar line above.

And the **gift** is **not like** the **result** of the one who sinned.
For after **one sin** there was the **judgment** that brought
condemnation;

acquittal = uh-KWIT-*l

but the **gift**, after **many transgressions**, brought **acquittal**.
For if, by the transgression of the **one**,
death came to reign **through that one**,

Slow down for "how much more . . . ."
abundance = uh-BUHN-duhnts
justification = juhs-tuh-fih-KAY-shun
Speak slowly again for the conclusion.

how much more will those who receive the **abundance** of **grace**
and of the **gift** of **justification**
come to reign in **life** through the **one Jesus Christ**.
In conclusion, just as through **one transgression**
condemnation came upon **all**,
so, through **one righteous act**,
acquittal and **life** came to **all**.

Inflect these words so that Paul's contrasts are clear: disobedience/obedience; the one man/the one; made sinners/made righteous.

For just as through the **disobedience** of the **one man**
the **many** were made **sinners**,
so, through the **obedience** of the **one**,
the **many** will be made **righteous**.

[Shorter Form: Romans 5:12, 17–19]

GOSPEL Matthew 4:1–11

A reading from the holy Gospel according to Matthew

Again, the narrator sets the stage.

At that time **Jesus** was **led by the Spirit** into the **desert**
to be **tempted** by the **devil**.
He **fasted** for **forty days** and **forty nights**,
and afterwards he was **hungry**.

READING II In the reading from Romans, Paul is teaching that Jesus Christ has reconciled the world to God. As today's reading concludes, this is stated twice: "through one righteous act acquittal and life came to all . . . through the obedience of the one, the many will be made righteous." The "one righteous act" and the "obedience of the one" both refer to Jesus' acceptance of his Passion and death, which led to his Resurrection. Through this act we have been saved.

In order to teach this profound truth Paul compares Jesus to the man in today's story from Genesis. Paul says that Adam is the "type of the one who was to come." To say that an Old Testament character is a type for a New Testament character is to say that one foreshadows the other. Adam is a type of Jesus, not in that he is like Jesus, but in that he is the polar opposite. One represents the sinfulness of the whole human race; the other brought about its redemption. One represents the pervasive nature of sin; the other redeemed the human race from slavery to sin.

Paul goes on to explain that humanity has always suffered from sin (from Adam to Moses), even before there was a law that clearly named what was sin and what was not. Because of sin, death reigned over everyone. All were guilty. Through Christ, all have been acquitted.

Paul's letter is difficult to read because Paul uses very complicated sentence structures. The tone is simply one of instruction. However, it will be necessary to read slowly and to pause at the end of each idea as it is presented. Be sure to

The devil's voice is challenging, authoritative.

Jesus' reply is not combative. Read Jesus' word with quiet authority.

Pause before each quotation, whether from Jesus or from the devil.

parapet = PAYR-uh-pit or PAYR-uh-pet

The devil continues to be challenging. He is offering Jesus a dare.

Pause here.

Jesus continues to speak with quiet authority.

Read this quotation slowly and with solemnity.

magnificence = mag-NIF-uh-s*ntz

Now the devil begins to plead.

prostrate = PROS-trayt

Jesus now speaks more firmly. Increase your volume and emphasize every word of "Get away, Satan!"

The narrator concludes the story.

The **tempter** approached and said to him,
"If **you** are the **Son of God**,
command that these **stones** become **loaves** of **bread**."
He said in reply,
"It is written:
One ***does not live*** *on* ***bread alone****,*
but on ***every word*** *that comes* ***forth***
from the ***mouth*** *of* ***God****."*

Then the **devil** took him to the **holy city**,
and made him **stand** on the **parapet** of the **temple**,
and said to him, "If **you** are the **Son of God**,
throw yourself down.
For it is written:
He will command his ***angels*** *concerning you*
and with ***their hands*** *they will* ***support*** *you,*
lest you dash your ***foot*** *against a* ***stone****."*
Jesus answered him,
"**Again** it is written,
You shall not put *the* **Lord**, **your God**, *to the* **test**."
Then the **devil** took him up to a **very high mountain**,
and showed him **all the kingdoms of the world**
in their **magnificence**,
and he said to him, "**All these** I shall give to **you**,
if you will **prostrate yourself** and **worship me**."
At this, Jesus said to him,
"**Get away**, **Satan**!
It is written:
The ***Lord****, your* ***God****, shall you* ***worship***
and ***him alone*** *shall you* ***serve****."*

Then the **devil** left him and, **behold**,
angels came and **ministered** to him.

study this reading so that you understand Paul's intent. If you do not understand the reading you will not be able to proclaim it effectively.

GOSPEL **Jesus, unlike the man and woman in the garden, does not succumb to temptation. The Gospel accounts of Mark, Matthew, and Luke all tell us that Jesus, before his public ministry began, overcame temptation. Mark, who is a source for the other two Gospel editors, simply says that "the Spirit drove him out into the desert, and he remained in the desert for forty days, tempted by Satan" (Mark 1:12-13a). Matthew and Luke both describe the kinds of temptation that Jesus overcame.**

In Matthew, Jesus overcomes the temptation to abuse his power, even to prove that he is the Son of God. First, the devil tempts Jesus to use his power to serve himself (turn stones to bread). Jesus refuses. Then, the devil tempts Jesus to use his power as a spectacle (to "throw yourself down"). Again, Jesus refuses. Finally, the devil tempts Jesus to use his authority to gain worldly power (all the kingdoms of the world). Once again, Jesus refuses.

We all have experience with temptation and sin. Today the Church reminds us that we do not have to be slaves to sin. We have been freed from that slavery by our savior, Jesus Christ.

In today's Gospel three people speak: the narrator, Jesus, and the devil. The narrator sets the scene and gives us information. The devil is a tempter, cunning and persuasive. Jesus speaks with authority.

2ND SUNDAY OF LENT

Lectionary #25

READING I Genesis 12:1–4a

The narrator's voice sets the stage

A reading from the Book of Genesis

Abram = AY-br*m

God speaks with gentle authority.

The LORD said to **Abram**:
"**Go forth** from the land of your **kinsfolk**
and from your **father's house** to **a land** that **I will show you.**

The promises are a proclamation.

"I will make of you a **great nation**,
and I will **bless** you;
I will make your **name great**,
so that you will be a **blessing**.
I will **bless** those who **bless you**
and **curse** those who **curse you**.

Say this with awe.

All the **communities** of the **earth**
shall find **blessing** in you."

The narrator concludes the story.

Abram **went** as the **LORD directed** him.

READING I As today's reading begins, God tells Abram (whom God will rename Abraham later in the story) to leave the land of his kinsfolk and go to a land that God will show him. After giving this direction, God makes promises to Abram: Abram will become the father of a great nation. In addition, "All the communities of the earth" shall find a blessing in him. As we read this promise we should remember that Abraham is considered the father in faith not only of Christians, but also of Jews and Muslims.

In addition to telling Abram that he will bless him, that Abram will be a blessing for others, and that those who bless Abram will be blessed, God says that he will "curse those who cruse you." Would God really curse anyone? Here God is described as though he were a human being; this is an anthropomorphic description of God. Blessings and curses were part of the culture, and God is pictured as acting according to the culture of Abram's time.

With these promises, the great story of God's covenant relationship with the people begins. Abram leaves his homeland and goes to Canaan, as God directs him. This is truly a great act of faith.

The words *covenant* and *testament* are synonyms. The Old Testament could be called the Old Covenant, and the remainder of the Bible is the rest of the story.

Only a narrator and God speak in this reading. God's words should be read as a proclamation. This is great good news, indeed.

READING II The letter entitled 2 Timothy is attributed to Paul. However, scripture scholars believe that the

READING II 2 Timothy 1:8b–10

A reading from the second Letter of Saint Paul to Timothy

Emphasize that Timothy is dear to the author.

Beloved:

Here the tone is sympathetic encouragement.

Bear your share of hardship for the **gospel**
with the **strength** that comes from **God**.

Now comes the explanation.

He **saved us** and **called us** to a **holy life**,
not according to our **works**
but according to his **own design**
and the **grace bestowed** on **us** in **Christ Jesus before time began**,
but **now** made **manifest**
through the **appearance** of our **savior Christ Jesus**,
who **destroyed death** and **brought life** and **immortality**
to light through the **gospel**.

bestowed = bih-STOH*D

manifest = MAN-ih-fest

Read these lines slowly and with authority.

letter is pseudonymous; that is, the letter was written well after Paul's death and attributed to Paul as a way of placing the author's ideas in the context of Paul's teachings. Timothy, to whom the letter is addressed, is the pastor of a church.

Evidently, Timothy is going through hardships in the name of the Gospel. As we learn later in the letter, some false teachers are denying life after death (see 2 Timothy 2:18). They think of life after Baptism as resurrection. In today's short passage, the author begins to argue against this false teaching. Jesus has "destroyed death and brought life and immortality to light."

The author reminds Timothy that Jesus not only saved us but calls us "to a holy life." At the same time, he makes it clear that we do not earn salvation. Salvation is a grace, something bestowed on us, not something we have earned: "He saved us . . . not according to our works but according to . . . the grace bestowed on us in Christ Jesus."

During Lent, the Church reminds us that we too have been called to live a holy life. We too live in holiness, not to earn salvation, which we have received as a gift, but to respond to God's love and to cooperate in the coming of God's kingdom on earth.

The author of Timothy is speaking words of love and encouragement. Timothy is being comforted by this letter, not called to task.

GOSPEL Our Gospel reading is Matthew's story of Jesus' Transfiguration. Jesus takes Peter, James, and John to a high mountain—the traditional place for an encounter with God. While on the mountain Jesus' appearance

GOSPEL Matthew 17:1–9

A reading from the holy Gospel according to Matthew

The narrator sets the stage.

Jesus took **Peter**, **James**, and **John** his brother,
and led them up a **high mountain** by **themselves**.

Here the tone changes to awe.
transfigured = trans-FIG-yerd

And he was **transfigured** before them;
his **face shone** like the **sun**
and his **clothes** became **white** as **light**.

Moses = MOH-zis
Elijah = ee-LĪ-juh

And **behold**, **Moses** and **Elijah** appeared to them,
conversing with **him**.
Then **Peter** said to **Jesus** in reply,
"**Lord**, **it is good** that **we are here**.

Peter is confused but trying to be helpful.

If you **wish**, I will make **three tents** here,
one for **you**, one for **Moses**, and one for **Elijah**."
While he was still speaking, **behold**,

The narrator's tone is still full of awe.

a **bright cloud** cast a **shadow** over them,
then **from the cloud** came a **voice** that said,

God speaks with authority. Emphasize that.

"**This** is my beloved Son, with whom I am **well pleased**;
listen to **him**."

prostrate = PROS-trayt

When the disciples **heard** this, they **fell prostrate**
and were **very much afraid**.
But Jesus came and **touched** them, saying,

Jesus speaks gently.

"**Rise**, and do **not be afraid**."
And when the disciples raised their eyes,
they saw **no one else** but **Jesus alone**.

As they were coming down from the mountain,
Jesus **charged them**,

This is an intimate warning.

"**Do not tell the vision** to **anyone**
until the **Son of Man** has been **raised** from the **dead**."

changes: his face shines "like the sun" and his garments become "white as light." Matthew is telling us that the disciples witnessed Jesus' glory, Jesus' divinity.

They also see Jesus talking with Moses and Elijah. Peter, overwhelmed, wants to put up tents for Jesus, Elijah, and Moses. However, a voice from a cloud, the voice that spoke at Jesus' baptism (see Matthew 3:17), says, "This is my beloved son . . . *listen to him*" (emphasis added). In other words, there is no need to put up tents for Moses and Elijah. They will not be staying to dwell with the people. It is Jesus to whom the disciples should listen.

Remember that Matthew is writing to a primarily Jewish audience. They want to be faithful to Judaism. Is becoming a disciple of Jesus being faithful or not? Matthew is teaching that it is. As Jesus himself had claimed earlier (Matthew 5:17), Jesus is the fulfillment of the law (Moses) and the prophets (Elijah). Matthew's audience can safely listen to Jesus.

As they come down from the mountain, Jesus tells his disciples not to talk about what they have seen until after the Resurrection. Jesus knows that they do not understand, and will not understand until "the Son of Man has been raised from the dead."

In the Gospel, we have four speakers: the narrator, Peter, the voice from the cloud, and Jesus. The narrator is not just setting the stage, but is describing something with great awe. Peter is confused and trying to be helpful. The voice from the cloud is loving and authoritative. Jesus speaks intimately, first with comfort, and then with firmness.

3RD SUNDAY OF LENT

Lectionary #28

READING I Exodus 17:3–7

A reading from the Book of Exodus

The people are very angry.

In those days, in their **thirst** for **water**,
the people **grumbled** against **Moses**,
saying, "**Why did you ever make us leave Egypt**?
Was it just to have us **die** here of **thirst**
with our children and our livestock?"

Moses is exasperated; he needs help and needs it now.

So Moses cried out to the LORD,
"What shall I **do** with this **people**?
A little more and they will **stone me**!"

God is reassuring.

The LORD answered Moses,
"Go over there in **front** of the **people**,
along with some of the **elders** of Israel,
holding in your hand, as you go,
the **staff** with which you **struck the river**.

Horeb = HOHR-eb
Here, God speaks with authority.

I will be standing there in front of you on the rock in Horeb.
Strike the **rock**, and the **water** will **flow** from it
for the people to drink."
This Moses did, in the presence of the elders of Israel.

Massah = MAS-ah or MAH-sah
Meribah = MAYR-ih-bah

The place was called **Massah** and **Meribah**,
because the Israelites **quarreled** there
and **tested** the **LORD**, saying,

Emphasize this question.

"Is the **LORD** in our **midst** or **not**?"

READING I In our reading from Exodus we join the Israelites in the desert at a moment when the people appear to have forgotten that God is with them. They are thirsty and blame Moses for their discomfort. Why did Moses lead them out of slavery in the first place? At least in Egypt they had water to drink. Was it just so that they could all die in the desert?

Notice Moses' reaction to the people's anger. He doesn't try to defend himself. He simply turns to God and asks, "What shall I do . . . ?" Moses, in contrast to the others, still trusts God's presence, God's love, and God's providential care.

God tells Moses to make sure that all the people are watching, especially the elders of Israel who will act as witnesses. Moses is to hold in his hand "the staff with which you struck the river." This is to remind the people of the central event of the Exodus experience, the parting of the sea. God had told Moses, "Tell the Israelites to go forward. And you, lift up your staff and, with hand outstretched over the sea, split the sea in two, that the Israelites may pass through it on dry land" (see Exodus 14:21).

God assures Moses that God is still with him and with the people. God says, "I will be standing there in front of you on the rock . . . ." God instructs Moses to strike the rock with his staff and water will flow from it. This Moses does—an act of great faith. Notice that the narrator feels no need to tell us that water did flow from the rock. That is a given. God does what he says he will do.

We are then told that the place where this event happened is called Massah and

READING II Romans 5:1–2, 5–8

A reading from the Letter of Saint Paul to the Romans

Brothers and sisters:
Since we have been **justified** by **faith**,
we have **peace with God through** our **Lord Jesus Christ**,
through whom we have gained **access** by **faith**
to this **grace** in which we stand,
and we **boast** in **hope** of the **glory** of **God**.

And **hope** does not **disappoint**,
because the **love of God** has been **poured out** into our hearts
through the **Holy Spirit** who has been **given** to us.
For **Christ**, while we were still **helpless**,
died at the appointed time for the **ungodly**.
Indeed, only with **difficulty** does one die for a **just** person,
though perhaps for a good person one might even find courage
to die.
But **God proves** his **love for us**
in that **while we were still sinners Christ died** for **us**.

Pause here.

Pause here again.

Say this line with conviction.

Read slowly.

This line is something of an afterthought.

Emphasize this line.

Meribah. The root word for *massah* means "to test"; the root word for *meribah* means "to quarrel." That is just what the Israelites did in that place: the Israelites "quarreled there and tested the Lord . . . ."

At Meribah, through their grumbling and quarreling, the people were asking, "Is God in our midst or not?" The answer they received was a resounding yes. As you proclaim this reading, try to make it clear that the people are quarreling and testing God, that Moses is still trusting God, and that God is reassuring and loving. The story is still being told today to reassure us that God is, indeed, in our midst.

READING II Like the author of the story from Exodus, Paul, in his letter to the Romans, is assuring his readers that God loves and saves them, even though they are sinners.

As the reading begins, Paul twice emphasizes a point that is central to all of Paul's teaching: "we have been justified by faith," not works. The result of that justification by faith is that "we have peace with God through our Lord Jesus Christ." It is through Christ that we have gained access to grace, but we must have faith to receive the gift: "we have gained access by faith to this grace." Because we have, through faith, received access to this grace, "we boast in hope of the glory of God." All of our hope rests in Christ.

Paul then goes on to proclaim that this hope, which rests in Christ, has not disappointed. Now, from experience, Paul knows that this hope results in the love of God being poured into our hearts "through the Holy Spirit," who also has been given to us.

GOSPEL John 4:5–42

The narrator's voice sets the stage.
Samaria = suh-MAYR-ee-uh
Sychar = SĪ-kahr

A reading from the holy Gospel according to John

Jesus came to a town of **Samaria** called **Sychar**,
near the plot of land that **Jacob** had given to his son **Joseph**.
Jacob's well was there.
Jesus, **tired** from his journey, **sat down** there at the well.
It was about noon.

Jesus' tone is conversational.

A woman of **Samaria** came to draw **water**.
Jesus said to her,
"**Give me a drink**."
His **disciples** had gone into the **town** to buy **food**.
The **Samaritan woman** said to him,

The woman is astounded.
6. Samaritan = suh-MAYR-uh-tuhn

"How can **you**, a **Jew**, ask **me**, a **Samaritan woman**,
for a drink?"
—For **Jews** use **nothing** in common with **Samaritans**.—
Jesus answered and said to her,

Jesus is still low key and inviting.

"**If you knew** the **gift** of God
and **who** is saying to you, 'Give me a drink,'
you would have asked **him**
and he would have given **you living water**."
The woman said to him,

The woman is getting friendlier.

"Sir, you do not even have a **bucket** and the **cistern** is deep;
where then can you get this **living water**?
Are you **greater** than our **father Jacob**,
who gave us this **cistern** and drank from it **himself**
with his **children** and his **flocks**?"

There is no question that our justification, that is, our peace with God, as well as the outpouring of love through the Holy Spirit, are unearned gifts. As Paul says, the human race was still helpless when Christ died, not for the godly, but for the ungodly. It would be amazing enough for Christ to have died to save us if we were just, but that is not what happened. Christ died for us while we were sinners. How, then, can anyone doubt God's love for his people?

We, too, are sinners. We are particularly reminded of this fact during Lent. The point is not to feel terrible about ourselves, but to realize that we are loved, we are saved, and, through the power of the Spirit, we can do better. Today's reading must be read slowly, with pauses after units of thought, to make the good news it proclaims understandable. The tone never changes, but pace and emphasis are very important.

GOSPEL In the reading from Exodus, the people are thirsty. In the Gospel, Jesus is thirsty. The woman whom Jesus meets at the well is also thirsty, but in a completely different meaning of the word. The woman is spiritually thirsty. To quote a well-known song, she was looking for love in all the wrong places.

In order to more fully understand today's reading it will be helpful to know a few things about the Gospel according to John. By the time John had written his account, at the end of the first century AD, Jesus' expected return was long overdue. The people were asking, "Where is he?" Their question was similar to the one the Israelites asked in today's reading from Exodus: "Is God in our midst or not?" John wrote to teach that Christ remains in our

Jesus' tone is becoming more serious.	Jesus answered and said to her, "Everyone who drinks **this water** will be **thirsty again**; but whoever drinks the water **I shall give** will **never thirst**; the water **I shall give** will become in him a **spring** of **water welling up** to **eternal life**."
The woman does not understand. She is not entirely serious.	The woman said to him, "Sir, **give me** this water, so that I may not **be thirsty** or have to keep **coming here** to draw **water**."
There is a challenge here.	Jesus said to her, "**Go call** your **husband** and come **back**."
Speak more softly here.	The woman answered and said to him, "I do not **have** a **husband**."
These words are factual and end affirming the woman, not accusing her.	Jesus answered her, "You are **right** in saying, 'I do not have a **husband**.' For you have had **five** husbands, and the one you have now is **not** your husband. What you have said **is true**."
Now the woman is serious and a little puzzled.	The woman said to him, "Sir, I can see that you are a **prophet**. Our **ancestors** worshiped on **this** mountain; but **you people** say that the place to worship is in **Jerusalem**."
Here Jesus speaks with authority.	Jesus said to her, "**Believe me**, woman, the hour is coming when you will worship the Father **neither** on **this mountain nor in Jerusalem**. You people worship what you **do not understand**; **we worship** what we **understand**, because **salvation** is from the **Jews**. But the **hour is coming**, and is now **here**, when **true worshipers** will worship the Father in **Spirit** and **truth**; and indeed the Father **seeks** such people to **worship** him.

midst, through the Church and through the sacraments.

As you read today's Gospel, try to keep two conversations in mind at the same time: the conversation between Jesus and the person to whom he is speaking in the story (for example, the woman at the well and the disciples) and the conversation between John and his end-of-the-century audience, which was asking, "Where is the risen Lord?" The main lesson of the Gospel comes from this second conversation.

Jesus is in a town in Samaria. To law-abiding Jews, Samaritans were unclean. It was entirely against custom for Jesus to initiate a conversation with a Samaritan, not to mention a Samaritan woman. However, that is exactly what Jesus does. Instead of treating the woman as unclean, Jesus asks her to give him a drink.

The woman is astounded at Jesus' inappropriate action. She says, "How can you, a Jew, ask me, a Samaritan woman, for a drink?" In response to this question, Jesus begins to speak metaphorically. He tells the woman that he could give her "living water." The woman misses the metaphor and takes Jesus' words literally. She asks him where he thinks he can get living water when he doesn't even have a bucket. Jesus goes on to explain that he means something other than well water. People who drink well water will be thirsty again. However, the water that Jesus will give will become "a spring of water welling up to eternal life."

If those in John's audience had not initially understood what Jesus meant when he referred to living water, they

God is **Spirit**, and those who **worship** him
must **worship** in **Spirit** and **truth**."
The woman said to him,

The woman is becoming more certain.

"**I know** that the **Messiah** is **coming**, the one called the **Christ**;
when he **comes**, he will tell us **everything**."
Jesus said to her,

This is a solemn statement.

"**I am he**, the one **speaking** with you."

At that moment his **disciples** returned,
and were **amazed** that he was talking with a **woman**,
but still no one said, "What are you **looking** for?"
or "Why are you **talking** with her?"
The woman left her water jar
and went into the **town** and said to the **people**,

This should be said with excitement.

"**Come** see a man who told me **everything** I have done.
Could he **possibly** be the **Christ**?"
They went out of the town and came to him.
Meanwhile, the disciples urged him, "**Rabbi**, **eat**."
But he said to them,

Jesus is thoughtful here.

"I have **food** to eat of which you **do not know**."
So the disciples said to one another,

The disciples are puzzled.

"Could someone have **brought** him something to eat?"
Jesus said to them,

This is said with great earnestness and some urgency.

"**My food** is to do the **will** of the **one who sent me**
and to **finish his work**.
Do you not say, 'In four months the harvest will be here'?
I tell you, **look up** and **see** the fields **ripe** for the harvest.
The reaper is **already** receiving payment
and **gathering crops** for **eternal life**,
so that the **sower** and **reaper** can **rejoice together**.

could not continue to misunderstand. The water that wells up to eternal life is Baptism. However, the woman continues to misunderstand. If there is water that cures thirst once and for all, she wants some. That way she won't have the arduous task of coming to the well to draw water every day.

Jesus then changes the subject to the woman's marital state, startling her by revealing that he knows she has had five husbands, and that the person with whom she now lives is not her husband. Now the woman takes the first step in what will be a process of coming to understand just who Jesus is. The woman concludes that Jesus is a prophet.

It is the woman's turn to change the subject. She asks Jesus whether or not, as Jews claim, Jerusalem is the only place where people should worship. Remember, by the time John is writing his Gospel the temple in Jerusalem no longer exists. (It was destroyed by the Romans in 70 AD.) Jesus denies that worship of God is dependent on a particular location. Since God is Spirit, those who worship God are not tied to a particular location, but worship in Spirit and truth. This statement reminds the woman of her expectation of a messiah. Jesus tells her, "I am he."

Next the disciples return. They had gone to find some food. Again, Jesus speaks metaphorically, but his listeners take him literally. Jesus tells the disciples that he has "food to eat of which you do not know." They take the word *food* literally and conclude that someone else must have brought Jesus some food. Jesus has to

For here the saying is verified that '**One** sows and **another** reaps.'
I sent you to **reap** what you have not **worked** for;
others have done the work,
and you are sharing the **fruits** of **their** work."

Many of the **Samaritans** of that town began to **believe** in him
because of the **word** of the **woman** who **testified**,

This is said with awe.

"He told me **everything** I have done."
When the Samaritans **came** to him,
they **invited** him to **stay** with **them**;
and he **stayed** there **two days**.
Many more began to **believe in him** because of his **word**,
and they said to the woman,

This is said with excitement and certitude.

"We no longer believe because of **your word**;
for we have **heard** for **ourselves**,
and **we know** that this is **truly** the **savior of the world**."
[Shorter Form: John 4:5–15, 19b–26, 39a, 40–42]

explain that the food to which he refers is to do the will of his Father.

Meanwhile, the woman has gone to town and told everyone about Jesus. Many townspeople decide to see for themselves. They go to Jesus and invite him to stay with them. Jesus stays for two days, and many more begin to believe in him. Because the woman was an excellent evangelizer, she not only gave witness to her own experience, but she brought others to know Jesus personally. Now the townspeople can say, "We know that this is truly the savior of the world."

Today's Gospel invites each of us to consider how the risen Christ is with us through Baptism. Like the woman at the well, we are called to give witness to Christ's presence to others so that they, too, based on their personal experience, can place their hope and trust in Jesus, the savior of the world. As you proclaim this reading, try to express Jesus' love and acceptance as he speaks both to the woman and to the disciples. Express also their total puzzlement at the meaning of his words. Then, as the woman comes to faith, try to express her astonishment, joy, and excitement. That woman's life will never be the same. Neither should ours.

4TH SUNDAY OF LENT

Lectionary #31

READING I 1 Samuel 16:1b, 6–7, 10–13a

Samuel = SAM-yoo-uhl
This direction is spoken with authority.
Jesse = JES-ee
Bethlehem = BETH-luh-hem

Eliab = ee-LĪ-uhb
This is a thought; speak softly.
anointed = uh-NOYN-t*d
Still soft, but with authority.
appearance = uh-PEER-uns
stature = STACH-er
Emphasize this very important insight.

Say this line gently; Samuel is disappointing Jesse.

Jesse is discounting the possibility that this son is important.
Now Samuel speaks with authority.
sacrificial = sak-ruh-FISH-uhl
banquet = BANG-kwet

A reading from the first Book of Samuel

The LORD said to **Samuel**:
"Fill your horn with **oil**, and be **on your way**.
I am **sending** you to Jesse of Bethlehem,
for **I have chosen my king** from among his sons."

As Jesse and his sons came to the sacrifice,
Samuel looked at Eliab and thought,
"**Surely** the **LORD's anointed** is here before him."
But the LORD said to Samuel:
"**Do not judge** from his **appearance** or from his **lofty stature**,
because **I have rejected him**.
Not as **man sees** does **God see**,
because **man** sees the **appearance**
but the **LORD** looks into the **heart**."
In the same way Jesse presented **seven sons** before Samuel,
but Samuel said to Jesse,
"The LORD has **not chosen any one** of these."
Then Samuel asked Jesse,
"Are these **all** the **sons** you have?"
Jesse replied,
"There is still the **youngest**, who is tending the sheep."
Samuel said to Jesse,
"**Send** for **him**;
we will **not begin** the sacrificial banquet until **he** arrives here."
Jesse **sent** and had the **young man** brought to them.

READING I The setting for today's reading from 1 Samuel is about 1020 BC. Samuel, to whom the Lord speaks, was not only a prophet, but a judge. As a prophet, he spoke for God and called the people to fidelity to covenant love. As a judge, he had administrative duties. Samuel assisted Israel greatly in its transition from a loose confederacy of twelve tribes to a nation with a king. The first king was Saul, and today's story takes place just at the end of his reign.

The Lord has told Samuel to fill his horn with oil and go to the home of Jesse, in Bethlehem, because God has chosen a new king from among Jesse's sons. Samuel will need to take oil because a king is anointed with oil. In fact, Samuel had previously anointed Saul as king (see 1 Samuel 10:1). However, Saul disobeyed the Lord, and a new king had to be chosen (see 1 Samuel 13:14). In his roles as prophet and judge, Samuel was to anoint the person who would become the next king.

Our Lectionary selection skips the next part of the story. After receiving this directive from God, Samuel says, "How can I go? . . . Saul will . . . kill me" (1 Samuel 16:2). God directs Samuel to take a heifer with him when he goes to the house of Jesse and to announce that he has come to offer a sacrifice to the Lord. He is to invite Jesse and his family to the sacrifice.

The Lectionary picks up the story again here. Jesse and his sons are at the sacrifice when Samuel spots Jesse's handsome son, Eliab, and thinks that he must be the Lord's chosen one. However, the Lord corrects Samuel, warning him not to judge from appearances: "man sees

Use an admiring tone here.

He was **ruddy**, a youth **handsome** to behold
and making **a splendid appearance**.
The LORD said,
"**There**—anoint **him**, for **this is the one**!"

Said in a decisive tone.

Speak with solemnity. An important ritual is being described.

Then Samuel, with the **horn of oil** in hand,
anointed David in the presence of his brothers;
and from **that day on**, the **spirit of the LORD rushed** upon **David**.

READING II Ephesians 5:8–14

A reading from the Letter of Saint Paul to the Ephesians

Brothers and **sisters**:
You were once **darkness**,
but **now** you are **light** in the **Lord**.

Paul's tone is encouraging. Things have changed for the better for the Ephesians.

Read this line slowly.

Live as children of **light**,
for light produces **every kind** of **goodness**
and **righteousness** and **truth**.

righteousness = RĪ-chuhs-n*s

Paul is advising, not accusing.

Try to learn what is **pleasing** to the **Lord**.
Take **no part** in the fruitless works of **darkness**;
rather **expose them**, for it is **shameful** even to **mention**
the things done by them in secret;

Emphasize the words "expose them."

but everything **exposed** by the **light** becomes **visible**,
for everything that becomes **visible** is **light**.

Read more slowly and increase the volume here.

Therefore, it says:
"**Awake**, O **sleeper**,
and **arise** from the **dead**,
and **Christ** will give you **light**."

Read this quotation as a proclamation.

the appearance but the Lord looks into the heart."

Based on this directive, Samuel refrains from selecting any of the seven sons whom Jesse presents to him. To Samuel's question about whether these are all of his sons, Jesse as much as says, "All that matter." But the youngest, who wasn't even invited to the sacrifice, is out tending the sheep. When this son appears the Lord tells Samuel that he is the chosen one, Samuel then anoints the boy, and "the spirit of the Lord rushed upon David."

This story was originally told to assure the people that David became king not through his own ambition but because he was chosen by God and filled with God's Spirit. The reading appears on this fourth Sunday of Lent because, as we shall soon see, it shares an important theme with the Gospel. The reading challenges us to ask ourselves, "What do we see? What do we fail to see?" Therefore, when reading this passage, the greatest emphases should be put on God's admonitions to Samuel. Help the assembly know that the Lord looks into our hearts, too.

READING II **Today's Second Reading is from the letter to the Ephesians—the community at Ephesus. While the letter is attributed to Paul, scripture scholars believe that it was written a generation after Paul and was later attributed to him as a way of honoring Paul and putting the author's teachings in the tradition of Paul's teaching.**

Like Paul, the author is addressing primarily Gentiles who are now Christians. At the beginning of today's reading, the author, whom we will call Paul, reminds his readers that they "were once darkness,

GOSPEL John 9:1–41

A reading from the holy Gospel according to John

The narrator sets the stage.

As **Jesus** passed by he saw a **man blind** from **birth.**
His **disciples** asked him,
"Rabbi, who sinned, this man or his **parents,**
that he was **born blind**?"

Rabbi = RAB-i

The disciples are puzzled.

Jesus answered,
"Neither **he nor** his **parents sinned**;
it is so that the **works** of **God** might be made **visible**
through **him.**

Jesus speaks with authority. Emphasize every word of this line.

We have to do the **works** of the **one who sent me** while it is **day.**
Night is coming when **no one** can **work.**
While I am **in the world,** I am the **light of the world."**

Use a softer voice here.

When he had **said** this, he **spat** on the **ground**
and made **clay** with the **saliva,**
and **smeared** the clay on his **eyes,** and **said** to him,
"Go wash in the Pool of **Siloam**"—which means **Sent**—.
So he **went** and **washed**, and came **back** able to **see.**

The narrator is simply giving information.

Jesus' order is given gently.

Siloam = sih-LOH-uhm

The narrator explains the meaning of Siloam. Drop your voice.

His **neighbors** and those who had seen him **earlier**
as a **beggar** said,
"Isn't **this** the one who used to **sit** and **beg**?"
Some said, **"It is,"**
but others said, **"No,** he just **looks** like him."
He said, **"I am."**
So they said to him, **"How** were your **eyes opened**?"
He replied,
"The man called Jesus made **clay** and **anointed** my eyes
and told me, '**Go** to **Siloam** and **wash.'**

Say this with firmness.

The man speaks with confidence.

but now you are light in the Lord." Notice, Paul does not say that now the people are in the light, but they *are* light in the Lord.

Next the Ephesians are encouraged to "Live as children of light." A person who lives as light will do his or her very best to "learn what is pleasing to the Lord."

Instead of taking part in the "fruitless works of darkness," the Ephesians should expose such behavior. When shameful behavior is exposed, it comes into the light; it "becomes visible." Then it can no longer continue.

As the reading concludes, Paul says, "Therefore, it says . . ." What is *it*? Scripture scholars surmise that the closing lines of today's reading are the words of a hymn sung at early Christian Baptisms. This hymn would have been familiar to the Ephesians and would have reminded them of their own recent baptisms: "Awake, O sleeper, / and arise from the dead, / and Christ will give you light." Baptism is the sacrament through which people die with Christ and emerge from the waters (arise from the dead) as a new person, a person of the light.

We who are baptized are to be the light of Christ to the world. Therefore, as the conclusion to today's reading is proclaimed, there should be an exultant tone, a rallying cry. We are the sleepers who have arisen from the dead and have been given the light of Christ. We are to be that light for the world.

GOSPEL As we read today's passage from the Gospel according to John, it will be very helpful to remember John's audience and John's purpose. John

So I **went** there and **washed** and was able to **see**."
And they said to him, "**Where is he**?"
He said, "I **don't know**."

Sabbath = SAB-uth

Again, the man speaks with confidence.

They brought the one who was **once blind** to the **Pharisees**.
Now **Jesus** had made **clay** and **opened** his **eyes** on a **sabbath**.
So then the **Pharisees** also asked him how he was able to **see**.
He said to them,

These lines are dismissive, disparaging.

"He put **clay** on my **eyes**, and I **washed**, and **now** I can **see**."
So some of the **Pharisees** said,

Here the tone is true puzzlement.

"This man is **not** from **God**,
because he does not **keep** the **sabbath**."
But others said,

There is a challenge in this question.

"**How** can a **sinful man** do such **signs**?"
And there was a **division** among them.
So they said to the blind man **again**,

This is a solemn proclamation.

"What do **you** have to say about him,
since he opened **your eyes**?"

Prophet = PROF-uht

He said, "**He** is a **prophet**."

Now the Jews did **not believe**
that he had been **blind** and **gained** his **sight**
until they summoned the **parents** of the one who had gained
his sight.
They asked them,

There is both a challenge and a threat in this question.

"**Is this your son**, who you say was **born blind**?
How does he **now see**?"
His **parents** answered and said,

The parents want to avoid trouble. They are somewhat wily.

"We **know** that this **is our son** and that he **was born blind**.
We do **not know** how he **sees now**,
nor do we know **who opened** his eyes.
Ask him, **he** is of **age**;
he can speak for **himself**."

is writing at the end of the century to people who are looking for the return of the risen Christ. His purpose is to help them see, that is, realize, that the risen Christ is already present to them in the Church and in the sacraments. There are two levels of conversation going on in John's account, the one we read in the text between Jesus and his contemporaries, and the one going on between John and his end-of-the-century audience.

In today's reading, John gives us a clear signal that we are to think of both of these levels of meaning at the same time. He does this by conflating the two settings: the setting of the plot, and the setting of the author and audience. When explaining why the blind man's parents act as they do, the narrator's voice tells us that his parents were afraid of being expelled from the synagogue. At the time Jesus was alive no one was being expelled from the synagogue for believing in Jesus. However, by the time John's Gospel was written, that is exactly what was happening. John is telling this story to teach his contemporaries how to see Jesus in their midst.

The words *blind* and *see* take on two levels of meaning as the story progresses. The blind man is blind in two different ways: he lacks physical sight, and he lacks spiritual insight. Jesus heals the lack of physical sight as the story begins. The account of the man's gradual coming to spiritual insight takes up the rest of the story. At the story's end, the blind man sees, and some of the Pharisees, who think they see, are called blind.

As is true of all of us, the blind man's growth into faith is gradual. Initially, he

Drop your voice as you say the narrator's lines. This is background information.

synagogue = SIN-uh-gog

His parents said this because they were **afraid**
of the **Jews**, for the **Jews** had already **agreed**
that if anyone acknowledged him as the **Christ**,
he would be **expelled** from the **synagogue**.
For **this reason** his **parents** said,
"**He** is of **age**; **question him**."

So a **second** time they **called** the man who had been blind
and said to him, "**Give God the praise**!

Say the words "Give God the praise" with false exuberance.

We know that this man is a **sinner**."
He replied,
"If he is a **sinner**, I do **not know**.

The once blind man speaks with quiet confidence.

One thing I **do know** is that I **was blind** and **now** I **see**."
So they said to him,
"What did he **do** to you?
How did he **open** your **eyes**?"
He answered them,
"I told you **already** and you did **not listen**.

A tone of impatience comes in here.

Why do you **want** to **hear** it **again**?
Do you **want** to **become** his **disciples**, **too**?"

disciples = dih-SĪ-p*lz

They **ridiculed** him and said,
"**You** are that **man's** disciple;
we are disciples of **Moses**!

This is said with arrogant superiority.
Moses = MOH-zis

We know that **God** spoke to **Moses**,
but we do **not know** where **this one** is **from**."
The man answered and said to them,
"This is what is **so amazing**,
that you do **not know** where he is **from**, yet he **opened** my **eyes**.

The man is being bolder now.

We know that **God** does **not listen** to **sinners**,
but if one is **devout** and does **his will**, he **listens** to **him**.
It is **unheard** of that **anyone ever** opened the eyes
of a person born **blind**.

Here the man speaks adamantly.

knows that Jesus healed him of his blindness, but he does not know who Jesus is. When questioned by the Pharisees, he simply recounts his experience. When asked what he has to say about Jesus, he concludes, "He is a prophet."

After questioning the man's parents to no avail, the Pharisees again question the once blind man. The Pharisees tell the man that they are disciples of Moses. Moses, of course, promulgated the Law. The Pharisees are legalists when it comes to obeying the law about the Sabbath. They insist on holding on to their understanding of the law even in the light of personal experience that challenges that understanding. They have concluded that Jesus is a sinner. Why? Because Jesus disobeyed the law by healing on the Sabbath.

While arguing with the once blind man, the Pharisees say, "we do not know where this one [Jesus] is from." Once more the reader of the Gospel understands a deeper meaning in the words than do the characters in the story. We readers of John's narrative do know where Jesus is from. As he began his account, John told us that Jesus is the Word who became flesh and dwells among us. Jesus is from God.

The once-blind man also concludes that Jesus is from God: he says, "If this man were not from God, he would not be able to do anything." However, the once blind man does not understand the same depth of truth in his words that the reader of the Gospel understands.

Later, the man comes to a full knowledge of Jesus' identity. After the man has been thrown out of the synagogue by the Pharisees, Jesus seeks him out and asks,

If this man were not from **God**,
he would not be able to do **anything**."
They answered and said to him,

The Jews are now outraged.

"You were born **totally** in **sin**,
and are **you** trying to teach **us**?"

Say this line with harshness.

Then they **threw** him **out**.

When **Jesus** heard that they had **thrown** him **out**,

Jesus speaks gently.

he **found** him and said, "Do you **believe** in the **Son of Man**?"
He answered and said,

The man is in awe.

"**Who is he**, **sir**, that I may **believe** in **him**?"
Jesus said to him,

Speak slowly, in a quiet voice.

"You have **seen him**,
and the one **speaking** with you is **he**."
He said,

Said with deep conviction.

"**I do believe**, Lord," and he **worshiped** him.
Then Jesus said,

Jesus speaks with firmness.

"I came into this world for **judgment**,
so that those who **do not see** might **see**,
and those who **do see** might become **blind**."

Some of the **Pharisees** who were with him heard this

The Pharisees are defensive.

and said to him, "Surely **we** are not also **blind**, are we?"
Jesus said to them,

Jesus speaks with quiet firmness.

"If you **were blind**, you would have **no sin**;
but now you are saying, '**We see**,' so your **sin remains**."

[Shorter Form: John 9:1, 6–9, 13–17, 34–38]

"Do you believe in the Son of Man?" The man wants to believe, but he does not know who the Son of Man is. Jesus says, "You have seen him, and the one speaking with you is he." With this revelation the man comes to full knowledge and belief: "He said, 'I do believe Lord,' and he worshipped him."

The man moves from blindness to sight, from darkness to the light of Christ. Some of the Pharisees, on the other hand, refuse to see the light, even when invited into the light by their own experience. They cling to the dark and thus become blind.

John's audience is invited to see ourselves in the characters in this story. Let us not be like the Pharisees who cling to their own misunderstandings and refuse to accept the light. Instead, let us be like the once blind man. We, like the blind man, have been washed in the waters (of Baptism) and have been sent (Siloam means "sent"). We, too, have been offered the great gift of seeing the Son of Man and knowing that he dwells in our midst.

Today's reading is a challenge for proclaimers because there are many characters with many different tones of voice: disciples, Jesus, neighbors, the blind man, the Pharisees, the parents, and the Jews. The tones range from puzzlement, to teaching, to anger, to belittlement, to awe. Try to draw your listeners into the story so that they will identify with the characters. Our Lenten challenge is to be like the blind man, to accept the gift of sight.

5TH SUNDAY OF LENT

Lectionary #34

READING I Ezekiel 37:12–14

Ezekiel = ee-ZEE-kee-uhl

A reading from the Book of the Prophet Ezekiel

Thus says the LORD God:
O my people, I will **open** your **graves**
and have you **rise** from them,
and bring you **back** to the **land** of **Israel**.
Then you shall **know** that **I am the LORD**,
when I open your **graves** and have you **rise** from them,
O my people!
I will put my **spirit** in you that you may **live**,
and I will **settle you** upon **your land**;
thus you shall **know** that **I am the LORD**.
I have **promised**, and I **will do it**, says the **LORD**.

God's words are full of love and assurance. Emphasize every word of "O my people."

Say this with great confidence. God is responding to the people's doubt.

This is joyful news, indeed.

Say the promise with certitude and solemnity.

READING II Romans 8:8–11

A reading from the Letter of Saint Paul to the Romans

Brothers and sisters:
Those who are in the **flesh cannot please God**.
But **you** are **not** in the **flesh**;
on the **contrary**, **you** are in the **spirit**,
if only the **Spirit** of **God dwells in** you.

This is stated adamantly.

Paul is complimenting the Romans as he teaches them.

READING I Ezekiel was a prophet in Judah from 593–571 BC during the second most traumatic time in the Israelites' history, the Babylonian exile (587–537 BC). Why was this time so terribly traumatic? Because events caused the Israelites to question their covenant relationship with God. Were they God's people or not?

From the time of Abraham (1850 BC), the Israelites had understood that God had promised them protection, land, and descendants. When Israel became a nation with a king like other nations (1000 BC), the people believed that God had fulfilled his promises. The 12 tribes were united, David was their king, and David had defeated their political enemies. The people believed that through Nathan, the prophet, God had promised David that his kingdom and his line would be secure forever.

Now all those expectations had been dashed. The kingdom had split, Assyria had conquered the Northern Kingdom, Israel, and during Ezekiel's lifetime, the Babylonians had conquered the Southern Kingdom, Judah. The leading citizens were in exile, the land was devastated, and the temple was destroyed. What did all of these horrible events mean? Was God their God or not?

In the very first words of the prophecy that we read today, Ezekiel begins to answer that question. The prophecy begins: "O my people . . ." The exiles are still God's people. God is still their God.

When Ezekiel, speaking for God, promises the people that God will "open your graves and bring you back to the land of Israel," Ezekiel is using the word graves metaphorically. Being in exile in Babylon is like being dead and buried. The Israelites

Again, this is an adamant statement.

Whoever does not have the **Spirit** of **Christ** does not **belong**
to him.

This is said with great reassurance.

But if **Christ** is **in** you,
although the **body** is **dead** because of **sin**,
the **spirit** is **alive** because of **righteousness**.

righteousness = RĪ-chuhs-n*s

This is Paul's great good news; speak with joy and confidence.

If the **Spirit** of the one who **raised Jesus** from the **dead**
dwells in **you**,
the One who **raised Christ** from the **dead**
will give **life** to **your mortal bodies also**,
through his **Spirit dwelling** in **you**.

GOSPEL John 11:1–45

A reading from the holy Gospel according to John

The narrator sets the stage.
Lazarus = LAZ-uh-ruhs
Bethany = BETH-uh-nee
Mary = MAHR-ee; Martha = MAHR-thuh
perfumed = per-FYOOM*D

Now a man was **ill**, **Lazarus** from **Bethany**,
the village of **Mary** and her sister **Martha**.
Mary was the one who had **anointed** the **Lord** with perfumed **oil**
and dried his **feet** with her **hair**;
it was **her brother Lazarus** who was **ill**.

There is a plea in these words.

So the **sisters** sent word to **Jesus** saying,
"**Master**, the **one you love** is **ill**."

Jesus is speaking thoughtfully and quietly. His words are mysterious.
glorify = GLOHR-ih-fī

When Jesus heard this he said,
"This **illness** is **not** to end in **death**,
but is for the **glory** of **God**,
that the **Son** of **God** may be **glorified** through it."
Now Jesus **loved Martha** and her **sister** and **Lazarus**.
So when he heard that he was **ill**,

Read this line slowly but in a matter of fact way.

he **remained** for **two days** in the place where he was.

do not begin to consider the possibility of life after death until about 200 years before Christ. Neither Ezekiel nor those to whom he prophesied rested their hope in a belief in life after life on earth. The hope Ezekiel is offering the people is that God will return them to the Promised Land: "I will settle you upon your land."

Why will God intervene on the Israelites behalf? We are told the answer to this question twice in today's reading: God tells the exiles: "Then you will know that I am the Lord." And again, "Thus you shall know that I am the Lord." Ezekiel is assuring the exiles that God will be faithful to his covenant promises.

The tone for today's reading is a mixture of confidence, reassurance, and hope. Ezekiel wants the exiles to know that although they are presently in a terrible situation, God has not deserted them. God will keep his promises.

READING II **Paul, unlike Ezekiel and his contemporaries, does believe in life after death. Paul knows from personal experience that Jesus Christ rose from the dead. Paul believes that he, too, will rise with Christ. In today's reading, Paul is assuring the Romans that if Christ's Spirit dwells in them, they, too, will have life, both on earth and in the life to come.**

As today's reading begins, Paul is drawing a contrast between those who are "in the flesh" and those who are "in the Spirit." Earlier in Romans, Paul has explained that through Jesus' Passion, death, and Resurrection, Jesus has freed human beings from living under the law and from slavery to sin. When Paul refers to those who are "in the flesh," he is referring to those who have not yet accepted

disciples = dih-SĪ-p*lz
The tone here is resolved; the time has come.
Judea = joo-DEE-uh or joo-DAY-uh
This is said with disbelief.
Rabbi = RAB-ī
Again, a quiet, thoughtful tone.

Then after **this** he said to his **disciples**,
"Let us go **back** to **Judea**."
The disciples said to him,
"**Rabbi**, the Jews were just trying to **stone** you,
and you want to go **back there**?"
Jesus answered,
"Are there not **twelve hours** in a day?
If one walks during the **day**, he does not **stumble**,
because he **sees the light** of this world.
But if one walks at **night**, he **stumbles**,
because the **light** is **not in him**."
He said this, and then told them,

This is said with great confidence.

"Our friend **Lazarus** is **asleep**,
but I am going to **awaken** him."
So the disciples said to him,

The disciples' tone is reassuring.
The narrator again explains things to us.

"**Master**, if he is **asleep**, he will be **saved**."
But Jesus was talking about his **death**,
while they thought that he meant **ordinary sleep**.
So **then** Jesus said to them **clearly**,

Say this slowly and solemnly.

"**Lazarus** has **died**.
And I am **glad** for **you** that I was not there,
that **you may believe**.

Speak more quickly here.
This is said with bravado.
Didymus = DID-uh-muhs

Let us **go** to **him**."
So **Thomas**, called **Didymus**, said to his fellow disciples,
"Let **us** also go to **die with him**."

The narrator continues the story.
Jerusalem = juh-ROO-suh-lem or juh-ROO-zuh-lem

When Jesus **arrived**, he found that Lazarus
had already been in the tomb for **four days**.
Now **Bethany** was near **Jerusalem**, only about **two miles away**.
And many of the Jews had come to **Martha** and **Mary**
to **comfort** them about their brother.

Christ and their new freedom from sin and from the condemnation of the law. Such people cannot please God.

In contrast to those still living in the flesh and under the power of sin are Paul's fellow Christians, those living in the Spirit. Paul assures his fellow Christians that although "the body is dead because of sin, the spirit is alive because of righteousness." In other words, although Paul's fellow Christians still live in the flesh, in mortal bodies, the flesh and sin no longer have power over them. The Spirit of Christ living in them has freed them from slavery to sin. They now live in righteousness.

As we read Paul's words, it will be helpful to remember his personal story. When Paul lived in the flesh, a slave to sin, he devoted himself to persecuting Christians. Even with the best of intentions he was not pleasing God. When Jesus appeared to Paul, Jesus asked him, "Why are you persecuting me?" Paul realized that he had been doing harm, not good. He also realized that the Spirit of Christ dwelled in those whom he had been persecuting. That is why Jesus asked why Paul was persecuting him, Jesus.

Once Paul accepted the Spirit of Christ into his life, Paul became a completely new person. He was no longer a slave to sin and to the law; he could live a life of righteousness in Christ Jesus.

Paul is teaching the Romans what he himself learned from personal experience. They have accepted the Spirit of Christ into their lives (they have been baptized). Now they can live completely new lives on

When Martha **heard** that Jesus was **coming**,
she went to **meet** him;
but **Mary** sat at **home**.
Martha said to **Jesus**,

Martha is full of grief. Speak slowly, with anguish.

"**Lord**, if **you** had **been here**,
my **brother** would **not** have **died**.

Now Martha speaks with hopeful faith.

But **even now I know** that **whatever you ask** of **God**,
God will **give** you."
Jesus said to her,

Jesus speaks gently and with love.

"Your **brother** will **rise**."
Martha said to him,

Martha speaks with confidence.

"I **know** he will rise,
in the **resurrection** on the **last day**."
Jesus told her,

resurrection = rez-uh-REK-shuhn

Emphasize every word of this line.

"**I am** the **resurrection** and the **life**;
whoever **believes** in **me**, even if he **dies**, will **live**,
and everyone who **lives** and **believes** in **me** will **never die**.

This question is not so much a challenge as it is encouragement.

Do you **believe** this?"
She said to him, "**Yes, Lord**.

Say this line with quiet conviction. Speak slowly.

I have come to **believe** that **you** are the **Christ**, the **Son of God**,
the one who is **coming** into the **world**."

When she had said this,
she went and called her **sister Mary secretly**, saying,

Say this line very quietly.

"The **teacher** is **here** and is **asking** for **you**."
As soon as she heard this,

Speak more quickly now.

she **rose quickly** and **went to him**.
For **Jesus** had not yet come into the **village**,
but was still where Martha had **met** him.

earth. In addition, they are promised eternal life: the one who raised Christ from the dead "will give life to your mortal bodies also, through his Spirit dwelling in you."

Paul's theological explanations must be read slowly, with appropriate pauses, in order to be understood. Practice reading the passage aloud repeatedly, making sure that you yourself understand it, and that you can help others understand it.

GOSPEL

Once more we are reading from the Gospel according to John, written near the end of the first century AD to respond to the question, "Where is the risen Christ?" Notice that the theme of Christ's apparent absence appears twice in the dialogue in today's Gospel. Both Martha and Mary greet the Lord with exactly the same words: "Lord, if you had been here, my brother would not have died."

These words express the sentiments of many in John's audience. Some of their number are undergoing persecution. Many relatives of those persecuted, and even martyred, are saying, "Lord, if you had been here our loved ones would not have died. Where are you?"

John's stories have more than one level of meaning. On the surface they are about Jesus and his contemporaries, in this case, Jesus and his friends, Lazarus, Martha, and Mary. However, they are, at the same time, about the risen Christ in the life of John's contemporaries. In order to accommodate both story lines, words very often take on double meanings.

Also, the author often says something at the literal level that doesn't quite make

So when the Jews who were **with** her in the house **comforting** her
saw Mary get up **quickly** and go **out**,
they **followed** her,
presuming that she was going to the **tomb** to **weep** there.

Read more slowly.

When **Mary** came to where **Jesus** was and **saw** him,
she **fell** at his **feet** and **said** to him,

Again, emphasize every word of this statement.

"**Lord, if you had been here**,
my **brother** would not have **died**."
When Jesus saw her **weeping** and the Jews who had come **with** her weeping,

perturbed = per-TERBD

he became **perturbed** and **deeply troubled**, and said,

Jesus says this with anguish.

"Where have you **laid** him?"
They said to him, "**Sir, come** and **see**."
And **Jesus wept**.

Pause here.

So the Jews said, "**See** how he **loved** him."
But **some** of them said,

Said with puzzlement and incredulity.

"Could not the one who **opened** the **eyes** of the **blind man**
have done **something** so that **this** man would **not** have **died**?"

So **Jesus**, **perturbed** again, came to the **tomb**.
It was a **cave**, and a **stone** lay across it.

This is said in a commanding voice.

Jesus said, "**Take away the stone**."
Martha, the dead man's **sister**, said to him,

Martha speaks with urgency.

"**Lord**, by now there will be a **stench**;
he has been **dead** for **four days**."
Jesus said to her,

Say this slowly and gently.

"Did I not **tell** you that **if you believe**
you will **see** the **glory** of **God**?"
So they **took away** the **stone**.

sense to the reader. The apparent inconsistency causes the reader to ask, "What does that mean?" On further examination the reader begins to understand John's deeper meaning.

For example, in today's reading the narrator's voice tells us: "Now Jesus loved Martha and her sister and Lazarus. So when he heard that he was ill, he remained for two days in the place where he was." One cannot read this without being taken aback. Our expectation is that the text would say, "So when he heard that he was ill, he rushed to be with those whom he loved."

Why does Jesus wait? It is this tardiness in Jesus' arrival that causes Martha and Mary to each express the central accusation of the story: "Lord, if you had been here our brother would not have died." Everything that follows flows from this plot element.

When Jesus explains his reasons for wanting to return to Judea to his disciples Jesus says, "Our friend Lazarus is asleep, but I am going to awaken him." Jesus uses the word *asleep* as a metaphor for death. From a Christian point of view, death is not really death. It is something from which those who believe in the risen Christ can be awakened.

The disciples do not understand Jesus' deeper meaning. They think *asleep* means "asleep." They respond, "Master if he is asleep, he will be saved." In case we missed the point, and the double meaning, the narrator explains it to us: "But Jesus was talking about his death, while they thought that he meant ordinary sleep."

This is not an intimate prayer but said to be heard by the crowd, to build the listeners' faith.

And **Jesus raised** his **eyes** and said,
"**Father**, I **thank** you for **hearing** me.
I know that you **always** hear me;
but because of the **crowd** here I have said this,
that **they may believe** that **you sent me**."
And when he had said this,
he **cried out** in a **loud voice**,

Raise your volume here.

"**Lazarus, come out**!"

Drop your voice for the narrator's lines. Read slowly and with awe.

The **dead man came out**,
tied hand and **foot** with burial bands,
and his **face** was **wrapped** in a **cloth**.
So Jesus said to them,

Said quietly and with great relief.

"**Untie him** and **let him go**."

The narrator makes a concluding remark to end the story.

Now **many** of the **Jews** who had come to **Mary**
and **seen** what he had done began to **believe** in **him**.
[Shorter Form: John 11:3–7, 17, 20–27, 33b–45]

By the time Jesus arrives Lazarus has been in the tomb for four days. There is no question that he has died. This fact is emphasized later in the story when Martha cautions Jesus, "Lord, by now there will be a stench; he has been dead for four days." What will Jesus do? The fact that Jesus seems to have arrived too late to do anything is again emphasized as some ask, "Could not the one who opened the eyes of the blind man have done something so that this man would not have died?" Surely it is too late for anyone to do anything now, even Jesus.

Jesus, however, is confident. He tells Mary, "I am the resurrection and the life; whoever believes in me, even if he dies, will live, and everyone who lives and believes in me will never die." This is John's message to his contemporaries who are in grief over their martyred loved ones. Jesus is present and has defeated death. Their loved ones are not really dead. Like Jesus, they have risen and are victorious over death.

The truth of Jesus' claim that he has authority even over death is then demonstrated. Jesus calls, "Lazarus, come out!" and Lazarus comes out. Through this story John is teaching his end-of-the-century contemporaries that the risen Christ is not absent, but present, and that he has power even over death.

Again, the Gospel reading has many voices: the narrator, Jesus, the disciples, Martha, Mary, and the Jews. In addition, the tones vary from perplexed, to anguished, to full of awe. As you proclaim the Gospel, try to help the assembly enter into both the grief and the joy of the characters in the story.

PALM SUNDAY OF THE LORD'S PASSION

Lectionary #37

GOSPEL AT THE PROCESSION Matthew 21:1–11

A reading from the holy Gospel according to Matthew

The narrator's voice sets the stage.
Jerusalem = juh-R<u>OO</u>-suh-lem or juh-R<u>OO</u>-zuh-lem
Bethphage = BETH-fuh-jee
Jesus is giving specific directions. Speak slowly and with authority.
tethered = TEH-th*rd

When **Jesus** and the **disciples** drew near **Jerusalem**
and came to **Bethphage** on the Mount of **Olives**,
Jesus sent **two disciples**, saying to them,
"Go **into the village** opposite you,
and **immediately** you will find an ass tethered,
and a colt with her.
Untie them and **bring them here** to **me**.
And if **anyone** should say **anything** to you, reply,
'The **master** has **need** of them.'
Then he will **send** them at **once**."
This **happened** so that what had been **spoken** through the **prophet**
might be **fulfilled**:
Say *to* **daughter Zion**,
*"**Behold**, your **king comes** to you,*
***meek** and riding on an **ass**,*
*and on a **colt**, the **foal** of a **beast** of **burden**."*
The disciples **went** and **did** as Jesus had **ordered** them.
They brought the **ass** and the **colt** and laid their **cloaks** over them,
and he **sat** upon them.
The **very large crowd** spread their **cloaks** on the **road**,
while **others** cut **branches** from the **trees**
and **strewed** them on the **road**.

Speak this line slowly.
Increase your pace here.
Now the narrator is speaking.

Read the quotation as a proclamation, slowly and with increased volume.
Zion = ZĪ-ahn

foal = fohl
The narrator continues to tell the story.

PROCESSION GOSPEL On Palm Sunday the universal Church re-enacts the crowd's celebration of Jesus' entrance into Jerusalem before his Passion and death. Holding palm branches, we hear Matthew's account of the crowd's reaction to Jesus: "Hosanna to the Son of David; / blessed is he who comes in the name of the Lord; / hosanna in the highest." The crowd proclaims, and we celebrate, Jesus as the messiah, the Son of David, the one who comes in the name of the Lord.

The account of Jesus' entry into Jerusalem appears in all four Gospels. During the present liturgical cycle, Cycle A, we read Matthew's account. However, Mark's account is the earliest, and was a source for Matthew. By comparing Matthew's account to Mark's we can discover Matthew's particular interests and emphasis as well as solve a mystery that puzzles many readers.

In today's reading Jesus instructs his disciples to find both an ass and a colt and bring them to Jesus. We then read: "They brought the ass and the colt and laid their cloaks over them, and he sat upon them." Did Jesus sit on two animals at once? This is a strange scene indeed. Why would Matthew say such a thing?

To solve this dilemma, scripture scholars compare Matthew's account to that of his source, Mark. In Mark, Jesus instructs his disciples to bring him a colt, which they do (see Mark 11:1–7). Jesus sits upon the colt as he is greeted by the crowds. It is obvious that Matthew changed his source. Why? As we seek the answer to this question we unlock both Matthew's method and his message.

The crowds **preceding** him and those **following**
kept **crying out** and saying:
Increase your volume as the crowd cries out.
"**Hosanna** to the **Son of David**;
blessed is **he** who **comes** in the **name** of the **Lord**;
hosanna in the **highest**."
And when he entered **Jerusalem**
Asked with great puzzlement.
the **whole city** was **shaken** and asked, "**Who is this?**"
And the **crowds** replied,
Said with conviction.
Nazareth = NAZ-uh-reth
Galilee = GAL-ih-lee
"This is **Jesus** the **prophet**, from **Nazareth** in **Galilee**."

Lectionary #38

READING 1 Isaiah 50:4–7

Isaiah = ī-ZAY-uh

A reading from the Book of the Prophet Isaiah

Speak slowly and with confidence.

The **Lord GOD** has given me
a **well-trained tongue**,
that I might know how to **speak** to the **weary**
a **word** that will **rouse** them.
rouse = rowz
Increase both volume and speed here.
Morning after **morning**
he **opens** my **ear** that I may **hear**;
Slow down with "have not rebelled."
and I have **not rebelled**,
have **not turned back**.
I gave my **back** to those who **beat** me,
my **cheeks** to those who **plucked** my **beard**;
my **face** I did **not shield**
buffets = BUF-its
from **buffets** and **spitting**.

Matthew, far more than any other Gospel writer, claims that Jesus' actions fulfill the words of the prophets. Matthew is writing primarily to Jews who want to be faithful to their two thousand year covenant relationship with God. Is becoming a disciple of Jesus Christ being faithful to that tradition, or not? Matthew insists that it is, as is evident from the fact that Jesus fulfills the words of the prophets. In Jesus, God's hidden plans for the chosen people are being carried out.

Today's reading is one of many occasions on which Matthew employs this fulfillment theme. Matthew tells us that Jesus' entry into Jerusalem "happened so that what had been spoken through the prophet might be fulfilled." In the passage attributed to the prophet, Matthew combines the words of not just one prophet, but two: Isaiah and Zechariah. Matthew alludes to Isaiah's words: "Say to daughter Zion / your savior comes!" (Isaiah 62:11), as well as to Zechariah's words: "See, your king shall come to you; / a just savior is he, / Meek, and riding on an ass, / on a colt, the foal of an ass" (Zechariah 9:9).

Scripture scholars surmise that Matthew altered Mark, adding the second animal, in order to more clearly allude to this passage from Zechariah. However, Zechariah, in fact, pictures only one animal. Zechariah is using a very common poetic device in Hebrew poetry called synonymous parallelism. In synonymous parallelism the same thought is expressed

Emphasize the word "my." Isaiah is naming the source of his wisdom and confidence.
Speak these last two lines with confidence and determination.
disgraced = dis-GRAYSD

The **Lord God** is **my** help,
therefore I am **not disgraced**;
I have set my **face** like **flint**,
knowing that I shall **not** be **put** to **shame**.

READING II Philippians 2:6–11

Philippians = fih-LIP-ee-uhnz

A reading from the Letter of Saint Paul to the Philippians

Read slowly, pausing at commas. Paul is giving an amazing explanation for that was considered a scandal.

Christ Jesus, though he was in the **form** of **God**,
did not regard **equality** with **God**
something to be **grasped**.
Rather, he **emptied** himself,
taking the form of a **slave**,
coming in **human likeness**;
and found **human** in **appearance**,
he **humbled** himself,
becoming **obedient** to the point of **death**,
even **death** on a **cross**.
Because of this, God **greatly exalted** him
and **bestowed** on him the name
which is **above every name**,
that at the name of **Jesus**
every knee should **bend**,
of those in **heaven** and on **earth** and **under** the earth,
and **every tongue confess** that
Jesus Christ is **Lord**,
to the **glory** of **God** the **Father**.

appearance = uh-PEER-unz

Emphasize this line. For the audience this is practically unbelievable.
Slowly increase both your tempo and your volume.
bestowed = bih-STOHD
Now, slow down again.

This is a proclamation. Emphasize every word.

twice, but in different words. In Zechariah the colt and the ass are one animal, not two.

What was Matthew's purpose in so obviously alluding to the passage from Zechariah? Matthew is teaching not only that Jesus is the expected messiah, but what kind of messiah Jesus will be. Although Jesus is a king, he comes not in victory but in humility: "meek and riding on an ass." Remember, this scene is leading up to Jesus' Crucifixion. Jesus, the messiah king, will not conquer the Romans who occupy the Holy Land, but will be crucified by them.

As those in the crowd greet Jesus, they use two messianic titles: "Son of David" and "he who comes." The messiah was expected to be of David's line. A form of the other phrace has been used earlier in Matthew when John the Baptist's disciples come to Jesus and ask, "Are you the one who is to come, or should we look for another" (Matthew 11:3)?

Both by illustrating that Jesus fulfills the words of the prophets and by having the crowd greet him using messianic titles, Matthew is teaching that Jesus is much more than "the prophet from Nazareth." Jesus is the Messiah, the one "who comes in the name of the Lord." Therefore, as you proclaim this reading, allow your voice to crescendo in order to emphasize the greeting of the crowd. It is through the crowd's greeting that Matthew makes clear the true identity of Jesus Christ.

READING I Today's first reading is from one of the suffering servant songs. There are four suffering servant songs in Isaiah 40—55, that part

PASSION Matthew 26:14—27:66

The Passion of our Lord Jesus Christ according to Matthew

The narrator's voice is a matter of fact.
Judas = JOO-duhs
Iscariot = is-KAYR-ee-uht
Judas is wily.

(1) One of the **Twelve**, who was called **Judas Iscariot**,
went to the **chief priests** and said,
"What are you willing to **give** me
if I hand him **over** to you?"
They paid him **thirty pieces of silver**,
and from **that time on** he looked for an **opportunity**
to **hand** him **over**.

unleavened = uhn-LEV-uhnd

Passover = PAS-oh-ver

Jesus is giving an order. Although his words are mysterious, he speaks with authority.

(2) On the **first day** of the **Feast** of **Unleavened Bread**,
the **disciples** approached **Jesus** and said,
"**Where** do you want us to **prepare**
for you to eat the **Passover**?"
He said,
"Go **into** the city to a **certain man** and **tell** him,
'The **teacher** says, "My **appointed time** draws **near**;
in **your house** I shall celebrate the **Passover**
with my **disciples**."'"
The disciples then **did** as Jesus had **ordered**,
and **prepared** the **Passover**.

When it was **evening**,
he **reclined** at **table** with the **Twelve**.
And while they were **eating**, he said,
"**Amen**, I **say** to you, **one** of you will **betray** me."

Jesus continues to speak with calm authority.
distressed = dis-TRESD
The tone here is both alarm and puzzlement.

Deeply distressed at this,
they began to say to him one after another,
"**Surely** it is not **I**, **Lord**?"
He said in reply,
"He who has **dipped** his **hand** into the **dish** with me
is the **one** who will **betray** me.

of the book of Isaiah known as Second Isaiah. Second Isaiah was a prophet to the Israelites who were forced to leave the Holy Land during the Babylon exile (587-537 BC). The exiles were indeed weary and needed a word that would rouse them.

If one were to ask, "Who is the servant in Isaiah's suffering servant songs?" the answer would differ depending on the context one is considering. Originally, the suffering servant was most probably the prophet himself. However, once the songs were inserted into the book of Isaiah, the songs were used to refer to the nation, Israel, living in exile. When placed in the context of the Lectionary on Palm Sunday, the words are understood to e refer to Jesus Christ.

The original suffering servant was the prophet known as Second Isaiah. As is often true with prophets, he has experienced persecution as a result of his preaching. He has been beaten and spit upon. However, he has not let this persecution undermine his confidence. Why? Because he is convinced that he is doing exactly what God has called him to do.

The prophet is not simply preaching his own opinions and insights. Rather, he has, morning after morning, listened to the Lord. It is the Lord's word that he is preaching. Given this, he still could not preach unless the Lord had given him another gift—a well trained tongue. Second Isaiah knows "how to speak to the weary a word that will rouse them." This is exactly what the exiles in Babylon need. Because they have lost their nation, their king, and their temple, they are in doubt about their very identity as God's beloved people.

The **Son of Man indeed goes**, as it is written of him,
but **woe to that man** by whom the **Son of Man** is betrayed.
It would be better for **that** man if he had **never been born**."
Then **Judas**, his **betrayer**, said in reply,

Judas is trying to deceive.

"**Surely** it is not **I**, Rabbi?"

Rabbi = RAB-ī

There is sadness more than blame in Jesus' response.

He answered, "**You have said so**."

(3) While they were **eating**,
Jesus took **bread**, said the **blessing**,
broke it, and **giving** it to his **disciples** said,

This is a solemn ceremony. Emphasize each word.

"**Take** and **eat**; **this is my body**."
Then he took a **cup**, gave **thanks**, and **gave** it to them, saying,
"**Drink** from it, **all** of you,

covenant = KUHV-eh-n*nt

for **this** is **my blood** of the **covenant**,
which will be shed on **behalf** of **many**
for the **forgiveness of sins**.

Lower your voice here. The tone is intimate.

I **tell** you, from **now on** I shall not **drink** this **fruit** of the **vine**
until the **day** when I **drink** it with **you new**
in the **kingdom** of my **Father**."

hymn = him

Olives = OL-ivz

Then, after **singing** a **hymn**,
they **went out** to the **Mount** of **Olives**.

(4) Then Jesus said to them,

Jesus' words are both a warning and a message of hope.

"**This night all of you** will have your **faith** in me **shaken**,
for it is written:
*I will strike the **shepherd**,*
*and the **sheep** of the **flock** will be **dispersed**;*
but after I have been **raised up**,

Galilee = GAL-ih-lee

I shall go **before** you to **Galilee**."
Peter said to him in **reply**,

Peter speaks with bravado.

"Though **all** may have their faith in you shaken,
mine will **never** be."

The prophet is a model for the nation as a whole. The fact that he is suffering does not mean that he is not God's prophet or that God has deserted him. Rather, the prophet is positive that the Lord is, and will continue to be, his help. He need not fear shame because he knows he is doing God's will.

The same is true of the exiles. They, too, can continue to live in confidence that they are still God's people. Their suffering does not change their identity as God's Chosen People.

We read this suffering servant song on Palm Sunday because what was true of the prophet and of the exiles is also true of Jesus Christ. That Jesus will suffer crucifixion and death does not alter his identity as the messiah. Jesus has also set his face like flint and knows that he will not be put to shame because he, too, is doing the will of his Father. Train your tongue well to proclaim Isaiah's words, so that you, too, may speak to the weary a word that will rouse them.

READING II

Our second reading is a hymn of high Christology, that is, it emphasizes Jesus' divinity. Paul includes it as part of his exhortation to the Philippians to act humbly and to regard others as more important than themselves (see Philippians 2:3b). He reminds them that acting with love toward others should be a fruit of their relationship with Jesus Christ. In addition he holds up Jesus as an example of one who humbled himself even to the point of death on a cross, the most ignominious death possible for a Jew.

Again, Jesus speaks with authority and sadness rather than anger or blame.

Peter is insistent.

Gethsemane = Geth-SEM-uh-nee

Zebedee = ZEB-uh-dee

Jesus is truly in distress.

prostrate = PROS-trayt

Jesus' humanity is completely evident. He truly does not want to die.

There is disappointment and accusation in Jesus' words.

Jesus still does not want to die, but he does want to do his Father's will.

Jesus said to him,
"**Amen, I say to you,**
this very night before the **cock crows**,
you will **deny** me **three times**."
Peter said to him,
"Even though I should have to **die** with you,
I will not deny you."
And **all** the disciples spoke likewise.

Then Jesus **came** with them to a place called **Gethsemane**,
and he said to his disciples,
"**Sit here** while I go **over there** and **pray**."
He took along **Peter** and the **two sons** of **Zebedee**,
and began to feel **sorrow** and **distress**.
Then he said to them,
"My soul is **sorrowful even** to **death**.
Remain here and keep watch with me."
He **advanced** a little and fell **prostrate** in prayer, saying,
"**My Father**, if it is **possible**,
let this cup **pass** from me;
yet, not as **I** will, but as **you** will."
When he **returned** to his **disciples** he found them **asleep**.
He said to Peter,
"So you could not keep **watch** with me for **one hour**?
Watch and **pray** that you may **not undergo** the **test**.
The **spirit** is willing, but the **flesh** is weak."
Withdrawing a **second** time, he **prayed again**,
"**My Father**, if it is **not possible** that this cup pass
without my drinking it, **your will be done**!"
Then he returned once **more** and found them **asleep**,
for they could not keep their **eyes open**.

There is no question that the hymn is an early expression of the Church's belief that "Jesus Christ is Lord." However, scholars debate the exact belief being expressed in the first lines. By proclaiming that, although Jesus was "in the form of God," he did not regard "equality with God" as "something to be grasped," is the community expressing its belief in Jesus as the pre-existent Word of God? Given the way in which the hymn ends, proclaiming Jesus as Lord and worthy of the adoration that belongs only to God, this is certainly a possibility.

However, a second interpretation is that Jesus is being compared to Adam. Adam was in the "form of God" in that human beings were created in God's image. In contrast to Jesus, Adam did regard equality with God as something to be grasped and thus disobeyed rather than obeyed. Jesus, on the other hand, was completely obedient to the will of his Father.

Jesus' willingness to empty himself, to take on the form of a slave, and to accept death on a cross did not end in death. Because Jesus did these things, God has greatly exalted him. The whole world—those "in heaven and on earth and under the earth"—should all confess that Jesus Christ is Lord.

By incorporating this hymn in his letter, Paul is persuading the Philippians that if Jesus, the Lord, could act humbly and for the good of others, surely the Philippians, who are united to Christ, can do the same. However, the Lectionary reading includes only the hymn, not the exhortations that

He **left** them and withdrew **again** and prayed a **third** time,
saying the **same thing again.**
Then he **returned** to his **disciples** and **said** to them,
"Are you **still** sleeping and **taking** your rest?

Now, Jesus is in charge and determined.

Behold, the **hour** is at **hand**
when the **Son of Man** is to be **handed over** to **sinners.**
Get up, let us **go.**
Look, my **betrayer** is at **hand.**"

While he was **still speaking,**
Judas, one of the **Twelve**, **arrived,**
accompanied by a **large crowd**, with **swords** and **clubs**,
who had come from the **chief priests** and the **elders** of the people.
His **betrayer** had arranged a **sign** with them, saying,

Lower your voice here. This is secret information.

"The man I shall **kiss** is the **one**; **arrest him.**"
Immediately he went over to Jesus and said,

"Hail Rabbi!" is obviously said with false friendliness.

"**Hail, Rabbi**!" and he **kissed** him.
Jesus answered him,

Jesus still speaks to Judas respectfully.

"**Friend**, **do** what you have **come** for."
Then **stepping forward** they laid **hands** on Jesus and **arrested** him.

Increase your pace here.

And **behold**, one of those who **accompanied** Jesus
put his hand to his **sword**, **drew** it,
and struck the **high priest's servant**, **cutting** off his **ear.**
Then Jesus said to him,

Jesus speaks with calm authority.

"Put your **sword back** into its **sheath,**
for all who **take** the **sword** will **perish** by the **sword.**
Do you **think** that I cannot call upon my **Father**
and he will not **provide me** at **this** moment

legions = LEE-juhnz

with more than **twelve legions** of **angels**?
But then how would the **Scriptures** be **fulfilled**
which say that it **must come** to **pass** in this way?"

accompany the hymn. Therefore, the passage should be read in an explanatory tone rather than as an exhortation. The Church is again centering our attention on the kind of messiah that Jesus turned out to be: a suffering servant messiah who submitted to death and who now reigns in glory.

PASSION **Today's Gospel is Matthew's account of Jesus' Passion and death. On Good Friday, we will read John's account. While the accounts have a great deal in common, they also differ in many respects. For instance, in Matthew there is an extended account of Jesus' agony in the garden. In John there is no agony in the garden. In Matthew, Jesus' last meal with his disciples is the Passover celebration, and Jesus institutes the Eucharist. In John, Jesus' last meal with his disciples is not the Passover celebration, and there is no institution of the Eucharist. The fact that the accounts differ calls us to be attentive to the ways in which each Gospel writer tells the story. Each addressed a particular audience, and so each wanted to emphasize certain truths. By noticing differences as well as similarities, we can better discern what each author wanted to teach his particular audience.**

Matthew is teaching primarily Jews. A faithful Jew might well ask how a person found guilty by the Sanhedrin, the Jewish governing body, and given the death penalty by the Roman court, could possibly be the expected messiah. As Matthew tells the story of Jesus' Passion and death, he emphasizes the faults and

There is a challenge in this question.

At **that hour** Jesus said to the **crowds**,
"Have you come **out** as against a **robber**,
with **swords** and **clubs** to **seize** me?
Day after **day** I sat **teaching** in the **temple** area,
yet you did not **arrest** me.
But **all this** has come to pass
that the **writings** of the **prophets** may be **fulfilled**."

Read this line slowly and with sadness.

Then **all** the **disciples left** him and **fled**.

Caiaphas = KĪ-uh-fuhs or KAY-uh-fuhs

(5) Those who had **arrested** Jesus **led** him away
to **Caiaphas** the **high priest**,
where the **scribes** and the **elders** were assembled.
Peter was **following** him at a **distance**
as far as the **high priest's courtyard**,
and going **inside** he sat down with the **servants** to see
the **outcome**.

Sanhedrin = san-HEE-druhn
Matthew is emphasizing the dishonesty of those in authority.
testimony = TES-tuh-moh-nee

The **chief priests** and the **entire Sanhedrin**
kept trying to obtain **false testimony** against Jesus
in order to **put him** to **death**,
but they **found none**,
though **many false witnesses** came forward.
Finally two came forward who stated,
"**This man said**, 'I can destroy the **temple of God**
and within **three days rebuild** it.'"
The **high priest** rose and **addressed** him,

This is said with arrogant authority.

"**Have you no answer?**
What are these men **testifying** against you?"

Read this slowly, with less volume.

But **Jesus** was **silent**.
Then the **high priest** said to him,

Use a demanding tone.

"**I order you** to **tell** us **under oath** before the **living God**
whether you are the **Christ**, the **Son of God**."

weaknesses of Jesus' disciples and the outright dishonesty of Jesus' adversaries in order to make it clear who was in the right and who was in the wrong. The man who was deserted, falsely accused, and killed was and is the messiah, the Son of God.

Today's reading has seven scenes: Judas' betrayal, the Passover meal, the agony in the garden, the trial before the Sanhedrin, the trial before Pilate, the Crucifixion, and events after the Crucifixion but before the Resurrection. Throughout these scenes, Matthew emphasizes the failure of just about everyone to support Jesus or to understand his true identity. When truthful statements are made about Jesus, they are made as accusations or as taunts, not as statements of faith. Also, throughout these scenes the author makes it abundantly clear to the audience that despite the lack of courage, understanding, or honesty on the part of his contemporaries, Jesus is the Son of God. Jesus fulfills the words of the prophets; he is the Messiah.

(2) Matthew, like Mark, his source, pictures Jesus' last meal with his disciples as being the Passover meal. The Passover celebration was, of course, a celebration of God's saving actions on Israel's behalf during the time of the exodus. During the last plague that preceded the Israelites' escape from slavery in Egypt, the Israelites were directed to put the blood of a lamb on the lintels of their doors. The angel of death, who would kill the first born of the Egyptians, would pass over the homes of the Israelites and not harm them.

Jesus said to him in reply,
"**You** have said so.
But I tell you:
From **now on** you will see the '**Son of Man**
seated at the **right hand** of the **Power**'
and '**coming** on the **clouds of heaven**.'"
Then the **high priest tore** his **robes** and said,
"**He has blasphemed**!
What **further need** have we of **witnesses**?
You have **now heard** the **blasphemy**;
what is your **opinion**?"
They said in reply,
"**He deserves** to **die**!"
Then they **spat** in his **face** and **struck** him,
while some **slapped** him, saying,
"**Prophesy** for us, **Christ**: **who** is it that **struck** you?"
(6) Now **Peter** was sitting **outside** in the **courtyard**.
One of the **maids** came over to him and said,
"**You too** were with **Jesus** the **Galilean**."
But he **denied** it in front of **everyone**, saying,
"**I do not know** what you are **talking** about!"
As he went out to the **gate**, **another** girl saw him
and said to those who were there,
"**This man** was with **Jesus** the **Nazorean**."
Again he **denied** it with an **oath**,
"**I do not know** the **man**!"
A little later the **bystanders** came over and said to Peter,
"**Surely** you **too** are **one** of them;
even your **speech** gives you away."
At that he began to **curse** and to **swear**,
"**I do not know the man**."
And **immediately** a **cock crowed**.

In contrast, Jesus speaks with quiet confidence.

Increase your volume here.

The high priest is outraged.
blasphemed = blas-FEEMD
blasphemy = BLAS-fuh-mee

This is said with anger.

Now they are taunting Jesus.
prophesy = PROF-uh-sī

The narrator is simply giving us information.
Galilean = gal-ih-LEE-uhn
This is an accusation.
Peter is defensive.

Again, an accusation.
Nazorean = naz-uh-REE-uhn
Now Peter is angry.

The bystanders are insisting.

Say this loudly and with anger.
Lower your voice and speak with sadness.

(3) While celebrating the Exodus, the greatest event in salvation history up until Jesus' time, Jesus takes the bread and wine and reinterprets them so that they become the basis for remembering, celebrating, and entering into the greatest saving act in all of history: Jesus' redemption of all of Creation through his Passion, death, and Resurrection. After blessing the bread, Jesus says, "Take and eat; this is my body." After blessing the cup, he says, "Drink from it, all of you, for this is my blood of the covenant, which will be shed on behalf of many for the forgiveness of sins."

For Catholics, these words are some of the most important in all of scripture. At every Mass, after the Liturgy of the Word, we celebrate the Liturgy of the Eucharist. We, too, give thanks, receive the bread and the chalice, eat, and drink. We believe that we are receiving the body and blood of Jesus, the new Lamb of God in the new covenant, whose blood gives life. However, the blood of the Passover lamb gave only an extended life on earth; Jesus' blood gives us eternal life.

(2) (4) Both before and after giving his disciples the great gift of Eucharist, Jesus speaks of betrayal. Before the institution of the Eucharist, Jesus declares that one will betray him. The disciples are all terribly distressed by this and each declares that it could not be he, including Judas. When Judas says, "Surely it is not I, Rabbi?" Jesus responds: "You have said so." These words will become something of a refrain on Jesus' lips. He will respond to the high priest and to Pilate in the same way.

Then Peter **remembered** the words that **Jesus** had **spoken**:
"Before the **cock crows** you will **deny me three times**."
He went **out** and began to **weep bitterly**.

Pause here.
The narrator resumes the story. Increase your tempo.

When it was **morning**,
all the **chief priests** and the **elders** of the people
took counsel **against** Jesus to **put** him to **death**.
They **bound** him, **led** him away,
and **handed** him over to **Pilate**, the **governor**.

Pilate = PĪ-luht

Speak slowly here.

Then **Judas**, his **betrayer**, seeing that Jesus
had been **condemned**,
deeply regretted what he had done.
He **returned** the thirty pieces of silver
to the **chief priests** and **elders**, saying,
"I have **sinned** in betraying **innocent blood**."

Judas is full of remorse.

They said,
"What is that to **us**?
Look to it **yourself**."

This response is flippant.

Flinging the money into the temple,
he **departed** and went off and **hanged** himself.

Speak slowly. This is a tragedy.

The **chief priests gathered up** the money, but said,
"It is not **lawful** to **deposit** this in the **temple treasury**,
for it is the price of **blood**."

Emphasize "lawful." The chief priests are legalists.

After **consultation**, they used it to buy the **potter's field**
as a **burial place** for **foreigners**.
That is why that field **even today** is called the **Field of Blood**.
Then was **fulfilled** what had been said through **Jeremiah**
the **prophet**,
*And they took the **thirty pieces** of silver,*
*the value of a man with a **price** on his head,*

Raise your volume to emphasize this line.
This is one of Matthew's main themes.
Jeremiah = jayr-uh-MĪ-uh

Notice that as Matthew tells the story there is no mystery about what is actually taking place. The author and the audience share knowledge of the truth that the characters in the story do not share. Matthew has already told us that Judas will betray Jesus. We know this, but the other apostles do not. The same will be true when Jesus is before the Sanhedrin and Pilate. We know what the characters in the story fail to understand. Therefore, the words spoken are full of irony. People who mean to ridicule, are, in the eyes of the reader, speaking a truth beyond the character's own comprehension.

(4) After the institution of the Eucharist, the theme of betrayal continues. Jesus tells the disciples that later that evening all of them will have their faith in Jesus shaken. Peter, with great bravado, tells Jesus that his faith in Jesus will never be shaken. In response, Jesus says that Peter will deny Jesus three times.

(6) Later we will hear Peter do just that. When accused of being one of Jesus' companions, Peter will curse and swear and declare, "I do not know the man." These words are full of tragic irony. Peter means to lie, but in fact, Peter is telling the truth. Peter will not fully know the man, the Son of God, until after the Resurrection.

Even before his denial, Peter, as well as James and John, have greatly disappointed Jesus. After the dinner, while in the garden of Gethsemane, Jesus asks these three to watch and pray with him. They know that Jesus is in terrible distress. Yet three times they fail to do as Jesus asks. Their failure continues at the

Israelites = IZ-ree-uh-lītz or IZ-ray-uh-lītz

*a price **set** by some of the **Israelites**,*
*and they paid it **out** for the **potter's field***
***just** as the **Lord** had **commanded** me.*

Pause before resuming the story.

(7) Now Jesus stood before the **governor**, and he **questioned** him,
"Are **you** the **king** of the **Jews**?"

Again, Jesus speaks with quiet confidence.

Jesus said, "**You** say so."
And when he was accused by the **chief priests** and **elders**,
he made no answer.
Then **Pilate** said to him,
"Do you not **hear** how many things they are testifying
against you?"

Say this with finality.

But he **did not answer** him **one word**,
so that the **governor** was **greatly amazed**.

This is background information. Increase your pace.

Now on the occasion of the feast
the **governor** was accustomed to release to the crowd
one prisoner whom they **wished**.

Barabbas = buh-RAB-uhs

And at **that time** they had a **notorious prisoner** called **Barabbas**.
So when they had assembled, **Pilate** said to them,

Pilate is trying to please the crowd.

"**Which one** do **you** want me to release to you,
Barabbas, or **Jesus** called **Christ**?"

This comment is an aside. Lower your voice.

For he knew that it was out of **envy**
that they had handed him over.
While he was **still seated** on the **bench**,
his **wife** sent him a **message**,

This is said with great alarm

"Have **nothing to do** with that **righteous man**.
I suffered **much** in a **dream** today because of **him**."
The **chief priests** and the **elders** persuaded the **crowds**
to ask for **Barabbas** but to **destroy** Jesus.
The governor said to them in reply,

Pilate is getting impatient.

"Which of the **two** do you want me to **release** to you?"

This is shouted.

They answered, "**Barabbas**!"

time of the arrest. Matthew tells us that all of the disciples left Jesus and fled.

Matthew, like his source, Mark, emphasizes Jesus' agony. (4) Jesus, prostrate, earnestly prays not to have to die. He says, "My Father, if it is possible let this cup pass from me; yet, not as I will, but as you will." As Jesus continues to pray he comes to terms with what lies ahead. His prayer changes slightly: "My Father, if is not possible that this cup pass without my drinking it, your will be done!"

When he returns to his disciples, rather than being crushed by their weakness and the inevitability of his death, Jesus is a strong leader. He tells the disciples to get up and get going because his betrayer is at hand.

Jesus greets his betrayer with warmth and confidence. He directs his disciples not to defend him with swords, and assures them that he is willing to do his Father's will. Jesus says: "it must come to pass in this way."

(5) (7) As Matthew tells the story of Jesus' trials, he makes it very clear to his readers that Jesus is innocent, and those who condemn him are guilty. The chief priests and the entire Sanhedrin are not presented as seekers after the truth who make a dreadful mistake. Rather, they have already decided the verdict: They want Jesus to have the death penalty. They are trying to find witnesses, false witnesses, to help them achieve their goal.

Also, the charge against Jesus changes from court to court, depending on that court's jurisdiction. When before the Sanhedrin, the court that deals with internal

Pilate said to them,
"Then what shall I do with **Jesus** called **Christ**?"
They all said,
"**Let him** be **crucified**!"

Again, this is shouted.

But he said,
"**Why**? What **evil** has he **done**?"

Pilate is challenging the crowd.

They only shouted the louder,
"**Let him be crucified**!"

The crowd keeps shouting.

When **Pilate** saw that he was not **succeeding** at **all**,
but that a **riot** was breaking out **instead**,
he took **water** and **washed** his **hands** in the sight of the crowd,
saying, "**I am innocent** of **this man's blood**.
Look to it **yourselves**."

Pilate is defensive and angry; not strong.

And the **whole people** said in reply,
"**His blood be upon us** and **upon our children**."

Said with great conviction.

Then he **released Barabbas** to them,
but after he had Jesus **scourged**,
he handed **him** over to be **crucified**.

scourged = skerjd
Pause here.
crucified = KROO-sih-fīd

Then the **soldiers** of the governor took **Jesus inside** the **praetorium**
and gathered the **whole cohort** around **him**.
They **stripped** off his **clothes**
and threw a **scarlet military cloak** about him.
Weaving a **crown** out of **thorns**, they **placed** it on his **head**,
and a **reed** in his **right hand**.
And **kneeling** before him, they **mocked** him, saying,
"**Hail**, **King** of the **Jews**!"
They spat upon him and took the reed
and kept **striking** him on the **head**.

The narrator continues the story.
praetorium = prih-TOHR-ee-uhm
cohort = KOH-hohrt

The tone is mocking, not praise.
Read quickly here. There is no rest.

Jewish matters, Jesus is charged with blasphemy. When before the Roman governor, Pontius Pilate, who deals with civil matters, Jesus is charged with claiming to be a king, a civil, rather than a religious, crime.

In both courts Jesus is reluctant to testify. When the truth is turned into a charge against him, Jesus replies as he did to Judas: "You have said so." The reader has no doubt: Jesus is "the Christ, the Son of God." as charged in the Jewish court; Jesus is "the King of the Jews," as charged in the Roman court. Jesus is found guilty for being who he is.

Neither the Sanhedrin nor Pilate could be painted in a worse light. In addition to seeking false witnesses against him, the members of the Sanhedrin and the chief priests spit on Jesus, strike him, and taunt him, obviously not part of any judicial process. Pilate has Jesus scourged and turns him over to be crucified even though he himself believes Jesus is innocent. Pilate is too weak to disappoint the crowd.

We can tell that Matthew is going out of his way to state Jesus' innocence because only he has the story of Pilate's wife, based on her dream, warning her husband to have nothing to do with Jesus, "this righteous man." Only Matthew has the story of Pilate trying to relieve himself of responsibility for his actions by washing his hands in front of the crowd. Matthew wants it abundantly clear that Jesus, although treated as though he were guilty, was not, in fact, guilty.

(8) Not only Jesus' disciples, the chief priests, the Sanhedrin, and Pilate abandon Jesus; so do the soldiers, the revolutionaries crucified with him, the scribes, and the elders. Jesus is reviled by all. In mocking

And when they had **mocked** him,
they **stripped** him of the cloak,
dressed him in his **own clothes**,
and **led** him off to **crucify him**.

Cyrenian = sī-REE-nee-uhn;
Simon = SĪ-muhn
Pause.

(8) As they were **going out**, they met a **Cyrenian** named **Simon**;
this man they **pressed** into service
to **carry** his **cross**.

Read more slowly here.
Golgotha = GOL-guh-thuh or GAWL-guh-thuh

And when they came to a place called **Golgotha**
—which means **Place of the Skull**—,
they gave Jesus **wine** to drink mixed with **gall**.
But when he had **tasted it**, he **refused** to **drink**.
After they had **crucified** him,
they **divided** his **garments** by casting **lots**;
then they **sat down** and **kept watch** over him there.
And they placed over his **head** the **written charge** against him:

Emphasize every word of this line.

This is **Jesus**, the **King** of the **Jews**.

revolutionaries = rev-uh-LOO-shun-ayr-eez

Two revolutionaries were crucified **with** him,
one on his **right** and the other on his **left**.

reviled = rih-VĪLD
This is both a taunt and a challenge.

Those passing by **reviled him**, shaking their heads and saying,
"**You** who would destroy the **temple** and rebuild it
in **three days**,
save yourself, if you **are** the **Son of God**,
and **come down** from the cross!"
Likewise the **chief priests** with the **scribes** and **elders mocked**
him and said,

The chief priests and scribes are having fun at Jesus' expense.

"He **saved others**; he cannot **save himself**.
So he is the **king** of **Israel**!
Let him come **down** from the cross **now**,
and **we will believe** in him.
He trusted in **God**;
let **him** deliver him **now** if **he** wants him.

They are confident that God does not want this person.

and taunting Jesus, many make true statements that they do not know are true: Jesus is the King of the Jews. Jesus is the Son of God.

In both Matthew and Mark's accounts, just before Jesus dies he calls out, "My God, my God, why have you forsaken me?" In saying these words, Jesus is expressing agony, but not abandonment. Jesus is praying a well known lament, Psalm 22. As is true of all laments, the prayer starts out with a plea for help, but then moves on to an expression of faith that as God has saved in the past, so will God save now.

After Jesus' death, Matthew alone tells us that the earth quaked, rocks split, and tombs were opened so that "the bodies of many saints who had fallen asleep were raised." This is Matthew's way of teaching his audience that Jesus' death was an earth-shattering event, the initial breaking in of a new age for all of creation. Matthew will again describe an earthquake when Mary Magdalene and the other Mary return to the tomb (see Matthew 28:1–2). The expectation that the dead would rise with the in-breaking of the new age is described in Daniel: on the day of the Lord "many of those who sleep in the dust of the earth shall awake" (Daniel 12:2).

In Matthew, as in Mark, the only people who sincerely express faith in Jesus Christ are Roman soldiers who do so only after Jesus' death. In response to the mighty signs following Jesus' death they say, "Truly, this was the Son of God." After the death we also learn that many women disciples of Jesus had been looking on from a distance, particularly Mary Magdalene, Mary, the mother of James and Joseph, and the mother of the sons of Zebedee, James and John.

For he said, '**I am** the **Son** of **God**.'"
The **revolutionaries** who were crucified **with** him
  also kept **abusing** him in the **same way**.

Read slowly.

From **noon onward**, **darkness** came over the **whole land**
  until **three** in the **afternoon**.

Eli, Eli, lema sabachthani = ay-LEE, ay-LEE, luh-MAH sah-bahk-TAH-nee

This is an anguished cry.

This is the narrator's voice explaining what Jesus said.

And about **three o'clock** Jesus **cried out** in a **loud voice**,
  "**Eli, Eli, lema sabachthani?**"
  which means, "**My God**, **my God**, why have **you** forsaken me?"

This is said with excitement and puzzlement.

Elijah = ee-LĪ-juh

Some of the **bystanders** who heard it said,
  "**This one** is calling for **Elijah**."
Immediately one of them ran to get a **sponge**;
  he soaked it in **wine**, and putting it on a **reed**,
  gave it to him to **drink**.
But the rest said,

This is said with urgency.

  "**Wait**, let us **see** if Elijah comes to **save** him."
But Jesus cried out **again** in a **loud voice**,

Emphasize "gave up." Jesus is choosing to do his Father's will.

  and **gave** up his **spirit**.

There is a lengthy pause here.

Here all kneel and pause for a short time.

These are remarkable events. Increase both your volume and your speed.

sanctuary = SANGK-choo-ayr-ee

And behold, the **veil** of the **sanctuary**
  was **torn** in **two** from **top** to **bottom**.
The **earth quaked**, **rocks** were **split**, **tombs** were **opened**,
  and the bodies of **many saints** who had fallen asleep
    were **raised**.
And coming forth from their **tombs** after **his** resurrection,
  they **entered** the **holy city** and **appeared** to **many**.

Now speak more slowly and softly.

centurion = sen-TOOR-ee-uhn or sen-TYOOR-ee-uhn

The **centurion** and the men **with him** who were **keeping watch**
    over Jesus
  feared greatly when they saw the **earthquake**
  and all that was **happening**, and they said,

Say this with awe and conviction.

  "**Truly**, **this** was the **Son** of **God**!"

(9) The two Marys are witnesses to the place where Joseph of Arimathea buries Jesus. They will return after the Sabbath and discover that the tomb is empty (Matthew 28:1–10).

Today's Gospel ends with another account that is unique to Matthew. The chief priests and Pharisees ask Pilate to help them make sure that Jesus' disciples do not steal Jesus' body and then later claim that a resurrection has occurred. Pilate gives them permission to seal the tomb and to post a guard. Here Matthew is assuring his Jewish audience that the claim that Jesus did not rise, but that his body was stolen, is not true (see Matthew 28:14).

Were we not already familiar with the story, the ending of today's Gospel would leave us in great suspense. However, we know that Jesus' death does not end in death, but in life, not only for Jesus but for us as well.

To proclaim today's Gospel effectively will require those who read to enter into the emotions of the characters described: Jesus in agony and then in charge, Peter full of bravado and then angry and cursing, Judas full of guile, the chief priests and Sanhedrin self-righteous and completely wrong, Pilate, persuasive and then defensively angry, the soldiers taunting and heckling, the centurion and his fellow soldiers full of awe, and the always present narrator moving the story along from one dramatic scene to another. Try to read so that the assembly—unlike the women in today's Gospel—does not watch from a distance until the very end, but become active participants in the story from the very beginning.

There were **many women** there, looking on from a **distance**,
who had **followed Jesus** from Galilee, **ministering** to him.
Among them were **Mary Magdalene** and **Mary** the mother of
James and **Joseph**,
and the mother of the **sons** of **Zebedee**.

Zebedee = ZEB-uh-dee
Pause with the change of scene.

(9) When it was **evening**,
there came a **rich** man from **Arimathea** named **Joseph**,
who was **himself** a **disciple** of Jesus.

Arimathea = ayr-ih-muh-THEE-uh

He went to **Pilate** and asked for the **body** of **Jesus**;
then Pilate **ordered** it to be **handed over**.
Taking the **body**, Joseph **wrapped** it in **clean linen**
and **laid** it in his **new tomb** that he had hewn in the rock.
Then he rolled a **huge** stone across the entrance to the tomb
and **departed**.
But **Mary Magdalene** and the **other Mary**
remained sitting there, **facing** the tomb.

This is important. The women will be witnesses.
Magdalene = MAG-duh-luhn or MAG-duh-leen or MAG-duh-lehn
Pause again.
Pharisees = FAYR-uh-seez

The next day, the one **following** the day of **preparation**,
the **chief priests** and the **Pharisees**
gathered before **Pilate** and said,
"Sir, we remember that this **impostor** while still **alive** said,
'After **three days** I will be **raised up**.'
Give orders, then, that the grave be **secured** until the **third day**,
lest his **disciples** come and **steal** him and say to the people,
'**He has been raised** from the **dead**.'
This **last** imposture would be worse than the **first**."

impostor = im-PAW-st*r
This is said with urgency and self-importance.
To the chief priests and Pharisees, this is a false, ridiculous claim.

Pilate said to them,
"The **guard** is **yours**;
go, **secure** it as **best** you **can**."
So they **went** and **secured** the tomb
by fixing a **seal** to the stone and **setting** the **guard**.

Pilate is acquiescing.
Say this in a firm voice.

[Shorter Form: Matthew 27:11–54]

HOLY THURSDAY

Lectionary #39

READING I Exodus 12:1–8, 11–14

Moses = MOH-ziz or MOH-zis
Aaron = AYR-uhn
Egypt = EE-jpt
God is giving instructions to Moses and Aaron, not giving a proclamation to the whole community. Read slowly and with moderate volume.
procure = PROH-kyoor

A reading from the Book of Exodus

The LORD said to **Moses** and **Aaron** in the land of **Egypt**,
"**This month** shall stand at the **head** of your **calendar**;
you shall reckon it the **first month** of the **year**.
Tell the **whole community** of **Israel**:
On the **tenth** of **this month every one** of your **families**
must procure for itself a **lamb**, **one apiece** for **each household**.
If a family is **too small** for a **whole** lamb,
it shall join the **nearest household** in **procuring** one
and shall **share** in the lamb
in proportion to the number of **persons** who **partake** of it.

partake = pahr-TAYK
blemish = BLEHM-ish

The lamb must be a **year-old male** and **without blemish**.
You may take it from either the **sheep** or the **goats**.
You shall **keep it** until the **fourteenth day** of **this month**,
and **then**, with the **whole assembly** of **Israel present**,
it shall be **slaughtered** during the **evening twilight**.

Emphasize "whole assembly of Israel." This is to be a community ritual.
Israel = IZ-ree-uhl or IZ-ray-uhl
slaughtered = SLAW-terd
lintel = LIN-t*l

They shall take some of its **blood**
and apply it to the **two doorposts** and the **lintel**
of **every house** in which they **partake** of **the lamb**.
That same night they shall eat its **roasted flesh**
with **unleavened bread** and **bitter herbs**.

unleavened = uhn-LEV-uhnd

READING I Today we read an account of God's instructions regarding how the Israelites are to celebrate Passover as "a perpetual institution." All succeeding generations are to re-member, that is, to once again join themselves to, and become participants in, the Exodus experience.

The Passover celebration developed after the actual exodus from Egypt. Scripture scholars think that these instructions were inserted by priestly editors into an already existing account of the ten plagues. The Passover celebration had become absolutely core to Israel's self understanding and self identity.

As the account now stands, we read the instructions regarding Passover after the tenth plague has been announced, but before it takes place. Moses has told Pharaoh that the first born of all the Egyptians will die. The firstborn of the Israelites will not die (see Exodus 11:4–8). The result of this final plague will be that the Pharaoh will not only let the Israelites leave, he will drive them away (Exodus 11:1).

The Passover celebration described in today's reading celebrates the Lord's passing over the houses of the Israelites so that their first born did not die during the tenth plague. This religious Passover celebration was a reinterpretation of an already existing Passover celebration. Originally, the Passover was a nomadic feast marking the passing over of shepherds and their flocks from the winter fields to the summer fields.

The month that stood at the head of their calendar was the month of the spring equinox. The blood that was to be applied to the two door posts and the lintel of every house was originally placed on the

Increase your pace here.

"This is **how** you are to **eat** it:
with your **loins girt**, **sandals** on your **feet** and your **staff** in **hand**,
you shall eat like those who are in **flight**.

Emphasize this line.

It is the **Passover** of the **LORD**.

God is reassuring Moses and Aaron, not threatening the Egyptians.

For on this **same night** I will go through **Egypt**,
striking down every firstborn of the **land**, both **man** and **beast**,
and **executing judgment** on **all** the **gods** of **Egypt**—
I, the **LORD**!

Emphasize "you."

But the **blood** will mark the **houses** where **you** are.
Seeing the **blood**, I will **pass over you**;

Again, emphasize "you."

thus, when I strike the land of **Egypt**,

Raise your volume for this conclusion.

no destructive blow will come upon **you**.

perpetual = per-PECH-oo-uhl

"**This day** shall be a **memorial feast** for you,
which **all your generations** shall celebrate
with **pilgrimage** to the **LORD**, as a **perpetual institution**."

READING II 1 Corinthians 11:23–26

Corinthians = kohr-IN-thee-uhnz

A reading from the first Letter of Saint Paul to the Corinthians

Read this with solemnity and reverence. Paul is recalling something holy.

Brothers and sisters:
I **received** from the **Lord** what I also **handed** on to **you**,
that the **Lord Jesus**, on the night he was **handed over**,

Emphasize Jesus' words of consecration.
remembrance = rih-MEM-bruhns

took bread, and, after he had **given thanks**,
broke it and said, "**This** is **my body** that is for **you**.
Do this in **remembrance** of **me**."

covenant = KUHV-eh-n*nt

In the **same way also** the **cup**, after supper, saying,
"**This cup** is the **new covenant** in **my blood**.

entrances to the nomads' tents as a way to ward off evil spirits who might affect adversely the fertility of the flocks or the lives of the newborn sheep. What was originally a nomadic feast was appropriated and reinterpreted to become a celebration of God's saving actions on the Israelites' behalf.

The Gospel accounts of Mark, Matthew, and Luke all picture Jesus' last meal as the Passover meal. At that meal Jesus once more reinterprets the meaning of the feast in the light of his own passing over through death to life. Jesus becomes the new Passover lamb whose blood gives life. As you proclaim this reading, emphasize those parts that foreshadow Jesus' last meal with his disciples: "It is the Passover of the Lord" and "This day shall be a memorial feast for you which all your generations shall celebrate."

READING II Our reading from 1 Corinthians is part of Paul's plea that the Corinthians remain united and recognize the poor in their midst. Evidently when the Corinthians gathered for Eucharist they gathered in a home and had an actual meal as part of the celebration. In describing their behavior, Paul says that "one goes ahead with his own supper, and one goes hungry while another gets drunk" (1 Corinthians 11:21). Paul asks how the Corinthians can possibly behave this way when they have gathered to celebrate Eucharist, given what Jesus had to say when he initiated this ritual. It is at this point that today's reading begins.

On the night before Jesus died he made it perfectly clear that he was giving his life in service to his disciples. When Jesus takes the bread he says, "This is my

Now it is Paul, not Jesus, who is speaking. This is Paul's concluding instruction.

Do this, as **often** as you **drink** it, in **remembrance** of **me**."
For as **often** as you **eat this bread** and **drink the cup**,
you proclaim the **death** of the **Lord** until he **comes**.

GOSPEL John 13:1–15

The narrator is giving us background information.
Passover = PAS-oh-ver

induced = in-DOOSD
Judas = JOO-duhs
Simon = SĪ-muhn
Iscariot = is-KAYR-ee-uht
Pause after, "So," then Raise your volume. We are starting the immediate drama here.

disciples = dih-SĪ-p*lz

Peter = PEE-ter
Peter is not just asking a question, but is objecting.
Jesus is reassuring Peter.

Peter is adamant.

Jesus is persuading.
inheritance = in-HAYR-ih-t*ns

A reading from the holy Gospel according to John

Before the feast of **Passover**, Jesus **knew** that his **hour** had **come**
to pass from **this world** to the **Father**.
He **loved** his **own** in the world and he **loved them** to the **end**.
The **devil** had already induced **Judas**, son of **Simon** the **Iscariot**,
to **hand him over**.
So, during **supper**,
fully aware that the Father had put **everything** into his power
and that he had **come from God** and was **returning to God**,
he **rose** from supper and **took off** his **outer garments**.
He took a **towel** and **tied** it around his **waist**.
Then he poured **water** into a **basin**
and began to **wash** the **disciples' feet**
and **dry** them with the **towel** around his **waist**.
He came to **Simon Peter**, who said to him,
"**Master**, are you going to wash **my** feet?"
Jesus **answered** and **said** to him,
"What **I am doing**, you do not understand **now**,
but you **will** understand **later**."
Peter said to him, "You will **never wash my feet**."
Jesus answered him,
"Unless I **wash** you, you will have **no inheritance** with me."

body that is for you." When Jesus takes the cup he tells the disciples to "Do this, as often as you drink it, in remembrance of me." Paul's point is that the Corinthians are not really celebrating Eucharist in remembrance of Christ if they are not, at the same time, living lives of self sacrifice in order to serve others. That is what Jesus did. That is what they must do.

Paul goes on to say that whoever "eats the bread or drinks the cup of the Lord unworthily will have to answer for the body and blood of the Lord" (1 Corinthians 11:27). In other words, neglecting the poor is just the same as mistreating Christ. Paul learned that mistreating others is the same as mistreating Christ at the time of his conversion. At the time, Paul was persecuting Christians. When the risen Christ appeared to him, Christ did not ask Paul, "Why are you persecuting my followers?" He asked, "Why are you persecuting me?"

Our Lectionary reading includes only Paul's account of Jesus' instituting the Eucharist, not the broader point Paul is making regarding service to the poor. Therefore, when you proclaim this reading do not use Paul's tone in the letter, one of exasperation, but read the passage as you would read a treasured and revered memory about a loved one. In this reading we have our earliest account of Jesus' great gift to us, his continued presence with us in Eucharist.

GOSPEL **As today's reading begins, John tells us that it is "Before the feast of Passover." In John's account of the Gospel, Passover and the Sabbath fall on the same day. Therefore, Jesus' last meal with his disciples is not the Passover meal. Rather, Jesus is killed**

	Simon Peter said to him,
This is said whole-heartedly.	"**Master**, then not only my **feet**, but my **hands** and **head** as **well**."
	Jesus said to him,
There is a warning in Jesus' words. bathed = baythd	"Whoever has **bathed** has no **need** except to have his **feet** washed, for he is **clean all over**; so you are **clean**, but **not all**."
This is an aside, said by the narrator.	For he **knew** who would **betray** him; for **this reason**, he said, "Not **all** of you are **clean**."
The story resumes here.	So when he had **washed** their **feet** and put his **garments** back **on** and **reclined** at **table** again,
Jesus speaks with gentle authority.	he said to them, "Do you **realize** what I have **done** for you? You call me '**teacher**' and '**master**,' and **rightly so**, for **indeed I am**. If **I**, therefore, the **master** and **teacher**, have washed **your feet**, **you** ought to wash **one another's feet**. I have given you a **model** to **follow**,
Read this final lesson slowly.	so that as I **have done** for **you**, **you** should **also do**."

at the same time the Passover lambs are being killed in preparation for the Passover meal. John is teaching that Jesus is the new Passover lamb.

John tells us that at Jesus' last meal with his disciples, Jesus taught them that they must model themselves after him and live in service to one another. This is the same message we heard from Paul in our selection from 1 Corinthians. In order to teach this lesson, Jesus washes his disciples' feet, a menial task. Jesus tells the disciples that they must wash each other's feet. As Jesus has done for them, they must do for each other.

As is nearly always true in John, his account has a double meaning. There is a meaning at the level of the plot, which we have just discussed, and an additional meaning about the presence of the risen Christ in the Church. Notice that when Peter objects to having his feet washed, Jesus says, "Unless I wash you, you will have no inheritance with me." Jesus then says that whoever has bathed "is clean all over." Here, John is referring to Baptism. Those who are baptized have an inheritance with Jesus. Because their sins have been forgiven, they are entirely clean.

As you proclaim this reading, the main emphasis should be on the baptismal passage, the conversation between Jesus and Peter, and on the conclusion. We are just as united to Christ through Baptism as were the disciples whose feet Jesus washed. We, too, are to model ourselves on Jesus and live lives of service to others.

GOOD FRIDAY OF THE LORD'S PASSION

Lectionary #40

READING I Isaiah 52:13—53:12

Isaiah = Ī-ZAY-uh

A reading from the Book of the Prophet Isaiah

Use an exultant tone. God is announcing good news.

See, my servant shall **prosper**,
he shall be **raised high** and **greatly exalted.**

Now the narrator is speaking and is drawing a contrast.

Even as many were **amazed** at him—

Lower your voice.

marred = mahrd

so **marred** was his look **beyond human semblance**

semblance = SEM-bl*ns

and his appearance **beyond** that of the **sons of man**—

With this line, increase your volume and sound jubilant.

so shall he **startle many nations,**
because of **him** kings shall stand **speechless**;
for those who have not been **told** shall **see**,
those who have not **heard** shall **ponder** it.

Now the kings of other nations are speaking. Their good news is almost unbelievable!

Who would **believe** what **we** have **heard**?
To whom has the **arm** of the **LORD** been **revealed**?

Again, this is a contrast. Lower your volume.

He grew up like a **sapling** before him,

parched = pahrchd

like a **shoot** from the **parched earth**;
there was in him **no stately bearing** to make us **look** at him,
nor **appearance** that would **attract** us to him.

spurned = spuhrnd

He was **spurned** and **avoided** by people,

infirmity = in-FER-mih-tee

a man of **suffering, accustomed** to **infirmity,**
one of those from whom people hide their **faces,**
spurned, and **we** held him in **no esteem**.

Speak with more volume and with authority. Now the truth is understood.

Yet it was **our infirmities** that **he bore,**
our sufferings that **he endured,**
while we thought of him as **stricken,**

smitten = SMIT-*n

as one **smitten by God** and **afflicted.**

READING I Today's first reading is from the prophet known as Second Isaiah (Isaiah 40—55), who prophesied to the Israelites during the Babylonian exile (587–537 BC). In order to understand the original meaning of this prophecy, we must understand both the role of a prophet in the life of the Israelites and the particular social situation in which the Israelites found themselves when Second Isaiah was preaching. A deeper understanding of the prophet's original message will make it clear why his words are proclaimed on Good Friday.

A prophet in Israel was not a fortune-teller, not a person who had the gift of foreseeing inevitable future events. Rather, the prophet was an inspired person who understood God's relationship with his Chosen People, who understood covenant love and called the people to fidelity to that love. If the people were sinning, the prophet warned of the inevitable suffering that would result unless the people repented. However, if the people were suffering, the prophet reminded them that God loved them and would be faithful to his promise to take care of them. He reminded them that there is never reason to lose all hope.

Second Isaiah was a prophet of hope. The Israelites were in desperate need of a hopeful message because during the Babylonian exile, they had been forced by events to question their understanding of their relationship with God. They had thought that their king, their nation, and their temple would be secure forever. Now they were in exile, the nation no longer existed, and the temple had been destroyed. Were they God's people, or not?

Speak slowly and with sorrow.

But he was pierced for **our offenses**,
  crushed for **our sins**;
upon **him** was the chastisement that makes **us whole**,
  by **his stripes we** were **healed**.

Say this with awe.

Increase your speed here.

We had **all** gone **astray** like **sheep**,
  each following his **own way**;

Again, read slowly to emphasize the contrast.

but the LORD laid upon **him**
  the **guilt** of us **all**.

Read this with sadness. This is a tragic turn of events.

Though he was **harshly treated**, he **submitted**
  and **opened not** his **mouth**;
like a **lamb** led to the **slaughter**
  or a **sheep** before the **shearers**,
  he was **silent** and **opened not** his **mouth**.

condemned = kuhn-DEMD

Oppressed and **condemned**, he was **taken away**,
  and **who** would have thought **any more** of his **destiny**?
When he was **cut off** from the **land** of the **living**,
  and **smitten** for the **sin** of his **people**,
a **grave** was assigned him among the **wicked**
  and a **burial place** with **evildoers**,

Emphasize the servant's total innocence.

though he had done **no wrong**
  nor spoken **any falsehood**.
But the LORD was pleased
  to **crush** him in **infirmity**.

This is the mystery. Why is the innocent servant, Israel, suffering?

Pause, and then speak with authority. The people are being assured that their suffering does have purpose.

descendants = dih-SEND-ntz

If he gives his life as an **offering** for **sin**,
  he shall see his descendants in a **long life**,
  and the **will** of the **LORD** shall be **accomplished**
    through **him**.

Yahweh is speaking. Proclaim these lines with hope and joy.

Because of his **affliction**
  he shall see the **light** in **fullness of days**;
through his **suffering**, my servant shall **justify many**,
  and their **guilt** he shall **bear**.

Had God deserted them? If not, what was the purpose of their suffering?

Second Isaiah assured the exiles that they were still God's people, and God was still their God. In addition, he taught them that their suffering had a purpose in God's plan for the world. If they accepted their suffering and remained faithful, they would realize, in hindsight, that through them God was bringing all nations to a knowledge of God.

As you seek to understand Isaiah's original meaning, it helps to realize that the voice speaking in today's prophecy changes as the reading progresses, as in a drama onstage. The original speaker is God. It is God who says, "See, my servant shall prosper." The word "my" would have been all-important to the exiles in Babylon. They are the servant about whom Isaiah is speaking, and the word "my" assures them that they still belong to God.

It is the kings of other nations who say, "Who would believe what we have heard?" They represent the people of the world who will finally benefit from the suffering of the exiles. They had initially thought that the Israelites' suffering, personified by the servant's suffering, was hardly worth noticing. However, they have come to understand that the Israelites were suffering for the sins of the whole world, and through their suffering the whole world would come to know God. This is the hope that Isaiah is offering the exiles. Their suffering has a purpose in God's plan.

Notice that Israel and her suffering are compared to the suffering of a lamb that goes to the slaughter with complete silence. Once again, the image of a lamb is being placed before us. On Holy Thursday

Therefore I will give him his **portion** among the **great**,
and he shall divide the **spoils** with the **mighty**,
because he **surrendered** himself to **death**
and was **counted** among the **wicked**;
and he shall take away the **sins of many**,
and win **pardon** for their **offenses**.

READING II Hebrews 4:14–16; 5:7–9

Hebrews = HEE-brooz

A reading from the Letter to the Hebrews

Brothers and sisters:

The tone of this reading is one of reasoned persuasion.

Since we have a **great high priest** who has passed through the heavens,

Emphasize this line.

Jesus, the **Son of God**,
let us **hold fast** to our **confession**.
For we do **not** have a high priest
who is **unable** to **sympathize** with our **weaknesses**,
but one who has **similarly** been **tested** in **every way**,
yet **without sin**.

Increase your tempo and speak with confidence.
similarly = SIHM-ih-luhr-lee

So let us **confidently approach** the **throne** of **grace**
to receive **mercy** and to find **grace** for **timely help**.

Pause. The author is introducing a new point.
supplications = sup-lih-KAY-shuhnz

In the days when **Christ** was in the **flesh**,
he offered **prayers** and **supplications** with **loud cries** and **tears**
to the one who was **able** to **save him** from **death**,
and he was **heard** because of his **reverence**.

Emphasize this conclusion.

Son though he **was**, he learned **obedience** from what he **suffered**;
and when he was made **perfect**,
he became the **source** of **eternal salvation** for **all** who **obey** him.

Increase your volume. This is a proclamation of good news, explaining the source of our confidence and hope.

it was the sacrificed Passover lamb who foreshadowed Jesus, the Lamb of God. Today it is the suffering servant, the lamb who is led to the slaughter and remains silent, who foreshadows Jesus.

As the reading ends, it is once more God who speaks. God says, "My servant shall justify many." Second Isaiah was assuring the exiles in Babylon that their suffering would justify many. The Israelites are God's people. God is their God. Their present circumstances are not without hope, nor are they without purpose.

After the scandal of Jesus' Crucifixion and death, his disciples tried to make sense of it all. For a while, they were like the Israelites in exile in Babylon. Their faith was challenged, and they were full of questions: had they completely misunderstood? Was there any meaning to be found in this terrible unfolding of events?

The early Christians found a way to understand and express what they believed to have been accomplished through Jesus Christ by turning to the words of the prophets, especially Second Isaiah and his prophecies about the suffering servant.

In the context of our Good Friday observance, Jesus is understood to be the suffering servant. In Jesus, Second Isaiah's words have been fulfilled; they have taken on a fuller meaning. Through Jesus' suffering, death, and Resurrection, all nations have been redeemed. Through Jesus, all nations will come to know God and God's love for his people.

As you proclaim this reading, put the greatest emphasis on the lines that express the hope that Second Isaiah is offering the exiles about the purpose of their suffering: a) "by his stripes we were healed"; b) "the

PASSION John 18:1—19:42

The narrator's voice begins the story. This is background information.
Kidron = KID-ruhn

Judas = JOO-duhs

Pharisees = FAYR-uh-seez

Emphasize this line. It is claiming Jesus' divinity.
Jesus speaks with calm authority.
Nazarene = naz-uh-REEN
Emphasize "I AM." This is another claim of divinity.
Drop your voice.
Pause after this line.

Again, emphasize "I AM."

This is the narrator giving us background information. Lower your voice.
Simon = SĪ-muhn
Peter = PEE-ter
Malchus = MAL-kuhs

The Passion of our Lord Jesus Christ according to John

Jesus went out with his **disciples** across the **Kidron valley**
to where there was a **garden**,
into which **he** and his **disciples entered**.
Judas his **betrayer also** knew the place,
because **Jesus** had **often met there** with his **disciples**.
So **Judas** got a band of **soldiers** and **guards**
from the **chief priests** and the **Pharisees**
and went there with **lanterns**, **torches**, and **weapons**.
Jesus, **knowing everything** that was **going** to **happen** to him,
went out and said to them, "**Whom** are you **looking for**?"
They answered him, "**Jesus** the **Nazorean**."
He said to them, "**I AM**."
Judas his **betrayer** was also with them.
When he said to them, "**I AM**,"
they **turned away** and **fell** to the **ground**.
So he **again** asked them,
"**Whom** are you **looking** for?"
They said, "**Jesus** the **Nazorean**."
Jesus answered,
"I **told** you that **I AM**.
So if you are looking for **me**, let **these** men go."
This was to **fulfill** what he had **said**,
"I have not lost **any** of those you **gave** me."
Then **Simon Peter**, who had a **sword**, **drew** it,
struck the **high priest's slave**, and **cut off** his **right ear**.
The slave's name was **Malchus**.

will of the Lord shall be accomplished through him"; c) "through his suffering, my servant shall justify many"; and d) "He shall take away the sins of many, and win pardon for their offenses." All of these hopes have been fulfilled in Jesus Christ.

READING II The reading from Hebrews is also addressing the meaning and purpose of Jesus' suffering and death. Today's selection begins with an exhortation to remain faithful to Jesus Christ: "let us hold fast to our confession." To what confession is the author referring? To the confession that Jesus is "the Son of God" and that Jesus has risen from the dead, "has passed through the heavens."

By referring to Jesus as "a great high priest," the author compares Jesus to the Jewish priests in the temple who offered sacrifice to God on behalf of the people. Jesus, the great high priest, experienced the same kinds of temptations that we experience, but he never sinned. Therefore, Jesus is able to "sympathize with our weaknesses," and we can confidently approach God and receive mercy.

The Lectionary reading then skips several verses of Hebrews and centers our attention on Jesus' suffering on the night before he died. The author tells us that Jesus prayed fervently to be saved from death and that "he was heard because of his reverence."

As we know, Jesus did die. Why, then, does the author of Hebrews claim that Jesus was heard? Jesus was not saved from his death on the cross, but he was saved from eternal death. Jesus' death did not end in death, but in life. Jesus was made perfect through his suffering and

scabbard = SCA-b*rd
Jesus is correcting Peter, but privately.

Jesus said to **Peter**,
"**Put your sword** into its **scabbard**.
Shall I **not drink** the **cup** that the **Father gave me**?"

Again, the narrator takes up the story.

So the band of **soldiers**, the **tribune**, and the **Jewish guards**
seized Jesus,
bound him, and brought him to **Annas** first.

Annas = AN-uhs
Caiaphas = KĪ-uh-fuhs or KAY-uh-fuhs

He was the **father-in-law** of **Caiaphas**,
who was **high priest** that year.
It was **Caiaphas** who had counseled the Jews
that it was better that **one man** should **die** rather than
the **people**.

Pause here.
Emphasize "another disciple." This is the beloved disciple.

Simon Peter and **another disciple followed** Jesus.
Now the **other disciple** was **known** to the high priest,
and **he** entered the courtyard of the high priest **with Jesus**.
But **Peter** stood at the gate **outside**.
So the **other disciple**, the **acquaintance** of the **high priest**,
went out and spoke to the **gatekeeper** and brought **Peter in**.
Then the maid who was the **gatekeeper** said to **Peter**,

This is said with incredulity.

"**You** are **not** one of **this** man's **disciples**, are you?"

This is said with firmness.

He said, "**I am not**."

The narrator continues the story.

Now the **slaves** and the **guards** were standing around
a charcoal **fire**
that they had made, because it was **cold**,
and were **warming** themselves.
Peter was **also** standing there keeping **warm**.

The **high priest questioned** Jesus
about his **disciples** and about his **doctrine**.
Jesus answered him,

Jesus speaks with calm authority.

"**I have spoken publicly** to the **world**.

thus "became the source of eternal salvation for all who obey him."

The author of Hebrews is holding Jesus up as a model. Jesus, our great high priest, sinless as he was, obediently accepted suffering, and his suffering was not in vain. Jesus passed from death to life and has paved the way for us to follow. Jesus understands our weaknesses, so we should not be afraid to approach God and receive both mercy and eternal life.

The author of Hebrews intended this passage to be an exhortation to his audience. As a living word, proclaimed on Good Friday to your assembly, the passage is also an exhortation. The tone for the reading should be both confident and persuasive.

PASSION Every Good Friday we read John's account of Jesus' Passion and death. John's narrative differs in many respects from those in other Gospels. By noticing these differences and asking, "Why does John tell the story this way?" we will better understand both John's motive and message.

John's is the latest of our four accounts of the Gospel, having been written near the end of the first century AD to people who were asking, "Where is the risen Christ?" The expectation had been that Christ would return in glory on the clouds of heaven during the lifetime of Jesus' contemporaries. Events did not confirm that expectation. Throughout his account, John is trying to help his readers understand that the risen Christ is not absent, but present. Christ is present in the Church, and in what we have come to call the sacraments. We will see evidence of this emphasis in today's reading.

synagogue = SIN-uh-gog

I have **always** taught in a **synagogue**
or in the **temple area** where **all** the **Jews gather**,
and in **secret** I have said **nothing**. **Why ask me**?
Ask those who **heard** me what I said to them.
They **know** what I said."

The narrator is speaking; lower your voice.

When he had **said** this,
one of the **temple guards** standing there **struck** Jesus and said,

This is said with outrage.

"**Is this the way** you answer the **high priest**?"
Jesus answered him,

Again, Jesus is calm and in control.

"If I have spoken **wrongly**, testify to the **wrong**;
but if I have spoken **rightly**, why do you **strike** me?"

The narrator is speaking again.

Then **Annas** sent him bound to **Caiaphas** the **high priest**.

Now **Simon Peter** was standing there keeping **warm**.
And they said to him,

This is said with incredulity.

"**You** are not one of **his** disciples, are you?"
He denied it and said,

Emphasize every word.

"**I am not**."
One of the **slaves** of the high priest,
a **relative** of the one whose ear **Peter** had cut off, said,

He is quite sure of what he saw.

"Didn't I see **you** in the garden with **him**?"
Again Peter **denied** it.

This is tragic. Pause after this line.

And **immediately** the **cock crowed**.

The narrator continues the story.

Then they brought Jesus from **Caiaphas** to the **praetorium**.
It was **morning**.

praetorium = prih-TOHR-ee-uhm
Passover = PAS-oh-ver
Pilate = PĪ-luht

And they **themselves** did **not enter** the praetorium,
in order not to be **defiled** so that they could eat the **Passover**.
So **Pilate** came out to them and said,

Pilate initially speaks with great authority.

"**What charge** do you bring against **this man**?"
They answered and said to him,

This is said with great anger.

"If he were not a **criminal**,
we would not have handed him over to **you**."

Another unique aspect of John's account of the Gospel is its high Christology. That is, John emphasizes Jesus' divinity more than do the other Gospel writers. This is not to say that the Gospel accounts disagree on the subject of Jesus' divinity. They do not. However in John, the divinity is emphasized in ways different from the other accounts. We will see evidence of John's high Christology in the Good Friday reading.

As the reading begins, Jesus is in the garden. Notice that John does not describe Jesus as suffering agony in the garden and praying that this cup might pass from him. Rather, Jesus seems eager to complete the work he has been sent to do. Jesus says to Peter, "Shall I not drink the cup that the Father gave me?"

During the arrest scene, we see more evidence of Jesus' divinity. First, John's Jesus is all knowing. John describes Jesus as "knowing everything that was going to happen to him." Jesus' complete understanding of all that is occurring, that he has come from the Father and will be returning to the Father, is a consistent theme throughout the Gospel. Of course, only God is all-knowing, so to describe Jesus as all-knowing is to claim that Jesus is God.

In addition, when Jesus asks the arresting soldiers for whom they are looking and they reply, "Jesus the Nazarene," Jesus says, "I AM," which is an allusion to the name God revealed to Moses at the burning bush. Moses asked God, "If they [the Israelites] ask me, 'what is his [God's] name?' what am I to tell them? God replied, 'I am who am.' Then he added, 'This is

Pilate wants no part of their plans.

This is the narrator giving background information. Drop your voice.

Again, Pilate is in charge and speaks with authority.

Jesus is not threatened. He, not Pilate, is actually in charge.

Pilate is interested.

Say this line quietly and earnestly.

Say this line with great interest.

Say this slowly and with solemnity.

Pause after this profound question.

At **this**, Pilate said to them,
"Take him **yourselves**, and judge him according to **your** law."
The Jews answered him,
"We do not have the **right** to **execute anyone**,"
in order that the word of **Jesus** might be **fulfilled**
that he said indicating the kind of **death** he would **die**.
So **Pilate** went back into the **praetorium**
and summoned **Jesus** and **said** to him,
"Are you the **King of the Jews**?"
Jesus answered,
"Do you say this on your **own**
or have others **told you** about me?"
Pilate answered,
"**I** am not a **Jew**, am I?
Your **own nation** and the **chief priests** handed **you** over to **me**.
What have you **done**?"
Jesus answered,
"**My** kingdom does **not belong** to **this** world.
If my kingdom **did** belong to **this** world,
my attendants would be **fighting**
to keep me from being **handed over** to the Jews.
But as it **is**, **my** kingdom is **not here**."
So **Pilate** said to him,
"Then you **are** a king?"
Jesus answered,
"**You** say I am a **king**.
For this I was **born** and for this I came **into** the **world**,
to **testify** to the **truth**.
Everyone who belongs to the **truth** listens to **my** voice."
Pilate said to him, "**What is truth**?"

what you shall tell the Israelites: I AM sent me to you'" (Exodus 3:13b–14).

Indeed, the arresting soldiers react as if they have seen Jesus' divinity: when Jesus says "I AM," the soldiers "turned away and fell to the ground." After portraying this remarkable scene, John continues the story as though this had never happened. He doesn't even tell us that the soldiers got back up. This is John's way of enabling the reader to see Jesus' divinity even as Jesus is arrested.

John does not have Jesus appear before the Sanhedrin, the Jewish court. Rather, Jesus appears before the high priests: first Annas, and then Caiaphas. Throughout Jesus' testimony, both before the high priest and before Pilate, Jesus remains calm, in authority, and truthful. After being struck by the temple guard Jesus says, "If I have spoken rightly, why do you strike me?" When questioned by Pilate, Jesus says, "For this I was born and for this I came into the world, to testify to the truth." During these trial scenes, by emphasizing Jesus' truthfulness, John is reminding his readers of what Jesus had said earlier, at his last meal with the disciples: "I am the way and the truth and the life" (John 14:6).

Another unique aspect of John's passion narrative is the appearance of the beloved disciple. This unnamed person appears twice in today's reading, once when Jesus enters the courtyard of the high priest and again at the foot of the cross.

When he had **said** this,
he again went out to the **Jews** and said to them,
"**I find no guilt** in him.

Emphasize every word. This is a refrain.

But you have a **custom** that I release **one prisoner** to you at **Passover**.
Do you want me to release to you the **King of the Jews**?"
They cried out again,
"Not **this** one but **Barabbas**!"

The crowd is angry.

Now **Barabbas** was a **revolutionary**.

This is the narrator's comment.
Barabbas = buh-RAB-uhs
revolutionary = rev-uh-LOO-shun-ayr-ee
scourged = skerjd

Then **Pilate** took **Jesus** and had him **scourged**.
And the **soldiers** wove a **crown** out of **thorns** and placed it on his **head**,
and **clothed** him in a **purple cloak**,
and they **came** to him and said,
"**Hail, King of the Jews**!"

The soldiers are having a good time making fun of Jesus. They don't know that their words are true.

And they **struck** him **repeatedly**.
Once **more Pilate** went out and said to them,
"**Look**, I am bringing him **out** to you,
so that you may know that **I find no guilt in him**."

Emphasize every word of this refrain ("I find no guilt . . .").

So **Jesus** came **out**,
wearing the **crown** of **thorns** and the **purple cloak**.
And he said to them, "**Behold**, the **man**!"

This is said in a mocking way, not in a respectful way.

When the **chief priests** and the **guards** saw him they cried out,
"**Crucify him**, **crucify him**!"

This is said with anger.

Pilate said to them,
"Take him **yourselves** and crucify him.
I find no guilt in him."

Again, emphasize every word of this refrain.

The Jews answered,
"We have a **law**, and according to that **law** he ought to **die**,
because he made **himself** the **Son of God**."

This is said with anger and outrage.

When Jesus is taken to the high priest, John tells us that "Simon Peter and another disciple followed Jesus." This other disciple (the beloved disciple) enters the courtyard of the high priest and then uses his influence to get Peter inside the gate, too. It is at this time that Peter is questioned about his relationship with Jesus and denies being Jesus' disciple.

In every instance where the beloved disciple and Peter appear together—at the Last Supper, in the high priest's courtyard, at the empty tomb, and at the post Resurrection appearance by the Sea of Tiberius—the beloved disciple is shown to be closer to Jesus than Peter. Scripture scholars believe that John's community had become wary of authority, represented by Peter, and had put much more stress on charismatic gifts, represented by the beloved disciple. This is John's way of teaching that love is more important than law. Later in John's story, Peter, who denied Jesus, will be given authority only after he declares his love three times (John 21:15–17).

In John, it is morning when Jesus is brought from Caiaphas to the praetorium. Here John makes it very clear that Jesus dies, not after celebrating the Passover meal, as he does in Mark, Matthew, and Luke, but on the day that the Passover lambs are being slaughtered in preparation for the Passover meal. John tells us that those who brought Jesus to the praetorium did not enter the praetorium "in order not to be defiled so that they could eat the Passover." This is John's way of teaching that Jesus is the new Lamb of God who takes away the sins of the world.

Now when Pilate heard **this** statement,
he became **even more afraid**,
and went back into the **praetorium** and said to **Jesus**,

Pause here. John's audience knows that Jesus is from God.

"**Where** are you **from**?"
Jesus did **not answer** him.
So Pilate said to him,

Pilate is both fearful and in disbelief.

"Do you not speak to **me**?
Do you not **know** that I have power to **release** you
and I have power to **crucify** you?"
Jesus answered him,

Jesus is still calm and unperturbed.

"You would have **no power** over me
if it had not been **given** to you from **above**.
For **this reason** the one who handed me **over** to you
has the **greater sin**."

The narrator continues the story.

Consequently, Pilate tried to **release** him; but the Jews cried out,

The crowd is angry and demanding.

"If you **release** him, you are **not** a **Friend** of **Caesar**.
Everyone who makes **himself** a **king opposes Caesar**."
When Pilate heard **these** words he brought **Jesus** out
and seated him on the **judge's bench**

Gabbatha = GAB-uh-thuh

in the place called **Stone Pavement**, in **Hebrew**, **Gabbatha**.
It was **preparation** day for **Passover**, and it was about **noon**.
And he said to the Jews,

Pilate is mocking, not honoring Jesus.

"**Behold**, your **king**!"
They cried out,

Again, the crowd is angry and insistent.

"Take him **away**, take him **away**! **Crucify** him!"
Pilate said to them,

Say this line with irony.

"Shall I **crucify** your **king**?"
The chief priests answered,

Say this line with great adamancy.

"We have **no king** but **Caesar**."

Drop your voice here.

Then he handed him over to **them** to be **crucified**.

Indeed, this is how John the Baptist has identified Jesus before Jesus' public ministry even began (see John 1:29b, 36b).

John leaves no room for doubt that Jesus is completely innocent. Pilate repeatedly says, "I find no guilt in him," even as the charge against Jesus changes. At first those who accuse Jesus simply say that he is a "criminal." Later the Jews say "He made himself the Son of God," and then that Jesus claims to be a king. It is true that Jesus, in response to Pilate's questions, acknowledges that he is a king. However, he also makes it clear that his kingdom is not "of this world."

While Jesus remains faithful to the truth, and Pilate fails out of weakness rather than out of dishonesty, the chief priests fail to remain true to their own beliefs. They live in an occupied country. They once had their own king, but now have only their messianic hope, their hope that God will once again intervene in events and send someone to save them. But when Jesus is presented to them and Pilate asks, "Shall I crucify your king?" they reply, "We have no king but Caesar." They deny their own messianic hopes.

There is no Simon of Cyrene in John's account. Jesus, the divine person, does not need help. Nor is Jesus deserted by all who love him. In John, Jesus' mother, several other women, and the beloved disciple are all at the foot of the cross. Jesus' mother, like the beloved disciple, goes unnamed. This is because she, like the beloved disciple, functions not only as a person but as a symbol.

Read slowly and with sadness.

Golgotha = GOL-guh-thuh or GAWL-guh-thuh

So **they took** Jesus, and, **carrying** the **cross himself**,
he went out to what is called the **Place** of the **Skull**,
in **Hebrew**, **Golgotha**.
There they **crucified him**, and with him **two others**,
one on either **side**, with **Jesus** in the **middle**.
Pilate also had an **inscription** written and put on the **cross**.
It read,

Read this as a proclamation.

"**Jesus** the **Nazorean**, the **King** of the **Jews**."
Now many of the Jews **read** this inscription,
because the place where Jesus was crucified was near the **city**;
and it was written in **Hebrew**, **Latin**, and **Greek**.
So the **chief priests** of the Jews said to **Pilate**,

The chief priests are ingratiating.

"Do not write '**The King** of the **Jews**,'
but that he **said**, 'I am the King of the Jews.'"
Pilate answered,

Pilate is fed up with the chief priests.

"What I have **written**, I have **written**."

Now the narrator speaks again.

When the soldiers had **crucified** Jesus,
they took his **clothes** and **divided** them into **four shares**,
a share for **each soldier**.
They also took his **tunic**, but the tunic was **seamless**,
woven **in one piece** from the **top down**.
So they **said** to one another,

The soldiers have no sense of tragedy. They are going about their business. Drop your voice here.

"Let's not **tear** it, but cast **lots** for it to see **whose** it will be,"
in order that the passage of **Scripture** might be **fulfilled**
that says:
They divided my ***garments*** *among them,*
and for my ***vesture*** *they cast* ***lots***.

Say this with sadness. Then pause.

This is what the soldiers ***did***.
Standing by the **cross** of Jesus were his **mother**
and his mother's sister, **Mary** the wife of **Clopas**,
and **Mary of Magdala**.

Clopas = KLEE-oh-puhs

Magdala = MAG-duh-luh

Jesus' mother appears twice in John's account: here, at the foot of the cross and earlier, at the wedding feast of Cana. Both times, Jesus addresses her as "Woman." This is one of many allusions to Genesis (the Gospel according to John and Genesis begin with identical words). In John, Jesus' mother becomes a symbol for the Church. She is the new Eve, the mother of all the living in the new spiritual order. That is why Jesus says to the beloved disciple: "Behold your mother." The Church is the mother of Jesus' disciples.

In John's account, Jesus does not call out, "My God, my God, why have you forsaken me?" as he does in Mark and Matthew's accounts (Mark 15:34; Matthew 27:46). After commending his mother and the beloved disciples to each other he says "I thirst," and then, "It is finished." John tells us that Jesus said "I thirst" in "order that the Scripture might be fulfilled." However, John does not tell us what Scripture is being fulfilled. Scripture scholars suggest that this is an allusion either to Psalm 22 or to Psalm 69.

Psalm 22 describes the suffering psalmist as saying, "As dry as a potsherd is my throat; / my tongue sticks to my palate; / you lay me in the dust of death" (Psalm 22:16). In Psalm 69 the psalmist is also suffering severe persecution and says, "Instead they put gall in my food; / for my thirst they gave me vinegar" (Psalm 69:22).

Notice that the sponge soaked in wine is lifted up to Jesus on "a sprig of hyssop." When Moses repeats the Passover instructions that he had received from God to the elders of Israel (see the Holy Thursday reading), he tells them to "take a bunch

Read Jesus' words slowly and clearly.

When Jesus saw his **mother** and the **disciple** there whom he **loved**
he said to his **mother**, "**Woman**, **behold**, your **son**."
Then he said to the **disciple**,
"**Behold**, your **mother**."
And from **that hour** the **disciple** took **her** into his **home**.

Pause here.

After **this**, aware that **everything** was now **finished**,
in order that the **Scripture** might be **fulfilled**,
Jesus said, "**I thirst**."

Jesus still speaks with authority.

There was a vessel filled with **common wine**.
So they put a **sponge** soaked in **wine** on a sprig of **hyssop**
and put it up to his **mouth**.

Emphasize hyssop; hyssop = HIS-uhp

When **Jesus** had taken the **wine**, he said,
"**It is finished**."
And **bowing** his head, he **handed over** the **spirit**.

Emphasize every word.
Speak slowly and with great solemnity.

Here all kneel and pause for a short time.

Speak more quickly here.

Now since it was **preparation** day,
in order that the bodies might not remain
on the **cross** on the **sabbath**,
for the **sabbath day** of that week was a **solemn one**,
the Jews asked **Pilate** that their **legs** be broken
and that they be **taken down**.
So the **soldiers** came and broke the **legs** of the **first**
and then of the **other** one who was **crucified** with Jesus.
But when they came to **Jesus** and saw that he was **already dead**,
they did **not break** his **legs**,
but one soldier thrust his **lance** into his **side**,
and **immediately blood** and **water flowed out**.

Say this with great conviction.

An eyewitness has **testified**, and his testimony is **true**;
he knows that he is speaking the **truth**,
so that **you also** may come to **believe**.

of hyssop, and dipping it in the blood that is in the basin, sprinkle the lintel and the two doorposts with this blood" (Exodus 12:22). By specifying hyssop, John is once more reminding us that Jesus is the new Passover lamb.

Jesus' final words are, "It is finished." He had come to earth from his Father to accomplish his Father's will. Now Jesus is returning to his Father. He has completed his work: "It is finished." Even in death Jesus is not a helpless victim. Rather, "bowing his head, he handed over the spirit."

As John tells us about what happened immediately after Jesus dies he continues to teach us that Jesus is the new Passover lamb whose blood gives life, and that the risen Christ remains present with us in the Church and in the sacraments. When Jesus' body is removed from the cross, the soldiers do not break his bones. This is once more an allusion to the Passover lamb. The Israelites, when eating the Passover lamb, were not to break any of its bones (Numbers 9:12).

However, one soldier stuck his lance in Jesus' side "and immediately blood and water flowed out." This is John's allegorical way of teaching that with Jesus' death the Church was born. Water and blood symbolize Baptism and Eucharist, the ways in which John's audience comes into relationship with the risen Christ. John's audience wants to know, "Where is Christ?" John is teaching them that Christ is in their midst.

Joseph of Arimathea then comes and asks for Jesus' body. Nicodemus is also present. We are reminded that Nicodemus

For this happened so that the **Scripture passage** might
be **fulfilled**:
*Not a **bone** of it will be **broken**.*
And again another passage says:
*They will look upon **him** whom they have **pierced**.*

The narrator's voice concludes the story.
Arimathea = ayr-ih-muh-THEE-uh

After this, **Joseph** of **Arimathea**,
secretly a **disciple** of Jesus for fear of the Jews,
asked Pilate if he could **remove** the **body** of Jesus.
And Pilate **permitted** it.
So he **came** and **took** his body.

Nicodemus = nik-oh-DEE-muhs
myrrh = mer; aloes = AL-ohz
This is amazing—a great extravagance.

Nicodemus, the one who had first come to him at **night**,
also came bringing a mixture of **myrrh** and **aloes**
weighing about **one hundred pounds**.
They took the **body** of **Jesus**
and bound it with **burial cloths** along with the **spices**,
according to the **Jewish burial custom**.
Now in the place where he had been **crucified** there was a **garden**,
and in the **garden** a **new tomb**, in which **no one** had yet
been **buried**.
So they **laid Jesus there** because of the **Jewish preparation** day;
for the **tomb** was **close by**.

is the one who had earlier come to Jesus at night. That was, of course, before Nicodemus realized that Jesus is the light of the world. Nicodemus is no longer in the dark. We know Nicodemus now realizes that Jesus is a king because he treats him as one would a king: he brings 100 pounds of myrrh and aloes with which to anoint Jesus. Joseph and Nicodemus carefully bind Jesus' body and place it in a new tomb in a nearby garden.

John's story of Jesus' Passion and death begins and ends in a garden. However, this garden story is in great contrast to the story of the garden that we read in Genesis. In John's garden, Jesus, a divine person, heals the divisions caused by human sin. Even as Jesus is buried, we know that Jesus, the pre-existent word, has returned to his Father. He has not left us orphans. Rather, he has "handed over the spirit," and remains in our midst.

As you read John's passion narrative, try to enter into the feelings of each of the characters: Peter, weak and fearful; the high priests, angry and accusing; Pilate, initially assertive with the crowd, but then giving in to their demands; Jesus' accusers, unreasonable and insistent; and Jesus, through it all, calm, purposeful, and truthful—a king whose glory shines through despite his terrible circumstances. Even as he tells the story of Jesus' Passion and death, John wants us to see a triumphant and present Christ. In the light of the Resurrection, John knows that what he is teaching is true, and that Jesus came to reveal that truth.

EASTER VIGIL

Lectionary #41

READING I Genesis 1:1—2:2

A reading from the Book of Genesis

The narrator's voice begins the story.

abyss = uh-BIS

In the **beginning**, when God created the **heavens** and the **earth**,
the earth was a **formless wasteland**, and **darkness covered** the **abyss**,
while a **mighty wind swept** over the **waters**.

Emphasize every one of God's words.
Drop your voice when the narrator speaks.

Then God said,
"**Let there be light**," and there **was** light.
God saw how **good** the light was.
God then separated the **light** from the **darkness**.
God called the **light** "**day**," and the **darkness** he called "**night**."
Thus **evening** came, and **morning** followed—the **first day**.

Pause here.

Read God's words as a proclamation.

Now, the narrator is speaking again.

Then God said,
"Let there be a **dome** in the **middle** of the **waters**,
to separate **one** body of water from the **other**."
And so it **happened**:
God made the **dome**,
and it separated the water **above** the dome from the water **below** it.
God called the **dome** "the **sky**."
Evening came, and **morning** followed—the **second day**.

Pause again.

Again, God proclaims.

Then God said,
"Let the **water under** the sky be gathered into a **single basin**,
so that the **dry land** may appear."
And so it **happened**:

READING I The Easter Vigil cannot be celebrated until after dark. As we gather in the dark to prepare to celebrate the Resurrection of the Lord, we recall many of the great stories of our ancestors in the faith, starting with the creation story in Genesis, in which God first creates light.

This story is obviously not trying to teach us anything of a scientific nature. We know that immediately because there are three days before there is a sun. A day, after all, is measured by the movement of the earth on its own axis in relation to the sun. In addition, the author, like his contemporaries, presumes that the earth is flat and that it has a dish over it, a dome in the sky. For centuries people believed that the earth was flat. This mistaken presumption does not make for good science, but it does not affect in any way the inspired author's insights and teachings on the subject he is addressing.

Neither does this story purport to be teaching history. Historical writing, by definition, is about events that have been witnessed and about which we have oral or written traditions. In today's story, human beings are not created until the sixth day. There is no one to witness what occurs on the first five days. Rather than an historical story, we have an imaginative and symbolic story that is teaching something very important about our origins.

Creation stories are rooted in universal experience, not in one specific historic event. The experience behind this story is that everything exists. Where did it all come from? The author is not interested in situating all of creation, and especially

This is now a refrain. Emphasize "happened."

This, too, is now a refrain. Emphasize "good."

Once more God proclaims.

Emphasize "happened."

Emphasize "good."

Pause again.

Say this with majesty.

luminaries = LOO-mih-nayr-eez

Emphasize "happened." God speaks and things happen.

the water **under** the sky was gathered into **its** basin,
and the **dry land appeared**.
God called the **dry land** "the **earth**,"
and the **basin** of the water he called "the **sea**."
God saw how **good** it was.
Then God said,
"Let the earth bring forth **vegetation**:
every kind of **plant** that bears **seed**
and **every kind** of **fruit tree** on **earth**
that bears **fruit** with its **seed** in it."
And so it **happened**:
the earth brought forth **every kind** of **plant** that bears **seed**
and **every kind** of **fruit tree** on **earth**
that bears **fruit** with its **seed** in it.
God saw how **good** it was.
Evening came, and **morning** followed—the **third day**.

Then God said:
"Let there be **lights** in the **dome** of the **sky**,
to separate **day** from **night**.
Let them mark the **fixed times**, the **days** and the **years**,
and serve as **luminaries** in the **dome** of the **sky**,
to shed **light** upon the **earth**."
And so it **happened**:
God made the **two great lights**,
the **greater** one to govern the **day**,
and the **lesser** one to govern the **night**;
and he made the **stars**.
God set them in the **dome** of the **sky**,
to shed **light** upon the **earth**,
to govern the **day** and the **night**,
and to separate the **light** from the **darkness**.
God saw how **good** it was.

human beings, in an historical or scientific context, but in a spiritual and moral context. The author asks such core questions as, "Who is God?", "Who are we?" and, most especially, "Who are we in relationship to God?" Because complete answers to these questions are beyond our comprehension, the author uses images and symbols to probe mystery. In doing so, he teaches both his original audience and us some universal truths.

What is the story teaching? A little more knowledge about the social setting of the original author and audience will help us answer this question. Scripture scholars think that this first story in Genesis is one of the later stories to develop in the Old Testament. It dates to the time after the Babylonian exile (587–537 BC) when the Israelites were rebuilding their temple and reestablishing themselves in the Holy Land.

While in Babylon, the Israelites had been exposed to many beliefs that completely contradicted the beliefs of their ancestors. Through this story the author was reaffirming long held truths that had been challenged during the Israelites' time in Babylon. The story was then placed at the front of the Israelites' existing faith narrative as a preface to all that follows.

The Babylonians believed in many gods, and that the sun and moon were gods. In this story one God creates all that exists, including the sun, the moon, and the stars. The sun and moon are not gods but material things that the one God created. The sun and moon do not rule human beings. Rather, they measure the night and the day.

Emphasize "good."

Pause after each day.

Emphasize "abundance."
abundance = uh-BUHN-duhntz
Emphasize "happened."

Continue to emphasize the words that stress abundance.

winged = wingd or WING-*d

Continue to emphasize "good." This refrain is central to the author's message.

Again, the author is describing abundance.

Emphasize "all kinds" all three times.

This line is important. Read slowly and solemnly.

Again, this is vital. Read these three lines slowly.

Evening came, and **morning** followed—the **fourth** day.
Then God said,
"Let the **water teem** with an **abundance** of **living creatures**,
and on the **earth** let **birds fly** beneath the **dome** of the **sky**."
And so it **happened**:
God created the **great sea monsters**
and **all kinds** of **swimming** creatures with which
the **water teems**,
and **all kinds** of **winged birds**.
God saw how **good** it was, and God **blessed** them, saying,
"Be **fertile**, **multiply**, and **fill** the **water** of the **seas**;
and let the **birds multiply** on the **earth**."
Evening came, and **morning** followed—the **fifth day**.
Then God said,
"Let the **earth bring forth all kinds** of **living creatures**:
cattle, **creeping** things, and **wild animals** of **all kinds**."
And so it **happened**:
God made **all kinds** of **wild animals**, all **kinds** of **cattle**,
and **all kinds** of **creeping things** of the **earth**.
God saw how **good** it was.
Then God said:
"Let us make **man** in our **image**, after **our likeness**.
Let them have **dominion** over the **fish** of the **sea**,
the **birds** of the **air**, and the **cattle**,
and over **all** the **wild animals**
and **all** the **creatures** that **crawl** on the **ground**."
God created **man** in **his image**;
in the **image** of **God** he **created** him;
male and **female** he **created** them.

The Babylonians believed that spirit was good, but matter was not. This story emphasizes over and over the goodness of the whole material world that God has created. After every day, God comments on just how good creation is. On the sixth day, the day on which God creates human beings, God looks at everything that God has made and finds it "very good."

In the Babylonian story of creation, human beings are made out of the corpse of a rebellious and defeated God. In the Genesis story, human beings, male and female, are made in the image of a loving and creative God. Human beings are, therefore, people of great dignity. Indeed, God gives them dominion over the rest of God's creation. Because they are created in God's own image, human beings have the potential to become loving people themselves. They are to use the dominion delegated to them by God not to exploit, but to nurture all that God has made and entrusted to their care.

While in Babylon the Israelites may well have failed to observe the Sabbath. The Babylonians did not observe the Sabbath, nor did the Israelites have their temple. The author teaches the returned exiles the importance of returning to this practice by showing that even God observed the Sabbath after the labor of creating the world.

Because the author is teaching that all of creation is God's work, he structures his story around a work week. On three days God divides things: light from darkness, water above the dome from water beneath the dome, and water from dry land under the dome. Then, in three days God populates that which God has divided: the

Now increase your tempo.

God **blessed** them, saying:
"Be **fertile** and **multiply**;
fill the **earth** and **subdue** it.

dominion = doh-MIN-yuhn

Have **dominion** over the **fish** of the **sea**, the **birds** of the **air**,
and **all** the **living things** that **move** on the **earth**."
God also said:

Emphasize "every" and "all." "All" is repeated five times.

"**See**, I give you **every seed-bearing plant all over** the **earth**
and **every tree** that has **seed-bearing fruit** on it to be your **food**;
and to **all** the animals of the land, **all** the birds of the air,
and **all** the living creatures that crawl on the ground,
I give **all** the green plants for food."
And so it **happened**.

Emphasize "very good." The refrain has been altered to emphasize just how good all of creation is.

God looked at **everything** he had made, and he found it **very good**.
Evening came, and **morning** followed—the **sixth day**.

Thus the **heavens** and the **earth** and **all** their **array**
were **completed**.

Emphasize "work." Creation is God's work.

Since on the **seventh** day God was **finished**
with the **work** he had been **doing**,
he **rested** on the **seventh** day from **all** the **work** he had
undertaken.

[Shorter Form: Genesis 1:1, 26–31a]

sun, moon, and stars go into the sky, fish fill the oceans, and birds fill the sky, and, finally, animals and human beings fill the dry land on the earth. After finishing all that work, God rests on the Sabbath, just as the Israelites should do.

What does the story teach? It teaches the returned exiles, and us, that there is one loving God who created all that exists, that all creation is good, especially human beings who are made in God's own image, and that the Israelites should observe the Sabbath. As you proclaim this reading, notice the refrains that reinforce the messages, especially the: "God saw how good it was." All of creation, especially humankind, is very good.

READING II Our Second Reading is the troubling story of the sacrifice of Isaac. Few people read this story without asking: "Why would God ask Abraham to sacrifice Isaac in the first place?" Once again, our Catholic approach to scripture, taking into consideration the kind of writing we are reading and the social context of the original author and audience, will help us understand just what this story is teaching.

The stories about Abraham are legends. A legend is neither fiction nor history. It is an imaginative story with an historical core. Abraham, the first character in the Bible to fall within the bounds of history, lived around 1850 BC. The stories that we have about Abraham rest on oral tradition. As they were told, generation after generation, they changed to meet the needs of successive generations. They took on new details and even changed in

READING II Genesis 22:1–18

Emphasize this first line. This is the narrator's interpretation of the story that follows.

Abraham = AY-bruh-ham

Abraham is eager to respond to the Lord.

Say God's words softly. God knows that this is terrible news for Abraham.

Isaac = Ī-zik

Moriah = moh-RĪ-uh

Now, the narrator is speaking. This is sad and mysterious.

saddled = SAD-ld

Abraham is not lying. He is walking in faith and speaking with calm assurance.

The narrator continues the story.

holocaust = HOL-uh-kawst or HOH-luh-kawst

Emphasize "son Isaac's shoulders." This foreshadows Jesus.

Emphasize "son." It will be repeated.

Isaac is excited and innocent. He has no sense of tragedy.

Abraham says this with great faith.

A reading from the Book of Genesis

God put **Abraham** to the **test**.
He called to him, "**Abraham**!"
"**Here** I **am**," he replied.
Then God said:
"Take your **son Isaac**, your **only one**, whom you **love**,
and go to the land of **Moriah**.
There you shall **offer** him **up** as a **holocaust**
on a **height** that I will **point out** to you."
Early the next morning Abraham **saddled** his **donkey**,
took with him his **son Isaac** and **two** of his **servants** as well,
and **with** the **wood** that he had **cut** for the **holocaust**,
set out for the place of which **God** had told him.

On the **third day Abraham** got **sight** of the place from **afar**.
Then he said to his **servants**:
"**Both** of **you stay here** with the **donkey**,
while the **boy** and I go on over **yonder**.
We will **worship** and then come **back** to you."
Thereupon Abraham took the **wood** for the **holocaust**
and laid it on his **son Isaac's shoulders**, while he **himself** carried the **fire** and the **knife**. As the two walked on **together**,
Isaac spoke to his father **Abraham**:
"**Father**!" Isaac said.
"**Yes**, **son**," he replied.
Isaac continued, "**Here** are the **fire** and the **wood**,
but **where is** the **sheep** for the **holocaust**?"
"**Son**," Abraham answered,
"**God himself** will **provide** the **sheep** for the **holocaust**."

focus. What the story taught to Abraham's contemporaries might be very different than what the story taught 500 years later. We see evidence of this fact in the story that finally became canonical and which we proclaim today.

If we had been contemporary with Abraham, we undoubtedly would have heard this story as one that illustrates how Abraham grew beyond a belief of his time—that God desired child sacrifice. Abraham is our very first ancestor in the faith. He lived in the Canaanite culture. In that culture, child sacrifice was not only accepted, but expected.

We know from earlier accounts in Genesis that Abraham had a very profound and personal experience of God. At that time, God had made a promise to Abraham that is restated in today's reading: "All the nations of the earth shall find blessing" in Abraham (see Genesis 12:3b). The fulfillment of this promise rested on Abraham having descendants. However, Abraham's wife, Sarah, was barren. We read about the promise that Sarah will have a son in Genesis 18, and about Sarah's giving birth to Isaac in Genesis 21. These earlier readings are necessary background information to our understanding of today's reading. How could God possibly ask Abraham to sacrifice Isaac when the fulfillment of God's covenant promises to Abraham depends on Isaac's survival?

Today's story pictures Abraham as faithful and obedient, and, at the same time, always confident that Isaac will not be killed. When Abraham and Isaac take leave of Abraham's servants, Abraham tells his servants that "we [Abraham and Isaac] will

Then the **two continued going forward.**

When they came to the **place** of which **God** had **told** him,
Abraham built an **altar** there and **arranged** the **wood** on it.

The narrator continues to build dread and suspense in the listeners.

Next he **tied up** his **son** Isaac,
and put him on **top** of the **wood** on the **altar.**
Then he **reached out** and **took** the **knife** to **slaughter** his **son.**
But the LORD's **messenger called** to him from **heaven,**
"**Abraham, Abraham!**"

This is said with urgency.

"**Here** I **am,**" he answered.

Abraham is calm. These are the same words he used in response to God's call.

"Do **not** lay your **hand** on the **boy,**" said the messenger.
"Do **not** do the **least thing** to him.

The messenger speaks with authority.

I **know** now how **devoted you** are to **God,**
since you **did not withhold** from **me** your **own beloved son.**"

As **Abraham** looked **about,**
he spied a **ram** caught by its **horns** in the **thicket.**
So he **went** and **took** the **ram**
and offered **it** up as a **holocaust** in **place** of his **son.**

Now the narrator is speaking. Lower your volume.

Abraham **named** the site **Yahweh-yireh;**
hence people now say, "**On the mountain** the LORD **will see.**"

Yahweh-yireh = YAH=way-YEER-ay

Again the LORD's **messenger** called to **Abraham** from **heaven**
and said:
"**I swear** by **myself,** declares the LORD,
that because you **acted** as you **did**
in **not withholding** from **me** your **beloved son,**

Again, the messenger speaks with great authority.

I will **bless** you **abundantly**
and make **your descendants** as **countless**
as the **stars** of the **sky** and the **sands** of the **seashore;**

Fill your voice with joy. This is great good news.

worship and then come back to you." When Isaac asks Abraham where the sheep for the holocaust is, Abraham responds with confidence that "God himself will provide the sheep for the holocaust." Abraham is not lying. Abraham is confident that God will keep his earlier promises.

Originally, then, this story was an imaginative dramatization of an internal dilemma: Even though Abraham's culture demanded child sacrifice, Abraham came to know a loving God who obviously did not desire child sacrifice. Abraham, confident in this knowledge, has the courage to grow beyond the understanding of his culture regarding this terrible practice. Years after Abraham, around 1250 BC, Abrahams' insight became part of the Israelites' law. The first fruits of human beings are not to be sacrificed, but are to be redeemed (see Exodus 13:11–14).

Once Israel no longer practiced child sacrificed, the story continued to be told through the generations. However, instead of being primarily about child sacrifice, the story became one about faithful trust and obedience to God. Abraham became the example of a person who walked in faith under the most difficult circumstances. Today's reading highlights this later focus on Abraham as an example of faith by beginning: "God put Abraham to the test."

Later generations, including ours, may not have to agonize over whether or not God desires child sacrifice, but each generation has to walk in love and trust, seeking to do God's will in the face of cultural expectations that are contrary to God's will. Abraham acts as the model of a

Say this with solemnity and awe. This is the core of God's covenant with his people.

descendants = dih-SEN-d*nts

your descendants shall take **possession**
of the **gates** of their **enemies**,
and in **your descendants all** the **nations** of the **earth** shall
find **blessing**—
all this because **you obeyed my command**."

[Shorter Form: Genesis 22:1–2, 9a, 10–13, 15–18]

READING III Exodus 14:15—15:1

Exodus = EK-suh-duhs

A reading from the Book of Exodus

God is empowering Moses, encouraging him to be a leader and act with authority.

Moses = MOH-ziz or MOH-zis

Israelites = IZ-ree-uh-lītz or IZ-ray-uh-lītz

The **LORD** said to **Moses**, "Why are you **crying out** to **me**?
Tell the **Israelites** to **go forward**.
And **you**, lift up your **staff** and, with **hand outstretched**
over the **sea**,
split the **sea in two**,
that the **Israelites** may **pass through it** on **dry land**.

God is assuring Moses that he need not fear the Egyptians.

Egyptians = ee-JIP-shuhnz

obstinate = OB-stih-nit

But I will make the **Egyptians** so **obstinate**
that they will go in **after** them.
Then I will receive **glory** through **Pharaoh** and **all** his **army**,
his **chariots** and **charioteers**.

Pharoah = FAYR-oh

Say, "I am the Lord," slowly and with authority.

The **Egyptians** shall **know** that **I am** the **Lord**,
when I receive **glory** through **Pharaoh**
and his **chariots** and **charioteers**."

charioteers = chayr-ee-uh-TEERZ

Now the narrator is speaking. At first we are given background information.

The **angel** of **God**, who had been **leading Israel's camp**,
now moved and went around **behind** them.

person who trusted in God's love and God's providence no matter how difficult the circumstances.

As you proclaim this reading, give special attention to the way you read the lines attributed to Abraham. Try to convey Abraham's complete trust in God's love from his first wholehearted response, "Here I am," to his words to Isaac, "God himself will provide the sheep for the holocaust." It is this faith and trust that we are called to emulate.

READING III Today's Third Reading describes the miraculous escape of the Israelites from slavery in Egypt. This story also has the characteristics of a legend. Although an historic event rests at its core, the storyteller feels perfectly free to include imaginative details in his account in order to teach his audience what he believes to be true. Both Jews and Christians believe that what the author intended to teach is true and foundational, and so it has an honored place in the canons of both traditions.

What core truth is the author teaching? This truth is stated very clearly as today's reading concludes: because the Israelites had a first hand experience of God's mighty, saving power, they "believed in him [the Lord] and in his servant Moses."

The Exodus experience, the experience of escaping from slavery in Egypt, is core to the self identity of the Israelites. The only explanation they could come up with to explain such an unbelievable turn of events was that God had intervened on their behalf. God was being faithful to the promises made to Abraham. Abraham's

column = KOL-uhm

The column of **cloud also**, **leaving** the **front**,
took up its place **behind** them,
so that it came **between** the camp of the **Egyptians**
and that of **Israel**.

Say this in a lowered tone.

But the **cloud** now became **dark**, and thus the **night passed**
without the **rival camps** coming **any closer together**
all night long.

At this point the story becomes marvelous. Raise your volume and speak with awe.

Then **Moses stretched** out his **hand** over the **sea**,
and the **LORD swept** the sea
with a **strong east wind throughout** the **night**
and so **turned** it into **dry land**.
When the **water** was thus **divided**,

Read with a slow pace and a victorious tone.

the **Israelites marched into** the **midst** of the **sea** on **dry land**,
with the **water** like a **wall** to their **right** and to their **left**.

Now increase your speed.

The **Egyptians followed** in **pursuit**;
all Pharaoh's **horses** and **chariots** and **charioteers**
went **after** them
right into the **midst** of the **sea**.

Now drop both your volume and your speed.

In the **night watch** just before **dawn**
the **LORD cast** through the column of the fiery cloud
upon the **Egyptian** force a **glance** that **threw** it into a **panic**;
and he so **clogged** their **chariot wheels**
that they could **hardly drive**.

Emphasize "Israel" and "them."

With **that** the **Egyptians sounded** the **retreat** before **Israel**,
because the **LORD** was fighting for **them** against the **Egyptians**.

God is not only instructing but encouraging Moses.

Then the **LORD** told **Moses**, "**Stretch out** your **hand over** the sea,
that the **water** may **flow back** upon the **Egyptians**,
upon their **chariots** and their **charioteers**."

The narrator is speaking. Again, this is marvelous.

So **Moses stretched** out his **hand** over the **sea**,
and at **dawn** the **sea** flowed **back** to its **normal depth**.

descendents were returning to the land that God had promised them.

The story of God's saving intervention was celebrated with the yearly Passover ritual, and the story was told from generation to generation. In today's reading we can see that several accounts of the story have been combined, because one storyteller adds imaginative details to make his point that another storyteller omits.

For instance, if we were to ask, "Exactly how did God intervene in events to save the Israelites?" we would find that today's reading gives us two different answers. One author tells us that God intervened through wind and tide: "the Lord swept the sea with a strong east wind throughout the night and so turned it into dry land." Another author gives Moses a more dramatic role. God tells Moses to lift up his staff and, "with hand outstretched over the sea, split the sea in two." Moses does as he is directed, and the sea does indeed split in two, "with the water like a wall to their right and to their left."

Scripture scholars believe that, over the years, several stories about this absolutely crucial and powerful experience developed. Later editors combined the stories rather than choosing between them. However, each author is teaching exactly the same thing. It was the Lord who "saved Israel on that day from the power of the Egyptians." It is this truth that we are remembering and affirming and that should be emphasized as the reading is proclaimed at the Easter Vigil.

READING IV In the Third Reading, the Israelites were escaping from slavery in Egypt (1250 BC) so that they could return to the land of their ancestors.

Increase your speed here.
hurled = herld
This is good news from Israel's point of view.

The **Egyptians** were **fleeing head on** toward the **sea**,
when the Lord **hurled** them **into** its **midst**.
As the **water flowed back**,
it **covered** the **chariots** and the **charioteers**
of **Pharaoh's whole army**
which had followed the **Israelites** into the **sea**.
Not a **single one** of them **escaped**.

Again, a triumphant tone is appropriate here.

But the **Israelites** had marched on **dry land**
through the **midst** of the sea,
with the **water** like a **wall** to their **right** and to their **left**.
Thus the **Lord saved Israel** on **that day**
from the **power of** the **Egyptians**.

Lower your volume and decrease your speed. This is the narrator drawing a lesson from the marvelous events.

When **Israel** saw the **Egyptians** lying **dead** on the **seashore**
and beheld the **great power** that the **Lord**
had shown **against** the **Egyptians**,
they **feared** the **Lord** and **believed** in **him**
and in his **servant Moses**.

Then **Moses** and the **Israelites** sang **this song** to the **Lord**:

This is said with great gratitude and joy.
triumphant = trī-UHM-f*nt

I will **sing** to the **Lord**, for he is **gloriously triumphant**;
horse and **chariot** he has **cast** into the **sea**.

READING IV Isaiah 54:5–14

Isaiah = ī-ZAY-uh

A reading from the Book of the Prophet Isaiah

Isaiah's tone is one of comfort and hope.
Emphasize "Lord of hosts."
Israel = IZ-ree-uhl or IZ-ray-uhl
Emphasize "God of all the earth."

The **One** who has become your **husband** is your **Maker**;
his name is the **Lord** of **hosts**;
your **redeemer** is the **Holy One** of **Israel**,
called **God** of **all** the **earth**.

God had intervened and kept the promises to Abraham. The Fourth Reading is from Second Isaiah, a prophet to the exiles in Babylon (587–537 BC). What has happened in the interval between the events described in these two readings?

After settling the holy land and becoming a united kingdom under King David (1000 bc), the Israelites were unable to maintain either their unity or their kingdom. First, they split into two kingdoms: Israel in the north and Judah in the south. Then, Israel was conquered by the Assyrians, and later, Judah was conquered by the Babylonians. All of the upper-class Israelites were forced into exile in Babylon. Their land was ravaged, their temple was destroyed, and their capitol, Jerusalem, was abandoned.

The people had understood their king, their kingdom, and their temple to be the external signs of their covenant relationship with God, a covenant that God had made with Abraham and renewed with Moses. The people were left asking, "Where are God and God's promises now?"

As our reading begins, the prophet is the speaker, and he is addressing Jerusalem, the holy city. Because Jerusalem has been abandoned and ravaged, the prophet compares her to a wife who has been cast off. First, the prophet assures Jerusalem that God, who is her maker, is also her redeemer. This redeemer, "the Holy One of Israel," is God not only of Jerusalem but of "all the earth." God's covenant relationship with Jerusalem is not over. Rather, God is using events to call Jerusalem back to faithful covenant love.

This is wonderful news.
grieved = GREEVD
abandoned = uh-BAN-duhnd
Now God is speaking. Read the "brief moment" quickly, the "great tenderness" line slowly.

Read quickly.

Read slowly.

God is explaining his reasons for no longer being angry.
Noah = NOH-ah
deluge = DEL-ooj or DEL-oozh or duh-LOOJ

This is a solemn promise.

This is what the exiles need to hear.
covenant = KUHV-eh-n*nt
unconsoled = uhn-kuhn-SOHL*D
This is extravagant love, indeed.
antimony = AN-tih-moh-nee
carnelians = kahr-NEEL-yuhnz
sapphires = SAF-īrz
rubies = ROO-beez
pinnacles = PIN-uh-k*lz
carbuncles = KAHR-bung-k*lz
This is wonderful news.

Speak with great confidence. This is a promise.

The LORD calls you **back**,
like a **wife forsaken** and **grieved** in **spirit**,
a wife **married** in **youth** and then **cast off**,
says **your God**.
For a **brief moment I abandoned** you,
but with **great tenderness** I will **take** you **back**.
In an outburst of **wrath**, for a **moment**
I **hid** my **face** from you;
but with **enduring love** I take **pity** on you,
says the **LORD**, your **redeemer**.
This is for **me** like the days of **Noah**,
when I swore that the **waters** of **Noah**
should **never again deluge** the **earth**;
so I have **sworn not** to be **angry** with you,
or to **rebuke** you.
Though the **mountains** leave their **place**
and the **hills** be **shaken**,
my love shall **never leave you**
nor my **covenant** of **peace** be **shaken**,
says the **LORD**, who has **mercy** on **you**.
O **afflicted one**, **storm-battered** and **unconsoled**,
I lay your **pavements** in **carnelians**,
and your **foundations** in **sapphires**;
I will make your **battlements** of **rubies**,
your **gates** of **carbuncles**,
and **all** your **walls** of **precious stones**.
All your **children** shall be **taught** by the **LORD**,
and **great** shall be the **peace** of your **children**.
In **justice** shall you be **established**,
far from the **fear** of **oppression**,
where **destruction cannot** come **near** you.

Next, God speaks. God acknowledges the disillusionment caused by the exile: "For a brief moment I abandoned you." "In an outburst of wrath, for a moment, I hid my face from you." However, that is now over. The exile does not signal that the Israelites' covenant relationship with God is over. Rather, God says, "with great tenderness I will take you back."

God is then pictured as comparing the present circumstances to the days of Noah and the deluge. At that time God promised never again to flood the whole earth. Now God is promising Jerusalem that God still loves her: "my love shall never leave you nor my covenant of peace be shaken."

God then describes the richness with which Jerusalem will be rebuilt. Her streets, gates, and walls will all be made of precious stones. Her children, presently exiles in Babylon, will return, will be taught by the Lord, and will live in peace. Then the exiles will have a complete change of fortune. Now they are "afflicted . . . storm-battered and unconsoled." Soon they will return to Jerusalem and live "far from . . . oppression, where destruction cannot come near" them.

Second Isaiah's prophecy is one of comfort and hope. The prophet, and then God, are assuring the exiles that God has not abandoned them. They are still God's people, and God will be faithful to his promises. As you proclaim this reading, give greatest emphasis to the lines that picture God assuring the exiles that the covenant still exists: "my love shall never leave you nor my covenant of peace be shaken."

READING V **The Fifth Reading is also from Second Isaiah and so comes from the same social setting as did**

READING V Isaiah 55:1–11

Isaiah = ī-ZAY-uh

A reading from the Book of the Prophet Isaiah

God is calling his people to return. Say "come" with longing. It is a refrain.

God is promising them a plentiful life after their return.

This is an ironic question. Why behave so foolishly?

God is pleading, not just inviting.

Thus says the LORD:
All you who are **thirsty**,
come to the **water**!
You who have **no money**,
come, receive **grain** and **eat**;
come, without **paying** and without **cost**,
drink **wine** and **milk**!
Why spend your **money** for what is **not bread**,
your wages for what **fails** to **satisfy**?
Heed me, and you shall **eat well**,
you shall **delight** in **rich fare**.
Come to me **heedfully**,
listen, that you may have **life**.

This line is all important. This is what the exiles need to hear.
covenant = KUHV-eh-n*nt
David = DAY-vid

God is teaching the exiles that their present suffering has not been without purpose. They, like David, are God's chosen witnesses.
Israel = IZ-ree-uhl or IZ-ray-uhl

I will **renew** with **you** the **everlasting covenant**,
the benefits assured to **David**.
As I made him a **witness** to the **peoples**,
a **leader** and **commander** of **nations**,
so shall **you summon** a **nation** you **knew not**,
and **nations** that knew **you** not shall **run** to you,
because of the **LORD**, your **God**,
the **Holy One** of **Israel**, who has **glorified you**.

Now, Second Isaiah is exhorting the people. The tone is one of invitation and encouragement, not blame.
scoundrel = SKOWN-druhl

Seek the LORD while he may be **found**,
call him while he is **near**.
Let the **scoundrel forsake** his **way**,
and the **wicked man** his **thoughts**;
let him **turn** to the **LORD** for **mercy**;
to our **God**, who is **generous** in **forgiving**.

our Fourth Reading: Second Isaiah is assuring the exiles in Babylon that they are still God's people and that their suffering in exile has a purpose other than punishment.

Isaiah's audience is thirsty; the exiles are spiritually thirsty. They feel separated from God. As our reading begins, God is calling out to his people to come: "Come to the water!" "Come, receive grain and eat." "Come, without paying." "Come to me heedfully, listen." God promises to give them exactly what they long for and need: "I will renew with you the everlasting covenant."

Events have challenged the Israelites' understanding that God is still their God and they are still God's people. After all, God had promised a nation ("the benefits assured to David"), yet here they are in exile. Second Isaiah is assuring the exiles that the covenant is everlasting and so is still in effect. He is inviting them to return to the Lord and experience the close relationship that they fear they have lost.

Next, Second Isaiah offers the exiles assurance that their suffering has not been in vain. God tells the exiles that, just as God called David and made him a witness to other nations, so has God called them to fulfill God's purposes in history. Other nations will come to a knowledge of God through the Israelites: "so shall you summon a nation you knew not, and nations that knew you not shall run to you."

Then the prophet's voice exhorts the people to "Seek the Lord." There is no question that God is calling them and remaining faithful to them. Will they respond? It is true that God's ways have been mysterious, beyond the exile's understanding. However, God's thoughts are not

Now the Lord is once more speaking.

For **my** thoughts are not **your** thoughts,
nor are **your** ways **my** ways, says the **LORD**.
As high as the **heavens** are above the **earth**,
so high are **my** ways above **your** ways
and **my** thoughts above **your** thoughts.

The rest of the reading is all one sentence. God is comparing the fruitfulness of rain to the fruitfulness of his word.

For just as from the **heavens**
the **rain** and **snow** come **down**
and do not **return** there
till they have **watered** the **earth**,
making it **fertile** and **fruitful**,
giving **seed** to the one who **sows**
and **bread** to the one who **eats**,

This is the second part of the comparison.

so shall **my word be**
that **goes forth** from **my mouth**;

Increase your volume and speak slowly as you proclaim this conclusion.

my word shall **not return** to me **void**,
but shall **do my will**,
achieving the **end** for which **I sent** it.

READING VI Baruch 3:9–15, 32—4:4

Baruch = buh-ROOK

A reading from the Book of the Prophet Baruch

Baruch is commanding attention. Proclaim these first two lines with energy.

Hear, O **Israel**, the **commandments** of **life**:
listen, and know **prudence**!

Israel = IZ-ree-uhl or IZ-ray-uhl

Now, drop your voice. Baruch is asking the exiles a question.

How is it, **Israel**,
that **you** are in the land of your **foes**,
grown **old** in a **foreign land**,
defiled with the **dead**,
accounted with those **destined** for the **netherworld**?

netherworld = NETH-er-werld

Pause after the question.

their thoughts. They are not capable of understanding all of God's ways.

The reading ends with a beautiful poem in which God assures the exiles that his word is never without effect. God compares the fruitfulness of his word to the fruitfulness of rain. Rain comes from the heaven and returns to the heaven, but not until it has first "watered the earth . . . giving seed to the one who sows and bread to the one who eats." Just so, God's word comes from God and returns to God, but not before achieving the end for which he sent it.

The good news in today's reading is God's fidelity to his covenant and the assurance that events are not outside of God's providence, but have a purpose in his saving plan for all nations. As you proclaim this good news, let your voice be filled with joy and confidence. Not only the exiles, but we also, need to hear it.

READING VI Our Sixth Reading claims to be from the prophet Baruch. Baruch was Jeremiah's scribe, and Jeremiah was a prophet for the forty years preceding the Babylonian exile (which began in 587 BC).

However, scripture scholars believe that the author of today's song in praise of wisdom actually lived in the first or second century BC. The author was writing to *diaspora* Jews, that is, Jews who were separated from the holy land and living under Greek rule. He attributed his work to Baruch, and chose the Babylonian exile as his setting, because he wanted to hold up the experience of the exiles as an example to his own contemporaries: the author is teaching the *diaspora* Jews that just as

Raise your voice. This is an accusation. This is one of the author's central points.

You have **forsaken** the **fountain** of **wisdom**!
Had you **walked** in the **way** of **God**,
you would have **dwelt** in **enduring peace**.

This is no longer an accusation but an appeal.

Learn where **prudence** is,
where **strength**, where **understanding**;
that you may **know also**

Pause after this line.

where are **length** of **days**, and **life**,
where **light** of the **eyes**, and **peace**.

Baruch poses a second question.

Who has **found** the place of **wisdom**,
who has **entered** into **her treasuries**?

Say this with gentle conviction.

The **One** who knows **all things** knows **her**;
he has **probed** her by his **knowledge**—
the **One** who established the **earth** for **all time**,
and **filled** it with **four-footed beasts**;

Fill your voice with awe.

he who **dismisses** the **light**, and it **departs**,
calls it, and it **obeys** him **trembling**;
before whom the **stars** at their **posts**
shine and **rejoice**;

The stars are always ready to serve.

when he **calls** them, they answer, "**Here we are**!"
shining with **joy** for their **Maker**.

Emphasize every word of this line.

Such is **our God**;
no other is to be **compared** to him:
he has traced out the **whole way** of **understanding**,

The "her" is personified wisdom.

and has given her to **Jacob**, his **servant**,
to **Israel**, his **beloved son**.

The "she" is also personified wisdom.

Since then she has appeared on **earth**,
and moved among **people**.
She is the **book** of the **precepts** of **God**,
the **law** that **endures forever**;
all who **cling** to **her** will **live**,
but those will **die** who **forsake** her.

God returned those who had been exiled in Babylon to the holy land, so could God return them. However, they must be faithful to Torah, to the law.

The author pictures Baruch asking those in exile, "How is it, Israel, that you are in the land of your foes, grown old in a foreign land?" Actually, the author is asking the *diaspora* Jews that question. Baruch answers it: the people "have forsaken the fountain of wisdom."

The rest of the reading is in praise of personified wisdom. A person who seeks out wisdom learns to walk in the ways of God. In wisdom lie prudence, strength, understanding, long life, and peace. God, the creator of the whole world, who orders even the stars, has given wisdom to Israel. Wisdom is "the law that endures forever."

The author of Baruch is urging the *diaspora* Jews not to succumb to the temptation of embracing Greek cultural values. Instead, they must continue to obey the law, where wisdom is to be found. When the author says, "Turn, O Jacob, and receive her. . . . Give not your glory to another," he is exhorting his fellow Jews to remain faithful to Torah and not to Greek beliefs and practices. He reminds them that they are greatly blessed because it is to Israel that God has chosen to reveal himself. He assures his readers that "what pleases God is known to us!"

The tone in this reading changes from proclamation, to questioning, to accusation, to awe, to exhortation, to a concluding proclamation of great blessing. Great emphasis should be given to the author's central points: those who walk "in the way of God," in wisdom's way, dwell "in enduring peace." Therefore, the *diaspora* Jews

Now Baruch is pleading with the people. This, too, is central to the author's purpose.
Jacob = JAY-kuhb

Baruch is reminding the Israelites that they are blessed because God has chosen to reveal himself to them. This is said with gratitude.

Turn, O **Jacob**, and **receive** her:
walk by her **light** toward **splendor**.
Give **not** your **glory** to **another**,
your **privileges** to an **alien race**.
Blessed are **we**, **O Israel**;
for what **pleases God** is **known** to **us**!

READING VII Ezekiel 36:16–17a, 18–28

Ezekiel = ee-ZEE-kee-uhl

God is explaining God's plan and purpose to Ezekiel. This is an explanation, not a condemnation.
Israel = IZ-ree-uhl or IZ-ray-uhl
defiled = dih-FĪLD

dispersing = dis-PERS-ing

Emphasize "profane my holy name."
profane = proh-FAYN
This line is spoken by the people of other nations. "People of the Lord" is said ironically.

A reading from the Book of the Prophet Ezekiel

The **word** of the **LORD came** to me, **saying**:
Son of man, when the **house** of **Israel** lived in **their** land,
they **defiled** it by their **conduct** and **deeds**.
Therefore I poured out my **fury upon** them
because of the **blood** that **they** poured out on the **ground**,
and because they **defiled** it with **idols**.
I scattered them among the **nations**,
dispersing them over **foreign lands**;
according to their **conduct** and **deeds I judged** them.
But when they came among the **nations wherever** they came,
they served to **profane my holy name**,
because it was **said** of **them**: "**These** are the **people** of the LORD,
yet they had to **leave** their **land**."
So I have **relented** because of **my holy name**
which the **house** of **Israel profaned**
among the **nations** where they **came**.

should not turn to the ways of "an alien race," but should cling to wisdom and live. So should we.

READING VII Our Seventh Reading is from the prophet Ezekiel, who prophesied to the exiles in Babylon from 593–571 BC. Ezekiel preached judgment and hope, both of which are evident in today's reading.

As the reading begins, God is explaining himself to Ezekiel. The reason the Israelites have lost their land, even though God promised them a land, is that they defiled the land while they had it: "they defiled it" with idols. God judged them "according to their conduct and deeds," and thus "scattered them among the nations."

However, this judgment had the effect of profaning God's name. The people of other nations said, " 'These are the people of the Lord, yet they had to leave their land.' " This remark dismisses the idea that the Israelites or their God are anything special. If they were, then the people would not have had to leave their land. God would have kept his promise to them.

Rather than allow his name to be profaned, God decides to prove his holiness by bringing the people back to their land. When Ezekiel pictures God saying, "Not for your sakes do I act, house of Israel, but for the sake of my holy name," Ezekiel is teaching the exiles that they will be saved, not because they earned or deserved to be saved, but because God is holy.

God, in his love, will not only bring the people back to their land, but will cleanse them from all their impurities and will put his own spirit within them. Then the people will once more live by God's

Now, God's words are addressed to the nation. They are an accusation.

Therefore say to the **house** of **Israel**: **Thus says** the **Lord GOD**:
Not for **your sakes** do I act, **house** of **Israel**,
but for the **sake** of my **holy name**,
which you **profaned** among the **nations** to which you **came**.
I will prove the **holiness** of **my great name**, **profaned**
among the **nations**,
in whose **midst** you have **profaned** it.

Emphasize these words. This is God's purpose.

Thus the **nations** shall **know** that **I am the LORD**,
says the **Lord GOD**,
when in **their sight** I **prove** my **holiness** through **you**.

The tone changes here to graciousness and mercy.

For I will **take you away** from among the **nations**,
gather you from **all** the **foreign lands**,
and **bring** you **back** to **your own land**.

Emphasize these lines since the Church will be celebrating Baptism and Confirmation at the Vigil.

cleanse = klenz

I will sprinkle **clean** water upon you
to **cleanse** you from all your **impurities**,
and from all your **idols** I will **cleanse** you.
I will give you a **new heart** and place a **new spirit within** you,
taking from your bodies your **stony hearts**
and giving you **natural hearts**.

statutes = STA-ch<u>oo</u>tz

I will put **my spirit** within **you** and make **you live** by **my statutes**,
careful to **observe** my **decrees**.

This is the good news that the exiles long to hear.

You shall **live** in the **land** I gave your **fathers**;
you shall be **my people**, and I will be **your God**.

statues and decrees. God assures the exiles that the covenant still exists. He says, "You shall live in the land I gave your fathers; you shall be my people, and I will be your God."

God's tone in the reading changes from explanation, to accusation, to great love and blessing. As the blessings are described—the cleansing water and God's spirit within the people—those who hear the readings at the Easter Vigil will realize that these words are being fulfilled in their midst through the sacraments of Baptism and Confirmation.

EPISTLE

In the reading from Paul's letter to the Christian community in Rome, he is in the midst of an explanation of the Christian life. He has previously explained that Christians are no longer slaves to sin and death because Christ has conquered both sin and death. In today's reading, Paul is reminding Roman Christians, who have already been taught what Paul is teaching, that because of their Baptism they have been united to Christ and now live an entirely new life.

Paul states his two major points three times in today's reading, both of which can be seen vividly in Baptism by immersion. Paul's two teachings are first, that Christians have joined themselves to Christ's death and therefore have died with Christ. Second, by joining Christ in his death, Christians have also joined Christ in his Resurrection.

The Roman Christians would likely have understood that these truths are expressed symbolically in Baptism by immersion: The person to be baptized joins Christ is his death by entering the water. The person joins Christ in his burial by

EPISTLE Romans 6:3–11

Romans–ROH-muhnz

A reading from the Letter of Saint Paul to the Romans

The overall tone of this reading is explanatory.
Paul is reminding the Romans of what they have previously been taught.
This is Paul's first point.

Brothers and sisters:
Are you **unaware** that we who were **baptized** into **Christ Jesus**
were **baptized** into his **death**?
We were indeed **buried with him** through **baptism** into **death**,
so that, just as **Christ** was **raised** from the **dead**
by the **glory** of the **Father**,

This is Paul's second point.

we too might **live** in **newness** of **life**.

Paul restates both points.

For if we have **grown** into **union with him** through a **death** like **his**,
we shall **also** be **united with him** in the **resurrection**.

Paul explains that Christians are no longer slaves to sin.

We know that our **old self** was **crucified** with **him**,
so that our **sinful body** might be **done away with**,
that we might **no longer** be in **slavery** to **sin**.
For a **dead person** has been **absolved** from **sin**.

Paul restates each point a third time.

If, then, we have **died** with **Christ**,
we **believe** that we shall also **live** with **him**.
We **know** that **Christ**, **raised** from the **dead**, **dies no more**;
death no longer has **power** over him.
As to his **death**, he **died** to **sin once** and for **all**;
as to his **life**, he **lives** for **God**.

Here Paul states the ramification of what he has taught. This is how the Romans should live.
consequently = KON-suh-kwent-lee

Consequently, **you too** must think of **yourselves** as being **dead** to **sin**
and **living** for **God** in **Christ Jesus**.

being submerged in that water. (In fact, early Christian fonts sometimes echoed the shape of tombs.) Finally the person joins Christ in his Resurrection by arising from the water.

What difference does Baptism make? Paul is teaching the Roman community that because of their Baptism they are new people. In Baptism they have not simply remembered and symbolically re-enacted Christ's victory over sin and death; they have been joined to Christ in that victory. They, too, are no longer slaves to sin. They can now live completely different lives. They live "for God in Christ Jesus." Nor are they slaves to death. They will share in Christ's victory over death, and will "be united with him in the Resurrection."

The tone of this reading is explanatory throughout. As you proclaim Paul's good news, put the greatest emphasis on Paul's two main points and on their ramification: Christians should understand that we are "dead to sin and living for God in Christ Jesus."

GOSPEL Two kinds of stories claim Jesus' Resurrection from the dead: empty tomb stories and post-Resurrection appearance stories. Today's Gospel has both.

At dawn on Sunday, Mary Magdalene and the other Mary, both of whom had witnessed the Crucifixion and the burial (see Matthew 27:56, 61), return to the tomb. As they arrive, there is an earthquake, just as there had been at Jesus' death (Matthew 27:51). This is Matthew's way of alerting us that earth-shattering events are occurring.

GOSPEL Matthew 28:1–10

A reading from the holy Gospel according to Matthew

The narrator begins the story.
Magdalene = MAG-duh-luhn or MAG-duh-leen
Now the narrator speaks with awe.

After the **sabbath**, as the **first day** of the **week** was **dawning**,
Mary Magdalene and the **other Mary** came to see the **tomb**.
And **behold**, there was a **great earthquake**;
for an **angel** of the **Lord** descended from **heaven**,
approached, **rolled back** the **stone**, and **sat upon it**.
His appearance was like **lightning**
and his clothing was **white** as **snow**.

Drop your voice here.

The **guards** were **shaken** with **fear** of him
and became like **dead** men.
Then the **angel** said to the **women** in reply,

Say this gently but with assurance.

"**Do not be afraid**!
I know that you are seeking **Jesus** the **crucified**.

Emphasize "he has been raised."

He is not here, for **he has been raised just** as he **said**.
Come and **see** the **place** where he **lay**.
Then go **quickly** and **tell** his **disciples**,

This is the central message. Jesus will repeat this message.
Galilee = GAL-ih-lee

'**He** has been **raised** from the **dead**,
and he is **going before** you to **Galilee**;
there **you** will **see him**.'
Behold, I have **told** you."

Now the narrator resumes the story. Speak more quickly.

Then they went away **quickly** from the **tomb**,
fearful yet **overjoyed**,
and **ran** to **announce** this to his **disciples**.
And **behold**, **Jesus** met them on their way and **greeted** them.
They **approached**, **embraced** his **feet**, and **did** him **homage**.

Jesus begins just as the angel did, with gentle reassurance, and then continues with the same instructions.

Then **Jesus** said to them, "**Do not** be **afraid**.
Go tell my **brothers** to go to **Galilee**,
and **there** they will **see me**."

An angel rolls back the stone of the tomb to illustrate that Jesus' body is no longer there.

The angel then explains the significance of the empty tomb: Jesus "has been raised just as he said." The women are admonished not to be afraid, are invited to see inside the empty tomb themselves, and are then sent on a mission to the apostles. They are to tell the apostles that Jesus has been raised from the dead, that Jesus is going before them to Galilee, and that they will see him there.

As the women go quickly to spread this absolutely amazing good news, Jesus himself appears to them. He is in bodily form, for the women "embraced his feet, and did him homage." Jesus then repeats the angel's commission to the women. They are to tell Jesus' apostles, whom Jesus now calls his brothers, to go to Galilee where they, too, will see the risen Christ.

As you proclaim today's Easter Gospel, emphasize the lines that are repeated because of their importance: "Do not be afraid," "He has been raised," and, "There you [they] will see him." The Church is reminding us to have no fear, Jesus has risen from the dead, and we, too, are invited to open our eyes, in faith, and see the risen Christ in our midst.

EASTER SUNDAY

Lectionary #42

READING I Acts 10:34a, 37–43

Apostles = uh-POS-*lz

A reading from the Acts of the Apostles

Peter = PEE-ter

Peter is reminding his listeners of past events.

Judea = joo-DEE-uh or joo-DAY-uh

Galilee = GAL-ih-lee

Nazareth = NAZ-uh-reth

Emphasize this line.

Peter proceeded to **speak** and said:
"**You know** what has happened **all over Judea**,
beginning in **Galilee** after the **baptism**
that **John preached**,
how **God anointed Jesus** of **Nazareth**
with the **Holy Spirit** and **power**.
He went about **doing good**
and **healing** all those **oppressed** by the **devil**,
for **God** was **with** him.

Emphasize "witnesses." This is important to Luke's purpose and will be repeated.

Jerusalem = juh-ROO–suh-lem or juh-ROO-zuh-lem

Say this slowly.

Now, speak more quickly and with joy and excitement.

Again, emphasize "witnesses."

We are **witnesses** of **all** that he **did**
both in the **country** of the **Jews** and in **Jerusalem**.
They put him to **death** by **hanging** him on a **tree**.
This man God raised on the **third day** and **granted**
that he be **visible**,
not to **all** the people, but to **us**,
the **witnesses chosen** by **God** in **advance**,
who **ate** and **drank** with him **after** he **rose** from the **dead**.

Emphasize "commissioned us."

These are the core truths. Say each line slowly and with conviction.

He **commissioned us** to **preach** to the **people**
and **testify** that **he** is the **one appointed** by **God**
as judge of the **living** and the **dead**.
To **him all** the **prophets** bear **witness**,
that **everyone** who **believes** in **him**
will receive **forgiveness** of **sins** through **his** name."

READING I The reading from Acts is part of a very important story: the beginning of the Church's mission to the Gentiles. Today's selection is part of Peter's speech in the house of Cornelius, a Roman centurion. Peter's original understanding had been that the good news of Jesus Christ was to be preached to the Israelites, not to the Gentiles. However, each of these two men had visions that caused them to seek out the other (Acts 10:1–33). As we join the story, Peter is, for the first time, preaching in the home of a Gentile.

In his speech, Peter teaches truths that are core to Christianity: that Jesus suffered, died, and rose from the dead, that Jesus fulfilled the words of the prophets, that Jesus is the messiah, that "everyone who believes in him [Jesus] will receive forgiveness of sins through his name," and that Jesus is "judge of both the living and the dead."

In addition to teaching these core truths, Peter describes the continuity that exists between Jesus' own mission and the mission of the apostles. He stresses that he and the other apostles are witnesses not only to Jesus' public ministry, but to his death and Resurrection. These chosen witnesses were commissioned by Jesus to do the work that Peter is now doing.

As you proclaim this reading, try to emphasize the core truths being taught, as well as the ramifications for us. We, too, are beneficiaries of this carefully handed down tradition. We know that through our faith in Jesus, we have received forgiveness of sins through Jesus' name.

READING II Colossians 3:1–4

Paul = pawl
Colossians = kuh-LOSH-uhnz

The author is imploring the Colossians.

Emphasize "what is above." This is stated for the second time.

Drop your voice for the explanation.

Now raise you voice and fill it with promise and joy. This is the Easter Good News.

A reading from the Letter of Saint Paul to the Colossians

Brothers and sisters:
If then you were **raised with Christ, seek** what is **above**,
where **Christ** is **seated** at the **right hand** of **God**.
Think of what is **above, not** of what is on **earth**.
For **you** have **died**, and **your life** is **hidden** with Christ in **God**.
When **Christ your life appears**,
then **you too** will **appear with him** in **glory**.

Or:

READING II 1 Corinthians 5:6b–8

Paul = pawl
Corinthians = kohr-IN-thee-uhnz

Here Paul is correcting the Corinthians. The tone is "Surely you must know this!"

dough = doh

This is a firm direction.

unleavened = uhn-LEV-uhnd

Drop your voice for this line.

paschal = PAS-kuhl

Now the tone changes to exhortation.

A reading from the first Letter of Saint Paul to the Corinthians

Brothers and sisters:
Do you **not know** that **a little yeast** leavens **all** the **dough**?
Clear out the **old yeast**,
so that **you** may become a **fresh batch** of **dough**,
inasmuch as **you** are **unleavened**.
For our **paschal lamb, Christ**, has been **sacrificed**.
Therefore, let us **celebrate** the **feast**,
not with the **old yeast**, the yeast of **malice** and **wickedness**,
but with the **unleavened bread** of **sincerity** and **truth**.

There is a choice of readings today. Speak with the liturgy coordinator or homilist to find out which readings will be used.

READING II **COLOSSIANS.** The reading from the letter to the Christian community at Colossae, like the reading from Acts, proclaims core creedal statements for Christians. Reviewing the context of today's passage will help us understand what the author is teaching.

Evidently, some false teachers were trying to persuade the Colossians that while worshipping Jesus was fine, it was not enough. They must practice asceticism—denying themselves physical comforts and restricting food and drink, and they must worship angels (see Colossians 2:18). The author of Colossians is insisting that Jesus is enough. Jesus is all they need.

When the author of Colossians says, "If then you were raised with Christ, seek what is above," he is reminding the Colossians that when they were baptized they died and rose with Christ. He has earlier taught them this very insight regarding Baptism when he said: "You were buried with him in baptism, in which you were also raised with him through faith in the power of God, who raised him from the dead" (Colossians 2:12).

When the author describes Christ as being "seated at the right hand of God" he is claiming that Jesus is the messiah. This statement, which, to this day, appears in our Creed, is an allusion to Psalm 110:1: "The Lord says to you, my lord: / 'Take your throne at my right hand.'" In the Gospels, Jesus is pictured as interpreting this passage as a reference to the Messiah (see Mark 12:35–37; Matthew 22:41–45).

GOSPEL John 20:1–9

A reading from the holy Gospel according to John

The narrator is setting the stage.
Magdala = MAG-duh-luh

On the **first day** of the **week**,
Mary of **Magdala** came to the **tomb early** in the **morning**,
while it was **still dark**,
and saw the **stone removed** from the **tomb**.

Say this with a puzzled and alarmed tone.
Simon = SĪ-muhn
Peter = PEE-ter
disciple = dih-SĪ-p*l
Mary is very upset.

So she **ran** and went to **Simon Peter**
and to the **other disciple** whom **Jesus loved**, and **told** them,
"They have **taken** the **Lord** from the **tomb**,
and we **don't know where** they **put** him."

Read more quickly here.

So **Peter** and the **other disciple** went out and **came** to the **tomb**.
They **both ran**, but the **other disciple** ran **faster** than **Peter**
and **arrived** at the tomb **first**;

Say this line slowly.
Now increase your pace again.

he **bent down** and **saw** the **burial cloths** there,
but **did not go in**.
When **Simon Peter** arrived **after** him,
he went into the tomb and **saw** the **burial cloths** there,
and the **cloth** that had **covered** his **head**,

burial = BAYR-ee-uhl
cloths = klawthz
Read these three lines slowly and solemnly, and then pause.

not **with** the burial cloths but **rolled up** in a **separate place**.
Then the **other disciple also** went in,
the **one** who **had arrived** at the tomb **first**,
and **he saw** and **believed**.

The narrator concludes the story with an explanation of the others' behavior.

For they did **not yet understand** the **Scripture**
that he had to **rise** from the **dead**.

As he reminds them of these two essential truths regarding their baptism and Christ's identity, the author exhorts the Colossians not to give in to the false teachers. The Colossians are to "think of what is above," that is, Christ at God's right hand, and not think of "what is on earth," that is, "seductive philosophy according to human tradition, according to the elemental powers of the world" (Colossians 2:8). These are the things about which the false teachers would have them be concerned.

The author assures the Colossians that, because of their Baptism, they have already risen with Christ. This truth is known in heaven, but not yet on earth: it is "hidden with Christ in God." However, when Christ appears in glory, so will the Colossians.

As you proclaim this reading, try to adopt the author's tone: both persuasive and reassuring. As you conclude, emphasize the Easter Good News: Resurrection is not limited to Jesus Christ. We, too, through Baptism, have risen with Christ to eternal life.

1 CORINTHIANS. Today's reading from Corinthians is Paul's conclusion to a warning that the Corinthians must not tolerate the sexual immorality that is taking place in their community: a man is living with his father's wife. Paul insists that the man should be expelled.

The "little yeast" that "leavens all the dough" is the immoral behavior of this man, behavior that can only have a negative effect on the whole community. To "clear out the old yeast" is to expel the man. To "become a fresh batch of dough" is to return the group to its purity.

The sources for Paul's imagery are the celebration of Passover and the Feast of Unleavened Bread. When Paul says, "Our

Lectionary #46

AFTERNOON GOSPEL Luke 24:13–35

A reading from the holy Gospel according to Luke

The narrator sets the stage.

That very day, the **first** day of the **week**,
two of **Jesus' disciples** were going
to a village seven miles from **Jerusalem** called **Emmaus**,
and they were **conversing** about **all** the **things**
that had **occurred**.

Jerusalem = juh-ROO–suh-lem or juh-ROO-zuh-lem
Emmaus = eh-MAY-uhs

And it happened that **while** they were **conversing** and **debating**,
Jesus himself drew near and **walked** with **them**,
but their **eyes** were **prevented** from **recognizing him**.

Slow your tempo here.
Emphasize this line. It is mysterious.

He asked them,
"**What** are you **discussing** as you **walk along**?"
They **stopped**, looking **downcast**.

Jesus appears just to be making conversation.

One of them, named **Cleopas**, said to him in **reply**,
"Are you the **only visitor** to **Jerusalem**
who does **not know** of the things
that have **taken place there** in **these days**?"

Cleopas = KLEE-oh-puhs
This is said with amazement andincredulity.

And he replied to them, "**What sort** of **things**?"

Again, Jesus appears just to be making conversation.

They said to him,
"The **things** that **happened** to **Jesus** the **Nazarene**,
who was a **prophet mighty** in **deed** and **word**
before God and **all** the **people**,
how our **chief priests** and **rulers** both **handed him over**
to a sentence of **death** and **crucified** him.

This is said with both conviction and sadness.
Nazarene = naz-uh-REEN

But we were **hoping** that **he would be the one** to **redeem Israel**;
and besides all **this**,
it is now the **third day** since this took place.

Say this slowly and thoughtfully.
Israel = IZ-ree-uhl; IZ-ray-uhl

paschal lamb, Christ, has been sacrificed," he is saying that Christ is the new Passover lamb who was killed at the time of Passover. When he says that the Corinthians are "unleavened" he is comparing their state of purity after Baptism to the unleavened bread eaten on the Feast of Unleavened Bread, after all the old yeast has been discarded. When the Israelites were nomads these two feasts were separate celebrations, but they later became combined and were celebrated together.

As you proclaim this short Easter homily, let your tone change from initial correction, to direction, to exhortation. We hope that we, through our Lenten resolutions, have thrown out the old yeast, whatever has been a block to our growing in holiness. We, too, are called to celebrate the feast, Easter, with the "unleavened bread of sincerity and truth."

GOSPEL John's empty tomb story has three main characters: Mary of Magdala, Simon Peter, and the "disciple whom Jesus loved." Only one of the three, the beloved disciple, "saw and believed" before any post-Resurrection appearance. The others will come to believe in time, but only the unnamed disciple "saw and believed" based solely on the empty tomb.

To understand the full significance of this account, we must know a little about the Gospel according to John. It was written near the end of the first century to respond to the question, "Where is the risen Christ?" Christ was expected to return in glory before the time John is writing. John wants his audience to understand that the risen Christ is in their midst. They must have eyes of faith to see him.

Speed up here.

Some **women** from our group, however, have **astounded** us:
they were at the **tomb early** in the **morning**
and **did not find** his **body**;
they came **back** and **reported**
that they had indeed **seen a vision** of **angels**
who **announced** that he was **alive**.

This is not an act of faith. It is a repetition of an unbelievable claim.
Say this slowly and with sadness.

Then some of those **with us went** to the **tomb**
and found things **just** as the **women** had **described**,
but **him** they **did not see**."
And he said to them, "**Oh**, how **foolish you are**!
How **slow** of **heart** to **believe all** that the **prophets spoke**!
Was it **not necessary** that the **Christ** should **suffer these things**
and **enter** into his **glory**?"

Now the narrator is speaking.

Then beginning with **Moses** and all the **prophets**,
he **interpreted** to them what **referred** to **him**
in **all** the **Scriptures**.

Pause before this line.

As they approached the **village** to which they were **going**,
he gave the **impression** that he was going on **farther**.

Say this with great earnestness.

But they **urged** him, "**Stay with us**,
for it is **nearly evening** and the day is **almost over**."
So he **went in** to **stay** with them.

Say the next three lines slowly. This is eucharistic language.

And it happened that, while he was **with them** at **table**,
he **took bread**, said the **blessing**,
broke it, and **gave it to them**.

Say this line with awe.

With **that** their **eyes** were **opened** and they **recognized him**,
but he **vanished** from their **sight**.
Then they said to **each other**,

This is said with great joy.

"Were not our **hearts burning within** us
while he **spoke** to us on the **way** and opened the **Scriptures**
to us?"

The disciple "whom Jesus loved," is unique to John's Gospel. He goes unnamed because, within the Gospel, he functions as a symbol. Scripture scholars surmise that John's community emphasized charismatic gifts over structured authority. This emphasis is dramatized in today's Gospel through the beloved disciple, who represents a direct and personal relationship with Jesus Christ, and Peter, who represents authority.

Both the beloved disciple and Peter receive exactly the same information: Mary Magdalene tells them that the tomb is empty. She has concluded that someone has taken the body. The beloved disciple and Peter both run to the tomb, but the beloved disciple, who represents love, gets there first. He respectfully waits for Peter, who represents authority, to arrive and enter the tomb.

Both see the same evidence in the tomb. The burial cloths are there, with the head cloth neatly rolled up in a separate place. This is evidence against Mary Magdalene's conclusion that someone has taken the body. Based simply on this evidence, not on a post-Resurrection appearance, the beloved disciple "saw and believed." It would take the others longer to understand that Jesus had risen from the dead.

John is teaching his audience, including us, to grow in our love and our personal relationship with Jesus Christ so that we, like the beloved disciple, will be able to see and believe, even though Jesus has not yet returned in glory on the clouds of heaven. As you proclaim this reading, give the greatest emphasis to the two most important lines: "he saw and believed" and "he had to rise from the dead." It is this good news that we are celebrating today.

This is the narrator again. Increase your tempo.

So they set out **at once** and **returned** to **Jerusalem**
where they found **gathered together**
the **eleven** and those **with** them who were saying,
"The **Lord** has **truly** been **raised** and has **appeared** to **Simon**!"

This is fantastic good news!
Simon = SĪ-muhn
The narrator concludes the story.

Then the two **recounted**
what had **taken place** on the **way**
and how **he** was **made known** to **them** in the **breaking** of **bread**.

Say the last line slowly so that those in the assembly are left with these words ringing in their ears.

AFTERNOON GOSPEL **Today we read Luke's famous post-Resurrection appearance story of the two disciples on the road to Emmaus. Through this story, Luke is teaching us the ways in which the risen Christ is still present to his disciples, even if we, like the two on the road, fail to recognize him.**

As the story begins, the two disciples are walking along, downcast. They are talking about Jesus and feeling his absence, unaware that when two or more are gathered in Christ's name, Christ is already among them. Soon, a stranger joins them, whom they welcome. Again, they are unaware that when they welcome a stranger in Christ's name, they welcome Christ. They fail to recognize him.

As they explain to Jesus why they are so dejected, it becomes evident that they have not believed the witness of the women who have told them that Jesus is alive. Jesus points out to them that they have also failed to believe the witness of the prophets. Jesus "interpreted to them what referred to him in all the Scriptures."

The two do not recognize Jesus until Jesus takes bread, blesses it, breaks it, and gives it to them. As soon as they recognize Jesus in Eucharist, he vanishes from their sight. However, they are now convinced. They not only believe the witness of others, that the Lord has risen, but they become witnesses themselves.

Through this story, Luke is teaching us to recognize the risen Christ in each other, in the stranger, in the word proclaimed, and in Eucharist. As you proclaim the reading, emphasize those lines that are as true for us as they were for the two disciples on the road: "The Lord has truly been raised," and has been made known to us "in the breaking of the bread."

2ND SUNDAY OF EASTER DIVINE MERCY SUNDAY

Lectionary #43

READING I Acts 2:42–47

Apostles = uh-POS-*lz

Luke is giving us an overview and a summary of life in the earliest Christian community. The initial tone is matter-of-fact.

communal = kuh-MYOON-*l or KOM-yoo-n*l

Say this sentence with awe.

Say this with joy.

Emphasize "devoted." This is being said for the second time.

Emphasize "breaking bread." This, too, is being stated for the second time.

exultation = eg-zuhl-TAY-shuhn

Speak slowly and with great joy.

A reading from the Acts of the Apostles

They **devoted** themselves
to the **teaching** of the **apostles** and to the **communal life**,
to the **breaking** of **bread** and to the **prayers**.
Awe came upon **everyone**,
and **many wonders** and **signs** were done through the **apostles**.
All who believed were **together** and had **all things** in **common**;
they would **sell** their **property** and **possessions**
and **divide** them among **all** according to **each one's need**.
Every day they **devoted** themselves
to **meeting together** in the **temple** area
and to **breaking bread** in their **homes**.
They ate their **meals** with **exultation** and **sincerity** of **heart**,
praising God and enjoying **favor** with **all** the people.
And **every day** the **Lord added** to their **number those** who were
being **saved**.

READING I In today's selection from Acts, we read a somewhat idealized description of life in the earliest Christian community. This is the first of a number of summary and transition statements that Luke makes in Acts as he tells us about the birth of the Church in Jerusalem, its spread to Samaritan towns, and finally, its spread to the ends of the then known world. Preceding today's reading, Luke has told us about Peter's first post-Pentecost speech to a crowd, after which 3,000 people were baptized. It is these new converts who are devoting themselves "to the teaching of the apostles and to the communal life" as today's reading begins.

As Luke describes it, the earliest Christians were devoted to study, worship, and community living. It is very important to Luke that his audience understand that what he is teaching is what the apostles originally taught. That we are an apostolic church is equally important today. We too devote ourselves to the teaching of the apostles as it has been faithfully passed on to us.

In addition, the earliest Christians devoted themselves to "the breaking of bread and to the prayers." The phrase "the breaking of bread" is a reference to Eucharist. In his account of the Gospel, Luke describes Jesus at the Passover meal taking bread, breaking it, and giving it to his disciples, saying, "This is my body, which will be given for you; do this in memory of me" (Luke 22:19). Also, in Luke's story of the disciples on the road to Emmaus, the disciples recognize Jesus "in the breaking of the bread" (Luke 24:35). The community still gathered in the temple areas; they

READING II 1 Peter 1:3–9

Begin with a strong, confident voice. The whole reading is only three long sentences, so read slowly, pausing at commas.

Say this line with great firmness, emphasizing each word.

inheritance = in-HAYR-ih-t*ns

imperishable = im-PAYR-ih-shuh-b*l

undefiled = un-dih-FĪL*D not in guide

Lower your voice here. The author is admitting that the present situation involves suffering.

genuineness = JEN-yoo-in-nes

perishable = PAYR-ish-uh-b*l

Now the author is complimenting his readers on their great faith.

indescribable = in-dih-SKRĪ-buh-b*l

Say this with a victorious tone.

A reading from the first Letter of Saint Peter

Blessed be the **God** and **Father** of our **Lord Jesus Christ**,
who in his **great mercy** gave us a **new birth** to a **living hope**
through the **resurrection** of **Jesus Christ** from the dead,
to an **inheritance** that is **imperishable**, **undefiled**,
and **unfading**,
kept in **heaven** for **you**
who by the **power** of **God** are **safeguarded** through **faith**,
to a **salvation** that is **ready** to be **revealed** in the **final time**.

In **this** you **rejoice**, although **now** for a little while
you may have to **suffer** through **various trials**,
so that the **genuineness** of your **faith**,
more **precious** than **gold** that is **perishable** even though **tested**
by **fire**,
may prove to be for **praise, glory**, and **honor**
at the **revelation** of **Jesus Christ**.
Although you have not **seen him** you **love him**;
even though you do not **see him now** yet **believe** in him,
you **rejoice** with an **indescribable** and **glorious joy**,
as you **attain** the **goal** of your **faith**, the **salvation**
of your **souls**.

were, of course, still faithful Jews. In addition, they gathered in each others' homes for the breaking of the bread.

Finally, the earliest Christians devoted themselves to communal life. Luke tells us that they lived much as religious orders do today. Property was communal property. They divided their resources "among all according to each one's need."

The community experienced the power and presence of the risen Christ not only in Eucharist but in "many wonders and signs" that were "done through the apostles," as well as through a constant influx of new members. No wonder the earliest Christians "ate their meals with exultation . ... praising God." We are invited to do the same. Today's reading has a single voice, Luke's. A joyful tone is appropriate throughout.

READING II We will better understand this reading from 1 Peter if we know the occasion for the letter. I Peter was addressed to a number of churches in Asia Minor who were suffering various kinds of ostracism from Roman society. The author refers to this suffering in today's reading when he tells his readers that they "may have to suffer through various trials."

Immediately before today's reading, the author refers to the recipients as *sojourners* or *exiles* of the *dispersion* (1 Peter 1:1), an implicit comparison to the Israelites who had been in exile in Babylon. He then offers his readers great hope: he blesses God who has given these suffering people "a new birth to a living hope through the resurrection of Jesus Christ." True, the people are suffering now. Nevertheless, the inheritance they have

GOSPEL John 20:19–31

A reading from the holy Gospel according to John

The narrator's voice sets the stage.
disciples = dih-SĪ-p*lz

On the **evening** of that **first day** of the **week**,
when the **doors** were **locked**, where the **disciples** were,
for **fear** of the **Jews**,
Jesus came and **stood** in their **midst**
and said to them, **"Peace be with you."**

Emphasize every word of Jesus' greeting. It will be repeated three times.

When he had **said this**, he **showed** them his **hands** and his **side.**
The disciples **rejoiced** when they **saw** the **Lord**.
Jesus said to them **again, "Peace be with you.**

Again, emphasize every word.

As the **Father** has **sent me**, so **I** send **you**."
And when he had **said** this, he **breathed** on them and said to them,
"**Receive** the **Holy Spirit**.

Emphasize this line. This is John's Pentecost.

Whose sins you **forgive** are **forgiven** them,
and whose **sins** you **retain** are **retained**."

Now, the narrator is speaking again. This is background information. Drop your voice.
Didymus = DID-uh-muhs

Thomas, called **Didymus**, one of the **Twelve**,
was **not with them** when Jesus **came**.

This is said with great excitement and joy.

So the **other disciples said** to him, "**We** have **seen** the **Lord**."
But he said to them,

Thomas is adamant. Speak slowly and raise your voice.

"Unless **I** see the **mark** of the **nails** in his **hands**
and put **my** finger into the **nailmarks**
and put **my** hand into his **side**, **I will not believe**."

Again, the narrator gives us background information.

Now a **week later** his **disciples** were **again inside**
and **Thomas** was **with** them.

Emphasize every word.

Jesus came, although the **doors** were **locked**,
and **stood** in their **midst** and said, **"Peace be with you."**

Jesus' tone is not a challenge but a loving invitation.

Then he said to **Thomas, "Put your finger here** and **see** my **hands,**
and **bring your hand** and **put it** into my **side**,
and **do not be unbelieving**, but **believe**."

received through Jesus Christ is "imperishable, undefiled, and unfading."

Why are the people suffering? The author suggests that their faith is being tested. He tells them that they may suffer through various trials "so that the genuineness of your faith . . . may prove to be for praise, glory and honor at the revelation of Jesus Christ."

The author then affirms the exiles for having such strong faith: "Although you have not seen him you love him . . . [you] believe in him." Because they have such strong faith, the exiles will overcome their difficulties and will "attain the goal" of their faith, "the salvation of [their] souls."

There is a single voice in this reading. From beginning to end, the author is giving his audience a pep talk. As you proclaim the reading, use a confident and joyful tone. You are assuring your listeners that no matter what their present difficulties, if they, like the exiles, live in hope and keep the faith, their inheritance, too, will be imperishable.

GOSPEL In the Gospel according to John, the disciples receive the Holy Spirit on the evening of the day that the empty tomb is discovered, the "first day of the week." The disciples are in a locked room when Jesus "stood in their midst." Of course, Jesus is always in their midst, but Jesus is not always visible to them. His first words to the disciples are: "Peace be with you." These words will be repeated three times in the course of this short reading. They are not merely a greeting, but a gift. Jesus is offering his disciples peace.

This is said with great awe.

Thomas answered and said to him, "**My Lord** and **my God**!"
Jesus said to **him**, "Have you **come** to **believe** because you have **seen** me?

Say this solemnly. This is John's point.

Blessed are those who have **not seen** and **have believed**."

The narrator speaks again.

Now, **Jesus** did **many other signs** in the **presence** of his **disciples** that are **not written** in this **book**.
But these **are** written that **you may come** to **believe**

Read the last two lines slowly and thoughtfully so that they remain with the listeners.

that **Jesus** is the **Christ**, the **Son** of **God**,
and that **through this belief you** may have **life** in his **name**.

Jesus commissions the disciples to carry on his mission: "As the Father has sent me, so I send you." Jesus has earlier been presented in John's account as the Lamb of God who takes away the sin of the world (John 1:29). Now the disciples are to extend Jesus' mission of freeing people from slavery to sin through preaching the Good News and through Baptism. They will be empowered to carry out this mission through the Holy Spirit.

Thomas is not present when the other disciples see the Lord. He does not believe, and insists that he will not believe unless he sees Christ and feels Christ's wounds himself. A week later, Jesus appears again and knows exactly what Thomas had said. In other words, Jesus is just as much with the disciples when they do not perceive his presence as he is when they do perceive his presence. Once invited to touch Jesus' wounds, Thomas has no need to do so. Thomas perceives Jesus' divinity and worships him. Jesus then says what John is teaching his audience: "Blessed are those who have not seen and have believed."

The reading ends with what is thought to have been the original conclusion to John's narrative. It clearly states John's purpose in writing his account: John wants his readers to believe "that Jesus is the Christ, the Son of God, and that through this belief [they] may have life in his name." As you proclaim this reading, remember that the Church has selected this reading today for the same reason: we, too, are called to have faith and believe so that we may have life in Jesus' name.

3RD SUNDAY OF EASTER

Lectionary #46

READING I Acts 2:14, 22–33

Apostles = uh-POS-*lz

This is the narrator's voice setting the stage.

Peter = PEE-ter

Like Peter, raise your voice and proclaim.

Jerusalem = juh-ROO-suh-lem or juh-ROO-zuh-lem

Say these two lines with urgency.

Israelites = IZ-ree-uh-līt or IZ-ray-uh-lītz

Now Peter wants to be persuasive.

Nazarene = naz-uh-REEN

This is not said angrily but with regret and sorrow.

The tone changes quickly to hope and encouragement.

David = DAY-vid

Peter is simply quoting a familiar text, Psalm 16.

exulted = eg-ZULHT-*d

netherworld = NETH-er-werld

A reading from the Acts of the Apostles

Then **Peter** stood up **with** the **Eleven**,
raised his **voice**, and **proclaimed**:
"You who are **Jews**, indeed **all** of you staying in **Jerusalem**.
Let **this** be **known** to you, and **listen** to my **words**.
You who are **Israelites, hear these words**.
Jesus the **Nazorean** was a man **commended** to you by **God**
with **mighty deeds, wonders**, and **signs**,
which **God** worked **through** him in **your** midst,
as **you yourselves know**.
This man, delivered up by the **set plan** and **foreknowledge**
of **God**,
you killed, using **lawless men** to **crucify** him.
But **God raised him up, releasing** him from the **throes of death**,
because it was **impossible** for him to be **held** by it.
For **David says** of him:
*I **saw** the **Lord ever before me**,*
*with **him** at my **right hand** I shall **not** be **disturbed**.*
Therefore** my heart has been **glad
*and my **tongue** has **exulted**;*
*my **flesh, too**, will **dwell** in **hope**,*
*because **you** will **not abandon** my **soul** to the **netherworld**,*
*nor will you **suffer** your **holy one** to see **corruption**.*
*You have made **known** to **me** the **paths of life**;*
*you will **fill** me with **joy** in your **presence**.*

READING I Today's reading from Acts is part of Peter's Pentecost speech. Peter is addressing his own people, the Israelites. Because it is the Jewish feast of Pentecost, many diaspora Jews have returned to Jerusalem. The travelers have just heard Jesus' disciples speak in their own languages. They are amazed and wonder if the apostles are drunk, and Peter will eventually explain that it is the work of the Holy Spirit (Acts 2:13, 15).

Peter speaks with a great deal of urgency. He insists that the people "listen to" and "hear" his words. Peter wants his fellow Israelites to know that Jesus Christ is the Messiah, now exalted at God's right hand, and that Jesus has poured the Holy Spirit on the disciples. What the Israelites "see and hear" is not drunkenness, but the Spirit working through Jesus' disciples.

In this first post-Pentecost speech, Peter teaches truths core to Christianity. However, we read only part of the speech. The intent of the words we read today is better understood when placed in the context of the whole speech.

Peter begins by accusing his listeners. He tells them that Jesus, during his public ministry was "commended to [them] by God with mighty deeds, wonders, and signs." However they killed him, "using lawless men to crucify him."

On first reading, we may think that Luke (the author of Acts), through Peter's speech, is attributing sole blame for Jesus' death to the Israelites. This would be a misunderstanding. Luke has Peter acknowledge the mystery of Christ's death by saying that Jesus was "delivered up by the set plan and foreknowledge of God." Luke also acknowledges that the Israelites, because they were living in an occupied

Now, Peter is speaking intimately with his listeners. He is as much as saying, "This is something we all know."
Patriarch = PAY-tree-ahrk
prophet = PROF-uht

Emphasize "resurrection of Christ."

Now raise your voice for the rest of the reading. These are Peter's main points.

"My **brothers**, one can **confidently** say to you
about the **patriarch David** that he **died** and was **buried**,
and his **tomb** is in our **midst** to this **day**.
But since he was a **prophet**
and **knew** that **God** had **sworn** an **oath** to him
that he would set **one** of his **descendants** upon **his throne**,
he **foresaw** and **spoke** of the **resurrection** of the **Christ**,
that **neither** was he **abandoned** to the **netherworld**
nor did his **flesh** see **corruption**.
God raised this Jesus;
of **this** we are **all witnesses**.
Exalted at the **right hand** of **God**,
he received the promise of the **Holy Spirit** from the **Father**
and **poured him forth**, as you **see** and **hear**."

READING II 1 Peter 1:17–21

This reading has a single speaker. He writes in long sentences so read slowly, pausing at commas.
Emphasize "If."
impartially = im-PAHR-sh*l-ee
Emphasize "conduct."
sojourning SOH-jern-ing
Drop your voice for these three lines.
ransomed RAN-suhmd

Now raise your volume, emphasizing each word.

A reading from the first Letter of Saint Peter

Beloved:
If you invoke as **Father** him who **judges impartially**
according to **each one's works**,
conduct yourselves with **reverence** during the time
of your **sojourning**,
realizing that you were **ransomed** from your **futile conduct**,
handed on by your **ancestors**,
not with **perishable things** like **silver** or **gold**
but with the **precious blood** of **Christ**
as of a **spotless unblemished lamb**.

country, did not have the authority to inflict the death penalty. Those who crucified Jesus were Romans.

The purpose of Peter's words is not to attribute sole blame to his own people but to call them to repentance and to assure them of God's forgiveness, a core theme in both Luke's Gospel and in Acts. This purpose is made clear in a part of the speech not included in the Lectionary. Peter says, "Repent and be baptized, every one of you, in the name of Jesus Christ for the forgiveness of your sins; and you will receive the gift of the holy Spirit" (Acts 2:38).

Luke then pictures Peter reinterpreting an Old Testament psalm as he teaches that Jesus is the Messiah and has risen from the dead. Reinterpretation of Old Testament texts was a common teaching method at the time. Peter is attributing Psalm 16:8–11 to David when he says, "David says of him." On David's lips, this psalm would have originally been expressing David's sure trust that God would be with him in battle and would help him be victorious. God would not allow God's "holy one to see corruption."

Reinterpreted in the light of Jesus' Resurrection, the psalm is seen to have an additional level of meaning. It is Jesus who was not abandoned to "the netherworld," nor did his body "see corruption." The psalm is no longer understood to be about David, who did die and whose tomb is right there. Rather, the psalm is about Jesus Christ. Through Jesus, God's promises to the house of David (see 2 Samuel 7:12–16) have been fulfilled. Jesus is now "exalted at the right hand of God." Jesus is the Messiah.

He was **known** before the **foundation** of the **world**
but **revealed** in the **final time** for **you**,
who through **him believe** in **God**
who **raised him** from the **dead** and **gave him glory**,
so that **your faith** and **hope** are in **God**.

Pause before and after "through him."
Emphasize this line. This is why we are reading this passage today.

GOSPEL Luke 24:13–35

A reading from the holy Gospel according to Luke

That very day, the **first** day of the **week**,
two of **Jesus' disciples** were going
to a village seven miles from **Jerusalem** called **Emmaus**,
and they were **conversing** about **all** the **things**
that had **occurred**.
And it happened that **while** they were **conversing** and **debating**,
Jesus himself drew near and **walked** with **them**,
but their **eyes** were **prevented** from **recognizing him**.
He asked them,
"**What** are you **discussing** as you **walk along**?"
They **stopped**, looking **downcast**.
One of them, named **Cleopas**, said to him in **reply**,
"Are you the **only visitor** to **Jerusalem**
who does **not know** of the things
that have **taken place** there in **these days**?"
And he replied to them, "**What sort** of **things**?"

The narrator sets the stage.

Jerusalem = juh-ROO–suh-lem or juh-ROO-zuh-lem
Emmaus = eh-MAY-uhs

Slow your tempo here.
Emphasize this line. It is mysterious.

Jesus appears just to be making conversation.

Cleopas = KLEE-oh-puhs
This is said with amazement and incredulity.

Again, Jesus appears just to be making conversation.

Jesus, the exalted one, the Messiah, has poured out his Spirit on his followers. That is what the Israelites have witnessed. Peter is imploring his fellow Israelites to believe, to repent, to be baptized, and to receive the Spirit themselves. As a lector, you will not only be reminding people of Peter's words, you will be imploring the people yourself. Jesus is the Messiah. We, too, are invited to believe, to repent, and to receive the Holy Spirit.

READING II In the selection from 1 Peter, the author is explaining to his readers how they are to live during a time when they are being ostracized by Roman society. That is what he means when he refers to their time of sojourning (see article on 1 Peter from the Second Sunday of Easter).

The author begins by reminding his readers that they address God as "Father," a very intimate way to speak to God. They also believe that their Father "judges impartially according to each one's works." Given this intimacy and this belief, the people should "conduct themselves with reverence," despite the difficulty of their present circumstances.

Why act with reverence even when being ostracized? Because the readers have been set free, "ransomed," from their "futile conduct," their past sinful behavior, by "the precious blood of Christ." Jesus, like the Passover lamb (see Exodus 12:15), was "spotless" and "unblemished." This Jesus, who has been revealed to them, God "raised . . . from the dead." It is because of Jesus that their "faith and hope are in God."

They said to him,

This is said with both conviction and sadness.
Nazarene = naz-uh-REEN

"The **things** that **happened** to **Jesus** the **Nazarene**,
who was a **prophet mighty** in **deed** and **word**
before **God** and **all** the **people**,
how our **chief priests** and **rulers** both **handed him over**
to a sentence of **death** and **crucified** him.

Say this slowly and thoughtfully.

But **we** were **hoping** that **he would be the one** to **redeem Israel**;

Israel = IZ-ree-uhl or IZ-ray-uhl

and besides all **this**,

sadness.

it is now the **third day** since this took place.

Speed up here.

Some **women** from our group, however, have **astounded** us:
they were at the **tomb early** in the **morning**
and **did not find** his **body**;
they came **back** and **reported**

This is not an act of faith. It is a repetition of an unbelievable claim.

that they had indeed **seen a vision** of **angels**
who **announced** that he was **alive**.
Then some of those **with us went** to the **tomb**
and found things **just** as the **women** had **described**,

Say this slowly and with sadness.

but **him** they **did not see**."

Say this with affection, not blame.

And he said to them, "**Oh**, how **foolish you are**!
How **slow** of **heart** to **believe** all that the **prophets spoke**!
Was it **not necessary** that the **Christ** should **suffer these things**
and enter into his **glory**?"

Now the narrator is speaking.
Moses = MOH-ziz or MOH-zis

Then beginning with **Moses** and all the **prophets**,
he **interpreted** to **them** what **referred** to **him**
in **all** the **Scriptures**.

Pause before this line.

As they approached the **village** to which they were **going**,
he gave the **impression** that he was going on **farther**.

Say this with great earnestness.

But they **urged** him, "**Stay with us**,
for it is **nearly evening** and the day is **almost over**."
So he went **in** to **stay** with them.

It is because of Jesus that our faith and hope are in God, too. As you proclaim this reading, give the greatest emphasis to Jesus' having been raised from the dead. It is because of this truth that we are proclaiming this reading today.

GOSPEL Today's Gospel, the story of Jesus' appearance to the two disciples on the road to Emmaus, is the same Gospel that was proclaimed on Easter Sunday afternoon (see the commentary for Easter Sunday). This story, which teaches us how to recognize the risen Lord in our presence, is of such significance that we proclaim it twice during the Easter season.

As the story begins, the disciples are dejected because their hopes have been dashed. Their situation is much more dire than that of the audience to whom 1 Peter was written. The disciples on the road to Emmaus are suffering not just ostracism, but total disillusionment. They had placed all their hopes in Jesus. Now their hopes have been completely dashed.

It is important to remember just how ignominious crucifixion was in the eyes of the Jews. The law put a curse on anyone who died on a tree (see Deuteronomy 21:22–23). That Jesus should die such a death brought into question whether he could possibly be the messiah. Would God allow his own son to die by crucifixion?

When Jesus joins the two disciples, they do not recognize him. After they explain to their unknown fellow traveler why they are so dejected, Jesus rebuilds their hope, just as the author of 1 Peter has done for his contemporaries. Jesus asks them: "Was it not necessary that the Christ should suffer these things and enter into his glory?"

Say the next three lines slowly. This is eucharistic language.

And it happened that, while he was **with them** at **table,**
he **took bread, said** the **blessing,**
broke it, and gave it to them.

Say this with awe.

With **that** their **eyes** were **opened** and they **recognized him,**
but he **vanished** from their **sight.**
Then they said to **each other,**

This is said with great joy.

"Were not our **hearts burning within** us
while he **spoke** to us on the **way** and **opened** the **Scriptures**
to us?"

This is the narrator again. Increase your tempo.

So they set out **at once** and **returned** to **Jerusalem**
where they found **gathered together**
the **eleven** and those **with** them who were saying,

This is fantastic good news!
Simon = SĪ-muhn

"The **Lord** has **truly** been **raised** and has **appeared** to **Simon!"**

The narrator concludes the story.
Say the last line slowly so that those in the assembly are left with these words ringing in their ears.

Then the two **recounted**
what had **taken place** on the **way**
and how **he** was **made known** to **them** in the **breaking**
of bread.

Here, Jesus is pictured affirming the same mystery that we saw affirmed in our reading from Acts: Jesus was "delivered up by the set plan and foreknowledge of God." The tragic event of Jesus' crucifixion is not evidence that Jesus is not the messiah. Rather, it is evidence that God's saving will for the human race is not thwarted by human evil and human failure. God's will can and has prevailed, despite human failings.

While teaching and comforting the disciples, Jesus "interpreted to them what referred to him in all the Scriptures." Here we see attributed to Jesus the same method of biblical interpretation that Peter used in today's reading from Acts. Old Testament passages are reinterpreted in the light of New Testament events, in the light of Jesus Christ. They are understood to have a second level of meaning, not previously understood, that reveals that God's promises to his chosen people have been fulfilled in Jesus Christ.

Later, after the disciples have recognized Jesus in the breaking of the bread, and Jesus has "vanished from their sight," the disciples say, "Were not our hearts burning within us while he spoke to us on the way and opened the Scriptures to us?" In hindsight, they realize that they should have recognized Jesus earlier, not just in the breaking of the bread.

As you proclaim this reading, remember that as Catholics, we believe that Jesus is present at the table of the word as well as at the table of the Eucharist. Our hearts, too, are burning within us as the word is proclaimed. The Lord has truly risen and is with us in many ways as we gather in his name.

4TH SUNDAY OF EASTER

Lectionary #49

READING I Acts 2:14a, 36–41

Apostles = uh-POS-*lz
The narrator sets the stage.
Peter = PEE-ter
You, too, should raise your voice and proclaim.
Israel = IZ-ree-uhl or IZ-ray-uhl
Emphasize this line.
Peter is not trying to antagonize, but to enlighten.
crucified = KROO-sih-fid
The Israelites are eager to do whatever is necessary.
This is an invitation, not a command.

The invitation is offered to all! This is wonderful news!

Drop your voice for the narrator's lines.
testified = TES-tuh-fid
Say this with urgency.
corrupt = kohr-RUPT
This is wonderful news! Say this with awe.

A reading from the Acts of the Apostles

Then **Peter** stood up **with** the **Eleven**,
raised his **voice**, and **proclaimed**:
"Let the **whole house** of **Israel know** for **certain**
that **God** has made both **Lord** and **Christ**,
this **Jesus** whom **you crucified**."
Now when they **heard this**, they were **cut** to the **heart**,
and they asked **Peter** and the **other apostles**,
"**What** are we to **do**, my brothers?"
Peter said to them,
"**Repent** and be **baptized, every one** of you,
in the name of **Jesus Christ** for the **forgiveness** of your **sins**;
and you will receive the **gift** of the **Holy Spirit**.
For the **promise** is made to **you** and to **your children**
and to **all those far off**,
whomever the **Lord** our **God** will **call**."
He **testified** with **many other arguments**,
and was **exhorting** them,
"**Save yourselves** from this **corrupt generation**."
Those who **accepted** his **message** were **baptized**,
and about **three thousand persons** were **added that day**.

READING I Today we continue to read Peter's sermon on Pentecost (see the commentary for the Third Sunday of Easter). That this is a later part of the same speech is made clear by the repetition of the first sentence. Notice, although it is Peter who is speaking, Peter is standing "with the Eleven." Peter and the eleven make up the twelve apostles, those who have witnessed Jesus' public ministry and post-Resurrection appearances and have been commissioned by Jesus to pass on this good news to others.

As we did last week, we hear Peter accuse his audience, the Israelites, of being instrumental in Jesus' death. This week we are provided with the context we need to understand Peter's purpose: Peter does not want simply to blame the Israelites, but to call them to conversion and to invite them to receive Baptism. Peter says, "Repent and be baptized, everyone one of you, in the name of Jesus Christ for the forgiveness of your sins; and you will receive the gift of the Holy Spirit."

Peter then reminds the Israelites that this invitation is offered to future generations, "your children," and to those not present now, "those far off." It is a universal invitation that extends through time and space. Peter says that the promise is made to "whomever the Lord our God will call." Peter will later understand that God is calling even Gentiles (see Acts 10). In response to Peter's preaching, 3,000 more people receive Baptism and become part of the early Church.

As you, like Peter, raise your voice and proclaim this reading, give special emphasis to the claim that God has made Jesus "both Lord and Christ," and to the

READING II 1 Peter 2:20b–25

A reading from the first Letter of Saint Peter

The author is trying not only to encourage, but to comfort his readers.

Beloved:
If you are **patient** when you **suffer** for doing what is **good**,
this is a **grace** before **God**.
For to **this** you have been **called**,
because **Christ also suffered** for **you**,
leaving you an **example** that you should **follow** in **his** footsteps.
***He committed no sin**, and **no deceit** was **found** in **his mouth**.*

Emphasize this line. This is the author's main point.
Here the author is quoting Isaiah.
deceit = dih-SEET
Speak gently here.

When he was **insulted**, he returned **no** insult;
when he **suffered**, he did **not threaten**;
instead, he **handed himself over** to the **one** who **judges justly**.
He himself bore **our** sins in **his** body upon the **cross**,
so that, **free** from **sin**, we might **live** for **righteousness**.
By **his** wounds **you** have been **healed**.
For **you** had **gone astray** like **sheep**,
but you have now **returned** to the **shepherd** and **guardian**
of your **souls**.

Emphasize this line, and then pause.
righteousness = RÍ-chuhs-n*s
Emphasize this line. This is wonderful news.
This is not an accusation, but ancient history. Now the people are living as disciples of Christ.

invitation to repent, be baptized, and receive the Holy Spirit. It is because of these themes that the reading has been chosen for today.

READING II The Second Reading is our third semi-continuous reading from 1 Peter. In today's selection, the author is teaching those who are presently suffering for their fidelity to Jesus Christ to look to Christ as their model.

Christ, too, suffered, not because he was guilty, but as an innocent person. Christ's suffering had redemptive power. The author assures his readers that "By his wounds you have been healed."

In teaching this truth, the author of 1 Peter reinterprets one of Isaiah's suffering servant songs. In Second Isaiah (40—55) we read a number of prophecies addressed to the Babylonian exiles (587–537 BC) in which Second Isaiah is offering the exiles hope that their suffering is not in vain. Rather, God is doing something new and wonderful: through them, other nations will come to know God.

The author of 1 Peter quotes Second Isaiah when he says: "He committed no sin, and no deceit was found in his mouth" (Isaiah 53:9b). The "he" referred to in Isaiah was the personified nation, Israel. The author of 1 Peter reinterprets Isaiah 53:4–12 and applies the words to Jesus. Jesus is the suffering servant whose suffering has redeemed the world.

The author of 1 Peter is reminding his readers that before they knew Christ they "had gone astray like sheep." Now they "have returned to the shepherd." They should remain faithful to Jesus Christ,

GOSPEL John 10:1–10

A reading from the holy Gospel according to John

This is said with great authority.

Say this with less firmness and more gentleness.

Here the tone changes again to warning.

Now the narrator is simply giving us information.

Pharisees = FAYR-uh-seez

Again, Jesus speaks with authority.

Emphasize this line

Emphasize this line. This idea is being repeated.

pasture = PAS-cher

slaughter = SLAW-ter

Read this line slowly so that it stays with your listeners.

Jesus said:
"**Amen, amen**, I **say** to you,
whoever does not enter a sheepfold through the **gate**
but climbs over **elsewhere** is a **thief** and a **robber**.
But whoever enters **through** the gate is the **shepherd**
of the **sheep.**
The gatekeeper **opens** it **for** him, and the **sheep hear** his **voice**,
as the **shepherd** calls his **own sheep** by **name**
and **leads** them out.
When he has driven out **all his own**,
he **walks ahead** of them, and the **sheep** follow **him**,
because they **recognize** his **voice**.
But they will **not follow** a **stranger**;
they will **run away** from him,
because they **do not recognize** the voice of **strangers**."
Although Jesus used this figure of speech,
the **Pharisees** did not **realize** what he was trying to **tell** them.

So Jesus said again, "**Amen, amen, I say to you**,
I am the **gate** for the **sheep**.
All who came **before** me are **thieves** and **robbers**,
but the **sheep** did not **listen** to **them**.
I am the **gate**.
Whoever **enters** through **me** will be **saved**,
and will **come in** and **go out** and **find pasture**.
A **thief** comes only to **steal** and **slaughter** and **destroy**;
I came so that they might have **life**
and have it **more abundantly**."

their Redeemer, even though they are suffering. Jesus has left them an example, and they should "follow in his footsteps."

As you proclaim this reading, give particular emphasis to the lines: "free from sin, we might live for righteousness," and, "By his wounds you have been healed." Whether or not we are presently suffering, these words are true for all of us.

GOSPEL In today's Gospel, Jesus is trying to teach the Pharisees something that they fail to understand. Immediately before today's passage, Jesus has given sight to a blind man. The Pharisees have concluded that Jesus could not be from God because he does not observe the Sabbath. Jesus has accused them of being blind. What is it that the Pharisees are unable to understand?

Jesus is trying to teach the Pharisees his own identity. In doing this, Jesus uses metaphorical language that he has appropriated from Ezekiel 34:1–31. In Ezekiel, God says that he "will look after and tend my sheep. . . . Thus they shall know that I, the Lord, am their God, and they are my people" (Ezekiel 34:11, 30a).

Jesus is telling the Pharisees that he is the good shepherd. Those who recognize his voice, like the once blind man, but unlike the Pharisees, will follow him. Jesus is also "the gate for the sheep." Whoever enters through this gate "will be saved." Jesus has come from God and is the way to God. Jesus has come in order to give life, and to give it more abundantly.

The Pharisees do not recognize Jesus' voice. As today's reading is proclaimed, we are invited to recognize Jesus' voice so that we may have life, and have it more abundantly.

5TH SUNDAY OF EASTER

Lectionary #52

READING I Acts 6:1–7

Apostles = uh-POS-*lz

The narrator is speaking. Emphasize "number of disciples continues to grow." This will be repeated.

Disciples = dih-SĪ-p*lz

Hellenists = HEL-uh-nist

Hebrews = HEE-brooz

A reading from the Acts of the Apostles

As the number of **disciples** continued to **grow**,
the **Hellenists** complained against the **Hebrews**
because their **widows**
were being **neglected** in the **daily distribution**.
So the **Twelve called together** the **community** of the disciples
and said,

The apostles are announcing a formal decision.

"It is **not right** for **us** to **neglect** the **word of God** to **serve**
at **table**.
Brothers, select from **among you seven reputable men**,
filled with the **Spirit** and **wisdom**,
whom **we shall appoint** to this task,
whereas **we** shall devote **ourselves** to **prayer**
and to the **ministry** of the **word**."

Emphasize "we shall appoint." The new leaders are accountable to the apostles.

The proposal was **acceptable** to the **whole community**,
so they chose **Stephen**, a man **filled** with **faith**
and the **Holy Spirit**,
also **Philip, Prochorus, Nicanor, Timon, Parmenas**,
and **Nicholas** of **Antioch**, a convert to **Judaism**.

Emphasize "whole community." Unity is being maintained.

Stephen = STEE-vuhn; Philip = FIL-ip; Prochorus = PRAH-kuh-ruhs; Nicanor = nih-KAY-ner or nī-KAY-ner; Timon = TĪ-muhn; Parmenas = PAHR-muh-nuhs; Nicholas = nik-oh-LAY-uhs; Antioch = AN-tee-ahk; Judaism = JOO-duh-is-*m or JOO-dee-iz-*m

They presented these men to the **apostles**
who **prayed** and **laid hands** on them.

Emphasize the apostles' role. It's very important to Luke.

The **word of God continued** to **spread**,
and the **number** of the disciples in Jerusalem increased **greatly**;
even a **large group** of **priests** were becoming **obedient**
to the **faith**.

Today's whole story is illustrating the growth of the disciples, the Church.

READING I In today's reading from Acts, Luke tells us how the early Christian community responded to a situation that threatened to destroy its unity. The solution put belief in Jesus Christ before cultural differences and resulted in the establishment of a new leadership role in the Church.

The problem arose because the "Hellenists" accused the "Hebrews" of neglecting their widows "in the daily distribution" of food. The Hellenists were diaspora Jews who spoke Greek, and the Hebrews were Jerusalem Jews who spoke Hebrew. The apostles were Hebrews, not Hellenists.

Rather than ignore the problem, or tell the Hellenists that they were welcome to leave if they were unhappy with the apostles' administration of community goods, the "Twelve" called a meeting to solve the problem. They instructed the Hellenists to choose seven men who would handle administrative affairs for the Hellenists, and the Twelve would formally appoint the men to this task. The solution gave the Hellenists their own leaders while preserving their unity with, and accountability to, the apostles.

Although there is an apparent distinction between the apostles' role, "the ministry of the word," and the soon to be appointed leaders' role, "to serve at table," this distinction is not maintained in the rest of Acts. Stephen and Philip, the only two of the seven who appear later in Acts, are both involved in the ministry of the word.

After the seven men are chosen, they are formally installed. The apostles "prayed and laid hands on them." This is not a ceremony of ordination (that will develop

READING II 1 Peter 2:4–9

A reading from the first Letter of Saint Peter

Beloved:

This is an exhortation. Speak with urgency.

Come to **him**, a **living stone, rejected** by **human beings**
but **chosen** and **precious** in the sight of **God**,
and, like **living stones**,
let **yourselves** be built into a **spiritual house**
to be a **holy priesthood** to offer **spiritual sacrifices**
acceptable to **God** through **Jesus Christ**.

Emphasize "holy priesthood" and "spiritual sacrifices." The author is helping the people find meaning in their suffering.

For it says in **Scripture**:
Behold, *I am laying a* ***stone*** *in* ***Zion***,
a ***cornerstone***, ***chosen*** *and* ***precious***,
and whoever ***believes*** *in* ***it*** *shall* ***not*** *be put to* ***shame***.

Now the author quotes scripture to support what he has already said. Read this with less affect.

Zion = ZĪ-ahn

Therefore, its **value** is for you who have **faith**, but for those
without faith:
The ***stone*** *that the* ***builders rejected***
has become the ***cornerstone***,
and
a ***stone*** *that will make people* ***stumble***,
and a ***rock*** *that will make them* ***fall***.
They **stumble** by **disobeying** the **word**, as is their **destiny**.

Emphasize "you who have faith." The author is drawing a contrast here.

The author is quoting Psalm 118.

Again, the author is quoting, this time Isaiah 8.

You are "a **chosen race**, a **royal priesthood**,
a **holy nation**, a **people** of his **own**,
so that **you** may announce the **praises**" of **him**
who called you **out** of **darkness into** his **wonderful light**.

Now raise your voice and speak with great confidence. These words are equally true of us.

later), but of commissioning. The formal installation of leaders had long been a custom among the Israelites (see Numbers 27:18–23). Nor do scripture scholars think that this scene is the birth of the deaconate. The newly chosen men were responsible not just to serve at table, but to equitably distribute community property, a responsibility that today belongs to bishops.

By seeking an equitable solution to the problem, the apostles succeeded in their main goal: "The word of God continued to spread." As you proclaim this reading, emphasize Luke's point, presented both as the reading begins and as it ends: the "number of disciples continued to grow."

READING II For the Fifth Sunday of Easter we are reading a selection from 1 Peter. However, today's passage precedes the one we read last week. In today's reading the author is weaving together a number of Old Testament texts from Exodus, Psalm 118, Isaiah, and Malachi to remind his readers of their new state of being, now that they have been called "out of darkness into his [God's] wonderful light."

As the passage begins, the author is referring to a verse from Psalm 118 that he later quotes: "The stone that the builders rejected / has become the cornerstone" (Psalm 118:22). He is identifying this rejected stone with Jesus Christ. The author exhorts his readers to come to this living stone (Jesus Christ), "precious in the sight of God," and become living stones themselves to "offer spiritual sacrifices acceptable to God through Jesus Christ."

After this exhortation, the author directly quotes or alludes to an array of

GOSPEL John 14:1–12

A reading from the holy Gospel according to John

disciples = dih-SĪ-p*lz

Jesus is consoling the disciples about his coming departure.

Emphasize this line. The exhortation to have faith will be repeated.

Jesus said to his **disciples:**
"**Do not** let your **hearts** be **troubled.**
You have faith in **God**; have faith **also** in **me.**
In my **Father's house** there are **many dwelling places.**
If there were **not,**
would I have **told you** that I am going to **prepare** a **place** for **you?**
And **if I go** and **prepare** a **place** for **you,**
I will **come back again** and **take you** to **myself,**
so that **where I am you also** may **be.**
Where I am going **you know** the **way.**"

Emphasize this line. Jesus' ongoing presence with his disciples is John's main theme throughout his Gospel account.

Thomas = TOM-uhs

Thomas is somewhat exasperated here.

Thomas said to him,
"**Master,** we do **not** know **where** you are going;
how can we **know** the **way?**"

Emphasize these two lines. Jesus is teaching the disciples that he is the way to the Father.

Jesus said to him, "**I am the way** and the **truth** and the **life.**
No one comes to the **Father except through me.**
If you **know me,** then you will **also** know my **Father.**
From now on you **do** know him and **have** seen him."

Old Testament texts, texts that originally referred to God's relationship with the Chosen People, Israel, and reinterprets them to apply to his audience, baptized Christians. He tells his readers that they are "a chosen race" (Isaiah 43:20–21), "a royal priesthood" (Exodus 19:6), "a holy nation" (Exodus 19:6), and "a people of his [God's] own" (Malachi 3:17). For them, Christ is not a stumbling block (Isaiah 8:14) as he is for nonbelievers. Rather, they now have the opportunity to "announce my [God's] praise" (Isaiah 43:21).

As we know, 1 Peter was written to Christians facing ostracism from Roman society because of their fidelity to Jesus Christ. In this passage the author is exhorting his readers to join their suffering to Christ's suffering. Joined to Christ as living stones (the Church), the people can, through their suffering, "announce the praises" of God, who has called them "out of darkness," their pagan past, to be God's own.

It will be important to read this passage to yourself several times until you completely understand it. Then you will be able to more effectively exhort those gathered for worship to realize that they, too, are God's own people.

GOSPEL Our reading from John is part of Jesus' farewell discourse to the disciples at their last meal on the night before Jesus dies. The reading both begins and ends with Jesus encouraging the disciples to have faith, both in him and in the Father. As the reading begins, Jesus says, "You have faith in God; have faith also in me." As the reading ends, he says, "whoever believes in me will do

Philip = FIL-ip

Philip is eager to know the Father.

Now, Jesus is exasperated, but he speaks gently.

Emphasize this line. Jesus and the Father are one.

Jesus is exhorting the disciples to believe.

Again, emphasize the words "believe in me."

Philip said to him,
"**Master, show** us the **Father**, and **that** will be **enough** for us."
Jesus said to him, "Have I been with you for so **long a time**
and you **still do not know me**, Philip?
Whoever has **seen me** has **seen** the **Father**.
How can you say, 'Show us the Father'?
Do you not **believe** that **I am in** the **Father** and the **Father** is
in me?
The words that I **speak** to you I do **not speak** on **my own**.
The **Father** who **dwells in me** is **doing his works**.
Believe me that **I am in** the **Father** and the **Father** is **in me**,
or else, **believe** because of the **works themselves**.
Amen, amen, I **say** to you,
whoever **believes** in **me** will do the **works** that **I do**,
and will do **greater ones** than **these**,
because **I am going** to the **Father**."

the works that I do, and will do greater ones than these."

Jesus also assures the disciples that his departure from them is not permanent. Rather, Jesus is going to prepare a place for the disciples and will return to them: "I will come back again and take you to myself, so that where I am you also may be." This promise to return is fulfilled in Jesus' post-Resurrection appearances to the disciples. Through these appearances the disciples will learn that the risen Christ continues to dwell in their midst.

Jesus also tries to help his disciples understand the unity that exists between himself and his Father. In answer to Thomas' question about "the way," Jesus says, "I am the way and the truth and the life. No one comes to the Father except through me." Jesus is not only the way to the Father, but Jesus is the revelation of the Father. Jesus tells Philip: "Whoever has seen me has seen the Father." Jesus explains to the disciples that he is in the Father and the Father is in him. Jesus is not speaking to the disciples on his own, but the Father, who dwells in Jesus, is doing the Father's works.

As John's account continues, we learn what Jesus means when he says that whoever believes in him will do greater works than Jesus has done. Jesus, because he is going to the Father, will send the Advocate, the Holy Spirit (see John 14:15). Through the power of the Spirit, Jesus' disciples, including us, will continue to do Jesus' work through the centuries. As you proclaim Jesus' words today, you also will be exhorting Jesus' disciples to have faith.

6TH SUNDAY OF EASTER

Lectionary #55

READING I Acts 8:5–8, 14–17

Apostles = uh-POS-*lz
There is a single voice in this reading. The narrator is teaching us about the growth of the Church.
Philip = FIL-ip
Samaria = suh-MAYR-ee-uh
Emphasize "the Christ."

A reading from the Acts of the Apostles

Philip went down to the city of **Samaria**
and **proclaimed** the **Christ** to **them**.
With **one accord**, the crowds **paid attention** to what was said by Philip
when they **heard it** and **saw** the **signs** he was doing.

Say these lines with awe and joy.
paralyzed = PAYR-uh-lizd

For **unclean spirits, crying out** in a **loud voice**,
came **out** of **many possessed** people,
and many **paralyzed** or **crippled** people were **cured**.
There was **great joy** in that **city**.

Pause here.
Emphasize "apostles."

Now when the **apostles** in **Jerusalem**
heard that **Samaria** had **accepted** the **word of God**,

Peter = PEE-ter
John = jon

they sent them **Peter** and **John**,
who went down and **prayed** for them,
that they might **receive** the **Holy Spirit**,

Lower your voice here. This is background information.

for it had **not yet fallen** upon **any** of them;
they had only been **baptized** in the **name** of the **Lord Jesus**.

Emphasize these two lines. Luke is teaching the importance of the apostolic witness in the growth of the Church.

Then they **laid hands** on them
and they **received** the **Holy Spirit**.

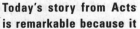

READING I **Today's story from Acts is remarkable because it demonstrates how the Church grew beyond Jerusalem to Samaritan lands. Preaching to the Samaritans was not a goal of the apostles. Rather, because Christians were being persecuted in Jerusalem, some of the new believers scattered and began evangelizing elsewhere (see Acts 8:1).**

Among those who fled was Philip, one of the seven Hellenists who had been selected as a leader for that community (see last Sunday's reading from Acts). Philip not only "proclaimed the Christ" to the Samaritans, but added authority to his words by "the signs [exorcisms and healings] he was doing."

Luke then tells us that upon hearing that "Samaria had accepted the word of God," the apostles sent Peter and John to the new converts. Although they had been baptized, it was only after these representatives of the apostles "laid hands on them" that the Samaritans "received the Holy Spirit."

This description of the reception of the Spirit occurring at a time separate from a baptism in Jesus' name appears several times in Acts, though it is not the rule. (For example, the two acts happen simultaneously in Acts 1:5; 11:16.) On occasion, the coming of the Spirit is pictured as occurring after baptism (today's reading and Acts 19:1–6), and, on other occasions, before (Acts 10:44–48).

Luke's purpose seems to be to emphasize that under the guidance of the Spirit, new understandings and new growth occurred in such a way that unity with the apostolic witness and tradition (represented by the *apostles* or the *twelve*) was maintained. So, as you proclaim this

READING II 1 Peter 3:15–18

A reading from the first Letter of Saint Peter

Beloved:
Sanctify Christ as **Lord** in your **hearts**.
Always be **ready** to give an **explanation**
to **anyone** who **asks** you for a **reason** for your **hope**,
but do it with **gentleness** and **reverence**,
keeping your **conscience clear**,
so that, when you are **maligned**,
those who **defame** your **good conduct** in **Christ**
may **themselves** be put to **shame**.
For it is better to suffer for **doing good**,
if that be the **will** of **God**, than for **doing evil**.
For **Christ also suffered** for **sins** once,
the **righteous** for the sake of the **unrighteous**,
that he might **lead you** to **God**.
Put to **death** in the **flesh**,
he was **brought** to **life** in the **Spirit**.

Say this with earnestness and firmness.

sanctify = SANGK-tih-fī

Speak firmly but gently in order to model what is being taught.

conscience = KON-shuhns

maligned = muh-LĪN*D

Don't say this vindictively. The Christians are not shaming others. The truth, once known, is bringing shame because of the maligners' false accusations.

Christ is being held up as a model.

righteous = RĪ-chuhs

Emphasize this line. This is an explanation for a Christian's hope.

reading, you will want to give special emphasis to the last two lines: "Then they [Peter and John] laid hands on them and they received the Holy Spirit."

READING II The reading from 1 Peter continues to teach early Christians how to act as they suffer ostracism from Roman society. Today's reading begins in the middle of a sentence. The author is encouraging the people not to fear and not to be intimidated. Instead, they should "Sanctify Christ as Lord" in their hearts.

Rather than respond in kind, Christians are to treat those who malign them with "gentleness" and "reverence," always being willing to give "a reason for [their] hope." Of course, a Christian's hope lies in Jesus Christ and his Resurrection from the dead. To give a reason for one's hope is to evangelize.

The author then remarks that it is better to suffer for doing good than for doing evil. Innocent sufferers should take Christ as their model. Christ was innocent and suffered, and his suffering had redemptive power. He suffered so that others might be lead to God. Christ was killed, but "was brought to life in the Spirit." The author is teaching that those who remain faithful to Christ and share in his suffering will also share in his Resurrection.

Emphasize this last line. Because of this truth—that Christ, and we who are faithful to Christ, are brought to life in the Spirit—this reading is placed in the Easter season.

GOSPEL Today's Gospel is a continuation of Jesus' farewell address to the disciples that we were

GOSPEL John 14:15–21

A reading from the holy Gospel according to John

Jesus said to his **disciples**:

"If you **love me**, you will **keep my commandments**.

Emphasize this line. It will be repeated.

And I will ask the **Father**,
and he will **give** you **another Advocate** to be **with you always**,
the **Spirit** of **truth**, whom the **world cannot accept**,
because it neither **sees** nor **knows** him.

Advocate = AD-voh-k*t
Emphasize "Spirit of truth."

But **you** know him, because he **remains with you**,
and will be **in you**.

Pause here.

I will not leave you orphans; I will **come** to you.

Say this slowly and with great love.

In a **little while** the world will no longer **see** me,
but **you will** see me, because **I live** and **you will live**.

This is the good news that both the disciples and John's audience long to hear.

On that day you will **realize** that **I am in** my **Father**
and **you** are **in me** and **I** in **you**.
Whoever has my **commandments** and **observes** them
is the one who **loves** me.
And whoever **loves** me will be **loved by** my **Father**,
and **I will love him** and **reveal** myself **to** him."

Read slowly here. This is being repeated and is the emphasis in today's reading.

reading last Sunday. As we rejoin Jesus and his disciples at their last meal together before Jesus dies, Jesus is reminding the disciples that if they love him, they will keep his commandments even after he has departed. If they do this, Jesus will ask his Father, and the Father will "give [them] another Advocate to be with [them] always."

Only in John is the Holy Spirit called an "Advocate." The term comes from a legal setting and means a defense attorney, one who defends and consoles another. This Advocate, "the Spirit of truth," like Jesus, will be accepted by the disciples but rejected by the world. The Spirit will remain with the disciples and will even dwell within them.

Jesus then promises the disciples that he "will not leave [them] orphans." Jesus says, "I will come to you." Remember that John's end of the century audience is wondering when the risen Christ will return in glory on the clouds of heaven. Here, John is assuring them, through Jesus' words to the disciples, that Jesus has returned and has never left. Through the Spirit, Jesus continues to dwell in and with the people.

Jesus then goes on to describe his unity with his Father ("I am in my Father . . ."). Those who love Jesus will be united to Jesus, to the Father, and to the Spirit who will dwell within them.

The reading begins and ends with the admonition that those who love Jesus will keep Jesus' commandments. As you proclaim the reading, emphasize that loving Jesus and keeping the commandments is what is necessary in order to receive the promised Advocate and to live in the presence of Jesus and the Father.

ASCENSION OF THE LORD

Lectionary #58

READING I Acts 1:1–11

Apostles = uh-POS-*lz

This is the author speaking. He is giving background information, connecting his two books together.

Theophilus = thee-OF-uh-luhs

Emphasize this line. This is very important to Luke.

Apostles = uh-POS-*lz

Pause after this line.

enjoined = en-JOYND

Jerusalem = juh-ROO-suh-lem or juh-ROO-zuh-lem

Now, Luke is quoting Jesus. Raise your volume and speak slowly.

Pause here.

The apostles are hopeful.

Israel = IZ-ree-uhl or IZ-ray-uhl

Jesus knows he is initially disappointing the apostles.

A reading from the Acts of the Apostles

In the **first book, Theophilus,**
I dealt with all that **Jesus did** and **taught**
until the day he was **taken up,**
after **giving instructions through** the **Holy Spirit**
to the **apostles** whom he had **chosen.**
He **presented himself alive** to them
by **many proofs** after he had suffered,
appearing to them during **forty days**
and **speaking** about the **kingdom** of **God.**
While **meeting** with them,
he **enjoined** them **not** to **depart** from **Jerusalem,**
but to **wait** for "the **promise** of the **Father**
about which you have **heard** me **speak;**
for **John baptized** with **water,**
but in a **few days you** will be **baptized** with the **Holy Spirit.**"

When they had **gathered together** they **asked** him,
"**Lord,** are **you** at **this time** going to **restore**
the **kingdom** to **Israel?**"
He answered them, "It is **not** for you to **know** the **times**
or **seasons**
that the **Father** has **established** by his **own authority.**

READING I Acts begins by reviewing what was taught in "the first book," that is, the Gospel According to Luke. Luke both concludes his account with the Ascension and begins Acts with the Ascension. The Ascension functions as the dividing point between Jesus' ministry, carried out both in the flesh and through post-Resurrection appearances, and Jesus' ministry, carried out in the Church through the power of the Holy Spirit.

Only in Acts does the Ascension take place 40 days after the Resurrection. In Luke's Gospel, the Ascension takes place on Easter Sunday evening (see Luke 24). Luke has separated what are aspects of a single Paschal Mystery—Jesus' Resurrection and Ascension—with the symbolic 40 days. The number 40 recalls the Israelites' 40 years in the desert and Jesus' forty days of temptation. The number 40 does not function as a number but means, *when the time was fulfilled.*

In Acts, the chosen apostles are told to wait in Jerusalem because "in a few days you will be baptized with the Holy Spirit." The apostles ask Jesus if he is, "at this time going to restore the kingdom to Israel." They are still thinking in terms of a political kingdom. Jesus tells them that it is not for them "to know the times or seasons that the Father has established." However, they will receive the Spirit and will be Jesus' "witnesses in Jerusalem, throughout Judea and Samaria, and to the ends of the earth."

The apostles then witness Jesus ascend into heaven. As was true in Luke's empty tomb story (Luke 24:4), two men in dazzling clothes (angels) are present to explain the significance of the event. The apostles are told that Jesus, who has been

Here, Jesus has wonderful news. Emphasize this line.

Judea = joo-DEE-uh or joo-DAY-uh
Samaria = suh-MAYR-ee-uh

Now the narrator is speaking. Fill your voice with awe.

The angels speak with joyful authority.
Galilee = GAL-ih-lee

Emphasize the promise of return.

But you will **receive power** when the **Holy Spirit** comes **upon** you,
and you will be my **witnesses** in **Jerusalem**,
throughout **Judea** and **Samaria**,
and to the **ends** of the **earth**."
When he had **said this**, as they were **looking** on,
he was **lifted up**, and a **cloud took** him from their **sight**.
While they were **looking intently** at the **sky** as he was **going**,
suddenly **two men** dressed in **white garments stood beside them**.
They said, "**Men of Galilee**,
why are you **standing there looking** at the **sky**?
This **Jesus** who has been **taken up** from you into heaven
will return in the **same way** as you have seen him going **into heaven**."

READING II Ephesians 1:17–23

Ephesians = ee-FEE-zhuhnz

Emphasize "God of our Lord Jesus Christ." All the following male pronouns refer back to God the Father.

Pause after each comma to make the three things the Ephesians are to know clear.
inheritance = in-HER-ih-t*ns

Pause again after this line.

A reading from the Letter of Saint Paul to the Ephesians

Brothers and sisters:
May the **God** of our **Lord Jesus Christ**, the **Father** of **glory**,
give you a **Spirit** of **wisdom** and **revelation**
resulting in **knowledge** of **him**.
May the **eyes** of your **hearts** be **enlightened**,
that you may **know** what is the **hope** that **belongs** to his **call**,
what are the **riches** of **glory**
in **his inheritance** among the **holy ones**,
and what is the **surpassing greatness** of his **power**
for **us** who **believe**,

taken up to heaven, will return. In the mean time, the apostles are not supposed to stand there, looking up at the sky, but are to follow Jesus' instructions.

As you read today's passage, emphasize those parts that are equally true of us. We, too, have been baptized with the Holy Spirit. We, too, know that Jesus will return. In the meantime, we, too, are to be Jesus' witnesses to the ends of the earth.

READING II Today's reading from the letter to the Christian community at Ephesus has only three sentences and uses complicated sentence structure. It will be very important that you understand the reading so that, by intonation, you make the reading understandable to others. Basically, today's passage is a blessing or prayer asking that the Ephesians come to understand God the Father, their call, and all that God has accomplished through Jesus Christ.

The use of "he" and "him" throughout the first half of the reading all refer back to "the God of our Lord Jesus Christ." The author is praying that God the Father will send the Ephesians the "Spirit of wisdom and revelation" so that they may know three things: "the hope that belongs to [God's] call [to them]," "the riches of glory in God's inheritance," and "the surpassing greatness of his power." All this has been made known through Jesus Christ, whom the Father has raised from the dead.

The description of the resurrected Christ makes this reading appropriate for the Ascension. Ephesians presents Christ as sitting at the Father's right hand in heaven, reigning above all of creation, even angels, and having authority over all things.

The author moves on to describe Christ's role in the Father's universal plan. Read slowly and with awe.

in accord with the exercise of **his great might**,
which he **worked** in **Christ**,
raising him from the **dead**
and **seating him** at his **right hand** in the **heavens**,

principality = prins-uh-PAL-uh-tee
dominion = doh-MIN-yuhn
The sentence finally ends here.

far above every principality, authority, power, and **dominion**,
and **every name** that is **named**
not only in **this age** but **also** in the **one** to **come**.

The author moves on to address the relationship between Christ and the Church.

And he put **all things beneath** his **feet**
and gave him as **head** over **all things** to the **church**,

Emphasize this line.

which is **his body**,
the **fullness** of the **one** who **fills all things** in **every way**.

GOSPEL Matthew 28:16–20

A reading from the holy Gospel according to Matthew

This is the narrator setting the stage.
disciples = dih-SĪ-p*lz
Galilee = GAL-ih-lee
Emphasize "worshiped."

The **eleven disciples** went to **Galilee**,
to the **mountain** to which **Jesus** had **ordered** them.
When they **saw** him, they **worshiped**, but they **doubted**.
Then Jesus **approached** and **said** to them,

Speak Jesus' words with great authority.
baptizing = BAP-tīz-ing or bap-TĪZ-ing

"**All power** in **heaven** and on **earth** has been **given** to **me**.
Go, therefore, and **make disciples** of **all nations**,
baptizing them in the name of the **Father**,
and of the **Son**, and of the **Holy Spirit**,
teaching them to observe **all** that I have **commanded** you.

Emphasize the last line. This is just as true today as it was in Matthew's time.

And **behold**, I am **with you always**, until the **end** of the **age**."

Christ is also the "head" of the Church, "which is his body." The Church is to be the fullness of Christ on earth. The Ephesians—and we, the Church—have been called to cooperate, through Christ and the Spirit, in God's redemptive plan for all of creation. The author of Ephesians prays that the Ephesians may come to know God the Father and their great call. You will help the Church, the gathered community, understand our call as you proclaim this reading.

GOSPEL **The Gospel, like the reading from Ephesians, states that "All power in heaven and on earth" has been given to the risen Christ. It also states that Christ's Resurrection and Ascension have not resulted in Christ's absence from us, but in Christ's presence. Jesus' last words to the eleven disciples are: "I am with you always, until the end of the age."**

That the risen, ascended Christ remains with us is stated both at the beginning and end of Matthew's Gospel. As the Gospel begins, in Matthew's Annunciation story, he says, " 'Behold, the virgin shall be with child and bear a son, / and they shall name him Emmanuel,' / which means, 'God is with us' " (Matthew 1:23).

The universal nature of God's saving plan is also proclaimed in today's Gospel. The disciples are told to "make disciples of all nations," not simply to go to the Israelites as they were previously instructed (see Matthew 10:6). As you proclaim this Gospel, emphasize this line because we too, as disciples of Jesus Christ, are called to make disciples of all nations.

7TH SUNDAY OF EASTER

Lectionary #59

READING I Acts 1:12–14

Apostles = uh-POS-*lz

There is a single voice in today's reading, telling us what occurred immediately after the Ascension.

Jerusalem = juh-ROO-suh-lem or juh-ROO-zuh-lem

Olivet = OL-ih-vet

Read each name slowly and distinctly. The apostolic witness is very important to Luke.

Peter = PEE-ter; Andrew = AN-droo; Philip = FIL-ip; Thomas = TOM-uhs; Bartholomew = bahr-THAHL-uh-myoo; Matthew = MATH-yoo; Alphaeus = AL-fee-uhs; Simon = SĪ-muhn; Zealot = ZEL-uht; Judas = JOO-duhs

Emphasize "Mary, the mother of Jesus." Luke, more than any other Gospel, gives Mary special mention and attention.

A reading from the Acts of the Apostles

After **Jesus** had been **taken up** to **heaven** the **apostles**
returned to **Jerusalem**
from the mount called **Olivet**, which is **near Jerusalem**,
a **sabbath day's journey** away.
When they **entered** the **city**
they went to the **upper room** where they were staying,
Peter and **John** and **James** and **Andrew**,
Philip and **Thomas**, **Bartholomew** and **Matthew**,
James son of **Alphaeus**, **Simon** the **Zealot**,
and **Judas** son of **James**.
All these devoted themselves with **one accord** to **prayer**,
together with some **women**,
and **Mary** the **mother** of **Jesus**, and his **brothers**.

READING I Today's reading follows immediately after the reading from Acts that the Church proclaimed on The Ascension. Luke tells us that the disciples returned from Mount Olivet to Jerusalem, which was "a sabbath day's journey away." That means that it was not a *journey* at all, as Jews would not travel on the Sabbath. The distance was about one half mile. In Luke's two volume work (Gospel and Acts), the post-Resurrection appearance and Ascension take place in and around Jerusalem.

Luke pictures the apostles doing as they were instructed to do: staying in Jerusalem to await the coming of the Spirit. Luke then names each apostle. The list of the apostles, minus Judas, includes the same people that Luke named in his Gospel (see Luke 6:14–16). It is very important to Luke that his readers know that the Church is faithful to the apostolic witness. He constantly emphasizes the apostles and the authority that was duly delegated to them and by them.

Luke then tells us that with the apostles were some women, including "Mary, the mother of Jesus, and his brothers." ("Brothers" could refer to half-brothers, cousins, or followers.) It is only in Luke's two volume work that we meet Mary rather than simply hear about her. That Mary is present here means that she is included in the group that Luke will soon describe who are gathered when the Spirit comes, descending on each one present.

As you proclaim this reading, read the names of the apostles slowly and carefully. Also emphasize who else was present: Mary, the mother of Jesus. Luke is

READING II 1 Peter 4:13–16

A reading from the first Letter of Saint Peter

Beloved:
Rejoice to the extent that you **share** in the **sufferings** of **Christ**,
so that when **his glory** is **revealed**
you may **also rejoice exultantly**.
If you are **insulted** for the **name** of **Christ**, **blessed** are you,
for the **Spirit** of **glory** and of **God rests upon** you.
But let **no one among** you be made to suffer
as a **murderer**, a **thief**, an **evildoer**, or as an **intriguer**.
But whoever is made to suffer as a **Christian** should **not be ashamed**
but **glorify God** because of the **name**.

The tone for this reading is one of encouragement and hope. Emphasize "rejoice." It will be repeated.

Emphasize "glory."

Emphasize "rejoice exultantly."

Now, drop your voice. The tone is comforting.

Now, begin to raise your volume.

intriguer = in-TREEG-*r

Again, emphasize "glorify God."

GOSPEL John 17:1–11a

A reading from the holy Gospel according to John

Jesus raised his eyes to **heaven** and said,
"**Father**, the **hour** has **come**.
Give **glory** to **your son**, so that **your son** may **glorify you**,
just as you gave him **authority** over **all people**,
so that **your son** may give **eternal life** to **all you gave him**.
Now **this** is **eternal life**,
that they should know **you**, the **only true God**,
and the one whom **you sent**, **Jesus Christ**.

Jesus is praying with faith and courage. He knows the Father hears him.

glory = GLOHR-ee

Pause here.

Speak these three lines slowly.

setting the stage for Pentecost, which we will be celebrating next Sunday.

READING II The author of 1 Peter continues to teach his audience how to act in their present difficult circumstances. The early Christians are being ostracized from Roman society because of their belief in Jesus Christ. Instead of being afraid of suffering or choosing infidelity over suffering, the author of 1 Peter insists that Christians should rejoice in their sufferings. Why? Because they are sharing "in the sufferings of Christ." Those who join Christ in his suffering will also join him in his Resurrection. Therefore, "When [Christ's] glory is revealed" those who have been faithful will "also rejoice exultantly."

The author goes on to say that it is a blessing to be "insulted for the name of Christ." People would have reason to be ashamed if they were suffering because they were murderers, thieves, or evildoers. But if people suffer because they are faithful disciples of Jesus Christ, there is no reason to be ashamed. This, rather, is reason to glorify God.

As you proclaim this reading emphasize the words "rejoice" and "glory." These words are repeated and emphasize the attitude Christians should have even in times of difficulty. We are to rejoice because we know that we, too, will share in Christ's glory.

GOSPEL The reading from John, part of Jesus' prayer at his last meal with his disciples, also centers our attention on Jesus' glory. As the prayer begins, Jesus says, "Father, the hour has come. Give glory to your son, so that your

Now, increase your tempo. Emphasize "glorified" which is being constantly repeated.
glorified = GLOHR-ih-fīd

I glorified **you** on **earth**
by **accomplishing** the **work** that you **gave** me **to do**.
Now **glorify me**, **Father**, **with** you,
with the **glory** that I **had** with you **before** the **world began**.

"I revealed **your name** to those whom **you gave me** out of the world.
They belonged to **you**, and **you** gave them to **me**,

Say this line slowly. We are also to do this.

and they have **kept** your **word**.
Now they know that **everything you gave me** is **from you**,
because the **words you gave** to **me I** have given to **them**,

Again, emphasize these lines.

and they **accepted** them and **truly understood** that **I came** from **you**,

Pause here.

and they have **believed** that **you sent me**.
I **pray** for them.
I do not pray for the **world** but for the **ones** you have **given** me,
because they are **yours**, and **everything** of **mine** is **yours**
and everything of **yours** is **mine**,

Again emphasize "gloryified."

and I have been **glorified** in **them**.
And now I will **no longer** be in the **world**,

Jesus ends on a note of great joy. He is returning to his Father.

but **they** are in the **world**, while **I am coming** to **you**."

son may glorify you." The "hour" to which Jesus refers is the hour of his death, Resurrection, and Ascension. Jesus came from the Father to accomplish a mission. Now the hour is come for him to do what he has been sent to do. Both Jesus' and the Father's glory, their divinity and power, will be manifest through Jesus' saving actions.

Jesus has been given "authority over all people," and will use that authority to "give eternal life to all [the Father] gave him." Eternal life rests in knowing "the only true God" and "the one whom [God] sent, Jesus Christ." Jesus prays that just as he glorified the Father on earth "by accomplishing the work" he was given to do, God will now glorify him with the glory that he had with the Father "before the world began."

Jesus then prays for his disciples, saying that they have understood what Jesus has taught them and have "truly understood" that Jesus came from the Father. Jesus does not pray for "the world." The world in this section of John refers to those who have rejected Jesus and therefore the Father. The disciples came from the world and will remain in the world after Jesus has returned to the Father, but they are not of the world.

As you proclaim this Gospel, you will be proclaiming it to modern day disciples of Christ. We, too, through Jesus Christ, have come to know the Father. We too, are in the world but not of the world, and are called to accomplish the work we have been given to do. Jesus' prayer, therefore, can be understood to be not only for the disciples who were with him at his last supper on earth, but also for us, disciples who celebrate Eucharist with Christ today.

PENTECOST: VIGIL

Lectionary #62

READING I Genesis 11:1–9

Genesis = JEN-uh-sis

The narrator is beginning to tell us a story.

Shinar = SHEE-nahr or SHĪ-nahr

The people are anxious to get started.

bitumen = bih-TOO-m*n or bih-TYOO-m*n

These are great plans! The people are full of themselves.

God is pictured as though a human being. God is offended at the peoples' prideful actions.

Emphasize this "Let us" in contrast to the people's "let us."

A reading from the Book of Genesis

The **whole world** spoke the **same language**, using the **same words**.
While the **people** were **migrating** in the **east**,
they came upon a **valley** in the land of **Shinar**
and **settled** there.
They said to one another,
"**Come**, let us **mold bricks** and **harden** them with **fire**."
They used **bricks** for **stone**, and **bitumen** for **mortar**.
Then they said, "**Come**, let **us** build **ourselves** a city
and a **tower** with its **top** in the **sky**,
and so make a name for **ourselves**;
otherwise we shall be **scattered all over the earth**."

The **LORD came down** to **see** the **city** and the **tower**
that the **people** had built.
Then the LORD said: "If **now**, while they are **one people**,
all speaking the **same language**,
they have started to do **this**,
nothing will later **stop** them from doing
whatever they presume to do.
Let us then **go down there** and **confuse** their **language**,
so that **one** will not **understand** what **another** says."

There is a choice of readings today. Speak with the liturgy coordinator or homilist to find out which readings will be used.

READING I **GENESIS. The Tower of Babel is one of four stories of sin in Genesis. These stories set the stage for the beginning of salvation history, the call of Abraham. In order to understand this story we must understand its literary form. Otherwise, we might misunderstand the story and think that the author is teaching us that God is petty, threatened by human achievement, and wants to keep human beings in their place.**

This story is an *etiology*—an imaginative story that explains why something is as one knows it to be from experience. Today's story was originally an etiology about why human beings speak different languages. However, the story was appropriated and edited so that it became a story about human beings' disobedience and pride, behavior that resulted in separation from God and from each other.

When God created the human race, he told the people to "fill the earth" (Genesis 1:28). Each group was to have its own land and its own language (see Genesis 10:5). In today's story the people disobey God; they decide to stay put and to try to make a name for themselves by building a city with a great tower. The tower would be like the ziggurat temple towers in Babylon.

In this imaginative story, God is pictured *anthropomorphically,* that is, God is pictured as a human being. God decides to go down and see the city and the tower. When he sees that the people are being disobedient, refusing to "fill the earth," God decides to confuse the language of

This is the narrator speaking.

Thus the LORD **scattered** them from there **all over** the **earth,**
and they **stopped building** the **city**.

Here the narrator is insulting Babylon.
Babel = BAB-*l or BAY-b*l

That is why it was called **Babel**,
because **there** the **LORD confused** the **speech** of **all** the **world**.
It was **from that place** that he **scattered them all over** the **earth**.

Or:

READING I Exodus 19:3–8a, 16–20b

Exodus = EK-suh-duhs

A reading from the Book of Exodus

Moses = MOH-ziz or MOH-zis

Moses went up the **mountain** to **God**.
Then the **LORD called** to him and said,

Here God initially speaks in terms of intimacy and gentleness.
Jacob = JAY-kuhb
Israelite = IZ-ree-uh-līt or IZ-ray-uh-līt
Egyptians = ee-JIP-shuhnz

"**Thus** shall you **say** to the **house** of **Jacob**;
tell the **Israelites**:
You have **seen for yourselves** how I treated the **Egyptians**
and how I **bore you up** on **eagle wings**
and brought you **here** to **myself**.

Raise your voice and speak slowly. This passage is core to the Israelites' self identity.

Therefore, if you **hearken** to my **voice** and **keep** my **covenant**,
you shall be my **special possession**,
dearer to **me** than **all other people**,
though **all** the **earth** is **mine**.

Emphasize this line.

You shall be to me a **kingdom** of **priests**, a **holy nation**.

Now drop your voice again.

That is what you must **tell** the **Israelites**."

Now, the narrator is giving us background information.

So **Moses went** and **summoned** the **elders** of the **people**.
When he set before them
all that the **LORD** had **ordered him** to tell them,
the people **all answered together**,

Say this with total conviction and commitment. Then pause.

"**Everything** the **LORD** has **said**, **we will do**."

these proud and disobedient people who want to make a name for themselves. By telling us that the place is called *Babel*, the author is using a play on words to make fun of the Babylonians. The word *baal*, in Hebrew means "confusion."

In the next chapter of Genesis we will read about the reversal of the situation presented in today's story—that human beings are separated from God and from each other and are unable to do anything about it. God will take the initiative and call Abraham, Abraham will agree to go where God sends him, and it will be God who makes Abraham's name great (Genesis 12:2).

There are three voices in today's story: the narrator's, the people's, and God's. Do not be afraid to enter into the spirit of the story and emphasize the people's pride, God's decision to punish them, and the narrator's pun regarding Babylon.

EXODUS. In this reading from Exodus, we join the Israelites as they are encamped at the foot of Mount Sinai. This section of Exodus is the absolute core of the Pentateuch (the first five books of the Bible), and describes events central to the Israelites' self identity. Here, we read about the Israelites' covenant relationship with God and their unique role in salvation history.

God tells Moses to invite the people to reflect on their experience: the Israelites escaped slavery in Egypt through God's direct intervention in history. God says, "'You have seen for yourselves . . . how I bore you up on eagle wings and brought you here to myself.' " God goes on to tell the people that if they "obey [God's] voice" and live in fidelity to the covenant, they

Read these lines with awe.

On the morning of the **third day**
there were **peals** of **thunder** and **lightning**,
and a **heavy cloud** over the **mountain**,
and a **very loud trumpet blast**,
so that **all** the **people** in the camp **trembled**.

Say this with confidence. After all, the people know they are dear to God.

But **Moses led** the **people** out of the camp to **meet God**,
and they stationed themselves at the **foot** of the **mountain**.

Now return to a tone of awe.
Sinai = SĪ-nī

Mount Sinai was all **wrapped** in **smoke**,
for the **LORD came down upon it** in **fire**.
The smoke **rose** from it as though from a **furnace**,
and the **whole mountain trembled violently**.

Let your voice get louder and louder, too.

The **trumpet** blast grew **louder** and **louder**,
while **Moses** was **speaking**,
and **God** answering him with **thunder**.

Drop your voice for the last two lines.

When the **LORD came down** to the **top** of **Mount Sinai**,
he summoned **Moses** to the **top** of the **mountain**.

Or:

READING I Ezekiel 37:1–14

Ezekiel = ee-ZEE-kee-uhl

A reading from the Book of the Prophet Ezekiel

Ezekiel is speaking. He is setting the stage for the conversation that follows.

The **hand** of the **LORD** came **upon** me,
and he **led me out** in the **spirit** of the **LORD**
and **set** me in the **center** of the **plain**,

Emphasize "bones."

which was now **filled** with **bones**.
He made me **walk among** the **bones** in **every direction**
so that I **saw** how **many they were** on the surface of the plain.

Say this with amazement.

How **dry they were**!

will be God's "special possession, dearer to [him] than all other people."

Why will the Israelites be God's special people? Because God has chosen them to have a role in his plan of salvation for the world. The Israelites will be "a kingdom of priests, a holy nation." In other words, they will become a worshipping nation. They will have the role among nations that priests have among the people. They will help bring others to God. The people promise to be faithful. They say, "Everything the Lord has said, we will do."

Today's selection then skips forward in Exodus to God's theophany, God's self-revelation. The images used to describe God's presence, holiness, transcendence, and power are smoke, fire, the mountain's violent trembling, and thunder. This is an appropriate reading for Pentecost, on which we celebrate the coming of the Spirit in wind and fire, a coming that results in people of many languages hearing the Good News.

As you proclaim the reading, emphasize both God's gentleness—bearing the people up on eagles' wings—and God's power—present through fire, smoke, and a volcanic mountain. These very different images are equally important and true.

EZEKIEL. Ezekiel, who prophesied from 593–571 BC, offered hope to the Israelites while they were in exile in Babylon. In today's reading, Ezekiel is assuring all of the Israelites scattered in other nations that God's promises are not dead, nor is Israel dead. The Lord will bring the exiles back to the land of Israel.

Today's reading includes both a description of Ezekiel's vision of dry bones and an interpretation of the meaning of the

He asked me:
Son of **man**, can **these bones** come to **life**?
I answered, "**Lord God, you alone know that**."
Then he said to me:
Prophesy over these **bones**, and **say** to them:
Dry bones, hear the **word** of the **Lord**!
Thus says the **Lord God** to these **bones**:
See! I will bring **spirit into** you, that you may **come** to **life**.
I will put **sinews upon** you, make **flesh grow over** you,
cover you with **skin**, and put **spirit in** you
so that you may **come** to **life** and **know** that **I am** the **Lord**.
I, **Ezekiel**, **prophesied** as I had been **told**,
and even as I was **prophesying** I **heard** a **noise**;
it was a **rattling** as the **bones came together**, **bone joining bone**.
I saw the **sinews** and the **flesh** come **upon** them,
and the **skin cover them**, but there was **no spirit in** them.
Then the Lord said to me:
Prophesy to the **spirit**, **prophesy**, **son** of **man**,
and say to the **spirit**: **Thus says the Lord God**:
From the **four winds come**, **O spirit**,
and **breathe** into these **slain** that they may **come to life**.
I **prophesied** as he **told** me, and the **spirit** came **into** them;
they came **alive** and stood **upright**, a **vast army**.
Then he said to me:
Son of **man**, **these bones** are the **whole house** of **Israel**.
They have been saying,
"Our **bones** are **dried up**,
our **hope** is **lost**, and we are **cut off**."
Therefore, **prophesy** and **say** to them: **Thus says the Lord God**:
O my people, I will **open** your **graves**
and have you **rise** from them,
and **bring you back** to the **land** of **Israel**.

God asks this question. God is testing Ezekiel's faith.

Ezekiel passes the test. He knows God can do anything.

God is speaking with great authority.

Emphasize "come to life."

Emphasize this whole line.

Now, drop your voice. Ezekiel is speaking.

Say this with awe.

Say this with disappointment.

God again speaks with great authority.

Emphasize "spirit."

Emphasize "come to life."

Say this with excitement and amazement.

Now God is explaining the meaning of the vision.

The people have been saying this with despair.

Now God is speaking with compassion and assurance.

vision. First, God asks Ezekiel if dry bones can come back to life. The expected answer would be no, but Ezekiel does not say no. Ezekiel believes that all things are possible with God.

Next Ezekiel is told to prophesy to the dry bones, telling them that they will come to life and know that God is the Lord. The bones do get sinew and skin, but not the spirit of life. Next, Ezekiel is to prophesy to the spirit, who is to breathe life into those slain. Ezekiel does as he is told, and the slain come to life.

Ezekiel is then told that "these bones are the whole house of Israel," those in exile who feel "lost" and "cut off." Ezekiel is to prophesy to the house of Israel and to assure them that God will open their graves, that is, free them from exile, and bring them "back to the land of Israel." Then the Israelites will once more know their God. After all, God has "promised" and God "will do it." As you proclaim the reading, emphasize God's faithfulness, which is stressed in the closing line and in the refrain: "know that I am the Lord."

JOEL. The prophet Joel lived in Judah after the Babylonian exile had ended, the people had returned to Judah, and the temple had been rebuilt. In the earlier part of the book, we read that the people had experienced a terrible plague of locusts that decimated their crops. Joel interpreted this event as a sign of the coming of the "day the Lord." He called the people to repent, they have repented, and now he is promising them good things when the day of the Lord finally comes.

Emphasize "O my people." It is being repeated here.

Say these concluding lines with earnestness. God is promising and God will keep his promises.

Then you shall **know** that **I am the LORD**,
when I **open** your **graves** and have you **rise** from them,
O my people!
I will put **my spirit** in **you** that **you may live**,
and I will **settle you** upon **your land**;
thus you shall know that **I am the LORD**.
I have **promised**, and **I will do it**, says the **LORD**.

Or:

READING I Joel 3:1–5

Joel = JOH-*l

A reading from the Book of the Prophet Joel

God is promising something wonderful! Emphasize "pour out my spirit." This is being repeated.

These are signs of God's presence. They are meant to instill great awe, not fear.

It is "great" for the audience, but "terrible" for other nations.

Thus says the LORD:
I will **pour out** my **spirit** upon **all flesh**.
Your **sons** and **daughters** shall **prophesy**,
your **old men** shall **dream dreams**,
your **young men** shall **see visions**;
even upon the **servants** and the **handmaids**,
in those days, I will **pour out** my **spirit**.
And I will work **wonders** in the **heavens** and on the **earth**,
blood, **fire**, and **columns** of **smoke**;
the **sun** will be turned to **darkness**,
and the **moon** to **blood**,
at the **coming** of the **day** of the **LORD**,
the **great** and **terrible** day.

When the day of the Lord comes, God will pour out his spirit on everyone, irrespective of age or class. There will be mighty signs in the sky, as there were during the Exodus: "fire, and columns of smoke."

Joel describes the day of the Lord as both "great" and "terrible." Why? Because on that day God will judge the nations. It will be a great day for those who call "on the name of the Lord," as have the Israelites by repenting. It will be a terrible day for other nations, who have not.

Although the reading sounds frightening, Joel means to comfort and give hope to his readers. They have repented and so will be among the survivors in Jerusalem when God pours out his spirit. Therefore, the tone when proclaiming this reading should not be one of frightening condemnation, but one of awe and of hope.

READING II In today's reading, Paul is in the middle of an explanation of the Christian life in the Spirit. In many ways it is an "already, but not yet" experience. Paul, the Romans, and we have already experienced the presence of the Spirit; we are the "firstfruits of the Spirit." Through Christ we have been redeemed and are no longer slaves to "the law of sin and death" (Romans 8:1). We are living in the Spirit right now.

At the same time, we, along with all of creation, are involved in an on-going birth process that will result in the redemption, not just of our spirits, but our bodies, not just of human beings, but of all of creation. All of creation is "groaning in labor pains" for the fulfillment of what has already begun. We, too, "groan within ourselves as we wait for adoption, the redemption of our bodies."

Those in Judah are the faithful survivors. This is good news for them.

remnant = REM-n*nt

Zion = ZĪ-ahn

Jerusalem = juh-ROO-suh-lem or juh-ROO-zuh-lem

Then **everyone** shall be **rescued**
who **calls** on the **name** of the LORD;
for on **Mount Zion** there shall be a **remnant**,
as the LORD has **said**,
and in **Jerusalem survivors**
whom the LORD shall **call**.

READING II Romans 8:22–27

A reading from the Letter of Saint Paul to the Romans

Speak slowly and emphasize "groaning in labor pains." This metaphor emphasizes the "already but not yet" nature of our life in the Spirit.

Brothers and sisters:
We know that **all creation** is **groaning** in **labor pains**
even until now;
and not only **that**, but **we ourselves**,
who have the **firstfruits** of the **Spirit**,
we also groan within **ourselves**
as we **wait** for **adoption**, the **redemption** of our **bodies**.

Say this with longing.

Now speak more quickly. With hope we can move forward.

For in **hope** we were **saved**.
Now **hope** that **sees** is **not hope**.
For who **hopes** for what one **sees**?
But if we **hope** for what we **do not see**, we **wait** with **endurance**.

endurance = en-DOOR-*ns or en-DYOOR-*ns

The Spirit's coming is very good news; our hope rests in the Spirit.

intercedes = in-ter-SEEDZ

The "one who searches hearts" is God. This is consoling news. It comforts us and adds to our hope.

In the **same** way, the **Spirit too comes** to the **aid** of our **weakness**;
for we **do not know how** to **pray** as we **ought**,
but the **Spirit himself intercedes** with **inexpressible groanings**.
And the one who **searches hearts**
knows what is the **intention** of the **Spirit**,
because he **intercedes** for the **holy ones**
according to **God's will**.

As part of this ongoing process, we believe that we have been saved in hope, and we continue to live in hope: "we wait with endurance" for the coming of the Spirit to be complete in us. In the mean time, "the Spirit . . . comes to the aid of our weakness." Although we do not yet know even how to pray, the Spirit intercedes with God for us "according to God's will."

On Pentecost we celebrate the coming of the Spirit. As you proclaim this reading, emphasize our longing and groaning to become what God wills us to become, and the Spirit's presence within us, already bringing all of our hopes to fulfillment.

GOSPEL Our reading begins: "On the last and greatest day of the feast." The feast is the Jewish Feast of Tabernacles (see John 7:2). Today's speech by Christ is set within the seven day celebration of this October harvest feast.

One part of the celebration involved the priest, on the seventh day, circling the altar seven times and then pouring water from the spring of Siloam. Jesus, on this day, is pictured as reinterpreting the symbolic meaning of water so that it refers to himself and the spiritual life received by those who believe in him.

Jesus exclaims, "Let anyone who thirsts come to me and drink." This statement recalls Jesus' earlier conversation with the woman at the well when Jesus told her, "whoever drinks the water I shall give will never thirst; the water I shall give will become in him a spring of water welling up to eternal life" (John 4:14). Here Jesus is pictured as talking about Baptism, the water that wells up to eternal life.

GOSPEL John 7:37–39

A reading from the holy Gospel according to John

The narrator's voice sets the stage.

On the **last** and **greatest day** of the feast,
Jesus stood up and **exclaimed**,

Jesus is exclaiming. So should you.

"Let **anyone** who **thirsts come to me** and **drink**.
As Scripture says:

Emphasize "living water" and "who believes in me."

Rivers *of* ***living water*** *will* ***flow*** *from* ***within him***
who ***believes*** *in* ***me***."

Emphasize "the Spirit." This is why we are reading this passage on Pentecost.

He said this in reference to the **Spirit**
that those who came to **believe** in **him** were to **receive**.

Drop your voice here. This is background information.
glorified = GLOHR-ih-fied

There **was**, of course, **no Spirit yet**,
because **Jesus had not yet** been **glorified**.

Jesus then quotes scripture: "Rivers of living water will flow from within him who believes in me." Scripture scholars debate what passage John was intending to cite. One possibility is from Isaiah: "I will pour out water upon the thirsty ground, / . . . I will pour out my spirit upon your offspring" (Isaiah 44:3). Another possibility is a passage from Zechariah that was read during the Feast of Tabernacles: "On that day, living waters shall flow from Jerusalem" (Zechariah 14:8a).

Scholars also debate whether the "rivers of living water" in the line Jesus quotes were intended to be flowing from Christ or from the believer. Our present translation favors the believer. Given Jesus' earlier conversation with the woman at the well, the idea that living water will flow from the believer is certainly plausible. The living water of Baptism not only wells up within the individual for eternal life, but sends that person on mission. We receive the Spirit, to whom we are told these words refer, at Baptism.

When John says that "There was . . . no Spirit yet," he is not speaking of the existence of the Spirit but of the reception of the Spirit. The disciples would not experience the reception of the Spirit until after Jesus had been "glorified."

Because this reading has been chosen for Pentecost, its most important part is that which refers to the Spirit. As you proclaim this reading, emphasize "the Spirit that those who came to believe in him were to receive." It is because of this line that we are proclaiming this reading on Pentecost.

PENTECOST: DAY

Lectionary #63

READING I Acts 2:1–11

Apostles = uh-POS-*lz

Pentecost = PEN-tih-kost
Emphasize "all" and "together." This is important to Luke.

Raise your voice here and increase your tempo.

Now speak more slowly and lower your voice.
tongues = tungs

Say this with amazement.

Emphasize "every nation under heaven."
Jerusalem = juh-ROO-suh-lem or juh-ROO-zuh-lem

The people ask this with amazement and confusion.
Galileans = gal-ih-LEE-uhnz

A reading from the Acts of the Apostles

When the **time** for **Pentecost** was **fulfilled**,
they were **all** in one place **together**.
And **suddenly** there came from the sky
a **noise** like a **strong driving wind**,
and it **filled** the **entire house** in which they were.
Then there appeared to them **tongues** as of **fire**,
which **parted** and came to rest on **each one** of them.
And they were **all filled** with the **Holy Spirit**
and began to speak in **different tongues**,
as the **Spirit enabled** them to **proclaim**.

Now there were **devout Jews** from **every nation** under **heaven**
staying in **Jerusalem**.
At this **sound**, they **gathered** in a **large crowd**,
but they were **confused**
because each one heard them speaking in his **own language**.
They were **astounded**, and in **amazement** they asked,
"Are not **all these people** who are **speaking Galileans**?
Then how does **each** of **us hear** them in his **native language**?

READING I Just as only Acts describes Jesus' Ascension occurring 40 days after his Resurrection, so only Acts pictures the coming of the Spirit on the Jewish Feast of Pentecost. As we will see when we read today's Gospel, in John, the Spirit is received on Easter Sunday evening.

In Acts, Luke separates various aspects of one event (the Resurrection, the Ascension, and the coming of the Spirit) and dramatizes them so as to better teach the multifold significance of the event. Luke signals that he is doing this when he says, "When the time for Pentecost was fulfilled." When Luke says that the "time is fulfilled," he means that an event of great importance is happening at the proper time in God's plan of salvation. God's promises and saving plans for his people are being fulfilled.

As Luke describes the coming of the Spirit, he uses the images that appear in descriptions of God revealing himself at Sinai: wind and fire (Exodus 19:16–20). These same images are used by Isaiah to describe the coming of the Lord: "Lo, the LORD shall come in fire, / . . . like the whirlwind / . . . I come to gather nations of every language" (Isaiah 66:15a, 18a).

Notice that Luke says that when they were "all in one place together" the tongues of fire "came to rest on each one of them." Luke has earlier told us who "all" includes some women, including Mary, Jesus' mother—all together about 120 people (Acts 1:14, 15). The Spirit is received by each person, not just by the apostles.

Luke then reinterprets the gift of tongues, *glossolalia,* as a gift to speak in foreign languages. Luke's purpose is to teach the significance of the coming of the Spirit: the Good News will be preached in every language to "every nation under

Parthians = PAHR-thee-uhnz;
Medes = meedz; Elamites = EE-luh-mīts;
Mesopotamia = mes-uh-poh-TAY-mee-uh;
Judea = joo-DEE-uh or joo-DAY-uh;
Cappadocia = kap-uh-DOH-shuh or kap-us-DOH-shee-uh; Pontus = PON-tuhs;
Asia = AY-zhuh; Phrygia = FRIJ-ee-uh;
Pamphylia = pam-FIL-ee-uh; Egypt = EE-jipt;
Libya = LIB-ee-uh; Cyrene = sī-REE-nee;
Judaism = JOO-du-iz-*m or JOO-dee-iz-*m;
Cretans = KREE-tuhns; Arabs = AYR-uhbz
Say this last sentence slowly and with awe.

We are **Parthians**, **Medes**, and **Elamites**,
inhabitants of **Mesopotamia**, **Judea** and **Cappadocia**,
Pontus and **Asia**, **Phrygia** and **Pamphylia**,
Egypt and the districts of **Libya** near **Cyrene**,
as well as travelers from **Rome**,
both **Jews** and **converts** to Judaism, **Cretans** and **Arabs**,
yet we hear them speaking in our **own tongues**
of the **mighty acts** of **God**."

READING II 1 Corinthians 12:3b–7, 12–13

Corinthians = kohr-IN-thee-uhnz

A reading from the first Letter of Saint Paul to the Corinthians

Brothers and sisters:

Emphasize "Holy Spirit". It is because this reading speaks of the Spirit that it has been chosen for Pentecost.

No one can say, "**Jesus** is **Lord**," **except** by the **Holy Spirit**.

Emphasize "same." It is repeated three times.

There are **different kinds** of **spiritual gifts** but the **same Spirit**;
there are **different forms** of **service** but the **same Lord**;
there are **different workings** but the **same God**
who produces **all** of them in **everyone**.

manifestation = man-ih-fes-TAY-shuhn

To **each individual** the **manifestation** of the **Spirit**
is given for some **benefit**.

Now, the word "one" is being repeated. Emphasize "one" all five times that it is repeated.

As a body is **one** though it has **many parts**,
and **all** the **parts** of the body, though **many**, are **one body**,
so also Christ.

Greeks = greekz
Say "one Spirit" with conviction. We want these words to remain in everyone's mind.

For in **one Spirit** we were **all baptized** into **one body**,
whether **Jews** or **Greeks**, **slaves** or **free persons**,
and we were **all** given to drink of **one Spirit**.

heaven." As you proclaim this reading, others in every nation and in every language will be proclaiming it, too. Lectors around the world, filled with the Spirit, will be "speaking in [their] own tongues of the mighty acts of God."

READING II The passage from 1 Corinthians addresses the problem of divisiveness. If people disagree, who is being faithful to the Spirit and who is not? Whose gifts are more important? In responding to these problems that arose among the Corinthians, Paul teaches us about the gifts of the Spirit and the unity that exists, despite diversity, in the body of Christ.

The first line of today's reading is addressing the question of the discernment of spirits. Paul is teaching that a person who says, "Jesus is Lord," an early creedal statement, is acting under the influence of the Spirit of Christ, not under the spirit of false idols.

Paul then stresses the absolute importance of remaining united. True, there are different gifts, but they are all gifts from the same Spirit. True, there are different kinds of service, but they are all services done in the name of the same Lord for the good of the community. True, there are different works, but it is the same God who is producing these good works in each person.

Just as a body has different parts with different functions but remains one body, so do the Corinthians, the body of Christ, have different parts with different functions. Nevertheless, by Baptism they are

GOSPEL John 20:19–23

A reading from the holy Gospel according to John

The narrator is setting the stage.
disciples—dih-SĪ-p*lz

On the evening of that **first day** of the **week**,
when the **doors** were **locked**, where the **disciples** were,
for fear of the Jews,
Jesus came and **stood** in their **midst**
and said to them, "**Peace** be **with you**."

Emphasize this line. It will be repeated. Jesus is not simply giving a greeting, but a gift.

When he had said this, he **showed** them his **hands** and his **side**.
The disciples **rejoiced** when they **saw** the **Lord**.
Jesus said to them again, "**Peace** be **with you**.
As the **Father** has sent **me**, **so I send you**."

Again, emphasize "Peace be with you." This is Jesus' commission to his disciples. Speak slowly and clearly.

And when he had said this, he **breathed** on them and said
to them,
"**Receive** the **Holy Spirit**.
Whose **sins** you **forgive** are **forgiven** them,
and whose **sins** you **retain** are **retained**."

On the feast of Pentecost, this is the most important line.

one. The Corinthians' unity in Christ trumps divisions such as Jews or Greeks, slaves or free. They have been given one Spirit and, therefore, must learn to appreciate each other's gifts and live in unity. Since this reading has been chosen for Pentecost, the constant mention of the source of that unity, the Spirit, should be emphasized.

GOSPEL In the Gospel according to John, the risen Christ gives the Spirit to his disciples on Easter Sunday evening. Jesus appears in the disciples' midst despite the fact that the doors are locked. His first words, which are repeated, are "Peace be with you." Jesus then shows the disciples the wounds on his hands and his side. This is to demonstrate that the same Jesus who was crucified and died has now risen and is in the disciples' midst in bodily form.

Jesus then commissions the disciples: "As the Father has sent me, so I send you." The disciples are to carry on Jesus' mission to the world. In order to fulfill this mission, the disciples are given the Holy Spirit. Just as at creation God breathed physical life into human beings (Genesis 2:7), so now Christ breathes spiritual life on his disciples. They are to give new life to others through Baptism, the sacrament through which sins are forgiven. To the extent that the disciples fail to fulfill their mission, people will remain slaves to sin; their sins will be retained.

As you proclaim this reading, emphasize the two gifts that Jesus gives his disciples: peace and the Holy Spirit. Because it is Pentecost, however, the greatest emphasis should be given to Jesus' gift of the Spirit.

MOST HOLY TRINITY

Lectionary #164

READING I Exodus 34:4b–6, 8–9

Exodus = EK-suh-duhs

Sinai = SĪ-nī

A reading from the Book of Exodus

Early in the morning **Moses** went up **Mount Sinai**
as the LORD had commanded **him**,
taking along the two stone tablets.
Having come down in a cloud, the LORD stood
with **Moses** there
and **proclaimed** his name, "LORD."
Thus the LORD passed before him and cried out,
"The LORD, the LORD, a **merciful** and **gracious** God,
slow to **anger** and **rich** in **kindness** and **fidelity**."
Moses at **once bowed** down to the ground in **worship**.
Then he said, "If I find **favor** with **you**, O LORD,
do come along in our **company**.
This **is indeed** a stiff-necked **people**; yet **pardon** our **wickedness**
and **sins**,
and **receive** us as your own."

Start out boldly proclaiming, "The Lord, the Lord" and then soften your voice as you speak of the Lord's merciful and gracious nature. Be deliberate in the pace of your proclamation on these phrases.

Proclaim Moses' words making eye contact with the assembly. Offer them as a prayer to the Lord.

READING I God had instructed Moses to cut two stone tablets so that the Lord could rewrite on them the same commandments which were on the original stones and which the Israelites had broken. The Lord then tells Moses that the next morning he is to go up the mountain alone bringing the tablets with him (Exodus 34:1–2).

This is the context for the covenant renewal scene in today's First Reading. God chooses to come to Moses in a cloud, a customary, but somewhat impersonal theophany (appearance of God). Yet by standing with Moses and revealing his name to Moses, the Lord makes the encounter personal. As the Lord describes himself to Moses, the prophet comes to know him more deeply and bows down to worship him. This action expresses how Moses recognizes the Lord as the one God and acknowledges the reverence that is due to him.

Moses' words which follow disclose the struggle he faces with the people, but also his trust that the Lord is who he says he is: "a merciful and gracious God, slow to anger and rich in kindness and fidelity."

By asking the Lord to receive his people as the Lord's own, Moses expresses his desire that they be in a deep relationship of communion with the Lord who initiated the call for them to be his people. Christians believe that the love of this gracious and merciful Lord is revealed and fulfilled in the sending of his Son, Jesus Christ who, today's Gospel tells us, came not to condemn the world but to save it. On today's solemnity, strive to convey the compassionate love of God that his name "Lord" implies.

READING II 2 Corinthians 13:11–13

Corinthians = kohr-IN-thee-uhnz

As you call those in the assembly to rejoice, let joy be heard in your voice and seen on your face.

Make eye contact with the assembly on each of the instructions. Offer the instruction to "live in peace" in a gentle tone of voice.

Proclaim the liturgical greeting clearly, keeping your voice strong through the end.

A reading from second Letter of Saint Paul to the Corinthians

Brothers and **sisters, rejoice.**
Mend your ways, **encourage** one another,
  agree with one another, **live** in peace,
  and the **God** of **love** and **peace** will be with **you**.
Greet one another with a **holy kiss**.
All the holy ones **greet** you.

The **grace** of the **Lord Jesus Christ**
  and the **love** of **God**
  and the **fellowship** of the **Holy Spirit** be with **all** of you.

READING II The six imperatives that begin this reading are appropriate instructions for today's parish communities, just as they were for the Christian community in Corinth. Coming at the conclusion of Paul's second letter to the Corinthians, these verses express his hope that the Corinthians can come together and live as a united body through Jesus Christ and in the communion of the Holy Spirit.

From 1 Corinthians we know the Christian community at Corinth was divided over social, cultural, economic, and religious issues. Paul faces opponents that could have been either Judaizers (those who wanted to hold fast to the Jewish traditions and require gentile Christians to observe them) or Hellinistic Jewish propagandists (those who believed their philosophies and ecstatic experiences of the spirit showed that they were in possession of the truth). Regardless of the identity of his opponents, we know Paul struggles to defend his authority and the Gospel he proclaims. At the time Paul is writing 2 Corinthians, the situation in the Corinthian community seems to have deteriorated further since his first letter. Thus, Paul is at pains to exhort the Corinthians to live in unity with one another.

Ponder the Trinitarian benediction which closes 2 Corinthians and concludes this reading—Paul's prayer for the community. Offer these words to the assembly as a reminder of the blessing that is theirs because their life together and their hope of overcoming any existing divisions are rooted in the life of the divine communion of persons. Be prepared to hear some in the assembly respond to your words with "And

GOSPEL John 3:16–18

A reading from the holy Gospel according to John

Take your time with the opening words "God so loved the world," pausing ever so slightly before the "that" clause.

God **so loved** the world that he gave his **only Son,**
so that **everyone** who **believes** in **him** might **not** perish
but might have **eternal life.**
For **God** did **not** send his **Son** into the **world** to **condemn**
the world,
but that the world might be **saved** through **him.**

Be strong and direct, but not harsh, in your proclamation of the consequences of believing and not believing.

Whoever believes in **him** will not be **condemned,**
but **whoever** does **not** believe has **already** been condemned,
because he has **not** believed in the **name** of the **only** Son
of God.

also with you" as they will be familiar with them as an opening greeting from Mass!

GOSPEL These three narrative verses interrupt Jesus' dialogue with Nicodemus, a Pharisee and Jewish leader (John 3:1–15). The verses tell both of the graciousness of God's love and the choice to accept the salvation freely given through his Son.

Only God (the Father) and his only Son, two of the divine persons of the Trinity, are mentioned in the Gospel's three verses. So understanding the importance of the Spirit in the whole of Jesus' conversation with Nicodemus (much of which does not appear in this Lectionary reading) helps complete the picture of why this Gospel is proclaimed on the solemnity of the Most Holy Trinity.

Attempting to engage Jesus in a debate, Nicodemus wondered how an old person could be born again. Beginning with a double "Amen," which signified the solemnity and seriousness of the words to follow, Jesus responded that a person has to be born of both water and Spirit. To be born of the Spirit, one must believe in the Son of Man. Through his sacrifice on the cross (described as being lifted up on the cross) salvation comes (3:14–15). The life-giving waters of the Spirit flow in the hearts of believers and continually invite non-believers to choose faith.

Proclaim this Gospel as an invitation to the different members in your assembly: those who are seeking to believe, desiring to grow in faith, and wavering in faith. Your invitation to them is to welcome the divine communion of persons into their lives and then to extend its love to the world.

MOST HOLY BODY AND BLOOD OF CHRIST

Lectionary #167

READING I Deuteronomy 8:2–3, 14b–16a

Deuteronomy = doo-ter-AH-nuh-mee

A reading from the Book of Deuteronomy

Proclaim this reading as if you are reminiscing about the desert experience with the assembly before you. Use a narrative tone of voice.

Moses said to the **people**:
"**Remember** how for forty **years** now the LORD, your **God**,
has **directed** all your **journeying** in the **desert**,
so as to **test** you by **affliction**
and find out whether or **not** it was your **intention**
to **keep** his **commandments**.
He **therefore** let you be **afflicted** with **hunger**,
and then **fed** you with **manna**,
a food **unknown** to you and your fathers,
in order to **show** you that not by bread **alone** does one **live**,
but by **every word** that comes forth from the **mouth**
of the LORD.

Emphasize that the Lord fed the Israelites. Be confident in your proclamation of the nourishment the word of the Lord gives.

"Do **not** forget the LORD, your **God**,
who **brought** you out of the land of **Egypt**,
that place of **slavery**;
who **guided** you through the **vast** and **terrible** desert
with its **saraph serpents** and **scorpions**,
its **parched** and **waterless** ground;
who brought forth **water** for you from the **flinty rock**
and **fed** you in the **desert** with **manna**,
a food **unknown** to your **fathers**."

Lower your tone of voice as you recall the challenges of the slavery and the desert. Strengthen your voice as you repeat that the Lord fed his people with manna. Maintain the strength until the end.

READING I This passage from Deuteronomy comes from the address of Moses to the people of Israel as they are approaching the Promised Land after 40 years of wandering in the desert. In it, Moses encourages the people to remember all that the Lord has done for them while they were in the desert. Moses reminds them how going without food and drink humbled them. Fed with manna and having their thirst quenched with water which flowed from rock, the Israelites came to know the Lord's love and care for them. Though they questioned the constancy of God's care for them, not only did God take care of the people's physical needs, but through his care the people learned, as Moses tells them again, that every word that comes from the Lord's mouth provides sustenance.

This passage has obvious connections to the solemnity of the Body and Blood of Christ. The manna is linked to the bread of the Eucharist and the water to the wine. But this passage also relates to the deeper liturgical truth that it is the one table of the Word and Eucharist from which we partake every time we participate in the Mass (*Dei Verbum,* Dogmatic Constitution on Divine Revelation, 21).

We, like the Israelites, face the danger of memory loss with regard to all the Lord has done for us. As you prepare to proclaim this reading, reflect on times when you have felt tested—when your resources seemed inadequate, when you felt criticized, or when you could not sense God's presence. Think about how those times humbled you. Remember how God has fed you personally and enabled you to move forward. Use your own recollection

READING II 1 Corinthians 10:16–17

Corinthians = kohr-IN-thee-uhnz

A reading from the first Letter of Saint Paul to the Corinthians

Pause significantly after the greeting.

Brothers and sisters:

Pause again at the comma. Ask the question making eye contact with the assembly. Pause again after the question. Repeat this pattern for the second question.

The cup of **blessing** that we **bless**,
is it **not** a **participation** in the **blood** of **Christ**?
The **bread** that we **break**,
is it **not** a **participation** in the **body** of **Christ**?

Closely follow the punctuation in the concluding verse and proclaim it slowly. Emphasize "we" looking up at the assembly.

Because the loaf of **bread** is **one**,
we, though **many**, are **one body**,
for we **all** partake of the **one loaf**.

GOSPEL John 6:51–58

A reading from the holy Gospel according to John

Jesus said to the **Jewish crowds**:

Proclaim Jesus' "I am" statement with a tone of hopefulness and the confidence of your own belief in the life he brings.

"**I am** the living **bread** that came down from **heaven**;
whoever eats this **bread** will live **forever**;
and the **bread** that I will **give**
is my **flesh** for the **life** of the **world**."

Ask the question the Jews raise with incredulity and a tinge of resentment in your voice.

The Jews **quarreled** among themselves, saying,
"**How** can this **man** give us his **flesh** to eat?"

Use a solemn tone to proclaim Jesus' words "Amen, amen."

Jesus **said** to them,
"Amen, amen, I **say** to you,
unless you **eat** the **flesh** of the **Son** of **Man** and **drink** his **blood**,
you do **not** have **life** within you.

of God's faithfulness as a basis for your proclamation of the word that feeds and gives life to those before you today.

READING II Today's very brief Second Reading begins with two rhetorical questions that remind the Corinthians of what they believe: in the Eucharist, the bread and wine are a participation in the body and blood of Christ. The Greek word *koinōnia,* translated as "participation," points to a deep union created among those who eat and drink of the body and blood of Christ. Their common action of eating and drinking identifies what they hold in common: belief in the one Lord, truly present in the eucharistic meal. He constitutes them as a body and will strengthen them to resolve the divisions they face.

Paul's reference to the cup of blessing and the bread that is broken in the eucharistic meal that the community celebrated (11:23–29) (and in the Eucharistic Prayer we pray today) supports the conclusion of his argument in the final words of the reading. The oneness of the loaf of bread signifies the unity of the one body of Corinthian believers. Though there are many and diverse members of the community, they are united by their participation in the Eucharist.

Most in the assembly you address will recognize the opening questions as rhetorical and a clear affirmation of what they believe about the Eucharist. The challenge you face is to communicate that our sharing in the Eucharist also has implications for our life together. Paul teaches us, as he did the Corinthians, that we live together as children of God in communion with him through Christ.

Whoever eats my **flesh** and **drinks** my **blood**
has eternal life,
and I will **raise** him on the **last day**.
For my **flesh** is **true food**,
and my **blood** is **true drink**.
Whoever eats my **flesh** and **drinks** my **blood**
remains in **me** and **I** in **him**.

With quiet confidence communicate the relationship between the Father and Jesus, and now those who feed on Jesus.

Just as the living **Father** sent **me**
and I have **life** because of the **Father**,
so also the one who **feeds** on **me**
will have **life** because of **me**.
This is the **bread** that came down from **heaven**.
Unlike your **ancestors** who **ate** and **still died**,
whoever eats **this** bread will live **forever**."

Emphasize "this bread" to contrast the experience of life in Jesus with that of the ancestors who ate and still died.

GOSPEL **Today's Gospel passage follows upon much discussion between Jesus and the crowds about the bread of God that comes down from heaven and gives life. Before the beginning of this passage, Jesus has previously identified himself twice in "I am" statements as the bread of life (John 6:45, 48) and noted that people who eat this read will never hunger and will not die.**

The third "I am" statement, identifying Jesus as the living bread that came down from heaven, which begins today's Gospel, follows upon Jesus' reference to the bread which the Israelites ate in the desert. This is an obvious connection to the First Reading in which Moses reminds the people how God fed them with manna in the desert. While the manna nourished the Israelites during their journey, Jesus, the living bread, now nourishes forever those who eat of his flesh.

Aside from the question the Jews raise as they argue amongst themselves about how Jesus can actually give his own flesh for them to eat, the rest of the Gospel is entirely Jesus' words. In these words, he speaks of the connection between sharing in his body and blood and being raised on the last day, the true food and drink that his flesh and blood are, the unity between him and the one who partakes of them, and the basis of this unity in the oneness between him and the Father. In the sending of his Son, Jesus, the Father meets forever our need for food and drink. This is truly the Good News of the Eucharist you proclaim to the assembly from today's Gospel!

14TH SUNDAY IN ORDINARY TIME

Lectionary #100

READING I Zechariah 9:9–10

Zechariah = zek-uh-RĪ-uh

Proclaim in a loud, joyful voice the opening lines calling Jerusalem to rejoice. Be careful, however, not to shout.

Lower your voice as you describe the savior's meekness.

Ephraim = EE-fra-im or EF-r*m

Proclaim the wideness of the savior's dominion with certainty and confidence.

A reading from the Book of the Prophet Zechariah

Thus says the LORD:
Rejoice **heartily**, O daughter **Zion**,
shout for **joy**, O daughter **Jerusalem**!
See, your **king** shall **come** to you;
a just **savior** is he,
meek, and **riding** on an **ass**,
on a **colt**, the **foal** of an **ass**.
He shall **banish** the **chariot** from **Ephraim**,
and the **horse** from **Jerusalem**;
the warrior's **bow** shall be **banished**,
and he shall proclaim **peace** to the **nations**.
His **dominion** shall be from **sea** to **sea**,
and from the **River** to the **ends** of the **earth**.

READING I We hear from the prophet Zechariah only twice in the three year Lectionary cycle of readings, once in Year A and once in Year C. Today's reading sounds more like an Advent reading than a reading for the Fourteenth Sunday in Ordinary Time. And if the reading sounds familiar to you, it is because it is quoted in the processional Gospel for Palm Sunday for both Year A and Year C.

Taken from the second half of the book of the prophet Zechariah, which is more poetic in nature and straightforward in its themes than the first half, this passage is part of a prophetic oracle. The oracle speaks of the divine judgment that will come upon the hostile powers of Syria, Phoenicia, and Philistia. Jerusalem itself will be the focus of the world's salvation, for a king will come to her.

The king will be humble and ride in on an ass, a sign of peace. This king will proclaim peace, a peace which will begin in Jerusalem but will extend to the nations. His reign will encompass the entire earth, but will be centered in Jerusalem.

Christians believe this prophecy to be fulfilled in Jesus. Although we await the fullness of his kingdom of peace, the Gospel today gives us hope because of the peaceful rest he already provides for those who come to him.

Proclaim this reading with as much joy and hope as you can. Allowing these emotions to be seen in your facial expressions, although not in an overly dramatic fashion, will assist in communicating the meaning of this prophecy to the assembly.

READING II With the resumption of Ordinary Time today, the Second Reading returns to the continuous

READING II Romans 8:9, 11–13

Emphasize "You" making eye contact with the assembly. Pause at the semi-colon. Soften the tone of your voice to communicate the contrast of the Spirit dwelling in the person who belongs to Christ.

A reading from the Letter of Saint Paul to the Romans

Brothers and sisters:
You are **not** in the **flesh**;
on the **contrary, you** are in the **spirit**,
if only the **Spirit** of **God** dwells in **you**.
Whoever does **not** have the **Spirit** of **Christ** does **not belong** to him.
If the **Spirit** of the one who **raised Jesus** from the **dead** dwells in **you**,
the one who raised **Christ** from the **dead**
will give **life** to **your** mortal bodies **also**,
through his **Spirit** that dwells **in** you.
Consequently, brothers and sisters,
we are not **debtors** to the **flesh**,
to live **according** to the **flesh**.
For if you live **according** to the **flesh**, you will **die**,
but if by the **Spirit** you put to **death** the **deeds** of the **body**,
you will **live**.

Emphasize the latter clauses of the conditional statements which conclude the reading ("you will die" and "you will live"). Do so by stressing each word and slowing down your proclamation.

reading of Paul's letter to the Romans which began over four months ago. Today's Second Reading and the readings for the next four Sundays come from chapter eight.

Paul's theology is dense in the three verses you will proclaim. At the heart of the matter, for Paul, are two human attitudes or motivations, one he calls "the flesh," which leads to death, and another he calls "the spirit," which leads to life and peace (8:6). Those who live in the flesh are hostile toward God, and those who live according to the Spirit, live in communion with God in Christ.

In the first verse of today's Second Reading, then, Paul tells the Romans that they are not in the flesh. For those who have been justified by faith and baptized in Christ live in the Spirit because they have the Spirit of God and the Spirit of Christ dwelling in them.

In the second verse, Paul instructs the Romans that the Spirit of God and Christ is the Spirit of the risen one. Life comes through this Spirit, whose source is God who raised Jesus from the dead.

In the third verse, Paul is realistic. He is under no illusions that the Romans—and any who are baptized (including us!)—will have an easy time of it staying away from works of the flesh. He sets out the reality: to live in the flesh is to die; to live by the Spirit is to live. Faith and Baptism in themselves do not remove us from the human propensity to choose sin. Yet because we belong to Christ, we can rely on his Spirit dwelling in us to help us choose life.

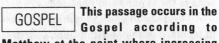

GOSPEL This passage occurs in the Gospel according to Matthew at the point where increasing opposition from Jewish leaders begins to

GOSPEL Matthew 11:25–30

A reading from the holy Gospel according to Matthew

Exclaim Jesus' praise of the Father in full voice. Be careful not to be too close to the microphone so the sound distorts. Begin to return to a moderate tone of voice as you speak of the Father's gracious will.

At that time **Jesus exclaimed**:
"I give **praise** to you, **Father, Lord** of **heaven** and **earth**,
for although you have **hidden** these things
from the **wise** and the **learned**
you have **revealed** them to **little ones**.
Yes, Father, such has been your **gracious will**.
All things have been **handed over** to me by my **Father**.
No one knows the **Son** except the **Father**,
and **no one** knows the **Father** except the **Son**
and **anyone** to whom the **Son** wishes to reveal **him**.

Continue in a similar voice through the explanation of the relationships of the Father, Son, and the believer.

"**Come** to me, **all** you who **labor** and are **burdened**,
and **I** will give you **rest**.
Take my **yoke** upon you and **learn** from me,
for I am **meek** and **humble** of heart;
and you will find **rest** for **yourselves**.
For my **yoke** is **easy**, and my **burden light**."

Offer Jesus' invitation in a kind and gentle voice. Use an unhurried pace throughout the entire stanza.

appear and Jesus reprimands the unrepentant people in the towns where his mighty deeds had been done (Matthew 11:20). Today's Gospel begins on a positive note. Jesus' praises the Father for revealing him to the "little ones," a term which refers to those who are simple, uneducated, or lack expertise in matters of the law. He also thanks the Father for keeping him hidden from the "wise and the learned," a reference to the scribes and Pharisees.

The second section, which appears to be more in the spirit of John's writing than Matthew's, comes from Q, an ancient source of Jesus' sayings that both Matthew and Luke use. These verses have served as the foundation for understanding the relationship between the Father and Son as the Church's Christology (understanding of Christ's nature) developed.

The third section contains the obvious connection to today's First Reading. Jesus identifies himself as meek and humble of heart. We, as Catholics, believe him to be the meek king who Zechariah prophesies will come to Jerusalem as the savior. By inviting people to come to him, Jesus extends the invitation to those who accept his yoke in place of the yoke of the law, to participate in his kingdom, a kingdom of peace.

Many in the assembly face burdens each day. Your unassuming and prayerful proclamation of this passage can lead them to recommit themselves to the revelation of the kingdom in Jesus, the Father's Son. Though his yoke will not take away life's challenges, it offers rest and comfort in moving through them.

15TH SUNDAY IN ORDINARY TIME

Lectionary #103

READING I Isaiah 55:10–11

Isaiah = ī-ZAY-uh

A reading from the Book of the Prophet Isaiah

Thus says the LORD:
Just as from the **heavens**
the **rain** and **snow** come down
and do not **return** there
till they have **watered** the earth,
making it **fertile** and **fruitful**,
giving **seed** to the one who **sows**
and **bread** to the one who **eats**,
so shall my **word** be
that goes **forth** from my **mouth**;
my word shall **not** return to me **void**,
but shall **do** my **will**,
achieving the **end** for which I **sent** it.

Pace yourself as you paint the beautiful picture of the earth bearing fruit and nourishing those who eat of its bounty.

Proclaim the purposeful work of the Lord's word with the certainty of faith, in a strong, but not overbearing, voice.

READING I The two verses which are today's First Reading are part of the Fifth Reading at the Easter Vigil. In Year B, they are also proclaimed on the feast of the Baptism of the Lord. Suitable to both these celebrations because they speak of the power and purpose of the word of the Lord, today they are paired with the well-known parable of the sower.

The prophecy from which today's two verses come is at the end of the book of comfort (Isaiah 40:1—55:13). In the verses before our reading begins, it offers an invitation to those who are thirsty, poor, and hungry to "Come to the water!" and receive life from the Lord. Those who are scoundrels are graciously encouraged to turn to the Lord for mercy. Life and mercy come through the word spoken by the Lord.

Using the natural cycle of precipitation and evaporation, the prophet explains the life-giving movement of the Lord's word. Just as rain and snow have a purpose—watering the earth so crops will grow and produce fruit—so too, the Lord's word has a purpose—to do God's will, bringing life to those who hear it. Thus, the coming of the word of the Lord is an event; it is not a passive occurrence on either the Lord's part or on the part of those who will receive it.

As baptized members of Christ's body, we believe the word of the Lord was made flesh in Jesus. The announcement of salvation contained in these two verses is fulfilled in him and through his life, death, and Resurrection. He himself, and the message of the kingdom he proclaims, are the precipitation which cultivates in believers and nonbelievers alike the willingness to build up the kingdom of God on earth.

READING II Romans 8:18–23

A reading from the Letter of Saint Paul to the Romans

Brothers and sisters:
I consider that the **sufferings** of this **present** time are as **nothing**
compared with the **glory** to be **revealed** for us.
For **creation** awaits with **eager expectation**
the **revelation** of the **children** of **God**;
for **creation** was made subject to **futility**,
not of its **own** accord but because of the one who **subjected** it,
in **hope** that **creation** itself
would be **set free** from **slavery** to **corruption**
and **share** in the **glorious freedom** of the **children** of **God**.
We know that **all creation** is **groaning** in labor pains
even until **now**;
and not only **that**, but **we ourselves**,
who have the **firstfruits** of the **Spirit**,
we also groan within **ourselves**
as we wait for **adoption**, the **redemption** of our **bodies**.

Let eagerness—tempered excitement—be heard in your voice as you proclaim creation's own eager expectation.

Contrast the images of slavery, corruption, and groaning, decay, and groaning with glorious freedom, adoption, and redemption.

End on a hopeful note: You and the assembly believe in the redemption of our bodies in Christ.

GOSPEL Matthew 13:1–23

A reading from the holy Gospel according to Matthew

On that day, Jesus went **out** of the **house** and sat **down** by the **sea**.
Such large **crowds** gathered **around** him
that he **got** into a **boat** and sat **down**,
and the whole **crowd** stood along the **shore**.

Throughout the Gospel, contrast the narrative lines (those at the beginning which describe the scene and those which introduce the words of Jesus and the disciples) with the spoken words.

As you prepare to proclaim the First Reading, remind yourself of the importance of the ministry you perform. You have the task, somewhat daunting at times, of proclaiming the word which will achieve the end described here. This one sentence reading provides beautiful images of God's word. The care and deliberateness with which you proclaim it will help express its meaning to an assembly open to its nourishment.

READING II Today's Second Reading begins on a somber note as Paul reflects on the sufferings of the present time. For him, the severity of the pain and trials of the present lessen when they are seen in relation to the glory that is to come.

The sufferings Paul speaks about are the struggles believers undergo as they are constantly faced with the decision whether to choose death through sin or life in the Spirit. Despite being drawn at times to sin, in the four verses between the end of last Sunday's reading and the beginning of this Sunday's, Paul offers the hope that belongs only to the children of God.

Led by the Spirit of God, these children have received a spirit of adoption, through which they can cry out, "Abba, Father!" (8:15). In the midst of suffering, we who are adopted children of God through Baptism in Christ, know that our sufferings are united to Christ's. United with him, we know, too, we will share in the glory of his Resurrection.

Imagine yourself as a storyteller as you communicate the parable of the sower to the assembly. Change expression slightly as you describe the different locations and consequences of where the seed falls. Pause after the bountiful harvest of the seed that fell on rich soil. Then boldly proclaim, "Whoever has ears . . . ."

And he **spoke** to them at **length** in **parables**, saying:
"A **sower** went out to **sow**.
And as he **sowed, some** seed fell on the **path**,
and **birds** came and **ate** it up.
Some fell on **rocky ground**, where it had **little soil**.
It sprang up **at once** because the soil was not **deep**,
and when the **sun** rose it was **scorched**,
and it **withered** for lack of **roots**.
Some seed fell among **thorns**, and the **thorns** grew up
and **choked** it.
But **some** seed fell on **rich soil**, and produced **fruit**,
a **hundred** or **sixty** or **thirtyfold**.
Whoever has **ears** ought to **hear**."

The **disciples** approached him and said,
"**Why** do you **speak** to them in **parables**?"
He **said** to them **in reply**,

Convey Jesus' explanation of his use of parable as a teacher would describe a complex concept to his or her students.

"Because **knowledge** of the **mysteries** of the kingdom
of **heaven**
has been **granted** to **you**, but to **them** it has **not** been granted.
To anyone who **has, more** will be **given** and he will grow **rich**;
from anyone who has **not**, even what he **has** will be
taken **away**.
This is why I **speak** to them in **parables**, because
*they **look** but do **not see**, and **hear** but do **not listen***
*or **understand**.*
Isaiah's **prophecy** is **fulfilled** in them, which says:

Differentiate between Jesus' lines and the quotations from Isaiah by pausing before the quotations, making eye contact on the quotations, and speaking them more insistently. End the second quotation on a gentle note as you speak of God's healing now accomplished in Jesus.

*You shall indeed **hear** but not **understand**,*
*you shall indeed **look** but never **see**.*
***Gross** is the **heart** of **this people**,*
*they will **hardly hear** with their **ears**,*
*they have **closed** their **eyes**,*

Yet because we live in our mortal bodies, we still face the temptation of sin; we still long for the day when we will be set free from even our inclination to choose sin.

In today's Second Reading Paul links our destiny with that of all creation. Creation, too, is waiting with "eager expectation" for that day when she will no longer be subject to futility. On this day, creation will share in the glorious new life of freedom that we as children of God already have tasted. Through our justification by faith and Baptism, we already know what it is like to live in the promise of the Spirit of redemption.

When you proclaim this reading, keep in mind that Paul understood the destiny of the created world to be linked to our destiny in Christ as adopted children of God. Thus, we too, are called to understand that our groaning, our desire for a life completely free from sin and suffering is related to the groaning of creation to be restored to her original beauty. Living in communion with God, others, and all of creation, we have a responsibility to choose life now and to be good stewards of all that God has given us in this world. Through our lives, we who have the first-fuits of the Spirit within us can offer the promise of redemption to our brothers and sisters, and indeed to all of creation.

GOSPEL Today's Gospel, the first part of the parable discourse in Matthew, has three sections. In the first, Jesus tells the large crowds at the shore the parable of the sower, so familiar to us today. The command to listen at the conclusion of the parable is also

lest they ***see*** *with their* ***eyes***
and ***hear*** *with their* ***ears***
and ***understand*** *with their* ***hearts*** *and be* ***converted,***
and I ***heal*** *them.*

"But **blessed** are **your** eyes, because they **see,**
and **your** ears, because they **hear.**
Amen, I say to **you, many prophets** and **righteous people**
longed to see what **you** see but did **not** see it,
and to **hear** what **you** hear but did **not** hear it.

The third section of the Gospel, with the explanation of the parable of the sower, begins. Return to the teacher-like tone of voice. Be explanatory, but not didactic or arrogant like a teacher who appears to know it all and lord it over his or her students.

"**Hear** then the **parable** of the **sower.**
The **seed** sown on the **path** is the one
who **hears** the **word** of the **kingdom** without **understanding** it,
and the **evil** one comes and **steals** away
what was **sown** in his **heart.**
The **seed** sown on **rocky ground**
is the one who **hears** the **word** and **receives** it at **once**
with **joy.**
But he has no **root** and lasts **only** for a **time.**
When some **tribulation** or **persecution** comes
because of the **word,**
he **immediately** falls away.
The **seed** sown among **thorns** is the one who **hears** the word,
but then **worldly anxiety** and the **lure** of **riches choke**
the word
and it bears **no fruit.**

Let enthusiasm for the one who hears, understands, and bears the fruit of the word be obvious in your voice. If you can do so with ease, memorize this verse and make as much eye contact with the assembly as possible.

But the **seed** sown on **rich soil**
is the one who **hears** the **word** and **understands** it,
who indeed bears **fruit** and **yields** a **hundred** or **sixty**
or **thirtyfold.**"

[Shorter Form: Matthew 13:1–9]

found in Matthew 11:15 and 13:43. Proclaim it to the assembly as a call to reflect further on the meaning of the parable and how it relates to their lives.

In the second section, the disciples pose a question to Jesus that perhaps many of us have wanted to ask about his style of teaching. In his reply, Jesus contrasts "the crowds" with the disciples. Those who follow Jesus sincerely have been granted knowledge of the desires of God; those who do not follow, do not know them. They have been closed to faith in him and lack the openness of true disciples.

The third section provides an explanation of the parable of the sower. As you come to the explanation, many in the assembly will have forgotten that this Gospel actually began with the parable! Notice the explanation of the parable shifts from what is originally expected. In the original telling of the parable, the seed appears to symbolize the kingdom of God. The seed now symbolizes a person and the person has responsibility for believing in Jesus and hearing and understanding the mysteries of the kingdom.

To help the assembly understand this shift, and understand that they are the ones who have chosen to hear the word and understand it, personalize your proclamation of the concluding verse by making eye contact with them and proclaiming it with confidence in their ability to bear fruit. Through them, even those who do not yet believe can be brought to faith, thus illustrating the truth of Jesus' explanation of the parable: the kingdom of God will flourish despite impediments to its growth.

16TH SUNDAY IN ORDINARY TIME

Lectionary #106

READING I Wisdom 12:13, 16–19

A reading from the Book of Wisdom

Throughout the reading, contrast power and might with care, leniency, and kindness. Try using a stronger tone of voice on the former and a lighter, softer (but still audible) tone on the latter.

temerity = tuh-MER-uh-tee

clemency = KLEM-*n-see

Treat the final sentence as a summary statement of why there is no god beside the Lord. Make eye contact with the assembly as much as possible: they are God's children who have good ground for hope!

There is **no god** besides **you** who have the **care** of **all**,
that you need **show** you have not **unjustly** condemned.
For your **might** is the source of **justice**;
your **mastery** over **all** things makes you **lenient** to **all**.
For you **show** your **might** when the perfection of your **power**
is **disbelieved**;
and in those who **know** you, you **rebuke temerity**.
But though you are **master** of **might**, you **judge** with **clemency**,
and with much **lenience** you **govern** us;
for **power**, whenever you **will, attends** you.
And you **taught** your **people**, by these **deeds**,
that those who are **just** must be **kind**;
and you gave your **children** good ground for **hope**
that you would permit **repentance** for their **sins**.

READING I Today's reading from the book of Wisdom comes from a section on God's power and mercy which follows a recounting of the ways God protected the Chosen People during the Exodus (Wisdom 11). The author is showing us the relationship between God's power and his care for all people. God used his power both to punish the enemies of Israel and to demonstrate his care to the Israelites when they questioned him. Despite God's might, he judges with clemency and leniency, even toward those who believe in him and still act with reckless audacity.

The author argues that because he judges with leniency, God shows he is master of his own might. His strength is the source of his justice. Reminiscent of the first commandment in the Decalogue, the opening line reminds us that there is no god besides the Lord. This means the Lord does not need to justify the judgments he renders.

All God asks, says the author of Wisdom in this digression, is that the justice and care he taught his people through his own actions on their behalf be the basis for their justice and kindness. God's people must be both righteous and kind. Yet if they fail, they still have good ground for hope in repentance for their sins.

Through your proclamation, strive to teach the assembly how their justice and kindness can be signs to others of God's justice and kindness. Proclaim the last verse in a manner which gives the assembly reason to hope that God's own power and mercy will always ground their attempts to act justly and kindly.

READING II Romans 8:26–27

A reading from the Letter of Saint Paul to the Romans

In a clear and direct manner, proclaim the opening line. Pause noticeably at the semi-colon. Doing both of these will help the assembly to hear the first main point of the brief reading.

Repeat the same pattern for the opening clause of the second main point, "And the one who searches hearts," in particular emphasizing "And the one who searches hearts" to signify the beginning of the next point. "He intercedes" refers to the intercession of the Holy Spirit.

Brothers and sisters:
The **Spirit** comes to the **aid** of our **weakness**;
for we do **not** know how to **pray** as we **ought**,
but the **Spirit** himself **intercedes** with **inexpressible groanings**.
And the **one** who **searches hearts**
knows what is the **intention** of the **Spirit**,
because he **intercedes** for the **holy ones**
according to **God's will**.

GOSPEL Matthew 13:24–43

A reading from the holy Gospel according to Matthew

Differentiate the narrative line from Jesus' words, which tell the first parable. Pausing at the colon will help to do this.

Within the parable, distinguish between the narrative lines and the words of slaves and the Master, using a pause, as above. Pause significantly after the first parable, so the assembly can begin to ponder its meaning.

Jesus proposed **another parable** to the crowds, saying:
"The **kingdom of heaven** may be likened to a **man**
who sowed **good seed** in his field.
While everyone was **asleep** his **enemy** came
and **sowed weeds** all through the **wheat**, and then **went off**.
When the crop **grew** and **bore fruit**, the **weeds** appeared **as well**.
The **slaves** of the **householder** came to him and said,
'**Master**, did you **not** sow **good seed** in your field?
Where have the **weeds** come from?'
He answered, 'An **enemy** has done this.'

READING II In two short verses, Paul gives us a lesson on prayer this Sunday. When we face weakness, which is for Paul the human propensity to choose to live according to the flesh rather than according to the Spirit, the Spirit will come to our aid.

Recall in the passage from Romans proclaimed last Sunday that creation and the children of God were both groaning as they awaited redemption. In today's passage, the Spirit comes to our assistance in prayer with "inexpressible groaning." The Greek word used by Paul suggests that the Spirit goes above and beyond in pleading with God on our behalf. The Spirit, in effect, understands and empathizes with our groanings to the extent that the Spirit, too, groans. Through the Spirit's own groanings, our desires are brought to God. When our hope is not enough, the Spirit helps us wait patiently for that new day when our sufferings will be replaced by the glory of the Resurrection.

Paul's lesson on prayer not only teaches us *that* the Spirit intercedes for us, but *how* the Spirit does so. The communion of the Spirit with God—the one who searches hearts (1 Kings 8:39; Psalm 7:11; 17:3; 139:1)—is so deep that God knows the intentions of the Spirit even before he intercedes for us. The Spirit's intercession follows God's plan of salvation.

Offer your proclamation in humility. To do so, think of the times when you have not known how to pray, when your needs and desires rather than God's will were at the center of your prayer. Then let confidence come through your proclamation as you convey the depth of empathy the Spirit has for us. The Spirit draws us into communion

His slaves **said** to him,
'Do you **want** us to **go** and **pull** them **up**?'
He replied, '**No**, if you pull up the **weeds**
you might uproot the **wheat** along **with** them.
Let them grow **together** until **harvest**;
then at **harvest** time I will **say** to the **harvesters**,
"**First** collect the **weeds** and tie them in **bundles** for **burning**;
but gather the **wheat** into my **barn**."'"

State the introductory sentence to the second parable matter-of-factly, pausing noticeably at the period to mark a shift from the narrative line to Jesus' words. Imagine yourself as a storyteller helping the assembly to picture themselves sewing the tiny mustard seed and nurturing it to full growth. Making your voice loftier and grander at the end of this parable will help you do this. Use the same technique to introduce the introductory sentence to the third parable.

He proposed **another** parable to them.
"The kingdom of **heaven** is like a **mustard seed**
that a person **took** and **sowed** in a **field**.
It is the **smallest** of **all the seeds**,
yet when **full-grown** it is the **largest** of **plants**.
It becomes a large bush,
and the '**birds** of the **sky** come and **dwell** in its **branches**.'"

He spoke to them **another** parable.
"The kingdom of **heaven** is like **yeast**
that a woman **took** and **mixed** with three **measures**
of wheat **flour**
until the whole batch was **leavened**."

Vary your tone of voice to separate the quotation from Psalm 78 from the surrounding text.

All these things Jesus **spoke** to the crowds in **parables**.
He **spoke** to them **only** in parables,
to **fulfill** what had been **said** through the **prophet**:
I will ***open*** *my* ***mouth*** *in* ***parables***,
I will ***announce*** *what has lain* ***hidden***
from the ***foundation*** *of the* ***world***.

with God because the Spirit himself longs with us for the day when we will know the redemption of our bodies and everything will be accomplished according to God's will for those of us who are his "holy ones."

GOSPEL The Gospel passage for this Sunday is composed of three parables, a section in which, like that in last Sunday's Gospel, Jesus explains why he teaches the crowds in parables, and a final section in which Jesus explains the parable of the weeds and the wheat.

In the parable of the weeds and the wheat, the Master surprisingly tells his slaves not to pull up the weeds lest they risk pulling up the wheat, too. Naturally concerned about keeping the field fruitful, the slaves were only asking to perform the practical gardening chore of removing weeds. Yet the Master, whom Jesus later reveals is the Son of Man, teaches them that the weeds and the wheat are to grow together until the harvest. At the time of the harvest, the time of the last judgment, the weeds will face the consequence of the evil they perpetrated and burn in the fiery furnace. On the other hand, the wheat, a symbol of those who have remained faithful despite the temptation of the evil weeds, will remain forever in the kingdom of heaven. The point about the kingdom in this parable, then, is that until the time of final judgment, wheat and weeds, good and evil, faithful ones and unfaithful ones, will coexist.

In the second parable, Jesus shows how the kingdom of heaven grows exponentially by using the symbol of the mustard seed. On average about two millimeters in diameter, this very tiny seed grows to be a

Lower your tone of voice as you come to the end of the narrative phrase introducing the disciples' request and again before you speak Jesus' reply.

Then, **dismissing** the **crowds**, he **went** into the **house**.
His **disciples** approached him and **said**,
"**Explain** to us the **parable** of the **weeds** in the **field**."
He **said** in reply, "He who sows **good seed** is the **Son** of **Man**,
the **field** is the **world**, the **good seed** the **children**
of the **kingdom**.

Contrast the ominous consequence the weeds (sinners) will face with the glorious outcome the wheat (righteous) will experience. Use a serious tone for the weeds and hopeful tone for the wheat.

The **weeds** are the **children** of the **evil one**,
and the **enemy** who **sows** them is the **devil**.
The **harvest** is the **end** of the **age**, and the **harvesters** are **angels**.
Just as **weeds** are **collected** and **burned up** with **fire**,
so will it **be** at the end of the **age**.
The **Son** of **Man** will send his **angels**,
and they will **collect** out of his **kingdom**
all who cause others to **sin** and all **evildoers**.
They will **throw** them into the **fiery furnace**,
where there will be **wailing** and **grinding** of **teeth**.
Then the **righteous** will **shine** like the **sun**
in the **kingdom** of their **Father**.

Be bold in exhorting the assembly to hear the message of the parable.

Whoever has **ears** ought to **hear**."

[Shorter Form: Matthew 13:24–30]

small tree in the area of the Holy Land. As the tree looks inviting to the birds of the sky who come to make their home in it, so too the kingdom of heaven is welcoming, opening itself universally to those who choose to believe.

In the third parable, the woman mixes yeast with flour and the leavening action of the yeast causes the entire batch to rise. In the Jewish tradition, leaven denoted the propensity of human persons to sin. Yet in this parable, the leavening agent symbolizes God's power. In the First Reading we learn God's power cannot be understood apart from his compassionate justice. This parable, then, shows us that because of this merciful power the kingdom will grow.

This week Jesus' explanation for speaking in parables shows us that Jesus knows God's plan—a plan that has been hidden since the beginning of the world. Jesus' words are based on Psalm 78:2, which is attributed to Asaph who is called "the prophet" in 2 Chronicles 29:30, although Matthew might be drawing from another source for the quotation. Regardless of the source, Jesus' explanation teaches the crowds and us that his announcement of the kingdom through parables fulfills the teachings of the prophets.

The explanation of the parable of the wheat and the weeds ends with the command for those who have ears to hear, a command which the assembly also heard last Sunday. Following upon the verses about the last judgment, your bold delivery of this command should leave the assembly ready to believe and act in accord with the Lord's compassionate justice.

17TH SUNDAY IN ORDINARY TIME

Lectionary #109

READING I 1 Kings 3:5, 7–12

Direct God's words to the assembly by making eye contact with them. Emphasize that God will give them what they ask. Speak Solomon's words describing himself with humility.

Offer Solomon's request of God as a prayer of petition, but do not come across as if Solomon is begging God.

Pause after proclaiming each item Solomon did not ask for, allowing the assembly to ponder whether they would ask for it or not.

Take your time proclaiming that the Lord will fulfill Solomon's request. Conclude with a note of pride in your voice as Solomon will rule filled with the gift of wisdom.

A reading from the first Book of Kings

The **LORD** appeared to **Solomon** in a **dream** at night.
God said, "**Ask** something of me and I will **give** it to you."
Solomon answered:
"O **LORD**, my **God**, you have **made** me, your **servant, king**
to succeed my father **David**;
but I am a mere **youth**, not knowing at **all** how to **act**.
I **serve** you in the midst of the **people** whom you have **chosen**,
a people so **vast** that it **cannot** be **numbered** or **counted**.
Give your **servant**, therefore, an **understanding heart**
to **judge** your **people** and to **distinguish right** from **wrong**.
For **who** is able to **govern** this vast **people** of yours?"

The LORD was **pleased** that Solomon made this request.
So God **said** to him:
"**Because** you have asked for **this**—
not for a **long life** for **yourself**,
nor for **riches**,
nor for the **life** of your **enemies**,
but for **understanding** so that you may know what is **right**—
I **do** as you **requested**.
I **give** you a **heart** so **wise** and **understanding**
that there has **never** been **anyone** like you up to **now**,
and **after** you there will come **no one** to **equal** you."

READING I Today's First Reading, a dialogue between God and Solomon occurring in a dream, expresses hope for the success of Solomon's reign. Solomon asks the Lord to grant him an understanding heart so as to discern right from wrong when judging the Lord's people. The author tells us that the Lord was pleased with Solomon's humble and thoughtful request, and granted it. In verse 13, which is not included in the First Reading, we learn that God also gives Solomon riches and glory such that no other king will be like him. Verse 14 tells us that so long as Solomon remains faithful to God's laws, he will be the beneficiary of a long life.

All of this may seem too good to be true for any human king, and in fact it is. Solomon is painted in a positive light in this passage, but in later days, described in 1 Kings, especially chapter 11, his sins become obvious. The prosperity of Solomon's reign ultimately comes to an end because of his infidelity to the same Lord who had granted his initial desire for an understanding heart.

The outcome of Solomon's tenure, however, need not take away from the message of this reading. The gift of God's wisdom is a treasure of great price, and we must always remember from whom it comes. Through your proclamation, call the assembly to see their own need to open themselves both to God's wisdom and the effective use of this great gift.

READING II The Second Reading begins with a verse that, on first hearing, probably does not match our actual experience of this world. But Paul is not saying that people of faith live an easy life in which everything fits neatly

READING II Romans 8:28–30

A reading from the Letter of Saint Paul to the Romans

Brothers and sisters:
We know that **all** things work for **good** for those who love **God**,
who are **called** according to his **purpose**.

Use a confident voice to convey Paul's first step in his argument about why things work for good for those who love God: "those he foreknew he also predestined."

For those he **foreknew** he also **predestined**
to be **conformed** to the **image** of his **Son**,
so that **he** might be the **firstborn**
among **many** brothers and sisters.

Use the same tone on the second point in Paul's argument: "And those he predestined he also called." Continue with the same intensity for the parallel phrases that advance Paul's line of reasoning.

And those he **predestined** he also **called**;
and those he **called** he also **justified**;
and those he **justified** he also **glorified**.

GOSPEL Matthew 13:44–52

A reading from the holy Gospel according to Matthew

Jesus **said** to his **disciples**:

Proclaim the first of three analogies of the kingdom of heaven with joy in your voice.

"The kingdom of **heaven** is like a **treasure** buried in a **field**,
which a person **finds** and **hides** again,
and out of **joy** goes and sells **all** that he has and **buys** that **field**.

Communicate the second analogy with a slightly higher degree of excitement and happiness.

Again, the kingdom of **heaven** is like a **merchant**
searching for **fine pearls**.
When he **finds** a pearl of **great price**,
he goes and sells **all** that he has and **buys** it.

together and there are no trials. Since earlier in the chapter he has spoken of the sufferings of the present world, we know Paul understands that even for those whom God calls as his adopted sons and daughters, life presents challenges. The truth Paul is suggesting is that all things will work together, if not always in the present, in the future when we will experience the full revelation of God's glory. (He expresses this clearly before our reading begins in 8:18.)

The second and third verses contain the complex concepts of foreknowledge and predestination that have been the subject of intense theological debates through the centuries. In simplest terms, by using the language of divine foreknowledge Paul is teaching that God has been at work even before the creation of the world. God knew us before we were born; God foresees our thoughts and actions; he knows our words before we speak them (compare Psalm 139). Even before the beginning of time, God's plan for the redemption of the world began.

The final verse is supremely hopeful. Build in confidence as you proclaim it. In doing so, call the assembly to trust that they truly are God's chosen ones whom he deeply desires to share in his glory at the end of time.

GOSPEL This is the last of three Sundays in which the Gospel passage comes from the parable discourse in Matthew 13. In this relatively short Gospel, there are five distinct sections.

In the first parable, Jesus teaches his disciples about the genuine and essential response of disciples who find the treasure of the kingdom of heaven. Disciples

Change the tone of your voice on the third analogy. Let contentment be evident as you describe what is good and let weightiness, even judgment, be heard in your voice as you speak about the bad.

Again, the kingdom of **heaven** is like a **net** thrown into the **sea**,
which collects **fish** of **every kind**.
When it is **full** they haul it **ashore**
and sit **down** to put what is **good** into **buckets**.
What is **bad** they **throw away**.

Announce the judgment at the end of the age with seriousness and some trepidation.

Thus it will **be** at the **end** of the **age**.
The **angels** will go out and **separate** the **wicked**
from the **righteous**
and throw them into the **fiery furnace**,
where there will be **wailing** and **grinding** of **teeth**.

Were the disciples bold in their response, or did they respond quickly, with some fear, to Jesus' question? Practice your proclamation both ways. Either way, they accepted the responsibility of teaching others about the kingdom.

"Do you **understand** all these things?"
They answered, **"Yes."**
And he replied,
"Then **every** scribe who has been **instructed** in the kingdom
of **heaven**
is like the **head** of a **household**
who brings from his **storeroom** both the **new** and the **old**."

[Shorter Form: Matthew 13:44–46]

realize that it offers opportunities for life that nothing else can. They will sacrifice everything to protect the treasure of the kingdom they have found.

The second parable of the pearl of great price presents much the same message as the first. The merchant's behavior points to the great value of the kingdom and the necessary sacrifice for the kingdom that a disciple must make.

In the third parable, the disciples learn that in the kingdom of heaven the good will be sorted out from the bad at the last judgment. This parable provides an image of the Church to which both saints and sinners belong until the time of judgment.

After the brief third parable, in the fourth section, Jesus explains to the disciples what will happen at the end of time. They learn that the wicked will be separated from the righteous. The deplorable consequence the wicked will face is the same that the evildoers face in the explanation of the parable of the wheat and the weeds heard last Sunday (Matthew 13:42, 50).

The final section of today's Gospel is understood both as general description of the Christian scribe's role and the evangelist's autobiographical statement of how he understands his own role. Almost a parable in itself, Jesus' reply to the disciples' affirmation of their understanding unites the Jewish scripture with his own teaching. The bringing together of the old and the new, which have the same roots, is unfolding in Matthew's community. This verse also looks forward to the completion of the union of the old and new in the kingdom of heaven—a kingdom already present in Jesus, but still yet to come.

18TH SUNDAY IN ORDINARY TIME

Lectionary #112

READING I Isaiah 55:1–3

A reading from the Book of the Prophet Isaiah

Stress all the imperative verbs of invitation and action and their repetitions: "come," "receive," "eat," "drink," "heed," and "listen." Try varying the strength and tone of your voice slightly on each so that your proclamation suggests the meaning of the words themselves, as if each of the words is an example of onomatopoeia.

Thus says the LORD:
All you who are **thirsty**,
come to the **water**!
You who have no **money**,
come, receive **grain** and **eat**;
come, without paying and **without** cost,
drink **wine** and **milk**!
Why spend your **money** for what is not **bread**;
your **wages** for what **fails** to **satisfy**?
Heed me, and **you** shall **eat well**,
you shall **delight** in rich **fare**.
Come to me **heedfully**,
listen, that **you** may have **life**.
I will **renew** with you the **everlasting covenant**,
the **benefits** assured to **David**.

Proclaim the Lord's promise with confidence based on your own experience and hope for the future: you and those in the assembly have already experienced benefits from coming to the Lord's banquet.

READING I These three verses are from the beginning of Isaiah 55, the culminating chapter of a section known as the book of consolation (Isaiah 40—55). On the Fifteenth Sunday in Ordinary Time, verses 10–11 from this same chapter were proclaimed and on the Twenty-fifth Sunday verses 6–9 will be proclaimed. Recall that the 11 verses which begin chapter 55 were proclaimed as the Fifth Reading at the Easter Vigil. Today Isaiah's words of invitation are heard in the context of Matthew's account of the beloved Gospel narrative of the loaves and fish.

Isaiah wrote near the end of the Babylonian exile and in these words he assures the Israelites that God has not forgotten them. God graciously invites those who are thirsty, poor, and hungry to the banquet. The attendees do not need to pay for any of the lavish nourishment on which they feast.

In beautiful, poetic imagery Isaiah tells us that those who heed and listen to the Lord will feast and have life. Moreover, the Lord himself will renew the covenant he made with them through David. Among the benefits the Lord promised to David in this covenant were that he would be famous, that a dwelling place would be fixed for the Israelites, that David's house and kingdom would last forever, and that his throne would stand firm until the end of time. God and David will be in a lasting father-son relationship such that if David does any wrong, the Lord will correct him but will not withdraw his love from him (2 Samuel 7:9–16).

Your task as a proclaimer of the word this Sunday is to communicate the Lord's

READING II Romans 8:35, 37–39

A reading from the Letter of Saint Paul to the Romans

Brothers and sisters:
What will **separate** us from the **love** of **Christ**?
Will **anguish**, or **distress**, or **persecution**, or **famine**,
or **nakedness**, or **peril**, or the **sword**?
No, in **all** these things we conquer **overwhelmingly**
through **him** who **loved** us.
For I am **convinced** that neither **death**, nor **life**,
nor **angels**, nor **principalities**,
nor **present** things, nor **future** things,
nor **powers**, nor **height**, nor **depth**,
nor any other **creature** will be able to **separate** us
from the **love** of **God** in **Christ Jesus** our **Lord**.

Speak the list of what potentially could separate us from the love of Christ slowly and seriously, pausing after each item. Remember to raise your voice slightly at the end of the question.

Proclaim Paul's answer resolutely.

Again, be deliberate as you list the ten risks to our communion with Christ. Pause noticeably after each, so people have a moment to mull it over.

Build in power and conviction as you approach the conclusion.

GOSPEL Matthew 14:13–21

A reading from the holy Gospel according to Matthew

When **Jesus** heard of the **death** of **John** the **Baptist**,
he **withdrew** in a **boat** to a deserted **place** by **himself**.
The **crowds** heard of this and **followed** him on **foot**
from their **towns**.
When he **disembarked** and saw the **vast crowd**,
his **heart** was moved with **pity** for them,
and he **cured** their **sick**.

Set the scene by using a narrative tone of voice.

care for his people and the miracle of the abundant nourishment that is theirs through him. As the Father's love never ceases, so too, the Lord will not abandon his people; he constantly offers the invitation to join him at his banquet.

READING II In the three verses which comprise the Second Reading, Paul answers the rhetorical question he asks the Romans and which you pose to the assembly today. His answer is an emphatic statement that nothing, not even the seven trials he names in the second rhetorical question, or the ten powers he lists in verses 38–39 (the last two verses of the reading) can separate us from God's love.

As adopted sons and daughters of God, we are able to conquer the obstacles we face because Christ himself has conquered death once for all. Justification is ours through his Passion, death, and Resurrection. In Baptism, we were baptized into his death so that we might also share in his Resurrection (Romans 6:3–4).

As you proclaim this reading, building in intensity will convey the steadfast nature of the love of Christ to the assembly. Not even the height or depth—astrological references to the enormity of the universe—can cut us off from his love, a love whose breadth and length and height and depth surpass anything we know (Ephesians 3:18). If your proclamation is successful, some in the assembly may respond "Amen" at its conclusion.

GOSPEL The Gospel begins by telling us that Jesus withdrew to a deserted place upon hearing of the death of John the Baptist (Matthew

Offer Jesus' instructions to the disciples in a direct, but not overly authoritative tone.

The disciples are simply stating the fact of how much food they have to Jesus. They are not arguing.

Communicate a sense of Jesus' command of the situation as he instructs the crowds to gather around him and the disciples to bring the food they have.

Take your time proclaiming the actions of Jesus that have an obvious Eucharistic connection. Pay particular attention in your proclamation to the action of the disciples who feed the crowds. Make eye contact with the assembly on this line.

Return to the narrative voice used at the beginning of the Gospel to proclaim the summary lines and the satisfaction of a people well fed and seeing the leftovers with which others can be fed.

When it was **evening**, the disciples approached him and said,
"This is a **deserted** place and it is already **late**;
dismiss the **crowds** so that they can go to the **villages**
and buy **food** for themselves."
Jesus **said** to them, "There is **no need** for them to go **away**;
give them some **food yourselves.**"
But they **said** to him,
"Five **loaves** and two **fish** are **all** we **have** here."
Then he said, "Bring them **here** to **me**,"
and he ordered the **crowds** to sit **down** on the **grass**.
Taking the five **loaves** and the two **fish**, and looking up
to **heaven**,
he said the **blessing, broke** the loaves,
and **gave** them to the **disciples**,
who in turn **gave** them to the **crowds**.
They **all ate** and were **satisfied**,
and they picked up the **fragments** left over—
twelve wicker baskets full.
Those who **ate** were about five **thousand** men,
not counting **women** and **children**.

14:1–12). It appears that Jesus was seeking solitude, but could not have it because the crowds followed him. Jesus lays aside his need to respond to their needs. The beloved miracle of the loaves and fish follows. Although often referred to as the multiplication of the loaves and fish, Matthew never describes how there came to be more than enough food for those gathered.

The narrative of the miracle begins with Jesus instructing the disciples to allow the people to stay and to provide food for them. After the disciples respond to Jesus' instructions by saying it would be impossible to feed the crowds with the small amount of food available, Jesus takes control of the situation.

Following the ritual of a Jewish meal, Jesus blesses, breaks, and gives the bread to the disciples, who in turn give it to the crowds. Notice how the disciples' action of giving mirrors Jesus' own action of giving. Observe also that the fish are not included in Jesus' action of breaking. This helps make the connection to Eucharist more evident.

In your proclamation of this miracle, draw particular attention to the facts that the disciples feed the crowds after Jesus performs the Eucharistic action of blessing, breaking, and giving and that there are leftovers. We still have the food of Jesus' body and blood with which we will be fed today. Both you and those in your assembly share in the vocation of feeding the peoples of the world with Jesus, though in different ways.

19TH SUNDAY IN ORDINARY TIME

Lectionary #115

READING I 1 Kings 19:9a, 11–13a

A reading from the first Book of Kings

Horeb = HOHR-eb
Elijah = ee-LĪ-juh

At the **mountain** of God, **Horeb**,
Elijah came to a **cave** where he took **shelter**.
Then the LORD said to him,
"Go outside and **stand** on the **mountain** before the LORD;
the LORD will be passing by."

Pause noticeably at the semicolon. Deliver the next phrase slowly: it sets the stage for the rest of the passage.

The next three sentences are parallel in structure. Pause significantly at the dashes and then communicate disappointment by the lowering the tone of your voice and softening its volume as the Lord was neither in the wind, the earthquake, or the fire. Proclaim the words "strong and heavy wind," "earthquake," and "fire," with strength, power, and intensity, respectively. Pausing slightly after the phrase "After the fire" will lead the assembly to expect a conclusion similar to the previous sentences. Significantly soften your voice, to an audible whisper, to signal the Lord's presence.

A **strong** and heavy **wind** was **rending** the **mountains**
and **crushing** rocks before the LORD—
but the **LORD** was **not** in the **wind**.
After the **wind** there was an **earthquake**—
but the **LORD** was **not** in the **earthquake**.
After the **earthquake** there was **fire**—
but the **LORD** was **not** in the **fire**.
After the **fire** there was a **tiny whispering sound**.
When he heard **this**,
Elijah **hid** his face in his cloak
and went and **stood** at the entrance of the cave.

READING I Elijah's long journey of 40 days and nights (1 Kings 19:1–8), reminiscent of the Israelites' own wandering in the desert and our Lenten journey, takes him to Mount Horeb, the same mount on which the Lord manifests himself to Moses (Exodus 19:1–23; Deuteronomy 4:10–15). The dramatic details of heavy wind, earthquake, and the fire are similar to the theophanies (appearances of God) experienced by Moses. Yet it is not in those dramatic events that Elijah encounters God. Instead God comes to Elijah unexpectedly in "a tiny whispering sound."

The reading never tells us that the Lord is in the whisper; we only know because the last verse describes Elijah's reaction. Without Elijah's openness to the Lord's coming in the whisper, he would not have recognized the Lord and received his new commission (1 Kings 19:15–17).

Vital to the proclamation of this reading will be your ability to create a sense of expectation in the assembly that the Lord will be in the wind, the earthquake, and the fire. The expectation should lead to a letdown when you communicate that the Lord was not there. The cycle of expectation and letdown will set the stage for the Lord's unexpected appearance in the whispering sound and help put across the main theme of the reading: the Lord is faithful in coming to us albeit in ways we might least expect. Our hearts, like Elijah's, must be open to receive him.

READING II Before you begin your proclamation of this reading, reflect on how Paul's opening line about the truth he speaks in Christ relates to your ministry of the word. In this ministry, you proclaim the truth of the word. The Holy

READING II Romans 9:1–5

A reading from the Letter of Saint Paul to the Romans

State the opening phrase firmly and with conviction: Paul and you speak the truth and do not lie.

Communicate how deeply Paul feels for the Israelites by increasing the intensity and passion in your voice as you proclaim the fact that he is willing to be cut off from Christ for the sake of his own people.

Paul uses Israelites, a religious title of honor rather than Jews, a political title. Take your time with the list of blessings. Build the intensity to the final line which is the climax. Very slowly proclaim the final words of praise and the "Amen," stressing each one equally.

patriarchs = PAY-tree-ahrks

Brothers and sisters:
I **speak** the **truth** in **Christ**, I do not **lie**;
my **conscience** joins with the **Holy Spirit**
in bearing me **witness**
that I have great **sorrow** and constant **anguish** in my **heart**.
For I could **wish** that I **myself** were **accursed** and **cut off**
from **Christ**
for the **sake** of my **own people**,
my **kindred** according to the **flesh**.
They are **Israelites**;
theirs the **adoption**, the **glory**, the **covenants**,
the **giving** of the **law**, the **worship**, and the **promises**;
theirs the **patriarchs**, and **from** them,
according to the **flesh**, is the **Christ**,
who is over **all, God blessed forever. Amen.**

GOSPEL Matthew 14:22–33

A reading from the holy Gospel according to Matthew

Use a narrative tone until the disciples speak.

After he had **fed** the people, **Jesus** made the **disciples** get
into a **boat**
and **precede** him to the other side,
while **he** dismissed the **crowds**.
After doing so, he went **up** on the **mountain** by himself to **pray**.
When it was **evening** he was there **alone**.

Spirit enables you to do so effectively just as the Spirit made possible Paul's witness to the same truth.

After five Sundays of the Second Reading coming from Romans 8, today we move on to a passage from chapter 9. In Romans 9—11, Paul focus on how the truth about justification by faith in Christ Jesus relates to the promises God made to his Chosen People, the Israelites. Paul's heart is torn apart and he experiences enormous grief because those Israelites who refuse to accept the Gospel are cut off from the salvific life it offers. Notice that the reference Paul makes is to the "Israelites," not to the "Jews." In using this term of address, he is honoring the heritage of the Chosen People and avoiding the political referent.

Christians believe that salvation has come through Christ Jesus. By reverencing the Israelite tradition, Paul shows how salvation has come through the Chosen People. This salvation is rooted in the seven privileges accorded to them that he lists. The climax of this list is "the Christ, who is over all" who comes from them.

The degree of Paul's sorrow is founded on his belief that Christ is the fulfillment of the promises given to Israel. Paul's sorrow for them is so intense that he himself would rather suffer for their sakes in imitation of Christ's suffering so that they might experience life.

As you proclaim, think of how your proclamation of the truth can lead others to faith. Like Paul, attempt to make your proclamation selfless and humble in nature. This will help those in the assembly who do not yet believe recognize God

Meanwhile the boat, already a few miles offshore,
was being **tossed about** by the **waves**,
for the **wind** was **against** it.
During the **fourth** watch of the **night**,
he came **toward** them **walking** on the **sea**.
When the disciples **saw** him **walking** on the **sea**
they were **terrified**.
"It is a **ghost**, " they said, and they **cried out** in **fear**.
At once Jesus **spoke** to them, "Take **courage**, it is **I**;
do **not** be **afraid**."
Peter said to him in **reply**,
"**Lord**, if it **is** you, **command** me to **come** to you
on the **water**."
He said, "**Come**."
Peter got out of the **boat** and began to **walk** on the **water**
toward **Jesus**.
But when he **saw** how strong the **wind** was
he became **frightened**;
and, beginning to **sink**, he **cried out**, "Lord, **save** me!"
Immediately Jesus **stretched** out his **hand** and **caught** Peter,
and **said** to him, "O **you** of **little faith**, why did you **doubt**?"
After they **got** into the **boat**, the **wind** died **down**.
Those who were **in** the boat did him **homage**, saying,
"**Truly**, **you** are the **Son** of **God**."

Fear and anxiety are evident in the disciples' words.

The calmness in your voice as you proclaim Jesus' reassuring words ought to contrast with the disciples' emotions.

Speak Jesus' one word command to Peter in a welcoming, not authoritative tone of voice. While a command, it is also an invitation to trust.

Peter is afraid: cry out, but do not shout so loudly the words become distorted by the sound system.

Allow a moment for the reverberations of Peter's cry to fade. Then calmly in the same reassuring tone as before, narrate Jesus' gesture and his question to Peter. Proclaim the statement of faith with the certainty of your own faith.

already present and at work in themselves as he was in the Israelites.

GOSPEL **Today's Gospel immediately follows the feeding miracle of the loaves and fish in Matthew. Matthew draws on Mark's original narrative, (Mark 6:45–52) but changes it in two significant ways.**

First, Matthew adds material that is unique to him—material that reflects an emphasis on Peter (Matthew 14:28–31). Peter trusts to the point of offering to walk on water if that is what the Lord commands him to do. Indeed, the Lord says to Peter "Come," often a word of invitation, but in this context, a command. Peter's response shows his obedience to the Lord and his expression of fear, his humanity. In the end, Peter's trust in the Lord is unqualified; Peter knows he can't save himself, only the Lord can.

Second, at the conclusion of the narrative in Matthew, the disciples in the boat resound together in their acclamation of Jesus' identity, whereas in Mark, the disciples' hearts remained hardened. They did not yet understand who Jesus is. Using the same words that the centurion and the men with him proclaimed upon the death of Jesus, the disciples' profession of faith in the Gospel according to Matthew shows how they, following Peter's example, believed in Jesus as the Savior of the world (Matthew 27:54).

20TH SUNDAY IN ORDINARY TIME

Lectionary #118

READING I Isaiah 56:1, 6–7

Isaiah = Ī-ZAY-uh

Pause noticeably after the introductory formula.

Maintain a tone of hopefulness and a sense of expectation throughout your proclamation.

profanation = proh-fuh-NAY-shuhn

Make eye contact with the assembly as you proclaim the Lord's house as a house of prayer for all peoples. Look around the assembly as you do so. Be careful your voice still projects properly through the microphone.

A reading from the Book of the Prophet Isaiah

Thus says the LORD:
Observe what is **right, do** what is **just**;
for my **salvation** is about to **come**,
my **justice**, about to be **revealed**.

The **foreigners** who join themselves to the LORD,
ministering to him,
loving the name of the LORD,
and **becoming** his **servants**—
all who keep the **sabbath** free from **profanation**
and **hold** to my **covenant**,
them I will **bring** to my **holy mountain**
and make **joyful** in my **house** of **prayer**;
their burnt **offerings** and **sacrifices**
will be **acceptable** on my **altar**,
for my **house** shall be **called**
a **house** of **prayer** for all **peoples**.

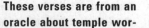

READING I These verses are from an oracle about temple worship for foreigners (Isaiah 56:1–8). Taken from the third part of the book of the prophet Isaiah, which includes chapters 56 through 66, the poem picks up the theme of the extension of God's salvation to all who follow him and observe his commands.

Addressed to the Jewish community upon their return from the Babylonian exile, this section emphasizes that those who faithfully observe the Sabbath will be brought to the Lord's holy mountain.

Neither race nor cultural heritage nor any other social condition is a prerequisite for knowing God's justice. Rather, loving the name of the Lord and following the time-honored tradition of keeping the Sabbath are the requirements. Those who adhere to these requirements will be happy in the Lord's house of prayer.

The sincerity with which you proclaim this reading will express the universal nature of the Lord's justice. While some in the assembly might not always keep the Lord's Day holy, still your proclamation invites them to hear once again that the Lord asks this of them. Moreover, in the midst of the diversity of people present in the many assemblies, what unites people together is their oneness in the Lord. Emphasizing the multiple occurrences of "all" will express this truth to your assembly. In God's house, all are welcome to be faithful to him.

READING II This is the last of eight consecutive Sundays of Ordinary Time for which the Second Reading comes from Romans. While last Sunday we heard of Paul's great sorrow because the Israelites have yet to accept

READING II Romans 11:13–15, 29–32

A reading from the Letter of Saint Paul to the Romans

Brothers and sisters:
I am **speaking** to you **Gentiles**.
Inasmuch as **I** am the **apostle** to the **Gentiles**,
I **glory** in my **ministry** in order to make my race **jealous**
and thus **save** some of them.
For if their **rejection** is the **reconciliation** of the **world**,
what will their **acceptance** be but **life** from the **dead**?

For the **gifts** and the **call** of **God** are **irrevocable**.
Just as you once **disobeyed** God
but have now **received mercy** because of **their** disobedience,
so they have now **disobeyed** in order that,
by **virtue** of the **mercy** shown to **you**,
they too may now **receive mercy**.
For God delivered **all** to **disobedience**,
that he might have **mercy** upon **all**.

Gentiles = JEN-tīls

Reconciliation and life from the dead are two goods. Only raise your voice slightly as you come to the end of the question.

irrevocable = eer-REV-uh-kah-b*l

Stress the repetition of both the forms of the word "disobey" and the word "mercy."

Stress both occurrences of "all" as you proclaim the concise summary of Paul's teaching in this section in a principled manner.

the Gospel, this Sunday we hear of his hope for their acceptance of it.

Paul speaks to the Gentiles, those who have at first rejected the God of Israel and who have now experienced the forgiveness and mercy of God because they have come to believe. Paul, an apostle called by God, personally experienced God's mercy because of his own disobedience. For Paul, Jews will come to believe through his preaching of the Gospel and the conversion of the Gentiles. The conversion of the Gentiles is the first stage in God's plan for the redemption of the world through Christ Jesus; the second is the acceptance of the Gospel by Jews.

Your proclamation of this passage is a balancing act this Sunday. As Paul is telling the Gentiles not to be arrogant because he is an apostle to them, he is also expressing his unity with his own "race." Thus, your proclamation needs to communicate both the promise of God's mercy available to all and the hope of the acceptance of the Gospel by all.

GOSPEL Today's Gospel of the healing of the Canaanite woman's daughter from a demon, is paired with the First Reading because of its emphasis on the extension of faith to Gentiles. Just as in the First Reading foreigners who joined themselves to the Lord were welcomed as part of the Lord's house of prayer, so too, the Gentile woman who professed her faith in Jesus, saw herself welcomed by the Lord through her daughter's healing.

The Gospel takes place in the region of Tyre and Sidon, Gentile territory. A woman from Canaan, a nation whose citizens were historically disregarded by Jews, comes to Jesus, asking him for pity. Matthew

GOSPEL Matthew 15:21–28

Tyre = tīr
Sidon = SĪ-duhn
Canaanite = KAY-nuh-nīt

Cry out the Canaanite woman's words as if you're pleading with Jesus. Lower the volume of your voice as you explain that the woman's daughter suffers because of a demon.

Convey irritation, even judgment, as you speak the disciples' words.

Jesus' response is filled with compassion.

Contrast the woman's second request of Jesus with her first by speaking her words with gentle insistence.

Jesus' reply borders on being indignant. Speak it in a moralizing tone.

Proclaim the woman's third request of Jesus strongly and persuasively: it is her surprising statement of faith.

Proclaim Jesus' praise of the woman's faith with delight. He is pleased to grant her request.

A reading from the holy Gospel according to Matthew

At that time, **Jesus** withdrew to the **region** of **Tyre** and **Sidon**.
And behold, a **Canaanite** woman of that district came
and **called out**,
"Have **pity** on me, **Lord, Son of David**!
My **daughter** is tormented by a **demon**."
But Jesus did not say a **word** in answer to her.
Jesus' disciples came and asked him,
"**Send** her **away**, for she keeps **calling out** after us."
He said in **reply**,
"I was sent **only** to the **lost sheep** of the **house** of **Israel**."
But the **woman** came and **did** Jesus **homage**, saying,
"**Lord, help** me."
He said in **reply**,
"It is **not right** to take the **food** of the **children**
and **throw** it to the **dogs**."
She said, "**Please**, Lord, for **even** the **dogs** eat the **scraps**
that **fall** from the **table** of their **masters**."
Then **Jesus** said to her in reply,
"O woman, **great** is your **faith**!
Let it be **done** for you as you **wish**."
And the woman's daughter was **healed** from that hour.

changes Mark's original Syrophoenician to a Canaanite woman in order to emphasize the woman's marginal status.

Yet despite her status, the woman's first statement is one of faith in which she recognizes Jesus' lineage. We can understand Jesus' silent response in light of the disciples' desire to send her away and Jesus' statement that he was sent only to the lost sheep of the house of Israel (Matthew 10:6). Apparently to Jesus' mind, healing a Gentile woman would take him beyond the limits of his mission. Notice that he will commission the disciples to go to all the nations at the end of Matthew (28:19).

Despite three rejections, the Canaanite woman is persistent, and asks a second time for Jesus' help. Jesus gives a response characteristic of Jews at the time. Referring to the woman with the harsh, derogatory language of "dog," he shows that salvation comes first to the Jews and then to the Gentiles. The woman does not miss a beat in her reply, letting Jesus know that she believes so strongly in him that if he would share even a little of who he is, her daughter would be healed.

The woman's articulation of her faith pays off. Jesus affirms her great faith, the only time in Matthew he refers to a person's faith in such terms, and heals her daughter.

In contrast to Mark's account of this narrative, which emphasizes the healing of the woman's daughter, Matthew emphasizes the conversation between Jesus and his disciples, and Jesus and the woman. Focus on differentiating the narrative lines from the dialogue in order to call your assembly to follow the example of the woman's bold and courageous faith.

ASSUMPTION OF THE BLESSED VIRGIN MARY: VIGIL

Lectionary #621

READING I 1 Chronicles 15:3–4, 15–16; 16:1–2

Chronicles = KRAH-nih-k*ls

In your proclamation of this reading, emphasize David's actions: "David assembled," "David also called together," "David commanded," and so on.

Aaron = AYR-uhn

Levites = LEE-vīts

lyres = lī¯rz

Narrate the conclusion of the ritual of presenting the Ark of the Covenant ("When David had finished . . .") and David's blessing of the people, using a reverent, sincere tone of voice. Make eye contact with the assembly as you speak of David blessing the people in the Lord's name.

A reading from the first Book of Chronicles

David assembled all **Israel** in **Jerusalem** to bring the **ark**
of the **LORD**
to the place that he had **prepared** for it.
David **also** called together the sons of **Aaron** and the **Levites**.
The **Levites** bore the ark of God on their **shoulders** with **poles**,
as **Moses** had **ordained** according to the word of the **LORD**.

David commanded the **chiefs** of the **Levites**
to appoint their **kinsmen** as **chanters**,
to play on musical **instruments, harps, lyres**, and **cymbals**,
to make a loud **sound** of **rejoicing**.

They **brought** in the ark of God and **set** it within the **tent**
which David had **pitched** for it.
Then they **offered** up burnt **offerings** and **peace** offerings to God.
When David had **finished** offering up the burnt offerings
and peace offerings,
he **blessed** the people in the **name** of the **Lord**.

READING I Initially, this reading may seem a puzzling choice for the Vigil of the Assumption. It is the Ark of the Covenant that makes it appropriate. For the Israelite people, the Ark of the Covenant represented God's presence with them. It was an ornate, rectangular box they carried with them from the time of the Exodus until the building of the Temple. Some traditions suggest that the Ark contained the written word of the law (1 Kings 8:9). Whatever was held within the Ark was so holy that only an authorized person could come in contact with it. Once the temple of Solomon was built, the Ark was placed in the Holy of Holies, a site only the high priest could enter. Prior to Solomon's reign, the Ark would be kept safe in a tent or tabernacle set up at each location where the Israelites' remained for a while.

In the scriptures, we can see a clear parallel between Mary and the Ark of the Covenant. The story of David bringing the original Ark of the Covenant into Jerusalem in 2 Samuel 6:4–16 is similar to Mary's visitation of Elizabeth in Luke 1:39–56, the narrative proclaimed tomorrow for the solemnity of the Assumption. Just as David journeys to Jerusalem with the Ark, Mary, pregnant with Jesus, journeys to Elizabeth. Thus, on the basis of scripture, the tradition of the Church has understood Mary as the Ark of the Covenant, the bearer of God's presence.

READING II This short passage from Paul's first letter to the Corinthians is part of Paul's response to questions raised earlier in chapter 15, verse 35, about the nature of the risen body and how the dead are actually restored to life. Drawing on Isaiah 25:8 and Hosea

Corinthians = kohr-IN-thee-unz

Pause slightly before and after the lines quoting Isaiah 25:8 and Hosea 13:14: "Death is swallowed up . . . ." Remember to raise your voice slightly as you near the end of the questions.

Proclaim the concluding verse in an exultant tone of voice filled with gratitude because you and the assembly before you have experienced this victory.

SECOND READING 1 Corinthians 15:54b–57

A reading from the first Letter of Saint Paul to the Corinthians

Brothers and sisters:
When that which is **mortal** clothes itself with **immortality**,
then the **word** that is **written** shall come **about**:
Death *is swallowed up in* ***victory.***
Where, *O death, is your* ***victory?***
Where, *O death, is your* ***sting?***

The sting of **death** is sin,
and the **power** of sin is the **law**.
But **thanks** be to **God** who gives **us** the **victory**
through our **Lord Jesus Christ**.

State the opening announcement ("A reading from . . .") clearly, in a strong tone of voice. Pause after the announcement, gaining the assembly's attention for the very brief Gospel that follows.

Pause slightly at the comma after "he replied." Proclaim Jesus' reply directly to the assembly, inviting them to follow Mary's example of hearing the word of God, by making eye contact with them.

GOSPEL Luke 11:27–28

A reading from the holy Gospel according to Luke

While **Jesus** was **speaking**,
a **woman** from the **crowd called out** and said to him,
"**Blessed** is the womb that **carried** you
and the **breasts** at which you **nursed**."
He **replied**,
"**Rather, blessed** are those
who **hear** the word of God and **observe** it."

13:14, Paul makes his point that death does not last; rather, God through Jesus Christ gives victory over death. The sting of death—sin—no longer has power over us.

Just as Saint Paul taught the Corinthian community that through Christ's Resurrection they will become a transformed body, bearing the image of the risen body of Christ, so too "the Assumption of the Blessed Virgin is a singular participation in her Son's Resurrection and an anticipation of the resurrection of other Christians" (*Catechism of the Catholic Church*, 966). Your proclamation of Paul's words on the eve of the Assumption can lead those in the assembly to understand that Mary's participation in Christ's Resurrection exemplifies the transformation that awaits all Christians at the end of our earthly life.

GOSPEL The two verses that compose the Gospel on the Vigil of the Assumption are found in the section of Luke that narrates the journey of Jesus and his disciples to Jerusalem (9:51—19:27). Prior to these verses, Jesus casts out a demon (11:14), speaks about Satan (11:18–19), and teaches about the effects of unclean spirits (11:24–26). In the midst of his teaching, an unidentified woman in the crowd interrupts Jesus, raises her voice and says, "Blessed is the womb . . . ." Jesus' response is not necessarily meant as a rebuke or denial. Instead his teaching is appropriately understood as completing the woman's words. The woman praises and honors Mary for her role as his mother. Jesus makes it clear that Mary is blessed because she heard the word of God and responded obediently to it. She is a model of holiness for us.

ASSUMPTION OF THE BLESSED VIRGIN MARY: DAY

Lectionary #622

READING I Revelation 11:19a; 12:1–6a, 10ab

Revelation = rev-uh-LAY-shuhn

Be clear in your announcement of the reading from "the book of Revelation," not Revelations.

A reading from the Book of Revelation

God's **temple** in heaven was **opened**,
and the **ark** of his **covenant** could be seen in the temple.

Let beauty and wonder be heard in your tone of voice as you narrate the words "A great sign appeared . . . ." Take your time painting the vision of the woman, allowing people time to engage their imaginations and make the connection to Mary and the child Jesus.

Pause before the dragon is introduced. Refrain from being overly dramatic in this scene.

A **great sign** appeared in the **sky**, a **woman** clothed with the **sun**,
with the **moon** under her **feet**,
and on her **head** a crown of twelve **stars**.
She was with **child** and wailed aloud in **pain** as she **labored**
to give **birth**.
Then **another** sign appeared in the sky;
it was a huge red **dragon**, with seven **heads** and ten **horns**,
and on its heads were seven **diadems**.
Its **tail** swept away a third of the **stars** in the **sky**
and **hurled** them down to the **earth**.
Then the dragon **stood** before the woman about to give **birth**,
to **devour** her child when she gave **birth**.
She gave **birth** to a son, a male child,
destined to rule all the **nations** with an iron rod.

Fill your voice with trust and faith as you narrate how the child and the woman were united with God in their respective ways.

Her child was **caught** up to **God** and his **throne**.
The woman **herself** fled into the **desert**
where she had a place **prepared** by God.

Boldly proclaim this entire verse without letting up on the strength of your voice.

Then I heard a loud **voice** in heaven say:
"**Now** have **salvation** and power come,
and the **Kingdom** of our God
and the **authority** of his **Anointed One**."

READING I The book of Revelation is a type of literature known as apocalyptic. It was probably written between 92 and 96 AD at the end of the reign of the Emperor Domitian. Through a dramatic, apocalyptic vision given by Christ to a man named John, the author expresses the belief that the world is corrupt and therefore will be destroyed. In the end, the righteous will be led to life in union with God. The audience for whom Revelation was written faced persecution by Roman leaders. The vision contained in Revelation urged them to stand up for their faith, for in doing so they would be rescued—if not in this life, then in the next.

Apocalyptic literature is usually replete with symbolism, as can be seen in today's First Reading. But this symbolism is not to be taken literally. For example, in the first section of the reading, the Catholic tradition has historically interpreted the "woman clothed with the sun" as Mary and the child the woman bears as Jesus. Yet the woman also symbolizes the heavenly Israel, the bringing together of God's Chosen People in the Old Testament with the new Israel, the Church, of the New Testament.

In the second section of the reading, the sign of the "huge red dragon" represents the power of the devil and the many forces of evil in the world that oppose the goodness of God and God's people, the Church. At the time of the writing of Revelation, the dragon most likely symbolized the Roman leaders who were putting down the nascent Church (see Revelation 12:13–18).

Finally, the third section of the reading shows that the child to whom the

READING II 1 Corinthians 15:20–27

Corinthians = kohr-IN-thee-unz

Make eye contact with the assembly.

Pause before the words "For just as in Adam . . . ." On the phrase "so too in Christ . . ." shift to a more hopeful tone of voice.

Build in intensity in your proclamation of Paul's argument from "then, at his coming . . ." until the conclusion.

A reading from the first Letter of Saint Paul to the Corinthians

Brothers and sisters:
Christ has been **raised** from the **dead**,
the **firstfruits** of those who have fallen **asleep**.
For since **death** came through man,
the **resurrection** of the dead came **also** through man.
For just as in **Adam** all **die**,
so **too** in **Christ** shall all be brought to **life**,
but each one in proper **order**:
Christ the **firstfruits**;
then, at his coming, those who **belong** to Christ;
then comes the **end**,
when he hands **over** the Kingdom to his God and **Father**,
when he has **destroyed** every **sovereignty**
and every **authority** and **power**.
For he must **reign** until he has put all his **enemies** under his **feet**.
The **last** enemy to be destroyed is **death**,
for "he subjected **everything** under his **feet**."

woman gives birth is protected by God and taken to his throne, a reference to the belief that Christ reigns forever with God through his Resurrection and Ascension. The woman, too, resides in a special place in the desert where God is present and where she is protected by him.

Because we understand the woman to symbolize Mary, the Mother of the Church, this vision also signifies that the Church will last throughout all time, a fundamental conviction held by the Christian community since its earliest days. The permanence of the Church is referred to as the Church's indefectibility and is rooted in the indestructibility of the core belief that Jesus, the Son of God and Son of Mary, is Lord for all time (*Lumen Gentium*, 9).

READING II Like the Second Reading for the Assumption Vigil, the Second Reading for the Assumption Mass during the Day comes from chapter 15 of Paul's first letter to the Corinthians. The focus of chapter 15 is Paul's teaching about the Resurrection of Christ and what it means for our Resurrection.

Paul develops his theology of Resurrection around two main points in today's Second Reading. First, the agricultural image of the "firstfruits," which Paul uses to understand the Risen Christ, refers to the part of the harvest that is offered in thanksgiving to God in anticipation of the whole harvest that will come. By speaking of Christ's Resurrection as the "firstfruits," Paul makes the connection between Christ's Resurrection and that of Christians. The "first" Resurrection anticipates the resurrection of Christians at the end of time.

GOSPEL Luke 1:39–56

As you narrate the opening lines, convey the sense of urgency in Mary's journey by placing some excitement and anticipation in your tone of voice.

2. Zechariah = zek-uh-RĪ-uh

Proclaim Elizabeth's words acknowledging Mary's identity as the acclamation they are by filling your voice with praise.

Pause after Elizabeth's acclamation of Mary and before her question. Humbly ask Elizabeth's question by lightening the tone of your voice.

Return again to the tone of praise—though somewhat more reserved than the tone used for the initial acclamation—on Elizabeth's second acclamation of Mary.

Proclaim the canticle of Mary (the Magnificat), "My soul proclaims . . ." with joy in your voice. You are praising God through these words and calling the assembly to do the same.

A reading from the holy Gospel according to Luke

Mary set out
and traveled to the **hill** country in **haste**
to a town of **Judah**,
where she entered the house of **Zechariah**
and greeted **Elizabeth**.
When Elizabeth heard Mary's **greeting**,
the infant **leaped** in her womb,
and **Elizabeth**, filled with the **Holy Spirit**,
cried out in a loud voice and **said**,
"**Blessed** are you among **women**,
and **blessed** is the **fruit** of your **womb**.
And **how** does this happen to **me**,
that the mother of my **Lord** should come to **me**?
For at the moment the sound of your **greeting** reached my **ears**,
the **infant** in my womb **leaped** for **joy**.
Blessed are you who **believed**
that what was spoken to you by the **Lord**
would be **fulfilled**."

And Mary said:

"My **soul** proclaims the **greatness** of the **Lord**;
my spirit **rejoices** in **God** my **Savior**
for he has **looked** with **favor** on his lowly **servant**.
From this day **all** generations will call me **blessed**:
the **Almighty** has done great **things** for me
and **holy** is his **Name**.
He has **mercy** on those who **fear** him
in **every** generation.

Second, Paul develops an Adam-Christ typology through which Christ is identified as a human being like Adam. Paul argues that since death (sin) came through Adam, then life must also come through a person like Adam—Christ. Thus, since we all have inherited the human condition of sinfulness from Adam, so at the second coming of Christ—the risen one who has destroyed sin—we too will be raised. But why proclaim this reading on the solemnity of the Assumption? Through Mary's Assumption into heavenly glory, she participates in a unique way in her Son's Resurrection and in doing so, anticipates our own Resurrection (*Catechism of the Catholic Church,* 966). From the Annunciation to the cross, Mary's role as Mother of God never ceased. Because of her closeness to Christ and to us, then, she intercedes for all Christians as we look forward to the gift of eternal salvation.

GOSPEL **In today's Gospel, the beloved narrative of the Visitation, Elizabeth praises Mary twice in her words of response to her greeting. First, Elizabeth's words ("Blessed are you among women, and blessed is the fruit of your womb") draw attention to Mary's election from among all other women to be the mother of the Lord. These words are a statement of faith regarding the child that Mary is carrying in her womb. They are also reminiscent of Jael's and Judith's liberation of their people in Judges 5:24 and Judith 13:18, respectively, and as such serve to show how Mary will contribute to the freedom of believers by giving birth to the Savior, Jesus Christ. Together with the angel Gabriel's words, "Hail, full of grace! The Lord is with you" (Luke 1:28), they form**

He has shown the **strength** of his **arm**,
and has **scattered** the proud in their **conceit**.
He has cast down the **mighty** from their **thrones**,
and has **lifted up** the **lowly**.
He has **filled** the **hungry** with **good** things,
and the **rich** he has sent away **empty**.
He has come to the **help** of his servant **Israel**
for he has **remembered** his promise of **mercy**,
the **promise** he made to our **fathers**,
to **Abraham** and his **children** for **ever**."

Pause after the canticle ends and before offering the concluding summary ("Mary remained . . .") slowly, in a reserved tone of voice.

Mary **remained** with her about **three months**
and then **returned** to her **home**.

the basis for the first half of the traditional prayer, the Hail Mary.

Second, at the conclusion of her response to Mary, Elizabeth praises Mary with the words "Blessed are you who believed that what was spoken to you by the Lord would be fulfilled." Elizabeth's words set Mary apart as a model believer whose obedience to the Lord's word we are to emulate.

The Gospel concludes with Mary's hymn of praise to God, placed by Luke at this point in his narrative to show how Mary's experience of the Lord's presence in her life, while unique, is extended by God to all. Notice how the first stanza of the Magnificat is Mary's praise of God for what God has done specifically for her (1:46–50) and the second stanza generalizes Mary's experiences and speaks of God's presence to all people, and in a particular way to the lowly, the hungry, and his servant Israel (1:51–55).

Mary's praise of God, which follows upon the praise of her given by Elizabeth, shows us that our praise and veneration of Mary is ultimately meant to draw us to a deeper praise and worship of God. As the popular devotional phrase attests, our faith goes "to Jesus through Mary." Mary's Assumption, body and soul into heavenly glory has placed her forever as our mother in the order of grace. She now intercedes on our behalf, leading us closer to Jesus and to union with the Father in the Holy Spirit. Thus, any celebration of Mary is first a celebration of her Son, Jesus Christ.

21ST SUNDAY IN ORDINARY TIME

Lectionary #121

READING I Isaiah 22:19–23

Isaiah = ī-ZAY-uh

1. Shebna = SHEB-nah

Eliakim = ee-LĪ-uh-kim
Hilkiah = hil-KĪ-uh

Judah = JOO-duh
Proclaim the giving of the key to Eliakim with confidence.
Pause after "no one shall shut" as if there was a period at the end of the phrase.

A reading from the Book of the Prophet Isaiah

Thus says the **Lord** to **Shebna**, **master** of the **palace**:
"I will **thrust** you from your **office**
and **pull** you **down** from your **station**.
On that **day** I will summon my **servant**
Eliakim, son of **Hilkiah**;
I will **clothe** him with your **robe**,
and **gird** him with your **sash**,
and **give over** to him your **authority**.
He shall be a **father** to the **inhabitants** of **Jerusalem**,
and to the **house** of **Judah**.
I will place the **key** of the **House** of **David**
on **Eliakim's** shoulder;
when he **opens**, no one shall **shut**,
when he **shuts**, no one shall **open**.
I will fix him like a **peg** in a sure **spot**,
to be a place of **honor** for his **family**."

READING I Today's First Reading recounts the demotion of Shebna and the promotion of Eliakim. Although not well known among biblical personages, both Shebna and Eliakim played important roles in the administration of King Hezekiah in the eighth century (Isaiah 36:3, 22; 37:2). Active during a time when the Assyrians were closing in on Jerusalem, Hezekiah commissioned Shebna and Eliakim, along with Joah, the son of Asaph, to negotiate with the enemy's commander, who represented the king of Assyria (2 Kings 18:18).

From this scene we learn that Eliakim is the son of Hilkiah, the master of the palace, and Shebna is a scribe. While today's passage does not provide any details as to what precipitated Shebna's demotion, Isaiah 22:18 reveals that something Shebna did brought disgrace to the master's house. Eliakim, however, is the Lord's servant. On the same day that the Lord removes Shebna from office, the Lord will call Eliakim and invest him with authority to govern the house of Judah.

Verses 22–23 are probably from an actual investiture ceremony. The key symbolizes Eliakim's new authority in the royal palace. Together with the reference to David, and the place of honor, the key connects Eliakim to the royal throne, introducing a messianic aspect to this oracle.

In your proclamation, pay attention to the Lord's own authority. All that happens with Shebna and Eliakim is the Lord's response to them, the Lord's doing. Even after Eliakim is given the keys, if he angers God and thus destroys his family's glory, the Lord says that catastrophe will befall him and his family (22:24–25). A balance of confidence, seriousness, and hope in your

READING II Romans 11:33–36

Grab the assembly's attention by proclaiming the opening line of the reading with a sense of wonder. Memorize this line if possible so you can make eye contact throughout it.

Proclaim the concluding doxology deliberately, pausing after each phrase and before the two occurrences of "and." Build in strength as you move through the doxology. Be prepared for those in the assembly to respond "Amen" with you!

A reading from the Letter of Saint Paul to the Romans

Oh, the **depth** of the **riches** and **wisdom** and **knowledge** of **God**!
How **inscrutable** are his **judgments** and how **unsearchable**
his **ways**!
*For **who** has known the **mind** of the **Lord***
*or **who** has been his **counselor**?*
*Or **who** has given the **Lord anything***
*that he may be **repaid**?*
For **from** him and **through** him and **for** him are **all** things.
To **him** be **glory** forever. **Amen**.

GOSPEL Matthew 16:13–20

Caesarea Philippi = sez-uh-REE-uh fih-LIP-ī

Ask the question directly to those gathered by making eye contact with them and panning around the assembly.

Elijah = ee-LĪ-juh

Jeremiah = jayr-uh-MĪ-uh

A reading from the holy Gospel according to Matthew

Jesus went into the region of **Caesarea Philippi** and
he **asked** his **disciples**,
"**Who** do people say that the **Son** of **Man** is?"
They replied, "**Some** say **John** the **Baptist**, others **Elijah**,
still others **Jeremiah** or one of the **prophets**."
He said to them, "But who do **you** say that **I** am?"
Simon **Peter** said in reply,
"**You** are the **Christ**, the **Son** of the living **God**."

proclamation will help convey the Lord's own authority and the new beginning Eliakim's service brings to the royal palace.

READING II The Second Reading contains Paul's reflections on the immense wisdom of God. In that wisdom, God has given faith to both Jews and Gentiles. Although beyond human understanding, God's plan of salvation includes both Jews and Gentiles. Through his Son, Jesus Christ, God extends salvation to all who believe.

After the opening exclamatory lines, two citations follow from Isaiah 40:13 and Job 41:3a, respectively. Paul uses these to show that no one can repay God for his gift of salvation. As the Lord delivered the Jews from exile, he needs no help, advice, or repayment for his gracious extension of salvation to all.

If he desires anything, it is simply that which the concluding doxology of the reading puts forward: the recognition that all that exists comes from him.

Your successful proclamation of this reading will communicate the beauty and generosity of God's wisdom to those in the assembly. Filled with your own praise of God, your proclamation of the doxology will invite the assembly to spontaneously respond with their own faith-filled "Amen" as you conclude the reading with the same word.

GOSPEL The focus of today's Gospel is Peter's confession of Jesus as "the Christ, the Son of the living God." Mark and Luke have parallels to Matthew's account, but Matthew adds Jesus' words in verses 16b–19 in order to

Speak Jesus' words to Simon with reverence in your voice. Strengthen your voice as you come to the words "upon this rock . . . ."

Simon = SĪ-muhn

Jonah = JOH-nuh

Jesus **said** to him in **reply**,
"**Blessed** are **you, Simon** son of **Jonah**.
For **flesh** and **blood** has not **revealed** this to you,
but my heavenly **Father**.
And so I **say** to **you**, you are **Peter**,
and upon this **rock** I will **build** my **church**,
and the **gates** of the **netherworld** shall **not prevail** against it.
I will **give** you the **keys** to the **kingdom** of **heaven**.
Whatever you **bind** on **earth** shall be **bound in heaven**;
and whatever you **loose** on **earth** shall be **loosed in heaven**."
Then he strictly **ordered** his **disciples**
to tell **no one** that he was the **Christ**.

Pause after Jesus' words and before offering the concluding line in a narrative tone of voice.

show how Peter's confession relates to the nature, growth, and structure of the Church.

This ecclesiological section focuses on Peter as the *rock* of the Church, *rock* being a word that plays on Peter's name. (In Greek, Peter is *Petros* and rock is *petra.* Both words are *kēphā* in Aramaic.) In all four accounts of the Gospel, the term *ekklesia* occurs only here and twice in Matthew 18:17. It is used by Matthew to show the relationship between the Church and the kingdom of heaven. Through the authority given to Peter, represented by the keys, and through his responsibility to bind and loose, the Church will proclaim salvation, grow, and be structured during this interim period before the fullness of the kingdom comes.

Later in Matthew, Jesus gives the authority to bind and loose to all the disciples (18:18). Yet Peter alone retains the unique role of being the Church's rock; only he has the keys. Binding and loosing are rooted in the rabbinical tradition of containing the devil during exorcism, making administrative decisions, and legally deciding who belongs to the community. The symbol of the keys is the clear link to today's First Reading. A second, more subtle connection is Peter's confession. By it, Peter, like Eliakim, shows he is faithful to God and is God's servant.

Your proclamation will help remind those in the assembly that Peter is the foundation of the Church and that his authority and that of the disciples will be succeeded in the Pope and Bishops. At its best, your proclamation will lead others to reaffirm for themselves that Jesus is the Christ and to live daily as his followers as members of the Church.

AUGUST 28, 2011

22ND SUNDAY IN ORDINARY TIME

Lectionary #124

READING I Jeremiah 20:7–9

Jeremiah = jayr-uh-MĪ-uh

Let Jeremiah's disappointment and frustration be heard in your voice.

A reading from the Book of the Prophet Jeremiah

You **duped** me, O LORD, and I **let** myself be **duped**;
you were too **strong** for me, and you **triumphed**.
All the **day** I am an **object** of **laughter**;
everyone mocks me.

Jeremiah is blaming the Lord's word for his derision. Express his resentment for the message he must carry in your tone of voice.

Whenever I **speak**, I must **cry out**,
violence and **outrage** is my **message**;
the **word** of the LORD has brought me
derision and **reproach** all the day.

Lighten your tone of voice as you speak Jeremiah's realization that he cannot contain the Lord's name. He will continue to trust in the Lord.

I say to myself, I will not mention him,
I will **speak** in his name **no more**.
But then it becomes like **fire burning** in my **heart**,
imprisoned in my **bones**;
I grow **weary** holding it **in**, I **cannot endure** it.

READING I **Jeremiah prophesied during the eighth century, after the Assyrians had conquered the northern kingdom of Israel and when the Babylonians were beginning to encroach on the southern kingdom of Judah. Called by the Lord to be a prophet to Judah, Jeremiah faced rejection from those in authority. His strong denunciation of idolatry and infidelity to the covenant, both of which had once again become common practice after a period of hopeful reforms initiated by Josiah, went unheeded by King Jehoiakim and his administration.**

Today's First Reading comes from the prophet's personal lament about the state of his ministry. In it, Jeremiah expresses his frustration with the Lord for seemingly having duped him into proclaiming the Lord's words, and accepting such a difficult vocation. Jeremiah also speaks about his frustration at having to endure ridicule at the hands of those he is trying to bring back to the Lord.

Yet all the persecution Jeremiah has suffered and his mounting frustration with the Lord are not enough to turn him away from his prophetic calling. Even in his private venting, in which he tries to convince himself not to speak the Lord's name, he cannot follow through with the idea. The prophet can no longer confine the Lord, who dwells within him as fire burning in his heart and as a prisoner in his bones. His words "I grow weary holding it in, I cannot endure it" are his submission to the power of the Lord acting in him and the power that the Lord's word will have over those who persecute him.

A few verses later in Jeremiah 20, the prophet praises the Lord with confidence.

The main clauses in the opening line are "I urge you" and "to offer your bodies as a living sacrifice." Use a stronger tone of voice on these and a lighter tone on the other parenthetical clauses.

Take your time with the lengthy sentence that is the second verse of this reading as Paul explains his thought step by step.

READING II Romans 12:1–2

A reading from the Letter of Saint Paul to the Romans

I **urge** you, brothers and sisters, by the **mercies** of **God**,
to offer your **bodies** as a **living sacrifice**,
holy and **pleasing** to **God**, your **spiritual worship**.
Do not **conform** yourselves to **this** age
but be **transformed** by the **renewal** of your **mind**,
that you may **discern** what is the **will** of **God**,
what is **good** and **pleasing** and **perfect**.

He is convinced the Lord will triumph over his enemies. While suffering in the Lord is the primary theme of this reading, this prophet and people of faith in general do not move through suffering without hope. Since this is the case, your proclamation will want to leave the assembly, not with a sense of the prophet's despair, but with the growing awareness of the Lord bursting forth from his very being.

READING II This Sunday's Second Reading comes from the beginning of a section of Romans that includes Paul's catechesis about what it means to live in Christ (12:1—15:3). The opening verse of today's reading shows us that the baptized are to bind themselves together as one living sacrifice. Together, as members of the one body of Christ, they will be strengthened by God in Christ to detach from the ways of this age.

When those who live in Christ offer themselves to God as a living sacrifice, two things are expected of them. First, Christians are not to conform or be molded to the present time because this age is passing away (Romans 12:11). Second, they are to be transformed through the renewal of their minds. This ongoing conversion occurs through prayer by distinguishing the will of God from other competing desires of the flesh and the world. The will of God is that which is good and pleasing and perfect. It is known through the common worship of brothers and sisters in Christ who journey together in pursuit of the good, of God's divine goodness. Through their shared sacrifice, Christians make themselves available to support others who seek to know and follow God's will.

GOSPEL Matthew 16:21–27

A reading from the holy Gospel according to Matthew

Use a narrative tone of voice on the opening sentence of the prediction of the Passion to set the context.

Jesus began to **show** his **disciples**
that he **must** go to **Jerusalem** and **suffer greatly**
from the **elders**, the chief **priests**, and the **scribes**,
and be **killed** and on the **third day** be **raised**.
Then **Peter** took Jesus aside and began to **rebuke** him,
"God **forbid**, Lord! **No** such **thing** shall **ever** happen to **you**."

Forcefully express Peter's words so as to convey the powerful sense of denial Peter was feeling.

He turned and said to Peter,
"Get **behind** me, **Satan**! You are an **obstacle** to me.
You are thinking **not** as **God** does, but as **human beings** do."

Give Jesus' reprimand of Peter in an even firmer voice.

Pause significantly as a transition to the next section.

Pause significantly after each of Jesus' sayings to allow the assembly time to ponder their meaning. Remember to raise the pitch of your voice slightly at the end of the questions.

Then Jesus **said** to his **disciples**,
"**Whoever** wishes to come after me must **deny** himself,
take up his **cross**, and **follow** me.
For whoever wishes to **save** his life will **lose it**,
but whoever **loses** his life for **my** sake will **find** it.
What **profit** would there be for one to gain the **whole world**
and **forfeit** his **life**?
Or what can one **give** in **exchange** for his **life**?
For the **Son** of **Man** will **come** with his **angels**
in his Father's **glory**,
and then he will repay **all** according to his **conduct**."

GOSPEL Last Sunday the Gospel was Peter's confession of Jesus as the Christ. In it, Peter appears as the disciple with utmost faith. In today's Gospel, Jesus refers to Peter as an obstacle to him because of his refusal to accept that Jesus the Christ will suffer and be killed.

This first prediction of the Passion (the other two are found in Matthew 17:22–23 and 20:17–19), links Jesus' impending suffering with that of his disciples. Those who follow Jesus must accept that he will suffer and die. To think this way, a disciple must try to think as God does and must not allow worldly attachments and fears to infiltrate their thoughts so that they become a stumbling block to Jesus.

After responding to Peter's rebuke of him, Jesus presents five sayings that focus on the life of discipleship. The essence of these sayings is that disciples must not make themselves the center of their lives. A disciple's life extends outward. Based on their faith in Jesus, they will be ready to give up their life as they know it in exchange for life in him. The final saying of Jesus in today's Gospel, then, reveals the judgment that will come at the end of time: the Son of Man will repay disciples according to their decision to take up the cross and follow him.

23RD SUNDAY IN ORDINARY TIME

Lectionary #127

READING I Ezekiel 33:7–9

Ezekiel = ee-ZEE-kee-uhl

A reading from the Book of the Prophet Ezekiel

Thus says the **LORD**:

Make eye contact with the assembly on "You." Direct the word to the assembly in a serious manner that conveys the significant responsibility they have to bring others to faith.

You, son of man, I have appointed **watchman** for the **house** of **Israel**;
when you hear me say **anything**, you shall **warn** them for me.

Again emphasize "you" to communicate the grave responsibility for others that the prophet and people of faith today have.

If I tell the **wicked**, "O **wicked** one, you shall **surely die**,"
and **you** do not speak **out** to **dissuade** the wicked from **his** way,
the **wicked** shall **die** for his **guilt**,
but I will hold **you** responsible for his **death**.

Express disappointment at the decision others make to turn from their evil ways. Contrast the disappointment with relief at the salvation of the watchman.

But if you **warn** the **wicked**,
trying to **turn** him from his **way**,
and he **refuses** to turn from his **way**,
he shall **die** for his **guilt**,
but **you** shall save **yourself**.

READING I Ezekiel prophesied in the sixth century BC. Taken into captivity by the Babylonians around 597 BC, he carried out his prophetic calling in exile.

Today's First Reading is from the second commissioning of the prophet Ezekiel (33:1–9). The first commissioning, the parallel to 33:1–9, is found in 3:16–21. Both include the theme of the watchman.

During war time, a watchman would blow his trumpet to alert people of the approaching enemy. Should he fail to give warning of the enemy, he would be held accountable for any deaths (33:2–6).

Verses 8–9 ("If I tell the wicked . . .") through to the end of the reading are parallel (almost identical) to 3:18–19. However, in the second commission, the situation has changed. The Babylonians are about to destroy Jerusalem. When it is destroyed, not even the righteous will be saved. As the watchman of the house of Israel, Ezekiel will be responsible for persuading the wicked to turn back to God who will take care of them as their good shepherd (34:1–31).

Through your proclamation, you serve as a watchman to the assembly, calling the people to contemplate the ways they have turned from God. The serious tone you use in the last two verses can aim to help them accept their responsibility to repent of their sins so as to live in the Lord. Through your well prepared and delivered proclamation, you will have fulfilled your role as the watchman and will have saved yourself.

READING II It might surprise you to find out that today's Second Reading is part of a chapter in Romans which begins with Paul's teaching about the Christian's responsibility toward civil

Take your time with the abbreviated list of commandments. Become even more deliberate as you approach the phrase "are summed up . . . ."

Make eye contact with the assembly as you solemnly proclaim the commandment "You shall love . . . ."

Again, be deliberate and make eye contact as you conclude the reading with a summary statement of Paul's main point, "love is the fulfillment . . . ."

READING II Romans 13:8–10

A reading from the Letter of Saint Paul to the Romans

Brothers and sisters:
Owe **nothing** to anyone, except to **love** one another;
for the one who **loves** another has **fulfilled** the **law**.
The **commandments**, "You shall not commit **adultery**;
you shall not **kill**; you shall not **steal**; you shall not **covet**,"
and whatever other commandment there may be,
are **summed up** in this saying, namely,
"You shall **love** your **neighbor** as **yourself**."
Love does no **evil** to the **neighbor**;
hence, **love** is the **fulfillment** of the **law**.

Speak step one, "If your brother sins . . . you and him alone" in a teacher-like tone of voice.

Use the same teacher-like tone of voice for step two, "take one or two others . . ." and again for step three, "tell the church."

GOSPEL Matthew 18:15–20

A reading from the holy Gospel according to Matthew

Jesus said to his **disciples**:
"If your brother **sins** against you,
go and tell him his **fault** between you and him **alone**.
If he **listens** to you, you have **won over** your brother.
If he does **not** listen,
take one or two **others** along **with** you,
so that 'every **fact** may be **established**
on the **testimony** of two or three **witnesses**.'
If he **refuses** to listen to them, tell the **church**.
If he **refuses** to listen **even** to the **church**,
then **treat** him as you would a **Gentile** or a **tax** collector.

authorities. In the verses which immediately precede today's passage, Paul speaks about Christians paying anyone to whom they owe dues—and also taxes.

With nothing other than the transitional phrase "Owe nothing to anyone," Paul moves his argument forward toward the main theme of this chapter. For Paul, the commandment of love is the fulfillment of the Mosaic law. His use of phrases from the Ten Commandments supports his belief (Exodus 20:13–17; Deuteronomy 5:17–21). Whether or not he is actually quoting a saying of Jesus (Mark 12:28–34), it is clear that Paul also links the fulfillment of the Mosaic law to the Lord. We see this later in Romans when Paul refers to Christ as the "end of the law" (Romans 10:4).

Through Jesus, Christians have a new standard for love. He taught and embodied the saving love that he uniquely offered through his life, death, and Resurrection. Thus for Christians, love entails not only following the commandments, but following a person.

In Old Testament times, "neighbor" referred to fellow citizens or fellow Jews. We see this in passages such as Leviticus 19:18 in which the saying "You shall love your neighbor as yourself" also occurs. In its new context, the saying calls Christians to extend their charity beyond members of their religious and ethnic communities, as Jesus' charity extended beyond religious and political boundaries. Christians must show to the world the love of their teacher.

GOSPEL The Gospel for this Sunday and next Sunday comes from the discourse on church order (18:1–35). This discourse deals with the ordering of the community life of Jesus' disciples.

For Jesus' two solemn teachings, use a serious tone of voice.

Amen, I say to you,
whatever you **bind** on **earth** shall be **bound** in **heaven**,
and whatever you **loose** on **earth** shall be **loosed** in **heaven**.
Again, **amen**, I say to you,
if **two** of you **agree** on earth
about **anything** for which they are to **pray**,
it shall be **granted** to them by my heavenly **Father**.

End on an optimistic note as the efficacy of prayer in Jesus' name provides hope for the sinner and the community of disciples.

For where **two** or **three** are **gathered** together in **my name**,
there am **I** in the **midst** of them."

In today's Gospel, Jesus presents three steps for relating to the sinner, which were common steps in trial proceedings at his time. All three steps are personal in nature, involving communication among people.

Out of respect for the individual, a disciple is first to speak to the sinner in private. If the sinner does not admit his wrongdoing, then a few others are to come along to help determine what transpired between them. If this does not work, then the disciple is to speak to the Church. Here, in contrast to Matthew 16:18, "the church" is a reference to the local community of believers. The use of "church" here, while not denying the institutional aspect of the Church, accentuates the fact that the Church is composed of disciples—human persons who follow Jesus. As followers of Jesus, those who belong to the Church have a responsibility to treat sinners with respect and lead them to repentance. They have a responsibility to respond to penitent sinners by reintegrating them into the community, and to avoid unrepentant sinners as was the customary response to Gentiles or tax collectors who were often separated from the community.

The use of the plural verbs for binding and loosing in Jesus' solemn teaching introduced with "Amen" signifies that Jesus grants his disciples the same power originally given solely to Peter (16:19b). That teaching concluding this reading makes it clear that this ministry is performed within the context of prayer. This prayer includes the prayer of the entire community as signified by two or three who gather in Jesus' name.

24TH SUNDAY IN ORDINARY TIME

Lectionary #130

READING I Sirach 27:30—28:7

Sirach = SEER-ak

Begin the reading in a firm, almost stern tone of voice. Lighten your tone as you speak of forgiveness.

Pause after each question allowing the assembly time to reflect on how they would respond.

Begin the proclamation of the final verses "Remember your . . ." in a slower pace and in a gentle tone of voice that will help the assembly ponder the last days, the commandments, and the covenant.

enmity = EN-mih-tee.

Enmity is hostility or antagonism.

A reading from the Book of Sirach

Wrath and **anger** are **hateful** things,
yet the **sinner** hugs them **tight**.
The **vengeful** will **suffer** the LORD's vengeance,
for he **remembers** their **sins in detail**.
Forgive your neighbor's **injustice**;
then when you **pray**, your **own** sins will be **forgiven**.
Could anyone nourish **anger** against **another**
and expect **healing** from the LORD?
Could anyone refuse **mercy** to another like himself,
can he seek **pardon** for his **own** sins?
If **one** who is but **flesh** cherishes **wrath**,
who will **forgive his** sins?
Remember your **last** days, set **enmity** aside;
remember **death** and **decay**, and **cease** from **sin**!
Think of the **commandments**, **hate not** your neighbor;
remember the Most High's **covenant**, and overlook faults.

READING I Today's reading is part of a lengthier passage in Sirach that describes how deceit, mistrust, betrayal, and suspicion can destroy a friendship and do lasting harm to the friends. Some scholars suggest that the passage refers to the story of Esther, to Haman's plot to kill Mordecai. Haman had been promoted to a high rank and Mordecai had refused to pay him homage. Then Haman refused to forgive Mordecai, but the tables turned on Haman and he suffered death because of his own wrath (Esther 3:1–6; 5:9; 7:9–10).

Paired with today's Gospel because of the theme of forgiveness, this reading argues that forgiveness of a neighbor's injustice comes first; after forgiving one's neighbor, in prayer, one can ask for the forgiveness of one's own sins. The rhetorical questions which follow this teaching serve to reinforce the point that anger and resentment toward others must give way to mercy.

The final verses of the reading teach us that the decision to forgive one's neighbor rather than continue to be angry is best made while thinking about the end of one's life and one's decision to follow the commandments. Your proclamation of these verses may lead those in the assembly to discern their own willingness to offer forgiveness and then to seek forgiveness in their relationships with God and others. As you prepare, reflect on the relationships in which you need to move from anger to forgiveness. This will give authenticity to the words you proclaim.

READING II This is the last Sunday of twelve counted Sundays in Ordinary Time in which the Second Reading

READING II Romans 14:7–9

A reading from the Letter of Saint Paul to the Romans

State the opening line emphatically.

Avoid a sing-song proclamation of the parallel lines about living and dying.

Give a lengthy pause after "came to life" as if the punctuation were a colon. This will prepare the assembly to hear what follows.

Brothers and sisters:
None of us **lives** for **oneself**, and no one **dies** for **oneself**.
For if we **live**, we **live** for the **Lord**,
and if we **die**, we **die** for the **Lord**;
so then, whether we **live** or **die**, we **are** the **Lord's**.
For **this** is why **Christ died** and came to **life**,
that he might be **Lord** of both the **dead** and the **living**.

GOSPEL Matthew 18:21–35

A reading from the holy Gospel according to Matthew

Emphasize the numbers in Peter's question and Jesus' response.

Use a narrative tone of voice as you give the introduction to the parable.

Emphasize "a huge amount."

Peter approached **Jesus** and **asked** him,
"**Lord**, if my **brother** sins **against me**,
how **often** must I **forgive**?
As many as **seven** times?"
Jesus answered, "I **say** to you, not **seven** times
but **seventy-seven** times.
That is **why** the **kingdom** of **heaven** may be **likened** to a king
who decided to settle **accounts** with his **servants**.
When he began the **accounting**,
a **debtor** was brought before him who **owed** him
a **huge** amount.

is from Romans. This Sunday's Second Reading, like last Sunday's, comes from the hortatory or catechetical section of Romans in which Paul teaches about what it means to live in Christ. In last Sunday's passage, Paul made the point that all the commandments are summed up in the saying "Love your neighbor as yourself." Recall also that Paul understood Jesus as the fulfillment of the commandments. In today's brief passage, Paul puts forward what could be considered the basics of love. The love of Christians for one another is founded on the Lord who lived, died, and rose for them. All that we do—our living and our dying—is done "for the Lord."

Controversies around whether or not to eat meat, observe certain festivals, and follow dietary laws of the Mosaic code form the backdrop to Paul's call for unity in the Lord. These controversies, like some today, can be understood generally as disagreements between those who wanted to hold onto the details of the law and those who wanted to maintain the spirit of the law.

Whatever the decision on the observance of particular components of the law, for Paul, the community must decide based on its life in the Lord. All our decisions, for Paul, must be guided by selflessness and love, the definition of living and dying in the Lord.

GOSPEL Today's Gospel begins with Peter's question to Jesus about how often he must forgive a brother who sins against him. Perhaps Peter is hoping Jesus will say that Peter would need to forgive no more than seven times. Unexpectedly and to Peter's dismay, Jesus

Since he had **no way** of paying it back,
his master **ordered** him to be **sold**,
along with his **wife**, his **children**, and all his **property**,
in **payment** of the **debt**.
At **that**, the servant fell down, did him homage, and **said**,
'Be **patient** with me, and I **will** pay you back in **full**.'
Moved with **compassion** the **master** of that servant
let him go and **forgave** him the loan.
When that **servant** had **left**, he **found** one of his **fellow** servants
who **owed** him a much **smaller** amount.
He **seized** him and started to **choke** him, demanding,
'**Pay back** what you **owe**.'
Falling to his **knees**, his fellow servant **begged** him,
'Be **patient** with me, and I **will** pay you back.'
But he **refused**.
Instead, he had the fellow **servant** put in **prison**
until he paid **back** the **debt**.
Now when his **fellow** servants **saw** what had **happened**,
they were **deeply disturbed**, and went to their **master**
and reported the whole **affair**.
His master **summoned** him and **said** to him, 'You **wicked** servant!
I forgave **you** your **entire debt** because you **begged** me to.
Should **you** not have had **pity** on your **fellow** servant,
as **I** had pity on **you**?'
Then in **anger** his master handed him over to the torturers
until he should **pay back** the **whole debt**.
So will my heavenly **Father** do to you,
unless **each** of **you forgives** your brother from your **heart**."

Let pleading be heard in your voice as you speak the servant's words.

Pause noticeably between scenes.

Emphasize "much smaller amount."

Let the same pleading be heard in your voice as was present when you spoke the first servant's words. The lines are almost identical.

Pause noticeably between scenes.

Try to balance firmness and compassion in your tone of voice as you proclaim Jesus' words about his heavenly Father.

responds that Peter must offer forgiveness 77 times, a number that symbolizes forgiveness without end. To illustrate this forgiveness, Jesus tells the parable of the unforgiving servant.

This parable has three scenes. In the first, the emphasis is on the king's compassion toward the debtor who owed him a large amount of money—literally 10,000 talents. The king's offer to repay his servant's debt in full is hardly realistic given the enormity of the money owed.

The second scene entails a turn of events. The servant to whom the master extended his generous offer to forgive his debt approaches a servant indebted to him. The servant's harshness and lack of compassion to the one who owed a much smaller amount than he owed the master, shows the human person's tendency toward sin.

The third scene involves the fellow servants and the king. These servants hold the unforgiving servant accountable to the master who in turn reminds the servant of his forgiveness and punishes him for not offering the same forgiveness when he had an opportunity to do so.

The parable needs no other explanation than Jesus' words about his heavenly Father. Disciples are to imitate the frequency and depth of divine mercy. The failure to do so has consequences at the final judgment. Though there are consequences, notice that the master's forgiveness of his servant's loan is not taken away. So, too, the Father's compassion for those who fail to forgive is never removed, yet he patiently waits for them to offer forgiveness to those who have wronged them.

25TH SUNDAY IN ORDINARY TIME

Lectionary #133

READING I Isaiah 55:6–9

Isaiah = ī-ZAY-uh

Elongate your enunciation of "seek" so that it reflects a sense of the word's meaning.

Pause significantly before the passage shifts to thoughts about the Lord's transcendence. Use a lighter tone of voice on these lines along with a deliberate pace.

A reading from the Book of the Prophet Isaiah

Seek the LORD while he may be **found**,
call him while he is **near**.
Let the **scoundrel** forsake his **way**,
and the **wicked** his **thoughts**;
let him **turn** to the LORD for **mercy**;
to our **God**, who is **generous** in **forgiving**.
For **my** thoughts are not **your** thoughts,
nor are **your** ways **my** ways, says the LORD.
As **high** as the **heavens** are above the **earth**,
so **high** are **my** ways above **your** ways
and **my** thoughts above **your** thoughts.

READING II Philippians 1:20c–24, 27a

Philippians = fih-LIP-ee-uhnz

Proclaim the opening line with purpose and conviction, believing that you magnify Christ in your body. Stress both occurrences of "life" and "death."

A reading from the Letter of Saint Paul to the Philippians

Brothers and sisters:
Christ will be **magnified** in my **body**, whether by **life** or by **death**.
For to me **life** is **Christ**, and **death** is **gain**.
If I go on **living** in the **flesh**,
that means **fruitful labor** for me.

READING I We have heard these verses proclaimed on three previous occasions: the First Reading on the Fifteenth and Eighteenth Sundays in Ordinary Time and the Fifth Reading of the Easter Vigil. The multiple proclamations of these verses remind us of God's never-ending invitation to seek him, come to his table, and be fed by his word. These three verses from Isaiah 55 hold two primary themes: the Lord is omnipresent and transcendent.

First, the prophet extends the invitation to all, in particular the scoundrel and the wicked, to discover the Lord by turning away from their sinful ways and thoughts. The opening phrase usually signaled the Israelites to come to the sanctuary. In this context, the phrase appears to mean that the Lord can be found in many places, not just the sanctuary. The use of this phrase here is similar to those in Jeremiah 29:13–14, in which the Lord, through the prophet, reminds his people in exile that when they look for him, they will find him and when they seek him with all their heart, they will know that he is with them.

Second, although we can seek and find a forgiving God with us, his thoughts and ways are not ours. Some scholars see in these words the prophet's explanation to the Israelites about the hope offered by the rise of the Persian emperor, Cyrus, who would conquer the Babylonians and send the exiles home.

Your proclamation can lead the assembly to see that the God they seek offers them hope of forgiveness and mercy. His forgiveness and mercy extend beyond any of our thoughts and ways—to heaven's heights.

Convey Paul's struggle between life and death with uncertainty in your voice. Let the uncertainty contrast with the confidence of the opening line.

And I do **not** know which I shall **choose**.
I am **caught** between the **two**.
I **long** to **depart** this life and be with **Christ**,
for that is **far better**.
Yet that I **remain** in the **flesh**
is **more necessary** for **your** benefit.

Make eye contact with the assembly on the concluding line. Proclaim it with the teacher-like authority of Paul.

Only, **conduct** yourselves in a way **worthy** of the **gospel** of **Christ**.

GOSPEL Matthew 20:1–16a

A reading from the holy Gospel according to Matthew

Jesus told his **disciples** this **parable**:
"The **kingdom** of **heaven** is like a **landowner**
who went out at **dawn** to hire **laborers** for his **vineyard**.
After **agreeing** with them for the **usual** daily wage,
he **sent** them into his **vineyard**.

Emphasize the time references throughout the Gospel.

Going out about **nine o'clock**,
the landowner saw **others** standing **idle** in the **marketplace**,
and he **said** to them, '**You too** go into my **vineyard**,
and I will **give** you what is **just**.'
So they went off.
And he went out **again** around **noon**,
and around **three o'clock**, and did **likewise**.
Going out about **five o'clock**,
the landowner found **others** standing around, and **said** to them,
'**Why** do you stand here **idle** all day?'

Ask the landowner's question inquisitively. Give the idle workers' reply with frustration and the landowner's response with urgency and encouragement.

READING II For the next four weeks, the Second Reading comes from Paul's letter to the Philippians. Philippi was a Roman town in the northeast area of Greece. Its population was Greek and Macedonian. A small number of Jews also resided in the town. Founded around 49 or 50 AD, the Christian community at Philippi was the first in Europe established by Paul, Silas, and Timothy. Paul wrote his letter to the Philippians while he was imprisoned in an unknown location (1:7, 13, 14, 17) and survived in fear of his life (1:20–23).

Chapter 1 begins with Paul's well-known and heartfelt expression of gratitude to the Philippians for their service as partners in spreading the Gospel (1:5). Today's passage, from the latter half of the same chapter, presents Paul's reflections on what lies before him, should he continue to live or should he die.

Although imprisoned and in danger of death, Paul presents life or death as a choice he has. Paul accepts the possibilities of both life and death in Christ. He is able to adopt such an attitude because he believes that Christ will be praised in his body, a reference to his entire person, not just the flesh, whether he lives or dies.

Ostensibly preferring death because he understands being with Christ forever as better than remaining in the flesh, Paul deems it necessary that he remain in the flesh—in his physical body—so that he can continue to preach the Gospel. This will profit the Philippians and encourage them as they continue their own work of evangelization.

GOSPEL Obviously, for the laborers who began the work at

They **answered**, 'Because **no one** has **hired** us.'
He **said** to them, '**You too** go into my **vineyard**.'
When it was **evening** the **owner** of the vineyard said
to his **foreman**,
'**Summon** the laborers and **give** them their **pay**,
beginning with the **last** and **ending** with the **first**.'
When those who had **started** about **five o'clock** came,
each received the **usual** daily wage.
So when the **first** came, they **thought** that they would
receive **more**,
but **each** of them **also** got the **usual** wage.
And on **receiving** it they **grumbled** against the **landowner**, saying,
'These **last** ones worked **only one** hour,
and **you** have made them **equal** to us,
who **bore** the day's **burden** and the **heat**.'
He said to **one** of them in **reply**,
'**My friend**, I am **not cheating** you.
Did you **not agree** with me for the **usual** daily wage?
Take what is **yours** and **go**.
What if I **wish** to give this **last** one the **same** as **you**?
Or am I **not free** to **do** as I **wish** with my **own money**?
Are you **envious** because I am **generous**?'
Thus, the **last** will be **first**, and the **first** will be **last**."

Reflect the workers' grumbling with frustration in your tone of voice.

Offer the landowner's words in an explanatory, non-confrontational manner. Remember to raise the inflection slightly at the end of each question. Pause noticeably after the last question, giving the members of the assembly time to answer the question for themselves.

Proclaim Jesus' concluding words emphatically and with expectation for the full realization of the kingdom of heaven.

dawn, the thoughts of the vineyard owner were not theirs! This unmistakable link with the First Reading reveals the focus of this first of two vineyard parables in Matthew: God's generosity is so overwhelming and incomprehensible that in the kingdom of heaven the last will be first, and the first will be last.

The concluding verse of this Gospel occurs in the previous chapter, but in reverse order (Matthew 19:30). Here it forms the conclusion to the scene where Jesus responds to a young man's question about what good he has to do to gain eternal life. After the young man has gone away disappointed, Jesus continues to teach his disciples about salvation. The main point of his instruction is that salvation is impossible for human beings, but possible for God.

Seen in light of today's Gospel, the laborers' view of the work they did can be interpreted as believing that salvation can be earned. But the landowner's generosity shows the falseness of this position. Salvation is a free gift from God and not possible for us as human beings. Whether one comes early or late to the vineyard of faith, does not increase or decrease chances for receiving this gift.

In Matthew's time, the early Church might have read this parable as speaking to the question of whether Jewish Christians or Gentiles would inherit the kingdom. Whether one comes to faith before or after someone else, according to this parable, does not matter. What matters is coming to work in the vineyard, keeping the commandments, selling one's possessions, and following Jesus (19:17–21).

26TH SUNDAY IN ORDINARY TIME

Lectionary #136

READING I Ezekiel 18:25–28

Ezekiel = ee-ZEE-kee-uhl

Proclaim the people's words loudly. Be careful not to shout into the microphone and cause feedback.

Ask the question about fairness in a nonjudgmental manner, allowing the assembly to conclude on their own that the people's ways are unfair.

iniquity = ih-NIK-wih-tee.

Iniquity is sin or evil.

Proclaim the first half of the final line in an exultant tone. After pausing slightly at the comma, lighten your tone of voice to express relief that the repentant sinner will not die.

A reading from the Book of the Prophet Ezekiel

Thus says the LORD:
You say, "The **LORD's** way is not **fair**!"
Hear now, **house** of **Israel**:
Is it **my** way that is **unfair**, or rather, are not **your** ways **unfair**?
When someone **virtuous** turns away from **virtue** to commit
iniquity, and **dies**,
it is **because** of the iniquity he committed that he must **die**.
But if he **turns** from the **wickedness** he has **committed**,
and **does** what is **right** and **just**,
he shall **preserve** his **life**;
since he has **turned away** from all the **sins**
that he has **committed**,
he shall **surely live**, he shall **not** die.

READING II Philippians 2:1–11

Philippians = fih-LIP-ee-uhnz

Use the punctuation as a guide for an understandable proclamation. Emphasize the virtues throughout the reading.

A reading from the Letter of Saint Paul to the Philippians

Brothers and sisters:
If there is **any encouragement** in **Christ**,
any **solace** in **love**,
any **participation** in the **Spirit**,

READING I At some point most of us have probably had the same thought expressed at the beginning of today's First Reading: "The Lord's way is not fair!" These words are followed by the Lord's question, spoken through the prophet Ezekiel, and by you today, which calls the people to reflect on the nature of what exactly is unfair—the Lord's way or human ways.

This passage is taken from Chapter 18, which is devoted to the theme of personal responsibility. The chapter begins with the prophet speaking the Lord's word, questioning the meaning of the proverb that says that because fathers have eaten green grapes, their children's teeth are on edge (18:1–2). This proverb expressed the wisdom of the day, which held that people are punished for the sins of their ancestors. In today's reading, however, the prophet, speaking for the Lord, transforms that wisdom and teaches that individuals must assume responsibility for their own choices. When people choose iniquity or sin, they will suffer death because of that choice. On the other hand, when people choose to do what is right and just, they will live.

Because today's reading is only four verses long, you will want to be sure you have the assembly's attention from the beginning, proclaiming boldly the people's belief in the unfairness of the Lord's way. Then do not shy away from clearly and directly laying out the personal choice between sin and death and justice and life to each and every person in the assembly.

READING II At the time Paul wrote his letter to the Philippians, the Christian community at Philippi was marred by internal divisions stemming

any **compassion** and **mercy**,
complete my **joy** by being of the **same mind**,
with the **same love**,
united in heart, thinking **one thing**.
Do **nothing** out of **selfishness** or out of **vainglory**;
rather, **humbly** regard **others** as **more important**
than **yourselves**,
each looking out not for his **own** interests,
but **also** for those of **others**.

Make eye contact with the assembly as you proclaim the line "Have in you the same attitude that is also in Christ Jesus," which is crucial to Paul's teaching in this reading.

Have in **you** the **same attitude**
that is **also** in **Christ Jesus**,
who, though he was in the **form** of **God**,
did not regard **equality** with **God**
something to be **grasped**.
Rather, he **emptied** himself,
taking the **form** of a **slave**,
coming in **human likeness**;
and found **human** in **appearance**,
he **humbled** himself,
becoming **obedient** to the point of **death**,
even **death** on a **cross**.

Build to the concluding doxology. State it with the boldness of your own faith, drawing the assembly into the confession.

Because of this, **God** greatly **exalted** him
and **bestowed** on him the **name**
which is **above** every name,
that at the name of **Jesus**
every **knee** should **bend**,
of those **in heaven** and **on earth** and **under** the **earth**,
and **every** tongue **confess** that
Jesus Christ is Lord,
to the **glory** of **God** the **Father**.

[Shorter Form: Philippians 2:1–5]

mainly from self-serving pride and arrogance among its members. These internal divisions lessened the community's ability to confront its opponents, who were denying the legitimacy of the Gospel of Jesus Christ. These opponents, more than likely, were pagans and fellow citizens of Philippi (Philippians 1:28–30).

Today's Second Reading can be divided into three sections: in the first, Paul urges the Philippians to turn away from their selfish ambition and serve others with humility by living "in Christ." For Paul, this means embodying the qualities of love, participation in the Spirit, compassion, and mercy that show that a believer has the same mindset (*phrōnein*) as Christ.

The second and the third sections contain the two parts of the Christological hymn that is proclaimed on Palm Sunday each year. The first part of the hymn recounts Christ's obedience to the point of death on the cross, a somber and holy journey of humility, seemingly a descent to the depths of despair. The second part of the hymn builds upward and climaxes with an exalted statement of faith—that because of Christ's humble obedience on the cross, the Father exalted him as Lord.

Through the use of this hymn, Paul intends to show the Philippians that through their own humility, modeled on Christ's, they too, will be exalted and glorified with him. By varying the tone of your proclamation in the three sections of this reading, you will help the assembly to understand the intent of Paul's writing. Try beginning with a serious and instructive tone, then shifting to a somber and solemn one, and concluding with a tone of optimism and praise for our life in Christ, the exalted Lord.

GOSPEL Matthew 21:28–32

A reading from the holy Gospel according to Matthew

Make eye contact with the assembly as you put forth Jesus' opening question, allowing the assembly to consider their opinion of the two sons in the parable which follows.

Jesus said to the chief **priests** and **elders** of the **people**:
"**What** is **your** opinion?
A **man** had two **sons**.
He came to the **first** and said,
'**Son**, go out and **work** in the **vineyard** today.'

State strongly the first son's refusal to work in the vineyard. Lighten your tone of voice to convey the fact that he changed his mind.

He said in reply, '**I will not**,'
but **afterwards** changed his **mind** and **went**.
The **man** came to the **other** son and gave the **same** order.
He **said** in **reply**, '**Yes**, sir,' but did **not** go.

Use the same technique as you give the second son's reply: state his "yes" boldly and then lighten your tone to convey the fact that he did not go.

Which of the **two** did his father's **will**?"
They answered, "The **first**."
Jesus said to them, "**Amen**, I **say** to you,
tax collectors and **prostitutes**
are entering the **kingdom** of **God before** you.

Proclaim Jesus' solemn teaching beginning with "Amen" in a serious tone of voice. Express disappointment and reproach in your proclamation of the final line "Yet even when you saw that . . . ."

When **John** came to you in the way of **righteousness**,
you did **not** believe him;
but **tax** collectors and **prostitutes did**.
Yet **even** when you saw **that**,
you did not later **change** your **minds** and **believe** him."

GOSPEL This parable is the first in a series of three on the judgment of Israel addressed to the chief priests and elders. It is the only one of the three unique to Matthew, and through it, Jesus teaches a message similar to that spoken through the prophet Ezekiel in the First Reading: if you convert to the Lord and his ways, you will have life with him.

The stage is set for this parable when the chief priests and elders challenge his authority. Yet in an ironic twist, through the parable the chief priests and elders challenge their own authority. Their response to Jesus' question about which son did the will of his father is a self-condemnation.

The two sons represent two different groups within Israel. The first symbolizes the religious outcasts, the prostitutes and tax collectors. The second corresponds to the religious leaders who questioned Jesus' authority and refused to believe in him. These unfaithful leaders, who refused to change and choose life, remain mired in their own sin. In contrast, those sinners who followed John and the way of righteousness he preached (the righteousness which came in Jesus), chose life in the kingdom of God.

As you prepare to proclaim this reading, consider having a conversation with the person who will proclaim the First Reading. Talk about how the proclamations of the readings can parallel each other in such ways as tone and emphasis. In this way, you can assist the assembly to make the connection between the two readings and to hear Jesus' call once again this Sunday—the call to choose life in Christ over death and sin.

27TH SUNDAY IN ORDINARY TIME

Lectionary #139

READING I Isaiah 5:1–7

Isaiah = Ī-ZAY-uh

Begin the song of the prophet's beloved and friend with joy and optimism, painting the beautiful picture of the vineyard. Conclude the song with disappointment, by lowering your tone of voice on the phrase "but what it yielded . . . ."

Judah = JOO-duh

Direct the Lord's words "Now, inhabitants . . ." to the assembly by making eye contact with them. Ask the questions to different parts of the assembly in an insistent tone of voice as if you are eliciting the responses, which you already know, from the people. Proclaim the stanza "Now, I will let you know . . ." with seriousness.

A reading from the Book of the Prophet Isaiah

Let me now **sing** of my **friend**,
my friend's **song** concerning his **vineyard**.
My **friend** had a **vineyard**
on a fertile **hillside**;
he **spaded** it, **cleared** it of stones,
and **planted** the choicest vines;
within it he built a **watchtower**,
and **hewed** out a **wine press**.
Then he looked for the **crop** of **grapes**,
but what it **yielded** was **wild** grapes.

Now, inhabitants of **Jerusalem** and people of **Judah**,
judge between **me** and my **vineyard**:
What **more** was there to **do** for my **vineyard**
that I had **not done**?
Why, when I **looked** for the crop of **grapes**,
did it bring forth **wild** grapes?
Now, I will let you **know**
what I mean to **do** with my **vineyard**:
take away its **hedge**, **give** it to **grazing**,
break through its **wall**, let it be **trampled**!
Yes, I will make it a **ruin**:
it shall not be **pruned** or **hoed**,
but overgrown with **thorns** and **briers**;

READING I **The chapter of Isaiah from which the first reading comes is often referred to as the song of the vineyard because of the first lines of the text. The prophet begins by telling us that he is speaking for his beloved, his love. The song of the vineyard is a parable in which the beloved is the Lord and, as we come to know at the end, the vineyard belongs to him and is the house of Israel.**

The prophet speaks incognito for the Lord and leaves the identity of the vineyard unknown until the conclusion of the song. This leads the inhabitants of Jerusalem and people of Judah, the parable's addressees, to indict themselves. Faced with the reality of a vineyard that had produced rotten grapes, the prophet's beloved asks the people whether he could have done more for the vineyard and why the vineyard produced as it did.

The people's response is implicit in the parable. They are reduced to silence, a silence through which they pass a negative judgment on themselves. They know there was nothing more for the beloved to do. Their sinful ways caused the vineyard to yield a bad harvest.

Now the inhabitants of the house of Israel must face the consequences of their sinfulness. The beloved will destroy the vineyard. This destruction seems to imply that the Lord will abandon his people to their own devices. Yet a second vineyard song in Isaiah 27:2–6 speaks of the Lord as the keeper of his pleasant vineyard, guarding it from its enemies, and watering it so that it will flourish. The Lord promises that Israel will blossom forth and provide fruit for the world in the future.

As you prepare to proclaim this reading, think of the assembly as inhabitants of

I will **command** the **clouds**
not to send **rain** upon it.

Express the Lord's dissatisfaction strongly, but temper it by reflecting his abiding compassion and justice. The Lord's people, including those in the assembly, are always his cherished plant.

The **vineyard** of the LORD of hosts is the **house** of **Israel**,
and the **people** of **Judah** are his **cherished plant**;
he looked for **judgment**, but see, **bloodshed**!
for **justice**, but hark, the **outcry**!

READING II Philippians 4:6–9

Philippians = fih-LIP-ee-uhnz

A reading from the Letter of Saint Paul to the Philippians

Express calmness throughout your proclamation of the first section of the reading.

Brothers and sisters:
Have **no** anxiety at all, but in **everything**,
by **prayer** and **petition**, with **thanksgiving**,
make your **requests** known to **God**.
Then the **peace** of God that surpasses all understanding
will **guard** your **hearts** and **minds** in **Christ Jesus**.

Take your time reciting the list of qualities worthy of praise. Emphasize each quality, not the repetition of "whatever is."

Finally, brothers and sisters,
whatever is **true**, whatever is **honorable**,
whatever is **just**, whatever is **pure**,
whatever is **lovely**, whatever is **gracious**,
if there is any **excellence**
and if there is anything worthy of **praise**,
think about **these** things.

Proclaim Paul's concluding instruction in an encouraging tone of voice, making eye contact with the assembly.

Keep on **doing** what you have **learned** and **received**
and **heard** and **seen** in me.
Then the **God** of **peace** will be **with** you.

the vineyard. Allow your proclamation to lead them to recognize that the Lord can do nothing more for them. Rather, they need to change their sinful ways so that the vineyard can produce good fruit. Be careful that your proclamation does not become so strong as to give the assembly the sense that their sinfulness is all God sees. They, like the house of Israel, forever remain his "cherished plant." One way to temper your proclamation is to pray the refrain of the Responsorial Psalm as part of your preparation during the week and your immediate preparation just prior to the liturgy. This is one of the few times in the Lectionary that the refrain is not from a psalm. In this case, it comes directly from Isaiah 5:7, a verse in the First Reading: "The vineyard of the Lord of hosts is the house of Israel."

READING II The opening verses of this reading are proclaimed on the Third Sunday of Advent in Year C (Philippians 4:4–7). In these verses, Paul calls the Philippians to let go of any anxiety they have, and through prayer, to bring their needs to God. The result, he tells them, is that the peace of God in Christ Jesus will be theirs.

At the time of Paul's writing, the Philippians faced antagonism from opponents who did not share their conviction about the Gospel (1:28–30). This opposition created strife within the community, rivalries fueled by pride.

In the second half of the reading, Paul instructs the Philippians to think about things worthy of praise. His instructions contain a list of common Greek Stoic virtues that Paul presents in order to assist the

GOSPEL Matthew 21:33–43

A reading from the holy Gospel according to Matthew

Make eye contact with the assembly as you invite them to hear another parable.

Emphasize the fact that the landowner chooses to send his son.

heir = ayr

Jesus said to the chief **priests** and the **elders** of the people:
"**Hear** another **parable**.
There was a **landowner** who planted a **vineyard**,
put a **hedge** around it, dug a **wine** press in it, and built a **tower**.
Then he **leased** it to **tenants** and went on a **journey**.
When **vintage** time drew **near**,
he sent his **servants** to the **tenants** to obtain his **produce**.
But the tenants seized the **servants** and one they **beat**,
another they **killed**, and a third they **stoned**.
Again he sent **other** servants, more **numerous**
than the first ones,
but they treated them in the same **way**.
Finally, he sent his **son** to them, thinking,
'They will **respect** my **son**.'
But when the **tenants** saw the **son**, they **said** to one another,
'**This** is the **heir**.
Come, let us **kill** him and acquire his **inheritance**.'
They **seized** him, **threw** him out of the vineyard, and **killed** him.
What will the **owner** of the vineyard **do** to those **tenants**
when he **comes**?"

Philippians with both of their struggles—with their opponents and their internal divisions. He uses the Stoic virtues because he knows the Philippians will be familiar with them and in themselves they are not in conflict with Christian life.

The reading concludes with Paul encouraging the Philippians in the Gospel way of life they have embraced. They have learned from Paul how he imitates the Lord in his life, and the Philippians are to continue to do the same. When they do, Paul tells them, in a reiteration of his point from the beginning of the reading, the God of peace will be with them.

Those in the assembly before you, each in their own way, experience anxieties in their personal lives and also in their common life in the faith community. Your gentle and loving proclamation of Paul's instructions and the encouragement to imitate him as he imitated Christ will provide them with a means to draw closer to God in Christ Jesus and to live in peace.

GOSPEL **The second of three parables of judgment in Matthew's account of the Gospel, this passage has as its background Isaiah's song of the vineyard in the First Reading. It is the second vineyard parable in Matthew; the first was proclaimed on the Twenty-Fifth Sunday in Ordinary Time (Matthew 20:1–16a). The passage has parallels in the accounts of both Mark and Luke (Mark 12:1–12; Luke 20:9–19). Whereas Mark concludes his version of the parable with the citation from Psalm 118, Luke ends with the warning that those who fall on the stone will be dashed to pieces and the stone will crush those on whom it falls.**

Give the reply of the chief priests and elders to Jesus in a harsh, judgmental tone of voice.

Let chastisement be heard in Jesus' introductory phrase to Psalm 118. Pause after the phrase and before proclaiming the verses from the Psalm in a deliberate pace.

Make eye contact with the assembly as you proclaim Jesus' words about the kingdom being given to people that produce its fruit.

They answered him,
"He will **put** those **wretched** men to a wretched **death**
and lease his **vineyard** to **other** tenants
who will give him the **produce** at the **proper times**."
Jesus said to them, "Did you never read in the **Scriptures**:
The ***stone*** *that the builders* ***rejected***
has become the ***cornerstone****;*
by the ***Lord*** *has this been done,*
and it is ***wonderful*** *in our eyes?*
Therefore, I say to **you**,
the **kingdom** of **God** will be taken **away** from you
and given to a people that **will produce** its **fruit**."

Matthew, in contrast to both of these accounts, includes a warning about the kingdom of God after Jesus' quotation of the psalm.

This parable is an allegory with characters who play important roles in salvation history. The landowner is God, Isaiah's beloved, the vineyard's tenants are God's Chosen People of Israel, and the servants are the prophets sent to Israel throughout her history. Each prophet is rejected in turn, and finally the landowner (God) sends his son to the tenants. The son in the allegory, of course, represents Jesus, and the son's death at the hands of the tenants, Jesus' Crucifixion. Traditionally, the "other tenants" to whom the vineyard is left, have represented the Gentile believers.

While some Jews did not believe in Jesus, and the believers in the early Church to whom Matthew wrote faced some opposition from Jews, the pairing of this Gospel with the First Reading also affirms that the Jews are forever God's Chosen People. Yet we who believe in Jesus see in him the fulfillment of God's promise for a Messiah to come. Thus, those who tend the vineyard of the kingdom—Jews and Gentiles alike—and who do not turn away the Servant when he comes, will inherit the kingdom.

For Matthew, the tending of the vineyard of the kingdom takes place now. It was this tending to which the chief priests and elders of the people were not faithful. It is this tending to which you call the assembly as you proclaim the parable.

28TH SUNDAY IN ORDINARY TIME

Lectionary #142

READING I Isaiah 25:6–10a

Isaiah = ī-ZAY-uh

Emphasize the parallel opening phrases of each stanza.

Follow the commas in the description of the rich food and choice wines and increase the confidence in your tone of voice on the repetition.

Describe the destruction of death with strength and the wiping away of tears with gentleness.

Make eye contact with the assembly as you boldly proclaim the testimony of faith: "Behold our God . . . ."

Emphasize "this mountain" to note the parallel with the opening phrases of the first two sections. Make eye contact with the assembly.

A reading from the Book of the Prophet Isaiah

On this **mountain** the **LORD** of **hosts**
will **provide** for **all** peoples
a **feast** of rich **food** and choice **wines**,
juicy, rich food and **pure**, choice **wines**.
On this mountain he will destroy
the **veil** that veils **all** peoples,
the **web** that is woven over **all** nations;
he will destroy **death forever**.
The Lord **GOD** will **wipe away**
the **tears** from **every** face;
the **reproach** of his **people** he will **remove**
from the **whole** earth; for the **LORD** has **spoken**.
On that **day** it will be **said**:
"**Behold** our **God**, to whom we looked to **save** us!
This is the **LORD** for whom we **looked**;
let us **rejoice** and be **glad** that he has **saved** us!"
For the **hand** of the **LORD** will rest on this **mountain**.

READING I Today's passage from Isaiah immediately follows three verses in which the Lord punishes the pagan elements of nature and the unfaithful kings of the earth. Then in the sight of the elders, the Lord himself reigns from Mount Zion, which is a symbol of the heavenly Jerusalem (24:21–23).

The verses you will proclaim continue this scene; they can be divided into three sections. The first portrays salvation at the end of time as a luscious feast of scrumptious food and tasty wine. (Note the repetition—for emphasis—of the description of the food and drink.)

The second section, which begins by repeating the phrase, "On this mountain," describes what the Lord will do to bring salvation. The veil, possibly a reference to the earth's surface covering the dead, he will destroy; tears that stream down people's faces, he will compassionately wipe away; and the criticism his people face, he will take away.

The Lord's actions lead to a hymn of praise, sung by his people in the third section. The Lord to whom they had turned for salvation has indeed saved them. His hand, which guided the return of the captives from Babylon and rescued them from their enemies, will remain forever with them, "on this mountain."

Proclaim this reading with particular emphasis on the parallel phrases which begin each section. Lead the assembly in their own hearts to sing praise to the Lord with you as you joyfully proclaim the words of the final section. Through your proclamation, let them experience the peace that comes from knowing that the hand of the Lord will also rest on them.

READING II Philippians 4:12–14, 19–20

Philippians = fih-LIP-ee-uhnz

A reading from the Letter of Saint Paul to the Philippians

Brothers and sisters:

Use a conversational tone of voice to offer Paul's reflections about himself to the assembly.

I know how to **live** in **humble** circumstances;
I know also how to **live** with **abundance**.
In **every** circumstance and in **all** things
I have learned the **secret** of being **well fed** and of **going hungry**,
of living in **abundance** and of being in **need**.

Strengthen your tone of voice and make eye contact with the assembly as you purposefully proclaim this main line of the reading.

I can do **all** things in **him** who **strengthens** me.
Still, it was **kind** of you to **share** in my **distress**.

Let the assembly know that God will supply whatever they need by making eye contact on this line.

My God will **fully** supply whatever **you** need,
in accord with his **glorious** riches in **Christ Jesus**.
To our **God** and **Father**, **glory** forever and **ever**. **Amen**.

GOSPEL Matthew 22:1–14

A reading from the holy Gospel according to Matthew

Jesus **again** in reply spoke to the chief **priests** and **elders**
of the people
in **parables**, saying,

Use a narrative tone of voice to tell the parable of the wedding feast.

"The **kingdom** of **heaven** may be likened to a **king**
who gave a **wedding feast** for his **son**.
He dispatched his **servants**
to summon the **invited** guests to the **feast**,
but they **refused** to come.

READING II **Today is the last of four Sundays on which the Second Reading comes from Paul's letter to the Philippians. The passage you proclaim occurs near the end of the letter. In this passage, Paul recounts how he has lived with both much and little at different times in his life. He is neither complaining to the Philippians nor crying, "Woe is me," because he experienced difficulties as he preached the Gospel. Rather, he is simply sharing his experiences so that they might learn from him. The lesson he wishes to teach the Philippians is that with faith in Christ, they can do all things.**

In this passage, Paul is thankful that the Philippians have shared in his suffering while he was in prison. Indeed, 4:10–20 is Paul's expression of gratitude for their generosity. While Paul strongly desired to be self-sufficient as a missionary and support himself through his own work (1 Thessalonians 2:5–9; 1 Corinthians 9:15–18), he humbly accepted gifts as he engaged in his missionary work (Philippians 4:16; Acts 17:1–9). The reading concludes with Paul's statement of faith that the God who has supported him will also provide for the people of his dearly beloved community at Philippi. While primarily a statement intended to convey God's providence in relation to the Philippians' spiritual needs, given the context of Paul's thanksgiving for the Philippians' monetary gift, it also connotes God's care in practical matters. Paul then offers a doxology of praise to God for his generous riches in Christ Jesus—an example to the Philippians and us of how we are to be thankful for all that we receive to strengthen us in faith and life.

Direct the king's line "come to the feast" to the assembly by making eye contact with them. Use an inviting, but strong, tone of voice. You want them to come.

Let disappointment be heard in your voice as you deliver the king's words that those who were invited were not ready to come. If possible on this lengthier line, make eye contact with the assembly. Some of them might not be ready to come to the feast.

Use a serious tone of voice to proclaim the consequences faced by the man who did not come dressed in a wedding garment.

Proclaim the concluding line matter-of-factly, making eye contact with the assembly.

A **second** time he sent **other** servants, saying,
'Tell those **invited**: "Behold, I have **prepared** my **banquet**,
my **calves** and fattened **cattle** are **killed**,
and everything is **ready**; **come** to the **feast**." '
Some **ignored** the invitation and **went away**,
one to his **farm**, another to his **business**.
The rest **laid hold** of his **servants**,
mistreated them, and **killed** them.
The king was **enraged** and sent his troops,
destroyed those murderers, and **burned** their city.
Then he said to his **servants**, 'The **feast** is **ready**,
but those who were **invited** were not **worthy** to come.
Go out, therefore, into the main roads
and **invite** to the **feast** **whomever** you find.'
The **servants** went out into the **streets**
and gathered **all** they **found**, **bad** and **good** alike,
and the hall was **filled** with **guests**.
But when the **king** came in to meet the **guests**,
he saw a man there **not dressed** in a **wedding garment**.
The king said to him, 'My **friend**, how is it
that you came in here **without** a wedding garment?'
But he was **reduced** to **silence**.
Then the king said to his attendants, '**Bind** his **hands** and **feet**,
and **cast** him into the darkness **outside**,
where there will be **wailing** and **grinding** of teeth.'
Many are **invited**, but **few** are **chosen**."

[Shorter Form: Matthew 22:1–10]

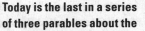

GOSPEL **Today is the last in a series of three parables about the judgment of Jerusalem addressed to the chief priests and elders of the people. The other two parables have been proclaimed on the previous two Sundays.**

A close look at this passage shows that it is composed of not just one parable, but two. The first is taken from the Q source and its parallel is found in Luke 14:15–24. It likens the kingdom of heaven to a wedding feast, an image that provides the direct link to today's First Reading. The parable details the king's preparation for the banquet and includes the invitation to the guests to "Come to the feast." We learn, then, that for various reasons the guests have rejected the invitation.

The second parable, included only in Matthew, emphasizes the preparation for the kingdom feast. It is linked to the first parable through the man who seems to have been one of the servants invited to come in off the streets to the banquet. But he is found to be dressed improperly. Missing the wedding garment, a symbol for repentance and the internal turning of the heart to belief in the Lord, the man faces the consequences of his lack of preparation. The parable serves as a warning to the members of Matthew's community—and us—that outward actions must grow out of the faith in one's heart.

Your proclamation can assist those in the assembly to see the need to prepare continuously to participate in the Lord's banquet, the eucharistic feast, both now and at the end of time. As you practice, reflect on your own invitation to the feast and recommit yourself to your preparation for the celebration.

29TH SUNDAY IN ORDINARY TIME

Lectionary #145

READING I Isaiah 45:1, 4–6

Isaiah = Ī-ZAY-uh

Cyrus = SĪ-ruhs

Speak the phrase "whose right hand I grasp" in a strong, but also personal, tone of voice.

Speak the line "I have called you by your name" in the same personal manner as before, though this time use a more compassionate tone of voice. Make eye contact with the assembly.

Proclaim the final repetition of the line "I am the Lord . . ." with the utmost confidence of faith in the one God. Throughout the reading, you will want to increase the emphasis you place on each repetition of the truth that there is no other God.

A reading from the Book of the Prophet Isaiah

Thus says the **LORD** to his **anointed**, **Cyrus**,
whose right **hand I grasp**,
subduing **nations** before him,
and making **kings** run in his service,
opening **doors** before him
and leaving the **gates** unbarred:
For the sake of **Jacob**, my **servant**,
of **Israel**, my **chosen** one,
I have **called** you by your **name**,
giving you a **title**, though you **knew** me **not**.
I am the **LORD** and there is no **other**,
there is **no God** besides **me**.
It is **I** who **arm** you, though you **know** me **not**,
so that toward the **rising** and the **setting** of the **sun**
people may **know** that there is **none** besides **me**.
I am the **LORD**, there is **no other**.

READING I This is the only passage in the Old Testament which refers to a Gentile ruler as the Lord's "anointed." The Hebrew word for "anointed one" is *meshiah,* from which the word "messiah" derives. The Greek translation of "messiah" is *Christos,* from which comes the title "Christ." Thus, using the term "anointed" in relation to Cyrus shows the divine mission of this king.

The Cyrus referred to in this reading is Cyrus the Great, who built the Persian Empire in the sixth century. For Second-Isaiah, the rise of Cyrus was a hopeful sign. In 539 BC, Cyrus defeated the Babylonians, who had taken many Israelites into exile five decades earlier. About three years after his victory, Cyrus allowed the exiles to return home. With his decree, the Babylonian exile was formally brought to an end, though the return of the exiles would occur throughout the next century.

This passage shows that the Lord works through *all* people, Gentile and Jew alike, to bring wholeness to his people. Only this Lord takes such a personal interest in knowing his anointed. We learn this in today's passage because Isaiah tells us that the Lord called Cyrus and gave him a title even before the ruler knew the Lord.

There might be some in your assembly who do not yet know the Lord. Perhaps they are the ones the Lord will call by name through your proclamation. The emphasis you place on the intimacy of the Lord's call to them and care for them as they accept his mission, might lead them to draw those who are already believers closer to the Lord as the Gentile Cyrus did for the Israelites.

READING II 1 Thessalonians 1:1–5b

Thessalonians = thes-uh-LOH-nee-uhnz

Silvanus = sil-VAY-nuhs

Proclaim the main clause "We give thanks to God always for all of you" in a strong tone of voice.

Emphasize the three characteristics of the efforts of the Thessalonians to live and spread the Gospel: faith, love, and endurance in hope. Proclaim these in an unhurried manner. Emphasize the Lord Jesus Christ, God and Father, and Holy Spirit to convey the Trinitarian character of faith and the gospel Paul preaches.

A reading from the first Letter of Saint Paul to the Thessalonians

Paul, **Silvanus**, and **Timothy** to the **church** of the **Thessalonians**
in **God** the **Father** and the **Lord Jesus Christ**:
grace to you and peace.
We give **thanks** to God **always** for all of you,
remembering you in our **prayers**,
unceasingly calling to mind your **work** of **faith** and **labor**
of **love**
and **endurance** in **hope** of our **Lord Jesus Christ**,
before our **God** and **Father**,
knowing, brothers and sisters loved by God,
how you were chosen.
For our gospel did **not** come to you in **word alone**,
but also in **power** and in the **Holy Spirit**
and with **much conviction**.

READING II For the next five Sundays, the Second Reading will come from Paul's first letter to the Thessalonians, the earliest of his letters which he wrote about 50 or 51 AD. The letter was occasioned by Timothy's report to Paul that the Christian community at Thessalonica was faithfully living and preaching the Gospel, but was also struggling with understanding the destiny of those who died (Thessalonians 4:15).

Today's passage, taken from the beginning of the letter, includes a customary opening greeting and thanksgiving. In the greeting, Paul, Silvanus, and Timothy are identified as the senders of the letter to the community in Thessalonica, a bustling commercial center and cosmopolitan area. The thanksgiving reveals their pride at the efforts of the Thessalonians to remain faithful and steadfast in the hope of Jesus Christ. Their labor on behalf of the Gospel is a labor of love.

The triad of faith, hope, and love occurs in other places in Paul's writings, most notably in 1 Corinthians 13:13 (see 1 Thessalonians 5:8). In today's reading, notice that the order of the triad is faith, love, and hope whereas in the verse from Corinthians the order is faith, hope, and love. In the reading you will proclaim, Paul emphasizes hope because the Thessalonians are concerned about their loved ones who have died before Christ's return. In the 1 Corinthians passage, he emphasizes love because love is the overall topic of 1 Corinthians 13. For him, love is contained in faith and hope, so that if faith and hope should fade away, the love of God and the love of brothers and sisters in Christ bound together by the Spirit will remain.

GOSPEL Matthew 22:15–21

Let your tone of voice suggest the sinister action afoot as you proclaim the opening line that sets the stage for the rest of the passage.

Herodians = her-OH-dee-uhnz

Speak the words of the disciples of the Pharisees as if they were attempting to flatter Jesus before they ask their question meant to entrap him.

Offer Jesus' response to their question with some annoyance in your tone of voice as he calls them "hypocrites."

Proclaim Jesus' conclusion "Then repay to Caesar . . ." in a teacher-like manner, without an air of superiority.

A reading from the holy Gospel according to Matthew

The **Pharisees** went off
and **plotted** how they might **entrap Jesus** in speech.
They sent their **disciples** to him, with the **Herodians**, saying,
"**Teacher**, we **know** that you are a **truthful** man
and that you teach the way of God in **accordance**
with the **truth**.
And you are **not** concerned with anyone's **opinion**,
for you do **not** regard a person's **status**.
Tell us, then, **what** is your **opinion**:
Is it **lawful** to pay the census **tax** to **Caesar** or **not**?"
Knowing their **malice**, Jesus said,
"**Why** are you **testing** me, you **hypocrites**?
Show me the **coin** that **pays** the census tax."
Then they handed him the Roman coin.
He said to them, "Whose **image** is this and whose **inscription**?"
They replied, "**Caesar's**."
At that he said to them,
"Then **repay** to **Caesar** what belongs to **Caesar**
and to **God** what belongs to **God**."

GOSPEL **The encounter in today's Gospel passage is a result of the chief priests and Pharisees seeing themselves as the indicted ones in the parables of the previous three Sundays. Thinking they could catch Jesus in his own words, they send to him their disciples along with a group of Herodians to pose the familiar question of the lawfulness of paying taxes.**

This group of diverse people has opposite views within it. The Herodians, who supported King Herod, a puppet of Caesar's administration, would have agreed with paying tax. On the other hand, the Pharisees would have opposed paying the tax because to do so meant paying allegiance to the Roman emperor, when in fact, their only allegiance should be to God.

Rather than taking sides and falling victim to the plot of this motley group of people, Jesus finds in their question a teachable moment. Jesus initially appears annoyed, as he calls them "hypocrites," but immediately moves to pose a question back to them. Interacting with them, he proceeds to answer their question by rationally explaining to them what is to be given to Caesar and what to God.

Jesus' response shows that our ultimate allegiance belongs to God. The role of the state is limited; God's power is universal. Although Jesus provides guidance to the questioners, his imprecise response surely left them unsatisfied. He instructed them, but as a good teacher does, left the decision for action up to them. Your proclamation should do the same: leave the assembly to ponder what decisions they will make when faced with seemingly competing allegiances.

30TH SUNDAY IN ORDINARY TIME

Lectionary #148

READING I Exodus 22:20–26

Exodus = EK-suh-duhs

A reading from the Book of Exodus

Thus says the **LORD**:
"You shall not **molest** or **oppress** an **alien**,
for **you** were once aliens **yourselves** in the land of **Egypt**.
You shall **not wrong** any **widow** or **orphan**.
If **ever** you wrong them and they **cry out** to me,
I will **surely** hear their cry.
My **wrath** will **flare up**, and I will **kill** you with the **sword**;
then your own **wives** will be **widows**,
and your **children orphans**.

Differentiate the first half from the second half of the conditional statements by proclaiming the first in a strong tone of voice and making eye contact with the assembly. Pause noticeably before the second half and lower your tone of voice for the rest of the sentence.

extortioner = ek-STOHR-shun-er

"If you **lend money** to one of your **poor** neighbors
among my people,
you shall **not** act like an **extortioner** toward him
by **demanding** interest from him.
If you take your neighbor's **cloak** as a **pledge**,
you shall **return** it to him before **sunset**;
for this **cloak** of his is the **only** covering he has for his **body**.
What **else** has he to **sleep** in?

Proclaim the Lord's compassion in a warm and empathetic voice.

If he **cries out** to me, I will **hear** him; for I am **compassionate**."

READING I This passage comes from the section of Isaiah called the Book of the Covenant that deals with social laws (Exodus 22:15—23:9). Two of them appear today: the treatment of "aliens," widows, and orphans and lending to the poor.

The word "alien" refers to people who take up residence in a land that is not their homeland. Today we refer to these people as immigrants. A number of Old Testament texts show us that the society recognized how much immigrants who were trying to make their way in a new land needed the special care and protection of God, just as widows and orphans did.

Notice the psychological insight in the Lord's words that command the Israelites not to subjugate newcomers. By referring to their own experience as foreigners in Egypt, the Lord personalizes his command and leads the Israelites to acknowledge its legitimacy. If the Israelites fail to show compassion to any of the three groups of people, the Lord himself will defend them. And those who are to bear God's compassion to others will face the Lord's wrath.

Immigrants, like the poor, often lacked financial resources. Thus, the Lord commands his people to lend money to their neighbors without taking advantage of them by charging an exorbitant amount of interest. Notice that the law does not completely forbid the collection of interest. Rather its emphasis is on the compassionate act of loaning money to a neighbor in need.

Both compassion and power should be emphasized in your proclamation of this reading: Compassion to express the Lord's own compassion and the compassion to which he calls his people, and power to

READING II 1 Thessalonians 1:5c–10

Thessalonians = thes-uh-LOH-nee-uhnz

A reading from the first Letter of Saint Paul to the Thessalonians

Make as much eye contact as possible as you speak the words "you" and "your" in the opening section of the reading.

Brothers and sisters:
You **know** what sort of **people** we were among you for your sake.
And you became **imitators** of **us** and of the **Lord**,
receiving the **word** in **great** affliction,
with **joy** from the **Holy Spirit**,
so that you became a **model** for **all** the **believers**
in **Macedonia** and in **Achaia**.

Macedonia = mas-eh-DOH-nee-uh
Achaia = uh-KEE-uh or uh-KAY-yuh

For from **you** the **word** of the **Lord** has sounded **forth**
not **only** in **Macedonia** and in **Achaia**,
but in **every** place your **faith** in **God** has gone forth,
so that we have **no need** to say **anything**.

Mark the three main points of this sentence by pausing before each occurrence of "and." Lower your tone of voice slightly on the parenthetical clauses which describe the Son from heaven.

For they themselves **openly declare** about us
what sort of **reception** we had among you,
and how you turned to **God** from **idols**
to serve the **living** and true **God**
and to await his **Son** from heaven,
whom he **raised** from the **dead**,
Jesus, who **delivers** us from the coming **wrath**.

express the Lord's authority and the consequences his people face when they do not care for those in need.

READING II A continuation of last Sunday's Second Reading, today's passage concludes Paul's thanksgiving for the faith of the Thessalonians. Two primary themes are imitation and conversion.

The Thessalonians became imitators of Paul, Silvanus, and Timothy, who themselves were imitators of the Lord. They all imitated the Lord in their embrace of the word, which brought them both affliction (*thlipsis*) and joy. While we do not know what affliction (or persecution) the Thessalonians faced, this reference suggests that through the affliction they were sharing in the cross of Christ. The joy with which the Thessalonians receive the word compels people throughout northwestern and southwestern Greece to imitate them, although Paul perhaps might be exaggerating slightly in reference to the geographical reach of the Thessalonians' example.

Paul's report of what others say about the Thessalonians indicates his satisfaction with the conversion at work in the region. The Thessalonians have turned from polytheistic practices to become monotheistic believers, followers of the risen Christ, who will protect them at the coming judgment.

As we approach the final month of the liturgical year, proclaim this reading with gratitude for how the assembly has imitated Christ and called you to the same imitation. Also be mindful of how they and

GOSPEL Matthew 22:34–40

A reading from the holy Gospel according to Matthew

Pharisees = FAYR-uh-seez
Sadducees = SAD-yoo-seez

When the **Pharisees** heard that **Jesus** had **silenced** the **Sadducees**,
they gathered together, and one of them,
a scholar of the law, **tested** him by asking,
"**Teacher**, which **commandment** in the **law** is the **greatest**?"

Ask the Pharisees' question with a hint of deceit in your tone of voice. They are trying to lure Jesus into an erroneous response.

He said to him,
"You shall **love** the **Lord**, your **God**,
with all your **heart**,
with all your **soul**,
and with all your **mind**.
This is the **greatest** and the **first** commandment.
The **second** is like it:
You shall **love** your **neighbor** as **yourself**.
The **whole law** and the **prophets** depend
on these two **commandments**."

Offer Jesus' response to the Pharisees' question slowly, emphasizing each way in which the Lord is to be loved. Make eye contact with various parts of the assembly as you do so.

Pause significantly after the colon. Then proclaim the second commandment with compassion, emphasizing "you" and making eye contact with the assembly. Pause noticeably after your proclamation of this commandment and before the concluding sentence.

you need to continue this imitation and conversion so that at the end of time deliverance can fully be yours through Christ in the joy of the Holy Spirit.

GOSPEL Last Sunday's Gospel marked the resumption of the controversies between Jesus and the Pharisees after Matthew had interrupted that story line with a few parables. Last week the Pharisees attempted to entrap Jesus in his own words with his response to the question about the lawfulness of paying taxes to Caesar. This Sunday, having heard that Jesus' explanation of the resurrection had left the Sadducees (who denied the resurrection) speechless, the Pharisees seek once again to invalidate Jesus' authority by asking him about the greatest commandment.

In his presentation of the greatest and first commandment (Deuteronomy 6:5) and the link he makes with the second commandment (Leviticus 19:18), Jesus trumps the Pharisees once again. He answers their question with more information than they asked for. They sought a prioritization of the commandments, a common concern among Jewish scholars at the time. Jesus employs the superlative in their question in his response, but he also places the second commandment, love of neighbor, on a similar plane ("The second commandment is *like* it").

As you proclaim this Gospel, read the second commandment with the same deliberate pace and strength in your voice as the first.

31ST SUNDAY IN ORDINARY TIME

Lectionary #151

READING I Malachi 1:14b—2:2b, 8–10

Malachi = MAL-uh-kī

Use an exclamatory tone of voice to proclaim the Lord's greatness. Make sure to lower your tone on the phrase which identifies the Lord as the speaker.

Make eye contact with the assembly as you tell them that the commandment which follows is for them to obey. Use a serious and stern voice, but not a loud voice, to give the commandment and the consequences for not obeying it.

Levi = LEE-vī

Let pleading be heard in your voice as you ask the first two rhetorical questions, to which you know the answer is "yes," but to which you desire to remind the assembly. Make eye contact with different parts of the assembly on each of the three questions. On the third question, let disappointment and a hint of sadness be heard in your voice.

A reading from the Book of the Prophet Malachi

A great **King** am **I**, says the LORD of **hosts**,
and my **name** will be **feared** among the **nations**.
And **now**, O **priests**, this **commandment** is for **you**:
If you do **not** listen,
if you do **not** lay it to heart,
to give **glory** to my **name**, says the **LORD** of **hosts**,
I will send a **curse** upon you
and of your **blessing** I will make a **curse**.
You have **turned aside** from the **way**,
and have caused **many** to **falter** by your **instruction**;
you have made **void** the **covenant** of **Levi**,
says the LORD of hosts.
I, therefore, have made you **contemptible**
and **base** before **all** the people,
since you do **not** keep my ways,
but show **partiality** in your **decisions**.
Have we not **all** the **one father**?
Has not the **one God** created us?
Why then do we **break faith** with one another,
violating the **covenant** of our fathers?

READING I We read from the book of the prophet Malachi only twice in the three-year Lectionary cycle of readings, once in Year A and again in Year C. Malachi (which means "messenger") is one of the minor prophets who was active in the post-exilic era after the Israelites had returned from the Babylonian exile and the temple had been rebuilt.

In today's reading, the Lord, through his prophet, offers a warning to the priests to listen to him and give glory to his name. Earlier in the chapter, the priests were criticized for offering polluted sacrifices of blind and lame animals (Malachi 1:8). The first part of verse 14, which is not proclaimed, extends this criticism to lay persons who bring the animals to the priests to be sacrificed. The point the prophet makes in the second half of verse 14, which opens today's reading, is that regardless of one's position, priest or lay person, the Lord is to be praised as King.

In the second part of today's passage, the prophet criticizes the priests because their instruction has not been faithful to the covenant of Levi. They have incorrectly interpreted the Torah and have shown partiality in the judgments they have made. Their partiality was evident in the decisions they made when two witnesses were not available, as the law required, and the priests cast lots to determine God's will for the outcome of the case.

The final lines of the reading come from the following section in Malachi, which addresses intermarriage between Jews and Gentiles. Malachi believes that intermarriage violates the covenant and breaks the unity of God's family.

Many in the assembly may hear this reading as a denunciation of priests. Your

READING II 1 Thessalonians 2:7b–9, 13

Thessalonians = thes-uh-LOH-nee-uhnz

A reading from the first Letter of Saint Paul to the Thessalonians

Speak the opening sentence with tenderness and care for the assembly seated before you so as to reflect the affection Paul, Silvanus, and Timothy had for the Thessalonians.

Brothers and sisters:
We were **gentle** among you, as a nursing **mother** cares
for her **children**.
With such **affection** for you, we were **determined** to **share**
with you
not only the **gospel** of God, but our very **selves** as well,
so dearly **beloved** had you **become** to us.

Shift your tone of voice to one that is serious and reflects the hard work of preaching the Gospel.

You recall, brothers and sisters, our **toil** and **drudgery**.
Working **night** and **day** in order **not** to **burden** any of you,
we **proclaimed** to you the **gospel** of **God**.

Shift your tone of voice to one that is optimistic and hopeful as you give thanks for the reception of the word of God among the people in the assembly. Make eye contact on the concluding phrase.

And for this **reason** we too give **thanks** to God **unceasingly**,
that, in receiving the **word** of **God** from hearing **us**,
you received not a **human word** but, as it truly **is**,
the **word** of **God**,
which is now at **work** in you who **believe**.

tone and the way you make eye contact with the members of the assembly will remind them that through Baptism, they share in Christ's priesthood and in the responsibility to praise God and treat everyone justly.

READING II In this reading, taken from the middle of the second chapter of Thessalonians, Paul again offers thanks to God for the Thessalonians. The reading begins with the plural "we" referring to Paul, Silvanus, and Timothy, those who had brought the Gospel to the Thessalonians (1:1). Paul compares the way they carried out their ministry to the way a nursing mother cares for her children. The three preachers of the Gospel cared so deeply for the Thessalonians that they wanted to nourish them not only with the Gospel, but also with themselves.

Chapter 2:1–12 is part of Paul's personal description of ministry among the Thessalonians. While Paul uses a feminine image in today's passage, in the same chapter (though not proclaimed today), he describes how he, Silvanus, and Timothy treated the Thessalonians as a father treats his children. The three encouraged them in right conduct according to the Gospel (1:11–12).

In the final section of today's reading, Paul is thankful because the Thessalonians have correctly discerned the Gospel. They have not simply heard the word the three preached as a human word. Rather, they have grasped it as God's word.

Your task as a proclaimer of the word is nothing less than Paul's. You want those in the assembly to hear the word you proclaim as the Word of God, not a human word.

GOSPEL Matthew 23:1–12

A reading from the holy Gospel according to Matthew

Jesus spoke to the **crowds** and to his **disciples**, saying,
"The **scribes** and the **Pharisees**
have taken their **seat** on the chair of **Moses**.

Look up at the assembly as you tell them in a stern tone of voice not to follow the example of the Pharisees.

Set off each of the practices of the Pharisees with a lengthy pause. This will help create a parallel effect when you come to Jesus' instructions to the crowds and the disciples as to how they are to act.

phylacteries = fih-LAK-tuh-reez

Therefore, **do** and **observe** all things **whatsoever** they **tell** you,
but do **not** follow their **example**.
For they **preach** but they do not **practice**.
They tie up heavy **burdens** hard to carry
and lay them on people's shoulders,
but **they** will not lift a finger to move them.
All their **works** are performed to be **seen**.
They **widen** their **phylacteries** and **lengthen** their **tassels**.
They love places of **honor** at **banquets**,
seats of **honor** in **synagogues**,
greetings in **marketplaces**, and the salutation **'Rabbi.'**

Emphasize "as for you" by making eye contact with the assembly on this phrase. Set off each of Jesus' imperatives with a lengthy pause. This will parallel the opposite actions of the Pharisees and give the assembly time to digest what is asked of them.

As for **you**, do **not** be called **'Rabbi.'**
You have but **one** teacher, and you are **all** brothers.
Call **no one** on earth your **father**;
you have but **one** Father in **heaven**.
Do **not** be called **'Master'**;
you have but **one** master, the **Christ**.
The **greatest** among you must be your **servant**.

Speak the verse on humility in an unassuming manner.

Whoever **exalts** himself will be **humbled**;
but whoever **humbles** himself will be **exalted**."

GOSPEL **Matthew 23:1–39, from which this Gospel passage comes, concludes a series of judgment parables and controversies between Jesus and the Pharisees, many of which have been proclaimed over the past weeks. In them we see a growing tension, even opposition, between Jesus and the Pharisees.**

What we need to understand, however, is that this opposition is more reflective of the opposition between Matthew's community and Pharisaic Judaism after the fall of Jerusalem. In other words, the harsh words Jesus' speaks in the first section of today's Gospel reflect more the historical and religious situation of the later part of the first century. The rhetoric is stronger than that found in Jesus' criticism of the Pharisees' hypocrisy during his own ministry and as reflected in the original sources of Mark and Q.

While many scripture scholars agree that Jesus' words in the second section of today's Gospel are addressed only to his disciples, the opening verse of the passage informs us that Jesus is also speaking to the crowds. Matthew provides no other remark, suggesting that the crowds at least hear Jesus' words and are themselves to heed them in their own life of faith.

The connection between this Gospel and the First Reading clearly lies in the consistency between the believer's spoken word of faith and his or her actions. Through both, the disciple is to cultivate humility and care for the unity of God's family, not his or her own self-importance.

ALL SAINTS

Lectionary #667

READING I Revelation 7:2–4, 9–14

Revelation = rev-uh-LAY-shun

Enunciate the opening words ("I, John"), which identify the first person narrator of this reading, clearly, observing the pauses at the commas.

"Do not damage . . ." is a lengthy sentence to proclaim in one breath without rushing through it and losing strength in your voice. Practice it aloud.

Pause before the words "After this." Build excitement in your voice from the beginning of this section through to "They cried out . . . ."

Pause at the semicolon after "They cried out in a loud voice" and then proclaim the words "Salvation comes . . ." boldly and confidently, increasing the volume in your tone of voice and making eye contact with the assembly.

A reading from the Book of Revelation

I, **John**, saw another **angel** come up from the **East**,
holding the **seal** of the living God.
He **cried out** in a loud **voice** to the four **angels**
who were given **power** to damage the **land** and the **sea**,
"Do **not** damage the **land** or the **sea** or the **trees**
until we put the **seal** on the **foreheads** of the **servants**
of our **God**."
I heard the **number** of those who had been **marked**
with the **seal**,
one **hundred** and forty-four **thousand** marked
from **every** tribe of the **children** of **Israel**.

After **this** I had a **vision** of a great **multitude**,
which no one could **count**,
from every **nation**, **race**, **people**, and **tongue**.
They stood before the **throne** and before the **Lamb**,
wearing **white robes** and holding **palm branches** in their **hands**.
They **cried out** in a loud **voice**:

"**Salvation** comes from our **God**, who is **seated** on the **throne**,
and from the **Lamb**."

READING I This passage from the book of Revelation is difficult to understand because it is an apocalyptic vision and is highly symbolic. However, it is appropriate for today's solemnity because it it announces the salvation of those faithful people chosen by the Lord.

The reading is actually a combination of two visions: the first comes from Revelation 7:1–8. In its use of the number 144,000 or 12 squared, which represents the 12 tribes of Israel of the Old Testament, the vision is symbolic of the new Israel, the people of God, the Church, who have been sealed as the new community of God's chosen ones.

Whereas the first vision seems to embrace symbolically a limited number of people who belong to the new Israel, the second vision ("After this . . . blood of the Lamb") extends the image of those who are made "white in the blood of the Lamb" (Revelation 7:9–17) to those of every nation, race, people, and language. Like the saints, these people are those who profess that salvation comes from God and from the Lamb, Jesus, who gave his life in the blood of the cross.

The Lord's description to John explains that the people of this multitude have experienced suffering, even persecution. Through their faithfulness to God and to the Lamb, they have been made pure. Through their own sufferings they have participated in Jesus' death and have been transformed into new spiritual people, a transformation symbolized by their white robes.

As you paint John's apocalyptic vision for the assembly through your proclamation, you will want to differentiate between

Pause after the words of the multitude and before the words "All the angels . . . ." Then lower your tone of voice to the usual tone you use for proclamation.

All the angels stood around the **throne**
and around the **elders** and the four living **creatures**.
They **prostrated** themselves before the throne,
worshiped **God**, and exclaimed:

Shift your tone of voice again to the exclamatory tone previously used for the words of the multitude as you proclaim the words "Amen. Blessing . . . ."

"**Amen. Blessing** and **glory**, **wisdom** and **thanksgiving**,
honor, **power**, and **might**
be to our God **forever** and **ever**. **Amen.**"

Pause before the words "Then one . . . ." Lower your tone of voice back down to your usual tone for proclamation.

Then one of the **elders** spoke up and said to me,
"**Who** are these wearing **white robes**,
and **where** did they **come from**?"
I said to him, "My **lord**, **you** are the one who **knows**."
He said to me,

Communicate the elder's words that conclude the reading in a softer tone of voice that is not a whisper, but rather one that gets across the relief and contentment of those who survived distress and have been made new in the Lamb.

"**These** are the ones who have **survived** the time
of great **distress**;
they have **washed** their **robes**
and made them **white** in the **Blood** of the **Lamb**."

the narrative lines and the spoken words of the various angels, elders, and John himself. In progression, these words reveal the belief that the servants of God are set apart for salvation from God, to whom all glory is due. Having survived times of suffering, they have been saved by the blood of the Lamb.

Prepare for your proclamation by considering how your faith in Jesus Christ, the Lamb of God, has helped you through times of suffering. Reflect on how you worship God and give him blessing through your proclamation of the word. Focus yourself on leading those in the assembly to praise of the Lamb this day.

READING II **The emphasis of this passage from 1 John is the identity of faithful Christians as the "children of God." Because Christians have believed and accepted the sign of God's love in the gift of his Son (John 3:16), they are God's children.**

At the time 1 John was written, the Christian community was divided. Some believed Jesus was not fully human; others suggested that he was not fully divine. The author recounts that some of these members left the community. In an earlier passage, he identifies those people as the antichrist (2:18–23). In contrast, those faithful, then, now, and in the future, who profess that Jesus is the Christ, belong to the family of God's children.

GOSPEL **The Alternative Opening Prayer in the Sacramentary for the solemnity of All Saints reads in part: "God our Father, source of all holiness, the work of your hands is manifest in**

As you proclaim this reading, take each line as it comes, being conscious not to rush from sentence to sentence. All the lines of the reading are in the first person plural ("we" and "us") except for the final line, so making eye contact with the assembly for as much of the reading as you can do so with ease will enhance your proclamation of the close bond between the Father and his children.

READING II 1 John 3:1–3

A reading from the first Letter of Saint John

Beloved:
See what **love** the Father has bestowed on **us**
that **we** may be **called** the **children** of **God**.
Yet so we **are**.
The reason the world does not **know us**
is that it did not **know him**.
Beloved, **we** are God's children **now**;
what we **shall be** has not yet been **revealed**.
We **do know** that when it is revealed we shall be **like him**,
for we shall **see him** as **he is**.
Everyone who has **this** hope based on him makes himself **pure**,
as he is pure.

your saints, the beauty of your truth is reflected in their faith. May we who aspire to have a part in their joy be filled with the Spirit that blessed their lives, so that having shared their faith on earth we may also know their peace in your kingdom."

The saints in this prayer are those men and women who exemplify the living out of the teachings in the Beatitudes proclaimed today. Through their actions, saints carried forth the Father's work and reflected the truth of the Christian faith. As Christian faithful, we pray for their intercession as we too try to manifest the virtues of the Beatitudes in our daily lives (*Catechism of the Catholic Church*, 1716–1729).

There are two versions of the Beatitudes, Matthew's account proclaimed today and the other in the Gospel according to Luke 6:20–26. Whereas in Matthew the Beatitudes are part of the "Sermon on the Mount" and addressed to his disciples as well as the crowds, in Luke, the Beatitudes are contained in the "Sermon on the Plain" and addressed only to Jesus' disciples. The first, second, fourth, and ninth Beatitudes in Matthew's account are paralleled, although with slight modifications, in Luke 6:20, 21b, 21a, and 22–23, respectively.

Because Matthew adds the words "in spirit" to the first Beatitude, some scripture scholars have suggested that he "spiritualizes" its teaching. Often this interpretation has a negative connotation, suggesting that Matthew did not recognize the material poor in his account of how Jesus announced the Beatitudes. Certainly it is true that Matthew's version of the Beatitudes is less concrete than Luke's (in 6:21, Luke adds a Beatitude for those who

GOSPEL Matthew 5:1–12a

Proclaim the opening lines, which set the scene for Jesus' teaching of the Beatitudes, in a narrative tone of voice.

Pause after the words "He began . . ." and before beginning the list of Beatitudes. Because the Beatitudes are parallel in structure, you will want to be careful to practice your proclamation of them so it does not sound "sing-song," that is, containing the same rise and fall in inflection for each Beatitude. Try pausing after each Beatitude and matching your tone of voice to the descriptive words in each one. For example, on "poor in spirit" use a slightly lighter tone of voice, and on "inherit the land" use a tone of voice that is fuller and firmer.

As you proclaim the final Beatitude, make eye contact with the assembly as the pronoun has changed from "they" to the personal "you." Maintain eye contact through "Rejoice and be glad" as you declare these commands of Jesus with joy in your voice, and perhaps even with a smile that expresses happiness.

A reading from the holy Gospel according to Matthew

When **Jesus** saw the **crowds**, he went **up** the **mountain**,
and after he had sat **down**, his disciples **came** to him.
He began to **teach** them, saying:

"**Blessed** are the poor in **spirit**,
for **theirs** is the Kingdom of **heaven**.
Blessed are they who **mourn**,
for they will be **comforted**.
Blessed are the **meek**,
for they will **inherit** the **land**.
Blessed are they who **hunger** and **thirst** for **righteousness**,
for they will be **satisfied**.
Blessed are the **merciful**,
for they will be **shown** mercy.
Blessed are the **clean** of **heart**,
for they will **see God**.
Blessed are the **peacemakers**,
for they will be called **children** of **God**.
Blessed are they who are **persecuted** for the sake
of **righteousness**,
for **theirs** is the Kingdom of **heaven**.
Blessed are **you** when they **insult** you and **persecute** you
and utter every kind of **evil** against you **falsely**
because of **me**.
Rejoice and be **glad**,
for **your reward** will be **great** in **heaven**."

are hungry now, and also includes three "woes"), but Matthew's version, with Jesus' addition of "in spirit" might mean simply that it is those, no matter their economic state—rich or poor—who believe in God's presence in Jesus, who belong to the kingdom of heaven.

One of Matthew's goals in writing to a predominantly Jewish Christian audience around 80 to 90 AD was to show how the reward of the kingdom of heaven is open to all—Gentiles included—who acknowledge Jesus as the Son of God. Matthew's version of the Beatitudes, and especially the particular beatitude "Blessed are the poor in spirit," serves his purpose of showing that the kingdom of heaven is available to Jew and Gentile alike.

The future passive tense of all but two of the Beatitudes in today's Gospel reveals Matthew's eschatological emphasis. Happiness, which comes from living out the Beatitudes (*beatitudo* in Latin means "happy"), is a reward that God *will* give in the future to those who have been, are, and will be faithful.

The first and tenth Beatitudes tell us that the kingdom of heaven is also available *now* to those who are dedicated to following Jesus and living by his teachings (the crowds), even if they are not part of the inner circle of disciples, or are not canonized saints. From these Beatitudes, those who are part of the multitude of the faithful can draw strength and inspiration, and thus grow closer to Christ (CCC, 956).

COMMEMORATION OF ALL THE FAITHFUL DEPARTED

Lectionary #668

READING I Wisdom 3:1–9

A reading from the Book of Wisdom

Proclaim the opening line in a confident tone of voice. Then lower the intensity in your tone of voice as you continue.

The **souls** of the **just** are in the **hand** of **God**,
and no **torment** shall **touch** them.
They seemed, in the view of the **foolish**, to be **dead**;
and their passing **away** was thought an **affliction**
and their going **forth** from us, utter **destruction**.

Communicate the line "But they are in peace" in a deliberate pace and with a gentle tone of voice, one slightly lower in volume than that used in the previous section.

But they are in **peace**.
For **if** before men, indeed, they be **punished**,
yet is their **hope** full of **immortality**;
chastised a little, they shall be greatly blessed,
because God **tried** them
and found them **worthy** of himself.
As **gold** in the **furnace**, he **proved** them,
and as sacrificial **offerings** he took them to **himself**.

Gradually build in intensity and confidence as you proceed through this section so that when you proclaim the concluding line of the reading the tone of your voice matches the opening line.

In the time of their **visitation** they shall **shine**,
and shall **dart** about as **sparks** through **stubble**;
they shall judge **nations** and rule over **peoples**,
and the LORD shall be their King **forever**.
Those who **trust** in him shall understand **truth**,
and the **faithful** shall abide with him in **love**:
because **grace** and **mercy** are with his **holy** ones,
and his **care** is with his **elect**.

The readings given here are suggestions. Any reading from the Lectionary for the Commemoration of All the Faithful Departed (#668) or the Masses for the Dead (#1011–1015) may be used. Consult with the liturgy coordinator or homilist about which readings will be used.

READING I This passage from Wisdom provides four references to God's love and care for the souls of those who have died. First, the opening lines convey the belief that "the wise"—those who trust in God now—can be confident that the souls of those who were just are now with God.

"The foolish," on the other hand, who simply believe that physical death is the end of all life, do not understand the peace in which the souls of the faithful reside.

Second, while the author states that the souls of the just are at peace, the words "For if in the sight . . ." suggests some ambiguity about their state immediately after they die. Some scholars see a reference to purgatory, the final purification of the elect in the slight chastisement that the souls undergo before they enter fully into the joy of life with God. However, this is not necessarily the intention of the author (see *Catechism of the Catholic Church*, 1030–1032).

The third reference is the allusion to God's judgment that is experienced at some point after death—an allusion in the phrase "In the time of their visitation." Whereas the souls of the just will live with God forever, those of the wicked will never be released from the snares of suffering and death (Wisdom 2:24; 3:10–12).

Fourth and finally, the reading concludes with a statement reiterating that

Address the assembly with the words "Brothers and sisters" by looking up and making eye contact. Continue your eye contact as you slowly and in an optimistic tone of voice proclaim the words "Hope does not disappoint." Be careful not to drop the inflection in your voice too much as you proceed with the clause after the comma ("because the love of God . . .").

"How much more then . . ." can sound like a question, but it is a statement. Proclaim it emphatically and do not raise the pitch of your voice when you come to the end of the statement. Do the same as you come to the second statement ("how much more, once reconciled . . .").

READING II Romans 5:5–11

A reading from the Letter of Saint Paul to the Romans

Brothers and sisters:
Hope does not **disappoint**,
because the **love** of **God** has been poured **out** into our **hearts**
through the **Holy Spirit** that has been **given** to us.
For **Christ**, while we were still **helpless**,
died at the appointed time for the **ungodly**.
Indeed, only with **difficulty** does one **die** for a **just** person,
though perhaps for a **good** person
one might even find **courage** to **die**.
But God **proves** his **love** for us
in that **while** we were still **sinners Christ died** for us.
How much **more** then, since we are **now justified** by his **Blood**,
will we be **saved** through him from the **wrath**.
Indeed, **if**, while we were **enemies**,
we were **reconciled** to God through the **death** of his **Son**,
how much **more**, once **reconciled**,
will we be **saved** by his **life**.
Not only **that**,
but we **also** boast of **God** through our **Lord Jesus Christ**,
through whom we have **now** received **reconciliation**.

Or:

the constant care of the Lord is always with those whom he has chosen ("his elect"). The statement's purpose is twofold: it comforts those who are concerned for their deceased loved ones who trusted in the Lord throughout their lives, and it provides hope for those of us who remain on earth.

READING II ROMANS 5. For Paul, the hope Christians have is genuine because it comes through the cross. Through Christ's death on the cross while we were still unjustified sinners, God's love was poured out on us. In Christ's sacrifice, we see God sharing his very self with us such that we might share in the divine life.

Paul sees Christ's death on the cross as the example par excellence of God's love being poured out for us. It is for Paul proof of God's tremendous love for us because it occurred while we were still "ungodly." Paul makes his argument in steps by explaining first that it would be hard to die, even for a just and righteous person. For a good person, it would still not be easy, but one could perhaps find the strength.

Finally, Paul's argument climaxes with his statement about the totally free and gratuitous nature of Christ's death. Christ died not on behalf of a just person or a good person, but on behalf of his enemies, those who were still sinful. Through his death, Christ offered reconciliation—a reunification of sinners with God. According to Paul, then, by reconciling us to himself, Christ saved those who were God's enemies.

On this day when we commemorate the souls of all the faithful departed, we can rejoice in and boast in the reconciliation Christ has offered. We joyfully profess

READING II Romans 6:3–9

A reading from the Letter of Saint Paul to the Romans

Address the opening greeting directly to the members of the assembly by looking up and making eye contact with them. Because the reading is in the second person plural ("we") in its entirety, strive to make as much eye contact with the assembly as you can without disrupting the flow of your proclamation.

Brothers and sisters:
Are you **unaware** that we who were **baptized** into **Christ Jesus**
were **baptized** into his **death**?
We were indeed **buried** with him through **baptism** into **death**,
so that, just as Christ was **raised** from the dead
by the **glory** of the **Father**,
we too might **live** in newness of **life**.

For if we have grown into **union** with him through a **death**
like **his**,
we shall also be **united** with him in the **resurrection**.
We **know** that our **old self** was **crucified** with him,
so that our **sinful body** might be done **away** with,
that we might no longer be in **slavery** to **sin**.
For a **dead** person has been **absolved** from sin.
If, then, we have **died** with **Christ**,
we **believe** that we shall also **live** with him.
We know that **Christ**, raised from the **dead**, dies no **more**;
death no longer has **power** over **him**.

Let the confidence of faith be heard in your proclamation of the conditional statement ("If, then, we have died . . .") through to the end of the reading. Keep your tone of voice strong through the final word. Then pause before saying, "The word of the Lord."

that one day we will all meet together in Christ, and live reconciled with our brothers and sisters for ever (*Order of Christian Funerals*, 175).

ROMANS 6. Paul wrote this passage from Romans as a response to a question posed by those who thought the Gospel promoted moral leniency (Romans 3:5–8, 23–24). The question was this: why not do evil if God's gift of justification comes to those who sin? In his response, Paul shows the foundation Baptism gives for a new relationship with Christ.

In Baptism, Christians are baptized "into Christ" (*eis Christon*). This phrase denotes that Christians are incorporated into Christ's person and, as such, participate in his death and Resurrection. Because Christ's death was death to sin, our unity with him in his death means that our old, sinful body is washed clean, and done away with.

Being freed from sin, then, the baptized person participates in the new life brought through Christ's Resurrection. It is this life in Christ that now has power and control over the newly baptized. This new life, Paul believes, impels the new Christian to live uprightly in relation to God and neighbor. Thus, moral laxity is no longer an option for the new self of the Christian. While ethical behavior for the old self might not have had any qualifiers, for the new self, it does. Christians must see to it that sin does not rule their bodies causing them to give in to human desires (6:12).

Paul concludes today's passage with a statement of belief in our future life with Christ. For Paul, it is our life on earth as those who were baptized into Christ's death and Resurrection that prepares us

GOSPEL John 6:37–40

A reading from the holy Gospel according to John

Jesus said to the **crowds**:
"**Everything** that the Father **gives** me will **come** to me,
and I will **not** reject **anyone** who comes to me,
because I came **down** from heaven not to do my **own** will
but the **will** of the one who **sent** me.
And **this** is the will of the one who sent me,
that I should not lose **anything** of what he **gave** me,
but that I should **raise** it on the last **day**.
For **this** is the will of my **Father**,
that everyone who **sees** the **Son** and **believes** in him
may have **eternal life**,
and I shall **raise** him up on the **last day**."

The first sentence is lengthy. Pausing at the commas and adding a minor pause after the words "own will" will help make for a smooth and understandable proclamation.

Communicate the reassuring line ("that I should not lose . . .") with a measure of hope in your voice, making eye contact with the members of the assembly to convey that they will not be lost by him.

Proclaim this climactic line of the Gospel with unwavering strength.

for the future. If we are interested in our future life with Christ, we must do our best now to live according to our new selves, baptized members of the body of Christ.

GOSPEL **As today's passage begins, Jesus teaches the crowd that he will not turn away anyone who approaches him. Earlier in John, "the Jews" had cast out from the synagogue those who believed in Jesus (9:34–35). Jesus does not welcome those who come to him simply of his own accord, but he does so because he is doing the will of the Father who sent him. Moreover, he recognizes that all who come to him also come from the Father. On the last day, then, Jesus will raise them up to be one with the Father so that they might have eternal life.**

The gift of eternal life is anticipated in the Eucharist in which the faithful departed have participated. Through their reception of the Bread of Life, they have professed their belief in Jesus. At their death, their "soul goes to meet God, while awaiting its reunion with its glorified body" on "the last day," when Christ comes again and those who died in Christ will rise (CCC, 997, 1001). The last verse of the Gospel explains the hope of believers for themselves and their faithful departed loved ones. As you prepare during the week to proclaim this Gospel, reflect on how this hope is evident in your own life. Your sanguine and self-assured proclamation will help strengthen the faith of others and lead them to continue to live in the hope of the Father's will for their eternal life brought through his Son's Resurrection.

32ND SUNDAY IN ORDINARY TIME

Lectionary #154

READING I Wisdom 6:12–16

Open your proclamation in a strong and bright tone of voice, thereby creating the impression of the glorious nature of wisdom.

Lighten your tone of voice and quicken your pace ever so slightly as you speak of wisdom hastening herself. Slow down as you tell of the person seeking wisdom finding her sitting nearby.

Proclaim the words about wisdom making rounds, seeking, appearing to, and meeting people worthy of her in a calm voice and measured pace.

A reading from the Book of Wisdom

Resplendent and **unfading** is **wisdom**,
and she is readily **perceived** by those who **love** her,
and **found** by those who **seek** her.
She **hastens** to make herself **known** in anticipation
of their **desire**;
whoever **watches** for **her** at **dawn** shall **not** be **disappointed**,
for he shall **find** her sitting by his **gate**.
For taking thought of **wisdom** is the **perfection** of **prudence**,
and **whoever** for **her** sake keeps **vigil**
shall **quickly** be **free** from **care**;
because she makes her own **rounds**, seeking those **worthy**
of her,
and graciously **appears** to them in the **ways**,
and **meets** them with all **solicitude**.

READING I Composed in the latter half of the first century BC, the book of Wisdom seeks to encourage Jews in their faith as they try to live observantly in the Hellenized (Greek) culture that permeated the many regions conquered by Alexander the Great. With growing scientific knowledge and a plurality of philosophical systems from which to seek wisdom, the Jews needed to see anew the wisdom in their own religious tradition.

Wisdom 6, from which today's reading comes, is an exhortation specifically to the kings and princes to seek wisdom (Wisdom 6:1, 9). The kings are in need of divine Wisdom, for though their authority has come from God, they have not judged rightly and have failed to adhere to the law (6:4). The princes need Wisdom to guide them away from sin (6:9).

Today's passage has three themes. First, it opens with an announcement of the glorious, magnificent, and everlasting nature of Wisdom. This announcement attests to Wisdom's divine origin. The second theme of the passage is Wisdom's availability to those who love her, seek her, and watch for her. Wisdom is so available that she will show herself even before a person desires her. Wisdom, like the Lord, who knew the psalmist in the womb (Psalm 139:13–16), is aware of our desire for her even before we reach out to her.

In the final section, the reading's third theme appears. Wisdom will look after those who are conscious of her and intentionally watch for her. These seekers will have no worries. Personified as a woman who walks the streets, making her rounds, Wisdom attentively cares for people as God's creations.

READING II Thessalonians 4:13–18

Thessalonians = thes-uh-LOH-nee-uhnz

Use an explanatory tone of voice to convey Paul's purpose for writing this passage.

Recall the Christian belief about Jesus' death and Resurrection and its relation to our own in an instructive tone, slightly stronger than the tone with which you began your proclamation.

Beginning with "For the Lord himself," build in strength and confidence to the truth that "the dead in Christ will rise first." Pause after that statement. Proclaim the concluding line with similar optimism, making eye contact with the assembly, assuring them that as believers, they too, will enter into eternal life with the Lord.

A reading from the first Letter of Saint Paul to the Thessalonians

We do not **want** you to be **unaware**, brothers and sisters,
about **those** who have fallen **asleep**,
so that you may not **grieve** like the rest, who have no **hope**.
For if we **believe** that Jesus **died** and **rose**,
so too will **God**, through **Jesus**,
bring **with** him those who have fallen **asleep**.
Indeed, we tell you this, on the **word** of the **Lord**,
that we who are **alive**,
who are **left** until the **coming** of the **Lord**,
will **surely** not **precede** those who have fallen **asleep**.
For the Lord **himself**, with a word of **command**,
with the voice of an **archangel** and with the trumpet of **God**,
will come **down** from **heaven**,
and the **dead** in **Christ** will rise **first**.
Then **we** who are **alive**, who are left,
will be caught up **together** with them in the **clouds**
to **meet** the **Lord** in the **air**.
Thus we shall **always** be with the **Lord**.
Therefore, **console** one another with these **words**.

[Shorter Form: 1 Thessalonians 4:13–14]

Your task is to make the three themes of the reading evident in your proclamation. You will want to begin by creating a sense of the glorious nature of Wisdom. One way to do this is to elongate your enunciation of the words. To convey the theme of Wisdom's accessibility to those who seek her, make eye contact as much as possible with those in the assembly. Finally, to communicate Wisdom's solicitude for the people, you might think of those in your assembly who "make rounds," especially doctors and nurses. Filling your voice with the compassion of those in the helping professions may enable those in the assembly to hear Wisdom's own compassion and increase their desire to seek her.

READING II It might seem strange to be hearing a reading about Christ's Resurrection and the resurrection of the dead at this time of year. However, a closer look at the reading in its context shows that Paul is speaking about what will happen at the end of time when Christ comes again in glory. The opening verse of this reading identifies the concern some in the Christian community at Thessalonica had about the fate of those who had died before Christ returned. Paul does not want them to remain in angst, without hope, like those who do not believe in the resurrection of the dead.

The second part of this apocalyptic passage expresses truths in which we believe, similar to a creed. Paul clearly states the relationship between Jesus' death and Resurrection and the death and Resurrection of those who believe in him. In the next section, he goes on to explain the authority of the Lord's word on which

GOSPEL Matthew 25:1–13

A reading from the holy Gospel according to Matthew

Jesus told his **disciples** this **parable**:
"The **kingdom** of **heaven** will be like ten **virgins**
who took their **lamps** and went out to **meet** the **bridegroom**.
Five of them were **foolish** and **five** were **wise**.
The **foolish** ones, when taking their **lamps**,
brought **no oil** with them,
but the **wise** brought **flasks** of **oil** with their **lamps**.
Since the **bridegroom** was long **delayed**,
they all became **drowsy** and fell **asleep**.
At **midnight**, there was a **cry**,
'**Behold**, the **bridegroom**! Come out to **meet** him!'
Then **all** those virgins got up and trimmed their **lamps**.
The **foolish** ones said to the **wise**,
'Give us some of **your** oil,
for **our** lamps are going **out**.'

Contrast "foolish" and "wise" so the focus of the parable is clear to the assembly from the start.

Announce the appearance of the bridegroom in a declarative voice.

Speak the words of the foolish virgins in a pleading manner. Respond dismissively with the words of the wise.

he proclaims this belief. At the Lord's command, an angel's voice along with the sounding of the trumpet will herald the Resurrection of those who have died believing in Christ.

The Thessalonians need not worry that their beloved who have already died have missed out on the Resurrection of the dead. Indeed, when Christ does return, they will be among the ones to rise first. Then those who are still alive will be brought to new life in Christ.

Your task is to encourage the assembly in the hope of the Resurrection and to leave them comforted by the concluding words of the reading. The knowledge that they and their beloved will always be with the Lord is a tremendous source of solace as we continue to live faithfully according to the Gospel until the parousia.

GOSPEL **The Gospel readings for the final Sundays of the liturgical year all come from Matthew 25, which is part of the evangelist's eschatological discourse. Today's Gospel, unique to Matthew and familiar to many, is often misunderstood to refer to the necessity of absolute vigilance for the full realization of the kingdom of heaven at the parousia. Yet in the parable, all ten virgins become drowsy and fall asleep, a situation that seems to be making a different point.**

A basic requirement for entering the kingdom of heaven when the Lord comes is readiness. Only the virgins who had oil for their lamps were ready. While others can help us be prepared, as symbolized by the merchants who would have sold oil to the virgins without it, preparedness for the kingdom is a personal responsibility. The

But the **wise** ones replied,
'**No**, for there may not be **enough** for us **and** you.
Go instead to the **merchants** and **buy** some for **yourselves**.'

Use a narrative tone of voice to convey what transpires after the foolish went off to buy oil.

While they went off to buy it,
the **bridegroom** came
and those who were **ready** went into the **wedding feast** with him.
Then the door was locked.
Afterwards the **other** virgins came and said,

Implore the Lord to open the door as the foolish virgins would have.

'**Lord**, **Lord**, open the **door** for us!'
But he said in reply,

Proclaim Jesus' words in a solemn and serious tone of voice. Remember to give a lengthy pause before the words "The Gospel of the Lord."

'**Amen**, I **say** to you, I do not **know** you.'
Therefore, **stay awake**,
for you **know** neither the **day** nor the **hour**."

unprepared virgins could have been ready in a timely fashion had they earlier taken responsibility for having oil for their lamps.

In the passage, the Lord himself discloses the symbolism of the oil when he says "I do not know you." The oil is all that we do to nurture our relationship with the Lord, personally and in our relationships with others. The wise virgins have realized this. The foolish, on the other hand, are procrastinators. At the last minute, they come to this same realization and attempt to build a relationship with the Lord all at once.

Salvation is indeed a free gift from the Lord; nothing we do can merit it. However, as the foolish virgins experienced, the door to salvation may be locked; entry into the kingdom of heaven is not a given. Readiness for the kingdom is essential.

In the final verse, the reference to staying awake was probably added to the original parable by Matthew and not meant to be taken literally, since both the wise and foolish virgins do fall asleep. The community to whom Matthew was writing his account of the Gospel was struggling to figure out how to live in the interim before the parousia—especially how to live in relationship to Jews who lived out of different expressions of Judaism.

Your proclamation of the final verse should leave the assembly wondering not only if they personally have the oil of preparedness for their own lamps, but how the oil of preparedness is present in their faith community. Does the Lord know them?

33RD SUNDAY IN ORDINARY TIME

Lectionary #157

READING I Proverbs 31:10–13, 19–20, 30–31

Proverbs = PRAH-verbz

Take each sentence one by one, proclaiming each with care and pausing noticeably after each.

distaff = DIS-taf
A distaff is a staff that holds un-spun flax or wool.

Express the contrasts between "charm" and "deceptive" and "beauty" and "fleeting."
End on a note of praise for the woman who loves the Lord.

A reading from the Book of Proverbs

When one **finds** a **worthy wife**,
her **value** is **far** beyond **pearls**.
Her **husband**, entrusting his **heart** to her,
has an **unfailing prize**.
She brings him **good**, and not **evil**,
all the **days** of her **life**.
She obtains **wool** and **flax**
and **works** with **loving** hands.
She puts her **hands** to the **distaff**,
and her **fingers** ply the **spindle**.
She reaches out her **hands** to the **poor**,
and extends her arms to the needy.
Charm is **deceptive** and **beauty fleeting**;
the **woman** who **fears** the **LORD** is to be **praised**.
Give her a **reward** for her **labors**,
and let her **works praise her** at the city gates.

READING I Just one week before the end of the liturgical year you might wonder why you are proclaiming a reading about the ideal wife. This passage, taken from the final chapter of Proverbs, can be seen as a summary for the entire book. It is thus a fitting prelude to the conclusion of the liturgical year next Sunday.

The reading is from an acrostic poem in which each verse begins with a letter of the Hebrew alphabet. Throughout the poem, we find some of the main themes of Proverbs. For example, the woman's priceless value to her husband reminds us of Wisdom's worth to those who seek and follow her. To those who remember her teaching, she is a tree of life (Proverbs 3:18); those who remain faithful to her, she will preserve (4:6). What greater value could there be than to have the blessing of life.

The reading concludes with the theme of fear of the Lord, which takes us back to the beginning of the book of Proverbs. In Proverbs 1, we hear that the fear of the Lord, or reverence for God, is the basis for knowledge, wisdom, and instruction. When we recognize that God is our Creator and we are not God, then our faith leads us to seek Wisdom all the days of our lives. The praiseworthy wife loves God for who he is, the loving Creator who has created his people in his image and likeness.

Some of the tasks the woman in this reading carries out will not be readily understood by those in your assembly. At the time of the writing of Proverbs, they were everyday, practical, domestic chores a woman performed. The smoothness with which you proclaim them, will help get across the point of the woman's faithfulness to her responsibilities. Comprehending

READING II 1 Thessalonians 5:1–6

Thessalonians = thes-uh-LOH-nee-uhnz

A reading from the first Letter of Saint Paul to the Thessalonians

Proclaim the opening lines with the confidence of faith: you and the assembly before you know that the day of the Lord will come unexpectedly.

Concerning **times** and **seasons**, brothers and sisters,
you have **no need** for **anything** to be written to you.
For you **yourselves know** very well that the **day** of the **Lord**
will **come**
like a **thief** at **night**.

Contrast the confidence of your proclamation in the opening lines, with the anxiety and fear of the sudden disaster for those who have not prepared for the coming of the day of the Lord.

When people are saying, "**Peace** and **security**,"
then sudden **disaster** comes upon them,
like **labor pains** upon a **pregnant woman**,
and they will **not** escape.

Make eye contact with the assembly as much as possible during the proclamation of the final stanza. Use a bright tone of voice. Offer the concluding line with encouragement for the assembly's ongoing journey of faith.

But **you**, brothers and sisters, are **not** in darkness,
for that **day** to **overtake** you like a **thief**.
For **all** of you are **children** of the **light**
and **children** of the **day**.
We are **not** of the **night** or of **darkness**.
Therefore, let us not **sleep** as the **rest** do,
but let us stay **alert** and **sober**.

the context of this passage as it appears within the entire book of Proverbs will also help you proclaim the reading so that it does not come across as one meant to focus solely on the woman's role in keeping the household functioning. Praise is due to her not for her unending daily activity, but because of her relationship with the Lord, which results in such good service to her household.

Keeping in mind that the wife in this reading might represent Wisdom caring for those who have sought and accepted her, a goal of your proclamation can be to communicate the Wisdom of all those who care for God's children. The value of those who do so is indeed far beyond pearls and an example to us as we prepare to end one liturgical year and begin another.

READING II Appropriately for this time in the liturgical year, today's Second Reading speaks of the coming of the end times. Using the image of the day of the Lord from the prophetic tradition, Paul exhorts the Thessalonians to remain alert for its coming. So long as the Thessalonians stay alert, they have nothing to fear because they are children of the light.

Believers in Christ are in the light, for Christ is the light of the world. In contrast, those who do not believe dwell in darkness. Those who are in Christ have no worries about the time when Christ returns in glory, for they have lived according to their faith; their actions will have announced the glory of Christ's second coming. Moreover, as Paul has previously reminded the Thessalonians, believers have faith in the Resurrection of the dead.

GOSPEL Matthew 25:14–30

A reading from the holy Gospel according to Matthew

Use a narrative tone of voice to tell the parable. Switch your tone when the master or the servants are speaking.

Jesus told his **disciples** this **parable**:
"A man going on a **journey**
called in his **servants** and entrusted his **possessions** to them.
To **one** he gave **five** talents; to **another**, **two**; to a **third**, **one**—
to **each** according to his **ability**.
Then he went away.
Immediately the one who received **five** talents went and **traded** with them,
and made **another** five.
Likewise, the one who received **two** made **another** two.
But the man who received **one** went off and dug a hole in the ground
and **buried** his master's money.

"After a long time
the **master** of those servants came **back**
and **settled accounts** with them.
The one who had received **five** talents came forward
bringing the **additional** five.
He said, '**Master**, you gave me **five** talents.
See, I have made **five** more.'
His master said to him, '**Well done**, my **good** and **faithful servant**.
Since you were **faithful** in **small** matters,
I will give you **great** responsibilities.
Come, **share** your master's **joy**.'
Then the one who had received **two** talents also came forward and said,
'**Master**, you gave me **two** talents.
See, I have made **two** more.'

The servant is proud; he has doubled the amount the master gave him.

Speak the master's words as a compliment. Offer his invitation with joy in your voice.

Similarly, the second servant is proud to have doubled the amount the master gave him.

When the day of the Lord suddenly comes, their beloved who have died in Christ will rise with him. And, after them, those who believe and are still alive will also rise. Although you are speaking about the sudden and unexpected coming of the day of the Lord—and the image of it coming like a thief in the night—this reading is optimistic in tone. Fill your proclamation with brightness and hope, for the people in the assembly are children of the light. Offer Paul's concluding exhortation as a gentle reminder to them that the way they live now prepares them for the Lord's return.

GOSPEL **The parable of the talents, which is the entirety of today's Gospel, is a well-known story. Proclaiming it as the liturgical year nears its close serves as a reminder that in the interim before the parousia comes and the final judgment occurs, we need to live faithfully, actively taking responsibility for the talents we have been given according to our abilities.**

In Jesus' time, a *talent* was a high-value unit of currency. It could vary in its worth based on its metal and where it was made. In the English language, we use the word "talent" to refer to a gift or skill one has. This use coincides with the relationship between the word "talents" and "ability" in the opening section of the Gospel. Notice that after having spoken with the servants, the master leaves, and then "After a long time" he comes back to settle accounts with his servants. Biblical exegetes in the early Church understood the master as Christ, his leave-taking as Christ's Ascension, and the master's return as Christ's second coming at the parousia.

How the servants acted in response to the talents they had been given provided

Speak the master's words, which are a repetition of his words to the first servant, again as a compliment. Similar joy should be heard in your voice as you offer the master's invitation to the servant.

His master said to him, '**Well done**, my **good** and **faithful servant**.
Since you were **faithful** in **small** matters,
I will give you **great** responsibilities.
Come, **share** your master's **joy**.'
Then the one who had received the **one** talent came forward
and said,
'**Master**, I knew you were a **demanding** person,
harvesting where you did **not plant**
and **gathering** where you did **not scatter**;
so out of **fear** I went off and **buried** your talent in the **ground**.
Here it is **back**.'

The third servant is also proud because he has done what he thought the master would want.

His master said to him in reply, 'You **wicked**, **lazy servant**!
So you **knew** that I **harvest** where I did not **plant**
and **gather** where I did not **scatter**?
Should you **not** then have put my **money** in the **bank**
so that I could have got it **back** with **interest** on my **return**?
Now then! **Take** the talent from him and **give** it to the one
with ten.

Proclaim the master's reply with anger in your voice. He is rebuking the servant, repulsed by his inaction.

For to **everyone** who **has**,
more will be **given** and he will grow **rich**;
but from the one who has **not**,
even what he has will be **taken away**.
And throw this **useless servant** into the **darkness** outside,
where there will be **wailing** and **grinding** of **teeth**.'"

Lower your tone of voice to an explanatory one as the master gives his instructions about what will happen to those who have and those who do not.

End on an ominous note.

[Shorter Form: Matthew 25:14–15, 19–21]

an example of how believers are to live in the time before the parousia. The first two servants were faithful to what they had been given. Their production of more talents led to the master giving them greater responsibilities and perhaps more significantly, as this Gospel is proclaimed near the end of the liturgical year, to their participation in the kingdom of God—their master's joy.

The third servant, the lazy servant, shows believers how not to live. Responsibility for living according to our faith cannot be put off. Idleness and apathy have consequences. The master's scolding of this servant leads to the most severe consequence: the servant is thrown into the darkness, presumably hell, for his irresponsibility. The master's words of final condemnation occur five other times in Matthew (8:12, 13:42, 50; 22:13, 24:51), and the Gospel of recent Sundays has included three of these.

The manner in which you differentiate in your proclamation between the words of the faithful servants and the master's responses to their actions, and the words of the lackluster servant and the master's response to him, will assist the assembly in hearing the message of this parable about the end times. As you proclaim the master's warning, remember this is the fourth time in recent weeks that it will be proclaimed. Perhaps, though, it might be the first time someone in the assembly takes it to heart and understands its meaning for his or her life. Through God's Spirit working in you, your proclamation can call this person to faithful living.

OUR LORD JESUS CHRIST THE KING

Lectionary #160

READING I Ezekiel 34:11–12, 15–17

Ezekiel = ee-ZEE-kee-uhl

Take your time as you proclaim this reading. Allow the Lord's care for his people to be evident in your voice.

A reading from the Book of the Prophet Ezekiel

Thus says the **Lord GOD**:
I **myself** will **look after** and **tend** my **sheep**.
As a **shepherd** tends his **flock**
when he finds himself among his **scattered sheep**,
so will **I** tend **my** sheep.
I will **rescue** them from **every place** where they were **scattered**
when it was **cloudy** and **dark**.
I **myself** will **pasture** my **sheep**;
I **myself** will give them **rest**, says the **Lord GOD**.

Pause after each phrase so that the assembly will be able to hear all the different people for whom the Lord has compassion.

Note the last phrase in the list speaks of the Lord's strong response to those who are deceptive and powerful. Switch your tone of voice appropriately.

The concluding verse is not so much a warning as a fact. Proclaim it straightforwardly, making eye contact with the assembly, the Lord's sheep.

The **lost** I will **seek out**,
the **strayed** I will **bring back**,
the **injured** I will **bind up**,
the **sick** I will **heal**,
but the **sleek** and the **strong** I will **destroy**,
shepherding them **rightly**.

As for **you**, my **sheep**, says the **Lord GOD**,
I will **judge** between **one** sheep and **another**,
between **rams** and **goats**.

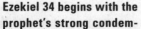

READING I **Ezekiel 34 begins with the prophet's strong condemnation of the shepherds of Israel (34:1–10). The Lord has instructed him to prophesy an oracle in which the Lord himself will come against these shepherds to save his sheep, the people of Israel.**

What had the shepherds, the leaders of Israel, done wrong? They had only taken care of themselves and they had done so at the expense of the people. The leaders had fed off their sheep's milk, worn their wool, and slaughtered their fatlings. In doing so, they had failed to take care of the weak, heal the sick, and treat the injured. Their lack of leadership resulted in their sheep being scattered throughout the land. The people of Israel were in exile. Having presented the Lord's words censuring the leaders of the people and his promise to pasture them himself, the prophet continues where today's reading begins. The tone of today's passage, filled with the Lord's message that he will take personal responsibility for tending his sheep, stands in stark contrast to the harsh words in the previous section.

In this reading, there are eleven "I" statements in which the Lord states what he will do for his sheep. Aside from the statement about the Lord destroying the sleek and the strong, and the concluding statement that details his role as judge and provides the obvious connection with today's Gospel, the other statements present the Lord as a kind and loving shepherd.

Because the Israelites had no king during the exile, they looked to the Lord as their king. The Lord was a different kind of king than those who led them astray. He gave them hope through the way in which

READING II 1 Corinthians 15:20–26, 28

Corinthians = kohr-IN-thee-uhnz

A reading from the first Letter of Saint Paul to the Corinthians

Boldly proclaim the opening line which states the truth of Christ's Resurrection.

Brothers and sisters:
Christ has been **raised** from the **dead**,
the **firstfruits** of those who have fallen **asleep**.

Lower your tone of voice to explain the parallels in the next two verses: death/life, Adam/Christ.

For since **death** came through **man**,
the **resurrection** of the **dead** came **also** through **man**.
For just as in **Adam** all **die**,
so too in **Christ** shall all be **brought** to **life**,
but **each one** in **proper order**:
Christ the **firstfruits**;
then, at his **coming**, those who **belong** to Christ;
then comes the **end**,
when he hands over the **kingdom** to his **God** and **Father**,
when he has **destroyed** every **sovereignty**
and every **authority** and **power**.

Speak about Christ' reign in a confident voice to help make the connection to today's solemnity.

For he must **reign** until he has put **all** his enemies under his feet.
The **last** enemy to be **destroyed** is **death**.

Proclaim the final stanza with a balance of confidence and peace: confident that God is all in all and peaceful that in the end, everything will come to rest in him.

When **everything** is **subjected** to him,
then the **Son** himself will **also** be **subjected**
to the **one** who subjected **everything** to **him**,
so that **God** may be **all** in **all**.

he cared for his people and through his promise to appoint his servant David as the one shepherd over them (34:23). The Lord will still remain God; David will be prince among them (34:24). On this day when we celebrate Christ the King, we recall the relationship between kings and shepherds that goes back historically at least to David's time. An upright king was to shepherd his people as the Lord proclaimed that he himself would. Christians believe that Christ the King is the fulfillment of the Lord shepherding his people.

READING II This reading presents Pauline theology at its best: profound themes of Christian faith, but difficult to understand. As a proclaimer of the word, it might be helpful for you to begin your preparation by reading the entirety of 1 Corinthians 15, focusing in particular on the section immediately preceding today's passage (1 Corinthians 15:12–19).

In these verses, Paul addresses those in the Corinthian community who deny the resurrection of the dead. While they believe in Christ's Resurrection, for some reason they are unable to see the relationship between his Resurrection and their own. Paul's fundamental argument is that if there is no resurrection of the dead, then neither has Christ been raised, and therefore, our preaching and faith are both empty (15:13–14).

Paul identifies Christ as the "firstfruits" of those who have died, because his Resurrection announces the Resurrection of all who believe. "Firstfruits" is a term used in Jewish rituals to refer to the first part of the harvest sacrificed to God. This offering was a sign that the entire harvest would eventually be given to him.

GOSPEL Matthew 25:31–46

A reading from the holy Gospel according to Matthew

Create an image of the Son of Man coming in glory by proclaiming the opening line in a glorious, expansive voice.

Jesus **said** to his **disciples**:
"When the **Son** of **Man** comes in his **glory**,
and all the **angels** with him,
he will **sit** upon his **glorious throne**,
and **all** the nations will be **assembled** before **him**.

The power of judgment belongs to the Son of Man; deliver these lines with authority, but not in a stern or threatening tone.

And he will **separate** them **one** from **another**,
as a **shepherd** separates the **sheep** from the **goats**.
He will place the **sheep** on his **right** and the **goats** on his **left**.
Then the **king** will say to those on his **right**,
'**Come**, you who are **blessed** by my **Father**.
Inherit the **kingdom prepared** for you from the **foundation** of the **world**.

Set off each of the actions of those who will inherit the kingdom by pausing as if the comma were a period.

For I was **hungry** and you gave me **food**,
I was **thirsty** and you gave me **drink**,
a **stranger** and you **welcomed** me,
naked and you **clothed** me,
ill and you **cared** for me,
in **prison** and you **visited** me.'
Then the **righteous** will **answer** him and **say**,

Ask the questions the righteous pose inquisitively.

'**Lord**, **when** did we **see** you **hungry** and **feed** you,
or **thirsty** and give you **drink**?
When did we **see** you a **stranger** and **welcome** you,
or **naked** and **clothe** you?
When did we **see** you **ill** or in **prison**, and **visit** you?'
And the **king** will say to them in **reply**,

Solemnly speak the king's response, making eye contact with the assembly on the entire line "whatever you did for one of the least . . . ."

'**Amen**, I **say** to you, **whatever** you **did**
for one of the **least** brothers of mine, you **did** for **me**.'

Paul then makes the connection between Adam and Christ. Because death (sin) came through Adam and we are linked to Adam because of our human nature, it was necessary that the resurrection of the dead also come through a man, through Christ. This new life can only come through him, who through his own death and Resurrection erased the stain of sin and triumphed over death. As a result of his Resurrection, he now reigns as King.

At the end of time, Christ, having brought all things under him, will himself be subjected to the One who drew all things to him. As it occurs in this passage, "subjected" does not carry a negative connation. Rather, it simply implies that everything is ordered to Christ first, and then to the Father. In the end, all will be one in God through Christ. Christ rose. Christ reigns. Christ will come again in glory. We will rise. The Lord is fully and completely God forever. This we celebrate on the solemnity that draws the Sundays of the liturgical year to a close.

GOSPEL In the Gospel according to Matthew, today's passage occurs at the end of the twenty-fifth chapter, after two parables about preparing oneself for the coming of the kingdom of heaven, which were proclaimed on the previous two Sundays. This Gospel also occurs immediately before Matthew's account of the Passion begins.

Jesus instructs his disciples that when the Son of Man comes in glory "all nations"—both Jews and Gentiles—will come before him. Then the Son of Man will separate the sheep (the righteous) from the goats (the accursed) as the Lord God in

Then he will **say** to those on his **left**,
'**Depart** from me, you **accursed**,
into the **eternal fire** prepared for the **devil** and his **angels**.
For I was **hungry** and you gave me **no food**,
I was **thirsty** and you gave me **no drink**,
a **stranger** and you gave me **no welcome**,
naked and you gave me **no clothing**,
ill and in **prison**, and you did **not care** for me.'
Then they will **answer** and **say**,
'**Lord**, **when** did we **see** you **hungry** or **thirsty**
or a **stranger** or **naked** or **ill** or in **prison**,
and **not minister** to your **needs**?'
He will **answer** them, '**Amen**, I **say** to you,
what you did **not do** for one of these **least** ones,
you did **not do** for **me**.'
And **these** will go off to **eternal punishment**,
but the **righteous** to **eternal life**."

Give the negative judgment faced by those on the Son of Man's left with some anger in your voice. Explain the reasons for the negative judgment in an explanatory tone.

Those facing the negative judgment are perplexed about their fate.

Make eye contact as you proclaim Jesus' final words. They were serious and instructive for believers in Matthew's time and are for the assembly before you today.

today's First Reading says he will judge between rams and goats.

The rest of the Gospel describes the basis on which the king (the Son of Man) will make his judgment. The parable shows the king carrying out his Father's will and thereby makes the connection to how Jesus does the will of the Father in his life, death, and Resurrection.

The criteria on which the king will judge the people are what Catholics have traditionally called the corporal works of mercy (notice, however, that burying the dead is missing). The way in which the people took care of others, akin to how the Lord will shepherd his people in the First Reading, reflects how they recognized and treated the king. It determines whether they will enjoy eternal life or suffer lasting punishment.

Jesus' message in this Gospel could not be clearer. Your proclamation as well should leave the assembly with little doubt as to the main point of the Gospel: At the final judgment, the Son of Man *will* examine their response to needy brothers and sisters. We are called to serve our brothers and sisters in need, not only in order to merit our salvation and not only because we recognize Christ in them. (Neither the righteous nor the accursed recognized Christ in the poor, although this is important to do.) We serve because, whether neighbor or stranger, they are in need. The Lord does no less in shepherding his people, and expects no less of us through whom he does it.